Warfare in History

THE ANGLO-SCOTS WARS
1513–1550
A Military History

Warfare in History

General Editor: Matthew Bennett
ISSN 1358–779X

Already published

The Battle of Hastings: Sources and Interpretations
edited and introduced by Stephen Morillo

Infantry Warfare in the Early Fourteenth Century:
Discipline, Tactics, and Technology
Kelly DeVries

The Art of Warfare in Western Europe during
the Middle Ages, from the Eighth Century to 1340 (second edition)
J. F. Verbruggen

Knights and Peasants:
The Hundred Years War in the French Countryside
Nicholas Wright

Society at War: The Experience of
England and France during the Hundred Years War
edited by Christopher Allmand

The Circle of War in the Middle Ages:
Essays on Medieval Military and Naval History
edited by Donald J. Kagay and L. J. Andrew Villalon

THE ANGLO-SCOTS WARS
1513–1550

A Military History

Gervase Phillips

THE BOYDELL PRESS

First published 1999
The Boydell Press, Woodbridge

ISBN 0 85115 746 7

The Boydell Press is an imprint of Boydell and Brewer Ltd
PO Box 9, Woodbridge, Suffolk IP12 3DF, UK
and of Boydell and Brewer Inc.
PO Box 41026, Rochester, NY 14604–4126, USA
website: http://www.boydell.co.uk

A catalogue record for this book is available
from the British Library

Library of Congress Cataloging-in-Publication Data
Phillips, Gervase, 1967–
    The Anglo-Scots wars, 1513–1550 : a military history / Gervase
Phillips.
        p. cm. – (Warfare in history, ISSN 1358–779X)
    Includes bibliographical references and index.
    ISBN 0–85115–746–7 (acid-free paper)
    1. Scotland – History – Stuarts, to the Union, 1371–1707.
2. Military art and science – Scotland – History – 16th century.
3. Great Britain – History, Military – 1485–1603. 4. Scotland –
Foreign relations – England. 5. England – Foreign relations –
Scotland. 6. Scotland – History, Military. 7. Flodden, Battle of,
1513. I. Title. II. Series.
DA784.P48   1999
941.104–dc21   99–30714

This publication is printed on acid-free paper

Printed in Great Britain by
St Edmundsbury Press Ltd, Bury St Edmunds, Suffolk

CONTENTS

ACKNOWLEDGEMENTS

I am grateful to the Research Committee of the Department of History and Economic History, the Manchester Metropolitan University, for the relief from my teaching duties in the Spring Term of 1998 that allowed me to concentrate on my research. Thanks are also due to the staff of the All Saints Library at MMU for their always helpful and efficient service. My parents, John and Dianne, provided encouragement and I.T. facilities, and my brother Carl offered technical support.

This book is dedicated to the memory of my grandmothers, Emma Phillips and Hattie Wearing.

GENERAL EDITOR'S PREFACE

At first glance, a volume covering the military history of barely a generation on the periphery of north-western Europe might seem a narrow subject for even a monograph. Yet what Gervase Phillips provides in his study of the Anglo-Scottish wars of the first half of the sixteenth century is something far more wide-ranging than a regional case study. As his first chapter explains, the period of the much-vaunted (and much misinterpreted) 'Military Revolution of the Sixteenth Century', as Michael Roberts first and famously described it, was far more complex than the 'revolutionary' terminology would suggest. In fact, it was a period of change within continuity. Developments in gunpowder weapons – artillery and hand-guns of various kinds – fortifications and siege techniques, the equipping and drilling of both horse and foot, tactical variations, strategic approaches, and much more all echoed developments of the preceding 'medieval' century. He surely hits the nail on the head when he says (p. 35): 'The avoidance of battle, the importance of siege warfare, the strategy of destruction of resources, all have been cited as features of the military revolution, yet all had long been features of medieval warfare.'

The analysis of the rival armies which follows is very richly evidenced – a positive goldmine for anyone interested in the practice of war in the sixteenth century. Once more Dr Phillips combines an understanding of the medieval inheritance within the context of sixteenth-century developments in a sophisticated and open-minded way. In addition there are enough details on arms and armour, weaponry (especially in the context of the bow versus firearms debate), the introduction of contemporary Continental styles of fortress construction and methods of siege warfare, recruitment, supply and support services (for example, medicine) to satisfy the most avid collector of military detail. Yet the analysis, like war itself, is not entirely to do with purely military activity. Too much military history has ignored the importance of naval and amphibious operations (which seems especially surprising in the light of the British kingdoms' island status). Dr Phillips shrewdly places the campaigns of the 1540s, and especially 1547, which led to the battle of Pinkie, within a wider historical context. He cites the expeditions of William I in 1072 and Edward I in 1296 as the only preceding operations to compare with the success of Somerset's expedition (to which might be added Athelstan in 934); and another century passed before Cromwell was able to emulate it.

Nor is war all about battles, of course. The long grind of Border warfare centred on raiding, ambushes, and grim sieges of garrisoned fortifications, ranging in size from small forts to substantial towns. Constant supplies of money were crucial to the maintenance of all this activity. In what effectively became a contest between the English and French fisc, there was to be no winner, but who held the upper hand depended greatly upon who put in the greater resources at a particular moment. Mercenaries played a significant role in the wars, as specialists providing up-to-date fortification and siege techniques, of course, but also as doughty fighters at the tactical level and dependable garrison troops. French arquebusiers and 'Almain' (German) pikemen, together with their experienced commanders, played crucial roles on more than one occasion.

Wars are won by words as well as swords, as the investigation of Protestant propaganda to convert the Scots' faith as well as their allegiance makes clear. When the tract writer James Henrisoun asked if it were better to win men's hearts at little cost or to expend great sums on fortifications (p. 219), he anticipates the modern British Army's 'hearts and minds' approach by almost half a millennium. Unfortunately, his masters did not listen and continued to prefer the sword to the pen, although, as Dr Phillips points out, the recourse to war was actually contrary to their perceived interests. This seemingly un-military conclusion is also a mark of how far military history has come, and how valuable a tool for historical exploration it can be in the hands of such a practitioner as the author of this book.

Matthew Bennett
Royal Military Academy Sandhurst
June 1999

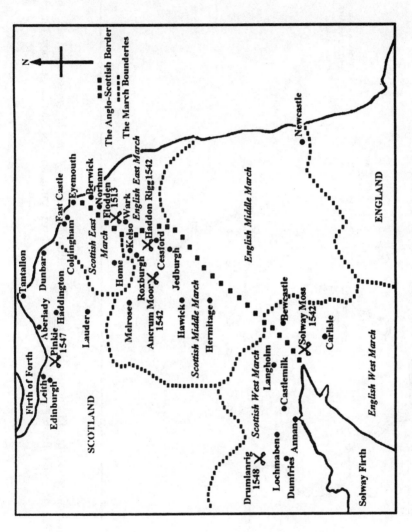

The Anglo-Scottish Border Marches in the sixteenth century.

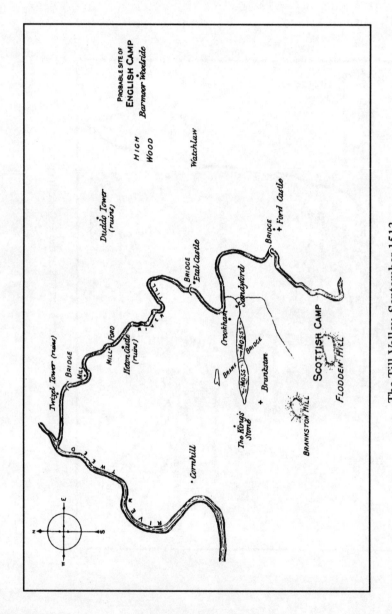

The Till Valley, September 1513.

(Originally published in Thomas Hodgkin, 'The Battle of Flodden', *Archaeologia Aeliana*, vol. 16 (1892), pp. 1–44. Reproduced by courtesy of the Society of Antiquaries of Newcastle upon Tyne.)

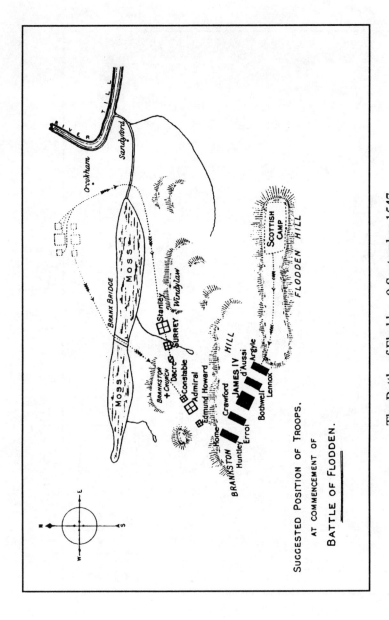

The Battle of Flodden, 9 September 1547.

(Originally published in Thomas Hodgkin, 'The Battle of Flodden', *Archaeologia Aeliana*, vol. 16 (1892), pp. 1–44. Reproduced by courtesy of the Society of Antiquaries of Newcastle upon Tyne.)

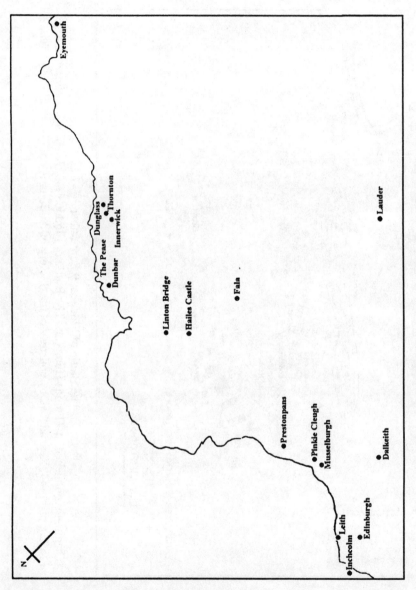

The Scottish East March and part of Lothian, September 1547.

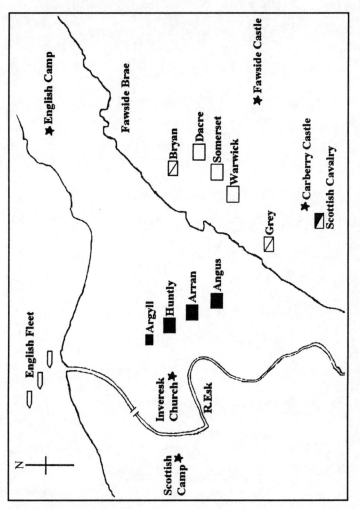

The Battle of Pinkie, 10 September 1547.

INTRODUCTION

This work is, without apology, a work of military history. Its focus is on the tactical and operational study of the conflicts between England and Scotland in the first half of the sixteenth century. Such a focus remains deeply unfashionable in academia, which has long been dismissive of the discipline of military history, regarded as the preserve of the retired army officer, limited in scope, methodologically primitive and lacking in intellectual rigour. The study of warfare is only worthy of the serious historian's attention if it is placed firmly in the context of 'war and society' and the broader development of political institutions.[1]

Academic historians have been confident that this broad canvas is the most appropriate framework to study the history of warfare. Colin Jones, for example, derided the 'traditional' approach which 'in the least competent hands, all too swiftly descended to the level of a chronicle of one damn battle after another, with interludes for the descriptions of uniforms'. In competition has arisen 'the new military history', which 'eschews narration and is essentially concerned with the social and institutional context of warfare. Military structures, logistics, the rank and file, relations with civilians, *mentalités* now take up position alongside *histoire événementielle*.'[2]

The new military historian moves swiftly away from the battlefield, to examine the impact of warfare on administrative procedure, on government, on finance, on social and political institutions. M.J.Braddick in his discussion of 'an English Military Revolution' goes so far as to 'leave aside the question of battlefield tactics' altogether in an examination of the fiscal and military performance of the Stuart regime.[3] His work focuses on administration and mobilisation, and it would surely be more legitimate to describe his topic as a governmental revolution rather than a military one. Indeed the move from the battlefield can be so swift that a genuine understanding of some military aspects of a topic can be compromised. As Brian Bond has observed, military history's

---

[1] For a full discussion of the nature of military history see the contributions of Michael Howard, Brian Bond, David Chandler, J.M.Stagg, John Childs, John Gooch, Geoffrey Best and John Terraine in 'What is Military History?', *History Today*, vol. 35 (1984), pp. 4–13. John Childs sums up the consensus with his observation that '. . . War and Society; civil-military relations; war and economy; armies and governments . . . [are the] . . . application of military history to other branches of the subject. Military history remains the study of armed forces, their institutions, methods and operations in time of war.'

[2] Colin Jones, 'New Military History for Old? War and Society in Early Modern Europe', *European Studies Review*, vol. 12, no. 1 (1982), p. 97.

[3] M.J.Braddick, 'An English Military Revolution?', *The Historical Journal*, vol. 36 (1993), p. 965.

'documentary sources, vast historiography and peculiar problems cannot easily be mastered in fleeting forays from other fields'.[4]

There will be no attempt to establish linkages between the tactics and technology of the battlefield and broader social and political developments in the British Isles during the first half of the sixteenth century. There are recent precedents for an approach in the style of the old military history. Paddy Griffiths has lamented the oversimplification, and consequent misunderstanding, of military practice in history by adherents of the war and society school, in their rush to discuss matters political or economic. There is, he has suggested, 'a crying need for the university to extend once again a welcome to the pure military historian'.[5] Similarly Matthew Bennett has emphasised the reintegration of the '. . . operational, tactical, technical and equipment aspects of the conduct of war, whilst not ignoring its impact on wider society. In this context, it becomes just as acceptable to study the history of particular campaigns or battles, as to investigate the social structures which made war-fighting possible.'[6]

The most effective methodology for studying military campaigns remains the narrative. The more thematic approach is a striking feature of the new military history, to the extent that its practitioners, as Colin Jones boasts, 'eschew narration'. This is dangerous talk, for narrative remains a defining technique of the historian. Interlopers in the discipline of history, social theorists and literary critics, also 'eschew narrative' and move quickly on to eschew the distinction between fact and fiction, throwing into question the very validity of the discipline itself. The incorporation of the dimension of time and progression into an explanation of cause and effect makes narrative one of the most powerful tools at the disposal of historians. They eschew it at their peril.[7]

This is particularly obvious in accounts of battles and campaigns. James McPherson, perhaps the leading historian of the American Civil War, has stressed the importance of contingency, of events being dependent upon earlier occurrences, in accounting for the military defeat of the Confederacy. For McPherson 'this phenomenon of contingency can best be described in a narrative format'.[8] It is striking to note that some of the strongest defences of narrative are emerging from those historians who are once again looking to science to provide effective models for studying the past. One might stress in particular the influence of chaos theory. As Donald McCloskey has reminded us, most historical events, and battles in particular, can hinge on the tiniest of chances, for 'little

---

4   Brian Bond *et al.*, 'What is Military History?', p. 6.
5   Paddy Griffiths, 'Some Limitations in the University Approach to Military History', Appendix 1, in *Battle Tactics of the Western Front: The British Army's Art of Attack, 1916–18* (London, 1996), pp. 201–203.
6   See Matthew Bennett's preface to Stephen Morillo (ed.), *The Battle of Hastings* (Woodbridge, 1996), p. vii.
7   For a robust defence of the discipline of History and its established methodology see Keith Windschuttle, *The Killing of History* (Paddington, Australia, 1996).
8   James McPherson, *The Battle Cry of Freedom* (Oxford, 1988), p. 858.

events can have big consequences'.[9] This is the essence of a chaotic system, where minuscule changes in initial circumstance can create massive differences in later conditions.

These changes do not occur at random. Events, as McPherson observes, are dependent on contingency. Historians may not be able to predict events in such a system but events can be explained after they have occurred. It may, of course, be possible that the causal relationship between a minuscule chance and a massive difference cannot be established by a historian. Those who have sought covering laws for history, or formulated elaborate paradigms to explain historical processes, have always been vulnerable to the charge that since their evidence is so fragmentary and their methodology so selective, their analysis must, at best, be incomplete, at worst utterly inaccurate. Here is one of narrative's greatest strengths. As George Reisch has commented:

> if puny and unknowable details do in fact play an essential role in some particular history, narrative accounts of that history need not have access to that detail. The narrator can still describe and emplot events and the effects of that detail even though the detail itself and its causal power is not recognised. As a causal explanation the resulting narrative would appear, from some ideal vantage, to be incomplete or incorrect. But at least it would remain parallel and in step with events that actually occurred.[10]

Narrative will, thus, be central to much of this study. Chapters 1 and 2 will be more thematic, looking at the development of military practice in Europe generally and at the rival military organisations of England and Scotland in particular. Chapters 3 to 6, which describe the military engagements between Scottish and English forces from Flodden in 1513 until the end of the Rough Wooing in 1550, will indeed be 'a chronicle of one damn battle after another'.

In many cases the study will focus in some detail on relatively minor incidents involving only a handful of men. The justification for this is two-fold. Firstly, in many instances small groups of soldiers had an impact out of all proportion to their numbers on the outcome of entire campaigns. Thus in 1523 Sir William Lisle defended the ancient walls of Wark Castle with just a hundred men against a Franco-Scottish army that probably numbered in excess of three thousand. Secondly, there has been a tendency for historians to underestimate the tactical ability of early sixteenth-century soldiers. Their battles are portrayed as clashes of mass against mass, in which lumbering formations of unskilled soldiers relied on simple brute force to achieve a decision.[11] In fact, for the average soldier, the pitched battle involving masses of men was a mercifully rare occur-

---

9 Donald McCloskey, 'History, Differential Equations and the Problem of Narration', *History and Theory*, vol. 30 (1991), p. 27.

10 George A. Reisch, 'Chaos, History and Narrative', *History and Theory*, vol. 30 (1991), p. 18. See also Stephen Morillo (ed.), *The Battle of Hastings* (Woodbridge, 1996), p. xix.

11 See, for example, the comments of Michael Roberts, 'The Military Revolution, 1560–1660', in *Essays in Swedish History* (London, 1967), pp. 195–223.

rence. He was more usually called upon to fight in relatively small engagements, the *camisado* assault in siege operations, the foray into enemy territory, the expedition to gather forage. He may even have been called upon to take part in counter-insurgency operations, against a rebellious peasantry or the hostile population of an occupied territory. The early sixteenth-century soldier had, therefore, to be far more skilled in small unit tactics than is often recognised. It is, therefore, worthwhile to pay some attention to the frequent but small-scale skirmishes that were central to the military experience.

Wherever possible, descriptions of that experience will be drawn from the testimony of contemporaries and, ideally, eye witnesses, using their words. This approach commends itself not only because their language is frequently more rich and expressive than I could ever hope to achieve, but also because elements of sixteenth-century military vocabulary can therefore be preserved. Nor would it be wise to ignore the influence of John Keegan who has observed 'that battles ought to be and are best described through the words of participants'.[12] The period offers plenty of scope for this approach. Soldiers of the day recorded events, both for posterity and in their reports for government officials. We are fortunate therefore to have some striking personal testimonies, such as William Patten's account of Somerset's campaign of 1547, *The Expedition into Scotland* (London, 1548), or the recollections of that garrulous Welsh professional soldier of the Calais garrison, Elis Gruffydd.[13] Regrettably, the vast bulk of these first-hand sources were written by those serving in English armies rather than by Scots. This will, unfortunately but unavoidably, colour the account given in this work, which will tend towards an English perspective of events. Hopefully, having recognised and acknowledged the tendency to give the soldier's-eye view from under the banner of St George, the overall picture will not become too distorted.

This will be a chronicle with a theme. J.R.Hale has commented that for the student of Tudor military affairs 'the middle decades of the sixteenth century are dark'.[14] The paucity of studies on Tudor warfare has, perhaps, led to a rather general neglect of the study of military activity within the broader framework of the history of the British Isles in the sixteenth century. Those studying the creation of the multi-national Tudor state have often neglected the fact that, for the early Tudors at least, armed conflict was a central element of English foreign policy.[15] Although Tudor England never adopted a strategy of outright conquest in pursuit of union with Scotland, the *chevauchée*, the expedition by Army Royal, and the seizure and occupation of key garrisons were all features of the drive for English hegemony. Nor was the recourse to war a uniquely English

[12] John Keegan, *The Face of Battle* (London, 1991), p. 33.
[13] Patten's work is reproduced in A.F.Pollard (ed.), *Tudor Tracts, 1532–1588* (Westminster, 1903). Elis Gruffydd's chronicles were edited and translated by M.B.Davis and were published in three parts in *Fouad I University, Bulletin of the Faculty of Arts*, vols 3, 11 and 12 (1944–1950).
[14] J.R.Hale, *Renaissance War Studies* (London, 1983), p. 247.
[15] Hale, p. 247.

response. Successive Scottish rulers, James IV, the Regent Albany, James V, all led or instigated military operations in the north of England. Although neither nation ultimately proved capable of achieving its strategic goals through military action, neither would they abandon war as an instrument of policy. Understanding the nature and limitations of military operations is, in many respects, a key to understanding the course of Anglo-Scots relations over the first five decades of the sixteenth century. It is a depressing and frustrating history of the repeated recourse to armed conflict in pursuit of political goals that failed again and again to deliver any decisive outcome.

Some aspects of Tudor military history have been well explored. Jeremy Goring's Ph.D. thesis, 'The Military Obligations of the English People, 1511–1558' (London University, 1955), is the standard work on the recruitment and mustering of early Tudor armies. C.S.L.Davies has done extensive work on the effectiveness of Tudor government in supplying its armies in the field.[16] One of the most exhaustive studies has been Gilbert John Millar's thorough and detailed examination of the employment by the English Crown of foreign soldiers, *Tudor Mercenaries and Auxiliaries, 1485–1547* (Charlottesville, 1980). The achievement of English military architects, particularly in the construction of sophisticated field fortifications, has been highlighted by J.R.Hale himself, by H.M.Colvin and, especially, by Marcus Merriman.[17] Beyond these areas, however, the actual performance of the early Tudor army has had scant attention for 'military activity in Scotland, Ireland and France was not on a scale, nor had lasting enough results to have encouraged its investigation in depth'.[18]

At least this has been the perception. The significance of the wars of the early Tudors has been largely overlooked. Mark Fissal has contrasted the ability of Henry VIII to wage war 'on a grandiose scale' with the inability of Charles I to do the same. In his work *War and Government in Britain, 1598–1650* (Manchester, 1991) he edits a collection of articles which highlight the relationship between government and war in Tudor, Cromwellian and Stuart Britain. The ability to sustain a campaign is a major theme, but there is not a single reference to the Lord Protector's three year campaign in Scotland, or its destructive impact on his government. This is a notable oversight. M.L.Bush has made the enormous financial strain imposed on Somerset's administration by the war abundantly clear. The Rough Wooing should figure prominently in any discussion of war and government in early modern Britain.[19]

[16] C.S.L.Davies, 'Provisions for Armies, 1509–50: A Study in the Effectiveness of Early Tudor Government', *The Economic History Review*, 2nd series, vol. 17 (1964–65), pp. 234–248.

[17] H.M.Colvin (ed.), *The History of the King's Works, Volume III, 1485–1660*, Part 1 (London, 1975), pp. 337–394 and *The History of the King's Works, Volume IV, 1485–1660*, Part 2 (London, 1982), pp. 607–728.

[18] Hale, p. 247. For a brief overview of the recent literature see Ian Roy, 'The British Army, 1500–1715: Recent Writing Reviewed', *Journal of the Society for Army Historical Research*, vol. 62 (1984), pp. 194–202.

[19] See M.L.Bush, *The Government Policy of Protector Somerset* (London, 1975).

Such a discussion, however, should begin with a careful consideration of the *military* history of the period, if it is to avoid the traps into which the new military historians so frequently wander. Charles Oman's *History of the Art of War in the Sixteenth Century*, originally published as far back as 1937, covers the main engagements, but pays little or no attention to campaigns as a whole. Charles Cruikshank, on the other hand, produced an excellent and comprehensive history of the 1513 invasion of France but sadly never turned his attention to the later wars in France, or the wars with Scotland.[20] Scotland itself has had even scantier treatment. The composition and performance of the Scottish armies that fought at Flodden, Solway Moss and Pinkie has led to their rapid dismissal as medieval, with the underlying assumption that medievalism equates with a primitive inefficiency and innate conservatism. More incisive studies of Scottish military history have been undertaken by David Caldwell, who has written what is the definitive account of the Battle of Pinkie, as well as looking closely at the arms and equipment of the early modern Scottish soldier.[21] Nevertheless, those who argue for the occurrence of a military revolution in early modern Europe, still place the British Isles firmly on its peripheries.

Even those who avoid the debate about changes in state administration and concern themselves with military practice alone, such as David Eltis, see the British Isles as essentially backward. Eltis argues strongly for a sixteenth-century military revolution associated with infantry formations of pike and shot, systematic training and the spread of military literature. His military revolution arrives in England only with that military literature, in the latter half of the sixteenth century.[22] For Scotland, change arrived even later. Geoffrey Parker contends that 'the full *trace italienne* only came to . . . Scotland . . . in the eighteenth century, with the construction of offensive bastion defences large enough to shelter a force capable of mounting a counter-attack in case of rebellion or invasion'.[23] Yet it was precisely this kind of 'offensive bastion' capable of sheltering a mobile force of cavalry that the English depended on to subdue Scotland in the period 1547 to 1550, *two hundred years before* Parker claims such fortifications were built.

The first fortification built in Scotland in the new style was constructed on the orders of Protector Somerset at Eyemouth in 1547.[24] It was quickly followed by others, which demonstrated an increasingly sophisticated design. At Had-

---

20 Both Oman and Cruikshank have been republished. Charles Oman, *A History of the Art of War in Sixteenth Century Europe* (London, 1991); Charles Cruikshank, *Henry VIII and the Invasion of France* (Stroud, 1990).

21 See David Caldwell (ed.), *Scottish Weapons and Fortifications, 1100–1800* (Edinburgh, 1981) and his chapter, 'The Battle of Pinkie', in Norman MacDougall (ed.), *Scotland and War, AD 79–1918* (Edinburgh, 1991).

22 David Eltis, *The Military Revolution in Sixteenth Century Europe* (Oxford, London, 1995).

23 Geoffrey Parker, *The Military Revolution* (Cambridge, 1988), p. 32.

24 M.Merriman, 'The Forts of Eyemouth: Anvils of British Union?', *The Scottish Historical Review*, vol. 67 (1988), pp. 142–155.

dington, Broughty and Lauder, English, French and Scottish soldiers contested possession of low-lying earthwork forts, resilient to bombardment and defended by artillery well placed in mutually supporting bastions in the most modern style. The *trace italienne* was not the only modern feature of Anglo-Scots warfare in the first half of the sixteenth century. Those rival infantries fought not just with the traditional bow, bill and axe, but with cannon, pike and arquebus. Mounted firearm troops were prominent in the English army at Pinkie in 1547 and throughout the ensuing campaign. The Scottish, for their part, had been committed to the assault by fast moving pike columns, the tactic of the Swiss and the *Landsknecht*, since Flodden in 1513. The arrival of those literary works on modern military theory in the late sixteenth century, emphasised by David Eltis, appears to have been pre-dated by the arrival of the actual military practice. Amongst the 'medieval', 'quasi-feudal' and allegedly 'backward' armies of early sixteenth-century Britain, there are so many modern features that one begins to question the extent to which the British Isles did lie on the peripheries of military development. My chronicle of 'one damn battle after another' will hopefully highlight the extent of development in military practice in England and Scotland in the first half of the sixteenth century.

Those developments were contingent on what had gone before, particularly in the late fifteenth century, and were governed by the context of insular warfare between Scotland and England. Contemporary political and military events on the continent did, however, impact significantly on events in Britain. Although the focus of this study will be on Anglo-Scots conflict, the relevant chapters will contain brief outlines of England's campaigns in France, since these are vital to understanding the nature of fighting within the British Isles itself. To give just one example, it was the lessons of the siege warfare around Boulogne in 1544–1545 that taught the English the value of modern earthwork fortifications. That lesson they took to Scotland in 1547. Similarly, the political context in which military events occurred has to be addressed, but only to the extent of providing a broad framework in which to place the histories of campaigns. No attempt will be made to follow in detail the convolutions of sixteenth-century politics.[25] For this study at least, social and political events will be secondary to the central focus of military conflict. This will highlight the change, innovation and gradual modernisation of English and Scottish military forces during those 'dark' years of British military history, 1513–1550. It will, hopefully, also demonstrate why, in spite of the growing sophistication of military practice, the recourse to war as an instrument of policy was proved so consistently futile.

[25] There are a number of excellent texts that do cover the political history of this period. Particularly useful are Gordon Donaldson, *Scotland, James V to James VII* (Edinburgh, 1965) and Marcus Merriman, 'The Struggle for the Marriage of Mary Queen of Scots: English and French Intervention in Scotland, 1543–1550' (London University Ph.D., 1974).

CHAPTER ONE

WARFARE IN EARLY MODERN EUROPE

A military revolution?

THE METHOD OF the new military historians is to place military history in its broadest possible context. For no period is this more true than in the study of early modern Europe. Michael Roberts' seminal thoughts on the *Military Revolution, 1560–1660*, first delivered in an inaugural lecture at Queen's University in Belfast in 1956, posit a thesis with the widest scope. In it, Professor Roberts argues that technological developments, most notably that of gunpowder weapons, resulted in sweeping tactical change on the battlefield. These weapons, Roberts argues, were adopted in the first instance because they economised on training. It took years of dedicated practice to make a skilled archer, but only a matter of days to train a man to use a gun. The cost, however, was paid in battlefield efficiency. The smoothbore, slow-firing gun was inaccurate even when fired at a ridiculously short range. The individually highly skilled infantry of medieval Europe was enfeebled by the adoption of firearms. Even those who shouldered the pike rather than the gun were less adept in the handling of their weapon than their forebears had been. The pikemen relied on brute strength not skill: 'if he inclined his pike in correct alignment and leaned heavily on the man in front of him, he had done almost all that could be required of him'. The unwieldy, deep mass formations adopted by sixteenth-century infantry also suggested to Roberts a decline in efficiency. They 'dispensed with the need for a large trained corps of officers, and required a less high morale, since it is difficult to run away with fifteen ranks behind you'.

Even the cavalry, traditionally the elite of medieval armies, were not spared from the malaise. Abandoning the lance, which like the bow required considerable skill to use, cavalry too adopted the fledgling and ineffective gun. So armed, they could no longer charge home, but galloped around the battlefield popping off their weakling pistols to little effect. The decisive battle became an impossibility, for troops armed with the ineffectual gun could not force a decision. According to Roberts, the great powers of Europe were all simultaneously involved in an expensive exercise to re-equip their soldiers with firearms, the outcome of which was to *diminish* the effectiveness of their armies.

This unlikely state of affairs ended, Roberts argues, with the 'revolutionary' military reforms of Maurice of Nassau, between 1590 and 1609, and Gustav Adolphus of Sweden, from 1617 to 1632. The most important of these reforms was the rediscovery of the lost Roman art of training. Highly drilled musket-armed troops could now fire in devastating volleys. They were drilled to operate in thin linear formations, maximising their firepower, but requiring both more officers and a higher degree of individual initiative. This well drilled infantry was supported by an altogether new innovation, mobile field artillery, and by a cavalry which had rediscovered the charge and was trained to close with the sabre. Roberts goes on to credit all kinds of further innovation to this revolution: the military map, standardisation of weapons, the introduction of uniforms and the first standing armies with a clearly defined hierarchy of rank. He also claims that there was an unprecedented and exponential growth in army size. The campaigning season extended, and commanders developed pan-continental strategies to envelop their enemies, their strategic vision extending over vast geographical areas. The guiding strategic objective became the devastation of the enemy's territory, achieved in campaigns of manoeuvre rather than by seeking battle. The bureaucracy needed to raise, supply and pay these enormous armies on their grand continental ventures laid the foundation for the modern nation state.[1] Roberts' thesis thus takes us swiftly from the battlefield to the nation and, in doing so, graphically illustrates the underlying flaw of the new military history. Every one of his initial assertions, from the idea that the adoption of guns actually reduced the firepower of European armies, through to the claims made for the revolutionary nature of Maurice and Gustav Adolphus's reforms, is open to question.

Yet the thesis has proved remarkably tenacious. Geoffrey Parker, whilst shifting much of the emphasis away from the tactical reforms of Maurice of Nassau and Gustav Adolphus, adopted and enhanced the central arguments of the original thesis. Parker's military revolution stretched from 1450 to 1800.[2] Parker does not underestimate the effectiveness of gunpowder weapons to the same extent as Roberts. His military revolution begins with the development of the angled bastion of the *trace italienne*, the new style artillery fortifications that countered the threat posed by modern siege cannon. Widening the scope of Roberts' thesis, Parker also pointed to the importance of military innovation in the rise of the West. For Parker it was military might that allowed Europeans to establish their first colonies abroad and lay the essential early foundations for the age of imperialism. He pays careful attention to the development of navies in early modern Europe, an area almost wholly neglected by Roberts. In the wake of Parker's contribution, the military revolution thesis has begotten an on-going debate which has proved both provocative and consistently fertile.

---

[1] Michael Roberts, 'The Military Revolution, 1560–1660', in *Essays in Swedish History* (London, 1967), 195–223. Roberts' thesis, together with related articles by a number of prominent historians working in the field, can also be found in Clifford J. Rogers (ed.), *The Military Revolution Debate* (Oxford, 1995), 13–35. See also M.Duffy (ed.), *The Military Revolution and the State 1500–1800* (Exeter, 1980), Kelly DeVries, 'Catapults Are Not Atomic Bombs: Towards a Redefinition of "Effectiveness" in Premodern Military Technology', *War in History*, vol. 4 (1997), pp. 454–470.
[2] Geoffrey Parker, *The Military Revolution, Military Innovation and the Rise of the West, 1500–1800* (Cambridge, 1988).

It cannot be denied that this has been a productive and fruitful framework for historical enquiry, but this manifestation of the new military history has its weaknesses. As an explanation for sweeping social, political, even global, change, Professor Parker's military revolution thesis is conspicuously mono-causal. To take but one example, the establishment of the European hegemony in the Americas owed more to the diseases carried by the conquistadors than it did to their muskets.[3] A further persistent criticism has been the underlying technological determinism of the military revolution hypothesis. Did the intro-duction of gunpowder weapons ultimately cause changes in state adminis-tration, or, alternatively, was it changes in state administration that made the creation of strong infantry-based forces possible? Siegfried Hoyer believes that it was increased commerce, enabling 'greater expenditure and payment of larger military units', not technological innovation, that was the dynamic behind devel-opments in warfare.[4] In a comparative study of Europe and Japan, Stephen Morillo has demonstrated that the Asian state underwent those changes associ-ated with the military revolution *before* gunpowder weapons were introduced to Samurai warfare in 1543.[5] Notes of caution have therefore been sounded on the tendency of some practitioners of the new military history to, in David Eltis's phrase, mix 'oversimplifications of the military aspects of the period with even more suspicious sweeping statements of political, economic and social linkages to . . . dramatic and varied visions of the "military revolution" '.[6]

Furthermore, medievalists have observed that many of the allegedly novel features of the military revolution were anticipated in the preceding centuries. To a great extent, belief in an early modern military revolution rests on the underlying assumption that medieval warfare was a deeply primitive affair. Wars were fought by individually highly skilled warriors, but without discipline, tactics, or strategic design. This, as medievalists have been quick to point out, is a modernist's conceit. Michael Prestwich has argued strongly that the early modern period has no monopoly on military innovation. The Crusades involved grand strategies to rival any formulated during the sixteenth or seventeenth cen-turies. Military architecture responded to improvements in siege techniques during the thirteenth and fourteenth centuries, just as it did in the fifteenth and sixteenth. Throughout those centuries large and tactically very competent armies, operating complex strategies backed by elaborate logistical arrange-ments, were made possible by credit finance and efficient government. Simi-larly Dennis Showalter has noted that 'the middle ages were characterised by growing institutional sophistication, and nowhere was this more apparent than

---

3 See Francis Jennings, *The Invasion of America* (New York, 1976).
4 Siegfried Hoyer, 'Arms and Military Organisation in the German Peasant War', in Bob Scribner and Gerhard Benecke (eds), *The German Peasant War of 1525 – New Viewpoints* (London, 1979), p. 99.
5 Stephen Morillo, 'Guns and Government: A Comparative Study of Europe and Japan', *Journal of World History*, vol. 6 (1995), pp. 75–106.
6 David Eltis, *The Military Revolution in Sixteenth Century Europe* (London, 1995), p. 11.

the craft of war. The image . . . of medieval warfare as featuring limited discipline, simple tactics, and no strategy at all, has given way to a growing appreciation of the complexity of military operations between the eighth and the sixteenth centuries.'[7] For the military revolution thesis to survive this growing awareness of the sophistication of the medieval military, it needs to extend its scope over several centuries. Eventually there comes a point when one has to ask how appropriate is the word revolution for such an extended time frame.[8] As Michael Prestwich has observed, 'the early modern military revolution has become less and less convincing as its chronological limits have expanded'.[9]

Even amongst proponents of the military revolution there has been little consensus on the overall chronology of the process. Michael Roberts' original thesis posits a one hundred year duration, from 1560 to 1660. Later studies have expanded this time frame even further. The importance of pre-sixteenth-century precedents has not been entirely overlooked, either by Parker or by others. Clifford Rogers has offered a paradigm of 'punctuated equilibrium evolution', a series of short bursts of rapid change in military practice, interspersed with long periods of near stasis. In the fifteenth century he identifies two important developments. The first is an infantry revolution, which witnessed feudal cavalry bested by foot soldiers, pre-eminently the dismounted man-at-arms/longbow combination of the English and the halberd/pike phalanx of the Swiss. The second development Rogers highlights is an artillery revolution, which saw an increase in the size and efficiency of gunpowder weapons. The first beneficiaries of artillery's new potency were the French, whose use of cannon facilitated the expulsion of the English from castle after castle during the final stages of the Hundred Years War.[10] Like Rogers, William McNeil has also stressed the significance of a fifteenth-century gunpowder revolution. McNeil points out that the effect was magnified by the French and Burgundian invention of truly mobile cannon between 1465 and 1477, almost two hundred years before Roberts credits Gustav Adolphus with the creation of field artillery.[11] Jeremy Black is yet another who sees the late fifteenth century as pivotal in the development of military practice, agreeing largely with Parker's emphasis on the impact of firearms and the corresponding response in defensive fortifications. Confusingly, however, he then suggests that a second, and far more significant, revolution took place, *after* 1660. For Black, Roberts' revolutionary century was in fact 'in relative terms one of limited change between two periods of greater

---

[7] Dennis Showalter, 'Caste, Skill, and Training: The Evolution of Cohesion in European Armies from the Middle Ages to the Sixteenth Century', *The Journal of Military History*, vol. 57 (1993), pp. 407–30. See also Michael Prestwich, *Armies and Warfare in the Middle Ages: The English Experience* (London, 1996) and Philippe Contamine, *War In The Middle Ages* (Oxford, 1984).

[8] Andrew Ayton (ed.), *The Medieval Military Revolution* (London, 1995), p. 17.

[9] Prestwich, p. 245.

[10] Clifford J. Rogers, 'The Military Revolutions of the Hundred Years War', in Rogers (ed.), *The Military Revolution Debate*, pp. 55–93.

[11] William McNeil, *The Pursuit of Power* (Chicago, 1982), p. 89.

importance'.[12] More recently David Eltis has focused on the period 1500 to 1600. He has wisely disassociated his 'military revolution in sixteenth-century Europe' from Roberts' original conception, avoiding the sweeping generalisations about impact on government and society. Instead he concentrates on the spread of military literature, theory, and the more systematic approach to training and discipline.[13] Yet even Eltis's focused thesis fails to recognise that many of the changes in military practice he identifies as revolutionary in fact pre-date 1500 by some margin.

Gunpowder small arms

Eltis's impressive grasp of military history allows him to dispose quickly of some seriously flawed elements in Roberts' original thesis. He quite rightly challenges the notion that by abandoning the bow in favour of firearms European armies sacrificed firepower. Roberts neglects entirely the stopping power of gunpowder weapons. The armourer's craft had, by 1500, largely defeated the bow. Superbly designed and crafted plate armour was practically impervious to longbow arrow or crossbow bolt except at extremely close range.[14] In contrast the 1988 test firings of selected early modern firearms at the *Landeszeughaus* (Provincial Armoury) in Graz, Austria, has demonstrated their ability to pierce plate armour. The two earliest weapons in the test, *doppelhaken* (heavy muskets) of 1571 could penetrate between 2 and 4 millimetres of steel (the thickness of a good breast plate) at 100 metres, although at that range they would cause disabling rather than lethal wounds in armoured men, since most of the ball's force would have been dissipated as it penetrated the armour.[15]

Eltis is, thus, absolutely correct to stress the significance of the firepower of gunpowder weapons. He does, however, rather overstate the overall revolutionary impact of the weapon. The Graz tests also revealed how inaccurate these weapons were. Only one of the thirteen guns tested demonstrated a significantly greater than chance probability of hitting the target at which it was aimed. Long-range harassing fire was used in the early modern period, but largely to disrupt enemy formations rather than cause casualties. John Smyth, an English veteran of Imperialist armies fighting in the Balkans, quotes a Spanish adage of the day, 'discharge afar off, to draw on and deceive dotterals'.[16] This use of

---

[12] Jeremy Black, 'A Military Revolution? A 1660–1792 Perspective', in Rogers (ed.), pp. 95–114.

[13] David Eltis, *The Military Revolution of the Sixteenth Century*, pp. 43–75.

[14] For useful overviews on the development of defensive armour, see Charles Ffoulkes, 'Some Aspects of the Craft of the Armourer', *Archaeologia*, vol. 79 (1929), pp. 13–28, and J.G.Mann, 'Notes on the Armour of the Maximilian Period and the Italian Wars', *Ibid.*, pp. 216–244.

[15] Peter Krenn, Paul Kalaus and Bert Hall, 'Material Culture and Military History: Test-Firing Early Modern Small Arms', *Material History Review*, vol. 42 (1995), pp. 103–105.

[16] J.R.Hale (ed.), *Certain Discourses Military by Sir John Smyth* (Ithaca, 1964), p. 63.

inaccurate long-range harassing fire was nothing new. It could be achieved with bows, and it would be wrong to overstate the impact of gunpowder small arms on contemporary tactics.

Yet Eltis evinces the same desire to identify a point of fundamental change that marks all proponents of the military revolution. For Eltis the significant point of departure from previous military practice was the period immediately after 1500. This presents a difficulty for, as Eltis himself is clearly aware, fire-arms were already common on European battlefields long before the turn of the century: 'by the 1470s large numbers were deployed by the leading armies of the day. The Sforzas [in Italy] had been using them since the 1440s.' Yet, whilst acknowledging their pedigree, Eltis argues that firearms had made little impact on European battlefields. This was because 'their effect was limited by design failings which were not satisfactorily cured until the early sixteenth century'.[17]

Chief amongst these failings was that early handguns were fired whilst rested against the breastbone, not the shoulder. This limited the size of the charge that could be used without the weapon's recoil injuring the firer. Yet, notwithstanding this limitation, handguns had been potential, and actual, battle winners for far longer than Eltis allows, when integrated into existing tactical systems. In the 1420s the Hussites, under the blind genius Jan Zizka, had rested their fire-arms on the wooden walls of their waggon-fortresses. The powder charge they had been able to use had been sufficiently heavy to bring charging German men-at-arms, encased in plate armour, crashing down. The formidable nature of the Hussite defensive *wagenburg* mirrors exactly the strengths of the defensive earthworks, bristling with gunpowder weapons, used at the battles of Cerignola (1503) and Bicocca (1522) that Eltis regards as revolutionary. This continuity is not surprising. As Bert Hall has observed, the handgun and the arquebus continued to be deployed in primarily defensive tactical formations throughout the fifteenth and sixteenth centuries, because of the length of the reloading cycle.[18] The weapon was most effective when used *en masse* at short range, supported by earthworks and infantry armed with staff weapons.

It may be that the impact of the Hussite system, which required an enemy obliging enough to hurl himself at the *wagenburg*, was too limited to have a major effect on European warfare. Nevertheless, the Hussites' initial success seems to have encouraged European armies in the use of handguns. The generally recognised point at which the Spanish adopted firearms in significant numbers is in the aftermath of their defeat at Seminara, Italy, in 1495. Here Gonsalvo de Cordoba suffered his first and only defeat. His heterogeneous Italian and Spanish army was swept from the field by Swiss pikemen in French service. Thereafter, it is assumed, 'the Great Captain' re-equipped his crossbow-men with the arquebus, an effective trigger-operated hand-held firearm. At Cerignola, in 1503, these arquebusiers, firing from entrenched positions, won their first notable success, allegedly revolutionising European warfare as they

---

[17] Eltis, p. 43.
[18] Bert S. Hall, *Weapons and Warfare in Renaissance Europe* (London, 1997), pp. 105–133.

did so.[19] In reality the Spanish had actually been committed to the use of hand-guns long before they arrived in Italy in 1495. Alfred D. McJoynt has argued that the final stages of the *Reconquista* was 'the launching pad for the Spanish army's preference for firearms'. McJoynt also draws attention to the carvings on the choir stalls of the cathedral of Toledo showing Spanish arquebusiers of the *Reconquista* in action. These show tough and disciplined Castilian infantry fighting alongside crossbowmen. They are aiming and firing their weapons *from the shoulder.* McJoynt concludes 'it appears that the handgun had by 1481 passed beyond the awkward, hand-held, match-lighting phase'.[20] R. Coltman Clepham noted that 'by the end of the fifteenth century, the handgun may be said to have attained, though roughly, the form we are familiar with. It was dis-charged generally from the shoulder, with or without a rest.'

Infantry firearms, with their heavy charges, developed increasingly curved stocks which allowed them to be braced against the shoulder. Lighter and straighter pieces, used by cavalry, continued to be braced against the cheek for greater accuracy. As late as the reign of Louis XIII, some French troopers were still firing their weapons in this manner. The technical development of the handgun itself was an on-going process. The sixteenth century did see advances in weapon design, notably the wheel-lock, rifling and the military pistol. Yet none of these developments seem of any more intrinsic significance than those of the fifteenth century.[21] All early modern firearms were limited in their battle-field potential by the inherent ballistic qualities of smoothbore weapons fired by a matchlock system, making them slow firing, inaccurate and most effective only at short range. Nor did the gun sweep aside the bow. Michael Mallet has suggested that it was not the arquebus's superiority as a weapon but its low cost that led Italian armies to adopt it in place of the crossbow in the late fifteenth century.[22] Indeed, the solid and reliable crossbow soldiered on with French armies until well into the sixteenth century. The Gascon Captain Blaise de Mon-luc's company was armed entirely with crossbows as late as 1523.[23] Twenty-one

[19] For a full account of the campaigns of the Great Captain, see D.M.R.Esson, 'The Italian Campaigns of Consalvo De Cordoba', Parts 1 and 2, *The Army Quarterly*, vol. 80 (1959–60), and vol. 81 (1960–61), pp. 235–246, pp. 105–120, and Gerald De Gaury, *The Grand Captain, Gonzalo de Cordoba* (London, 1955).

[20] Albert D. McJoynt (ed.), *The Art of War in Spain: The Conquest of Granada, 1481–1492* (London, 1995), pp. 36–37.

[21] R. Coltman Clephan, 'The Military Handgun of the Sixteenth Century', *The Archaeologi-cal Journal*, vol. 67 (1910), pp. 110–111. Rifling may have been invented in the closing years of the fifteenth century. See Coltman Clephan, 'An Outline of the History of Gunpowder and that of the Hand-Gun, from the Epoch of the Earliest Records to the end of the Fifteenth Cen-tury', *The Archaeological Journal*, vol. 66 (1909), p. 170.

[22] Michael Mallet, *Mercenaries and their Masters* (London, 1974), p. 158.

[23] Ian Roy (ed.), *Blaise de Monluc, the Valois-Habsburg Wars and the French Wars of Relig-ion* (London, 1971), p. 41.

years later English besiegers of Boulogne noted the presence of crossbowmen amongst the defending garrison.[24]

The longbow had an even greater longevity, and not just in English hands. The rapid fire possible with a bow made it an ideal weapon to complement fire-arms, to provide covering fire for arquebusiers as they reloaded. For this reason the Venetian navy continued to recruit bowmen throughout the sixteenth century. Galleys arming in Crete in 1538 were instructed to take on 'good, reli-able and skilled archers'. A Venetian galley's inventory of 1556 lists twenty arquebuses and twenty of the older style *schioppi* handgun together with fifty bows. This combination of bows and firearms enabled missile infantry to main-tain a constant barrage of fire. Only with the increasingly widespread use of the longer and more powerful musket in the latter half of the century did the Vene-tians take the decision to phase out the bow, choosing range and armour penetra-tion over rapidity of fire. Even then some captains continued to favour the archer. As late as 1617 the Venetian Senate protested against the continued use of 'bows and arrows which are useless and superfluous weapons'.[25]

The emphasis here is on the continuity between fifteenth- and sixteenth-century warfare. The handgun itself evolved technologically but always within certain inherent limitations. The early fifteenth-century handgun gave way to the arquebus with its curved stock and heavier charge, to give marginal improve-ments in range and penetrative power. In the latter half of the sixteenth century similar marginal improvements were achieved by the large calibre musket, which fired a heavier ball but at the expense of mobility. The weapon was so large it required a rest for its barrel when fired and most infantry continued to favour lighter pieces, the arquebus or the caliver. These weapons were always startlingly inaccurate and unlikely to kill at ranges of 100 metres or more. To pick a date, or even a century, when the impact of such weapons was revolution-ary is problematic in the extreme. The previous precedents and essential conti-nuity in military practice will always surface. Were the Hussites military revolutionaries? Zizka's use of firearms may have been novel but his basic tactic of using effective missile weapons from a strong defensive position was not new. Zizka had fought for France at Agincourt. He may well have learnt from the English the value of disciplined, self-confident infantry using missile weapons from a well defended position.[26] Firearms, one could argue, did not revolution-ise warfare but slotted neatly into existing tactical systems.

[24] John Leslie (ed.), 'Diary of the Siege and Capture of Boulogne, 1544', *Journal of the Society of Army Historical Research*, vol. 1 (1922), p. 196.
[25] J.R.Hale, 'Men and Weapons: The Fighting Potential of Sixteenth-Century Venetian Gal-leys', in Hale, *Renaissance War Studies* (London, 1985), p. 322.
[26] McJoynt, *Art of War in Spain*, pp. 18 and 73.

Pole arms and staff weapons

On the battlefield arquebusiers were usually protected by bodies of infantry armed with the pike. Highly drilled and rapidly moving columns of close order pike could swiftly overrun enemy infantry formations. Opposing cavalry could be easily fended off, their lances out-reached by the longer infantry pike. The pike column could thus manoeuvre with confidence on the battlefield in the face of both rival infantry and cavalry. This, David Eltis has argued, was a decisive break from the past.[27] Successful medieval infantry relied on an enemy with enough misplaced confidence to throw himself headlong at a highly defensible position. This had been the case with the English at Crécy, Poitiers and Agincourt during the Hundred Years War. It was also true of the Hussites and their victories at Luditz and Kütenberg in 1421. The pike, on the other hand, gave infantry an offensive capability. This seems to have been its revolutionary contribution to warfare.[28]

Yet, once again, one must question whether a truly decisive break with existing tactical practice had actually taken place. At Courtrai in 1302 and Bannockburn in 1314, blocks of spearmen had behaved very much as pike phalanxes, overrunning even mounted opponents.[29] Eltis dismisses these precedents, because he believes they were unique cases, dependent on favourable terrain. Both the Scots and the Flemish had advanced against an enemy disorganised by protective pits or broken ground. Eltis believes that it was the 'achievement of the Swiss to use pikemen effectively, even in the face of horse' and to do this 'without a terrain advantage'. However, as with gunpowder weapons, the precise nature of this infantry revolution has been misunderstood. Eltis claims that 'the Swiss had gradually changed their weapons and tactics in the course of the later middle ages, adopting the pike phalanx in the course of the fourteenth century'.[30] They had gone on to win a series of decisive victories, most notably at Morgarten in 1315 and at Laupen in 1339 against mounted Austrian men-at-arms.

Yet these victories were not won with the pike, but with the halberd, a pole arm perhaps 2 metres in length, but of considerably less reach than a pike. As late as the battle of Arbedo in 1422 the majority of Swiss infantry still carried the halberd rather than the pike. At Morgarten in 1315 the Austrian cavalry had been caught in a narrow defile. They found it impossible to form up for a charge, and the halberd-armed Swiss had swarmed amongst them, hamstringing horses, hooking riders from their steeds, knocking them to the ground, and hammering them to death. This was, of course, an ambush in favourable terrain, which may make Morgarten an exceptional case. On an open field halberdiers

---

[27] Eltis, *Military Revolution in Sixteenth-Century Europe*, p. 45.
[28] Eltis, pp. 23–24.
[29] Sir Charles Oman, *The Art of War in the Middle Ages*, vol. 2 (London, 1992), pp. 84–100 and 113–116.
[30] Eltis, p. 44.

could not face cavalry, or so, at least, the chivalry of Europe assured itself. At Laupen, however, in 1339, Swiss halberdiers proved the opposite. Here, on a gentle slope well suited to cavalry action, Austrian men-at-arms were once again routed by halberd-armed infantry. The halberdiers had, it must be admitted, struggled to keep the men-at-arms at bay, and valuable assistance had been rendered to them by spear-armed allies. Yet in the aftermath Swiss armies still retained a higher proportion of halberds than pikes. The impact of Laupen was so great that the next time an Austrian army faced the Swiss in a major battle, at Sempach in 1386, they chose, like the French at Poitiers, to dismount. As for the Swiss, their willingness to take the battle to the enemy pre-dates their wholesale adoption of the pike.

When the Swiss did begin to increase the proportion of pikemen in their ranks it was not in response to the threat posed by cavalry, but a result of a rare defeat inflicted upon them by dismounted Italian *condottieri* at Arbedo in 1422. The Swiss Confederates had been pushing across the Alps into the northern valleys of the tributaries of the River Po. An Italian army comprising six thousand horse and several thousand infantry had raced to meet one marauding force of four thousand men of Uri, Unterwalden, Zug and Lucerne. Desperately outnumbered, the Swiss halberdiers and pikemen (comprising only about a third of their infantry) had fended off Italian cavalry charges with their usual ease. For their next attack, the Italians dismounted and attacked in column, using their lances effectively as pikes. This time the Swiss themselves were overrun. It was in response to this, the danger posed by heavily armed and well disciplined infantry, that the Swiss originally chose to adopt the pike as their main infantry weapon.[31]

The pike may well have given the Swiss a more effective weapon system than the halberd, but it did not revolutionise their tactics. Their ferocity, self-confidence, discipline and willingness to carry the battle to any opponent had been features of their tactics whilst the halberd was still their primary weapon. Social context had a far greater impact than technology upon the Swiss military system. The Swiss economy could not afford to keep large masses of men under arms for long periods of time while crops rotted in the fields. They had to win their battles quickly. Mountainous Switzerland did not produce large numbers of heavy cavalry comparable to the shock arm of rival European armies, but was dependent on foot soldiers. The poor Swiss mountaineer could not afford expensive body armour. His best hope of protection lay in closing quickly and dispatching his enemy. For these reasons the Swiss developed a cohesive, confident infantry-based force which won its victories by advancing rapidly on its enemies with an unparalleled ferocity.[32] Siegfried Hoyer has summed up the Swiss military system as 'dictated by the composition of the . . . popular army, for it was

---

[31] Oman, *Art of War in the Middle Ages*, vol. 2, p. 263.
[32] Dennis Showalter, 'Caste, Skill, and Training: The Evolution of Cohesion in European Armies from the Middle Ages to the Sixteenth Century', *The Journal of Military History*, vol. 57 (1993), pp. 423–425.

difficult for those left behind in the towns and villages to dispense with the labour power of the warriors under arms, and simultaneously to support the army for any length of time'.[33]

The emergence of 'pike and shot' units: an adaptive response

Initially, therefore, the use of the pike as the primary infantry weapon was fundamentally tied to an underlying commitment to an offensive doctrine that promised a swift and favourable decision on the battlefield. Yet, despite the early successes, use of the pike could not guarantee victory. On the continent pike columns came to grief at Cerignola (1503), Ravenna (1512), Marignano (1515) and Bicocca (1522). Their nemesis was usually entrenched gunpowder weapons, but not always. At Ravenna pike-armed *Landsknechte* (German infantry) had tumbled into Imperial trenches defended by Spanish sword and buckler men. In the ensuing mêlée the swordsmen slaughtered the unfortunate pikemen who struggled to use their unwieldy weapons effectively.[34] Bert Hall has argued that, in the aftermath of these disasters, the pike's primary function on the later sixteenth-century battlefield was, ultimately, defensive and that Bicocca was the last time the weapon was used offensively.[35] Such an assertion requires modification, for the pike retained its offensive capability as long as it remained in service. The Scots utilised the assault by close-order pike column at Pinkie in 1547. Peter Englund has suggested that the Swedish army, with its 'almost doctrinaire mistrust of firepower' continued to base offensive tactics around large numbers of pikemen as late as the Great Northern War of 1700–1721.[36]

Where the pike proved most effective was in those armies which integrated it into existing tactical systems. The most striking example is that of the Spanish. Already committed to the use of firearms, they were highly proficient in the combination of pike, shot and field fortification. This combined arms approach was soon to make Spain the dominant military power in Europe. No one single factor had revolutionised their tactical system; their success in the sixteenth century has its roots in the developments of the preceding decades, if not centuries. The strong links between the *Reconquista* and the Great Italian Wars can be seen, for example, in the often unappreciated role played by the *Santa Hermandad* in the Italian campaigns of 1495 to 1498. This 'brotherhood' was originally drawn from the militia of fortified cities but during wars with the Moors had frequently mixed with royal troops. As royal authority grew in Spain so the

---

[33] Siegfried Hoyer, 'Arms and Military Organisation in the German Peasant War', in Bob Scribner and Gerhard Benecke (eds), *The German Peasant War of 1525 – New Viewpoints* (London, 1979), p. 99.

[34] See F.L.Taylor, *The Art of War in Italy 1494–1529* (London, 1993), pp. 180–204.

[35] Bert S. Hall, *Weapons and Warfare in Renaissance Europe*, pp. 213–214.

[36] Peter Englund, *The Battle of Poltava* (London, 1992), pp. 90 and 98–99. According to Englund, a 150-strong Swedish company of 1709 would comprise one hundred musketeers and fifty pikemen.

monarchs continued to use these same men as part of their army, both in Spain and abroad. In 1493 *Hermandad* soldiers accompanied Columbus to the New World. More significant still were the *Hermandad* captains who accompanied Gonzalo de Cordoba to Italy. Eventually these troops merged completely into the regular army.[37]

The Spanish army had not re-invented itself in Italy; it had adapted. The requirements of a war against disciplined Franco-Swiss infantry and heavy men-at-arms were different to those of a war against Moorish and Granadine armies built largely around light cavalry. Thus the Spanish strengthened their own cavalry arm with Italian *condottieri*. They increased the proportion of their infantry who carried pikes, and maintained their established commitment to hand-held firearms. They also took advantage of their expertise in building field fortifications. In short, the troops of the *Reconquista* took the necessary steps to meet the changed circumstances of the war in Italy. 'Adaptation' is surely a more appropriate description for this process than 'revolution'.

Adaptation was also the key word in the development of Italian military practice. As with the *Hermandad*, Italian military institutions enjoyed a long continuity of experience. Michael Mallet has documented the development of standing forces in fifteenth-century Italy, which grew from the garrison troops of the leading city states. These included the infantry *provisionati* and permanent cavalry forces, the household guard of the *famiglia ducale* and the *lanze spezzate* (broken lances), individuals employed directly by the state. In the face of demonstrations of foreign military might, the Italians adapted their own techniques. The infantry forces gradually swapped their swords, spears and bucklers for pikes and their crossbows for handguns, then arquebuses. Mounted *condottieri* conducted some of the earliest experiments involving the use of firearms from horseback. Italian gunners, like the Spanish, became adept at utilising entrenchments, making the use of their cannon viable on the battlefield.[38]

This same adaptive patten is visible in the development of infantry tactics throughout the early modern period. Whilst qualitative differences remained amongst Europe's infantry (the Swiss, followed by the *Landsknechte* and the Spanish, were generally held to be the most reliable), the general trend was towards standardisation in tactics and equipment. Throughout the fifteenth and sixteenth centuries, classical precedents were cited as the most important authorities on tactics. The *De Re Militari* of Flavius Renatus Vegetius remained the most popular work, but Frontius, Polybius and Caesar were all avidly consulted. The employment of Roman missile infantry, armed with javelin and sling-shot, as originally described by Aelian in about AD 100, was supposedly the inspiration for many of the reforms instigated by Maurice of Nassau in 1594. In particular, a Roman precedent was cited for the counter-march, the technique

---

[37] Paul Stewart, 'The Santa Hermandad and the First Italian Campaign of Gonzalo de Córdova, 1495–1498', *Renaissance Quarterly*, vol. 28, part 1 (1975), pp. 29–37.
[38] Michael Mallet, *Mercenaries and their Masters* (London, 1974), p. 110.

by which successive ranks of musketeers fired volleys and then marched to the rear of the formation to reload.[39]

Yet, much as the order and discipline of Roman armies continued to be a positive example, it would be wrong to overestimate the tactical debt to classical authorities. The contents of classical works on military theory must have been interpreted in the light of current practice. Aelian's skirmishes cannot have operated in close order as an early modern commander would have understood the concept. A javelin or a sling-shot requires a considerable amount of room to the rear of the thrower or slinger to be used effectively. Instructions for troops armed with javelins and slings cannot have provided a literal model for those armed with muskets. Maurice may have cited the classical precedent of Aelian to give his reforms intellectual respectability.

It would seem possible that what he actually did was refine tactics that had already developed in Europe over the preceding century. In broad terms, the tactics of Aelian's missile troops, who operated in rotating ranks to deliver continuous fire, were already being mirrored by European troops well before Maurice of Nassau's reforms. An English 'Captain's Handbook' of 1562 describes how small bodies of arquebusiers could discharge their weapons in sequence to maintain constant fire.[40] This work also describes a 'snail' formation, whereby successive ranks of arquebusiers fire their weapons then wheel away to the flank. This snail formation, an obvious precursor of the counter-march, probably had its origins in the late fifteenth century. According to Hans Delbrück, units of handgunners were being instructed to fire alternately as early as 1477. In Spain Cardinal Ximenez's militia, established in 1516, were trained 'in forming up and in the caracole'. Later in the century the word 'caracole' would be particularly associated with pistol-armed cavalry, but here it indicates that militiamen were being drilled to fire in sequence, one rank firing then stepping back to reload whilst another rank stepped forward to take their place. In 1515, at the Battle of Marignano, French and Italian arquebusiers had practised this technique in action, using 'snail fire' against the Swiss.[41] Not only did this technique allow arquebusiers to maintain a continuous barrage of fire, but the simultaneous discharge of weapons maximised the effectiveness of the gun. The devastating effect of volley fire would also seem to have been well known in the first half of the sixteenth century. Blaise de Monluc describes how French and Italian arquebusiers advanced swiftly on English troops outside Boulogne in 1545, discharged their weapons simultaneously and then charged into the mêlée with their swords.[42] Nor could classical authors offer much useful advice on the deployment of pike with firearms. Most commanders strove to achieve a balance

---

[39] Geoffrey Parker, 'The "Military Revolution" – A Myth?', in Rogers (ed.), *Military Revolution Debate*, p. 39.

[40] J.R.Hale, 'On a Tudor Parade Ground: The Captain's Handbook of Henry Barrett, 1562', in J.R.Hale, *Renaissance War Studies*, p. 257.

[41] Hans Delbrück, *The Dawn of Modern Warfare* (London, 1990), p. 148.

[42] Roy (ed.), *Blaise de Monluc*, p. 130.

between the proportion of pike and shot in their armies. Arquebusiers unsupported by pikemen would be ridden down by enemy cavalry. Blocks of pikemen unsupported by arquebusiers would be shot down by the enemy's firearm troops and cannon. In the early decades of the sixteenth century most armies maintained more pike than shot. Writing during the reign of Edward VI, an English military theorist, Thomas Audley, suggested that one third shot to two thirds pike was the correct proportion for a 'small' force, whilst 'larger' forces might have only a fifth of their infantry armed with missile weapons. He bases his tactical ideas on French and German practice and describes in detail the operation of a sixteenth-century infantry 'battle' (unit) in action.

What is particularly striking is the extent to which Audley's pike and shot formation mirrors the tactical deployment of fifteenth-century infantry. The gun has replaced the bow in tactical formations that had, as yet, remained largely unchanged. The battle was the standard tactical unit of infantry. Traditionally armies in the fields were divided into three battles, the vanguard, the main battle and the rearward. From the late fifteenth century onwards the trend was increasingly towards a slightly larger number of smaller battles, perhaps six to eight. Infantry, Audley wrote, was best deployed in a regular formation, either exactly square, or twice as broad as it was deep. The individual battle was to be composed of five distinct parts. The first five or six ranks were to be pike. To give this formation an advantage if it clashed head on with a rival pike battle, Audley suggests that a rank of shot might be included behind the first rank of pike. This could fire a volley over the pikemen's heads, at short range, into the enemy column.

There is nothing revolutionary about this use of a missile weapon in close conjunction with pike. This particular tactic had been developed in the fifteenth century by longbowmen serving in the Burgundian army. In his military ordinance of 1473 Charles the Bold had ordered that pikemen be trained to:

> ... advance in close formation in front of the ... archers, kneel at a sign from them, holding their pikes lowered to the level of a horse's back so that the archers can fire over the said pikemen as if over a wall. Thus, if the ... pikemen see the enemy are breaking rank, they will be near enough to charge them in good order according to their instructions ... [43]

In the sixteenth century rival infantries simply retained the tactic, substituting arquebuses and pistols for bows. Famously, the method was utilised by both French and Imperialists at Ceresoles in 1544.

Behind the initial ranks of pike in his battle, Audley placed a core of men, armed with bills, halberds or two-handed swords. Although the proportion of men armed with these shorter weapons declined steadily over the century, they remained useful in the confines of the mêlée. Once the pikes had locked, swords and short pole arms were handy weapons, as had been demonstrated at Ravenna.

[43] Philip Vaughan, *Charles the Bold, the Last Valois Duke of Burgundy* (London, 1973), p. 210.

Behind the shorter weapons was another rank of pike, and behind them another rank of halberds, protecting the battle's standards. The final rank, guarding the rear of the battle, would again be composed of pike. The whole formation was surrounded by a sleeve of 'shot', men armed with arquebus or musket.

Again, this deployment of missile troops has earlier precedents. Both Matthew Bennett and E.M.Lloyd have pointed out the similarities between the tactics of the fifteenth and sixteenth centuries. The deployment of a core of infantry flanked by sleeves of missile troops in Audley's battle closely resembles the combination of dismounted men-at-arms supported by flanking 'herses' (units) of archers that was standard practice during the Hundred Years War.[44]

This element of continuity with fifteenth-century infantry formations did not preclude tactical ability. Even large formations were capable of manoeuvre and redeployment. Audley's sleeve of shot could, if threatened by oncoming horse, shelter beneath the outstretched pike. Alternatively, arquebusiers could file through the ranks of pike, to the safety of the middle of the formation as it redeployed as a square. Component sections of the battle could function independently if called upon to do so. Beyond the sleeve of shot was the skirmish line of missile infantry. This 'forlorn hope' maintained a constant barrage of harassing fire on enemy formations, advancing or retreating as necessary, utilising natural cover to its best advantage. The terrible effectiveness of such skirmishers at Pavia in 1525, where they broke up formations of French men-at-arms, demonstrates the flexibility and efficiency of small-unit tactics in the early sixteenth century. Well before the reforms of Maurice of Nassau, European infantry could operate efficiently in units ranging in size from the 100-strong band of English armies through to the 400-strong *landsknecht Fähnlein* or the 3000-strong Spanish *tercio*, which emerged in the 1530s. Early sixteenth-century infantry warfare was not simply a question of mass against mass.[45]

The mounted arm: heavy cavalry

The sophistication of infantry warfare was matched by the mounted arm. The role of cavalry in early modern warfare has again been much debated. Here David Eltis has, once again, dealt very effectively with the misconceptions concerning cavalry that occur in the Roberts' thesis, and are, to an extent, perpetuated by Parker. Cavalry, whilst it could be held at bay by determined infantry, continued to be an effective force on the early modern battlefield. Indeed heavy

[44] Matthew Bennett, 'The Development of Battle Tactics in the Hundred Years War', in Anne Curry and Michael Hughes (eds), *Arms, Armies and Fortifications in the Hundred Years War* (Woodbridge, 1994), p. 8. E.M.Lloyd, 'The "Herse" of Archers at Crécy', *English Historical Review*, vol. 10 (1895), pp. 539–40.

[45] Thomas Audley, 'A Treatise on the Art of War', *The Journal of the Society of Army Historical Research*, vol. 6 (1927), pp. 65–78, 129–133. For the clash at Ceresoles between rival columns of pike and shot, see Ian Roy (ed.), *Blaise de Monluc*, pp. 104–117. For Pavia, see Angus Konstam, *Pavia 1525* (Osprey, London, 1996).

cavalry had undergone something of a renaissance of its own during the fifteenth century. Reliable infantry armed with pike, or protected by some form of
stockade, be it sharpened stakes or waggon fortress, had generally been able to
defy the mounted charge. This continued to be the case, but cavalry still had a
vital battlefield role, particularly in favourable circumstances. Unprotected
missile infantry on open ground was terribly vulnerable to horse. Poor quality
infantry, which doubted its own courage, could break and flee before oncoming
horse, for the psychological effect of the charge was often the man-at-arms'
most potent weapon. Infantry that had been shaken by bombardment or prolonged mêlée might also prove unable to withstand a well timed charge. Cavalry
that could deliver that charge to an unprotected flank stood an excellent chance
of success, even against sound infantry. Similarly, infantry was vulnerable as it
manoeuvred. An advance could be prevented by charging cavalry, since infantry
would have to halt and form up in close ranks to prevent the horse from penetrat-
ing their formation.

In short, cavalry remained an essential element of the early modern army.
Indeed, an army without cavalry was unlikely to achieve a decisive victory on
the field of battle. Mounted troops were vital if a beaten enemy was to be
pursued and destroyed. At Granson in 1476, Charles the Bold was able to withdraw his Burgundian army with only minimal casualties, for his victorious
Swiss opponents had few, if any, horse of their own. A year later at Nancy, Charles's army was utterly destroyed, for following the Swiss infantry's success on
the battlefield the Burgundian army was ridden down by the Swiss's Italian
allies.[46]

Late fifteenth-century men-at-arms had their effectiveness boosted by
improvements in armour that rendered them less vulnerable to arrows or crossbow bolts, and by the adoption of the *arrêt de cuirasse*, the lance rest. With
heavy lances weighing up to 16 kilograms it was a difficult task to lower, aim
and balance the weapon in a charge. On collision with an opponent the shock of
impact might cause the lance to splinter, or break the lancer's arm. The *arrêt de
cuirasse* solved this problem. The weight of the lance was now supported on a
prong attached to the breastplate. This lance rest acted as a fulcrum for the
lance, so it could be lowered from vertical to horizontal whilst the horse moved
at speed. On impact the lance was braced effectively against the whole breastplate, absorbing recoil and keeping the weapon firmly on target. Malcolm Vale
has commented that 'the introduction of such technical innovations in the use of
the lance had served to make the mounted man into a form of living projectile
whose force of impact against both horse and foot was greater than it had ever
been'. The device was in widespread use by 1420, giving the fully armoured
mounted man-at-arms a new lease of life which lasted well into the next
century.[47]

[46] Malcolm Vale, *War and Chivalry* (London, 1981), p. 127.
[47] Vale, pp. 114–119. François Buttin, 'La lance et l'arrêt de cuirasse', *Archaeologia*, vol. 99
(1965), pp. 77–177.

The 'English' tactic of dismounting men-at-arms to strengthen infantry for-mations, in fact widely practised throughout Europe, survived, but was far from obligatory. In 1465, when Charles the Bold's Burgundians clashed with the French at Montl'hery, he first dismounted his knights, then had most of them remount, trusting his luck ultimately to the charge. Charles's decision to have his men-at-arms fight mounted is indicative of cavalry's potential as the decisive arm. When Charles VIII of France invaded Italy in 1494 over half of his army was composed of heavily armoured, lance wielding *gendarmerie*.[48] This renais-sance of heavy cavalry was ultimately limited by the presence of skilled and self-confident infantry on the battlefield, supported by artillery and whose pike and shot formations were able to combine fire and shock action. The deaths of the talented French commander Gaston de Foix at Ravenna in 1512, at the hands of Spanish pikemen, and of Pierre du Terrail, the Chevalier Bayard, shot by a Spanish arquebusier in 1524, symbolise the man-at-arms battlefield vulnerabil-ity. From this point on, the proportion of cavalry in west European armies declined steadily. This has been interpreted as one of the central features of the military revolution, yet it is little more than a return to the status quo of 1415. Europe's nobles began to fight dismounted again, content to trail a pike and seek positions of honour as captains of foot, like the Gascon cavalier Blaise de Monluc 'who ever had an inclination for foot service'.[49]

Heavy cavalry did not disappear from the battlefield entirely. The develop-ment of more sophisticated firearms, especially the pistol, allowed some heavy horse to transform itself 'from an instrument of shock into one of mobile fire-power'.[50] Horsemen had experimented with firearms from a surprisingly early date. A Munich manuscript of about 1460 shows a German knight in the unlikely act of firing a *Faustrohr*, an early form of short handgun, from horse-back at a fleeing enemy's back.[51] Ignited by placing a piece of tinder directly into the touch-hole, such a weapon would have been incredibly difficult to dis-charge from horseback and practically impossible to reload. The development of the matchlock firing mechanism was a considerable improvement. Yet even the arquebus was a cumbersome device to use whilst mounted, only really practical for light cavalry unencumbered by plate armour. It was the wheel-lock that allowed heavy cavalry to adopt a truly effective firearm, the pistol.

The first effective pistols, still referred to as *Faustrohr*, seem to have appeared first in Germany in the 1520s. Throughout the sixteenth century the German mercenary *Reiter* carried the weapon across Europe. By mid-century the pistol was in widespread use, being adopted by French cavalry in 1544. During the same decade the weapon, usually referred to as a dagge, was intro-

---

48 Sir Charles Oman, *A History of the Art of War in the Middle Ages*, vol. 2, pp. 429–430. Vale, p. 128.
49 Roy (ed.), *Blaise de Monluc*, p. 39.
50 Michael Howard, *War in European History* (Oxford, 1976), p. 34.
51 R. Coltman Clephan, 'The Military Handgun of the Sixteenth Century', p. 145.

duced to the British Isles. Several are recorded in the inventory of the Tower of London taken in 1547.

Its use in action was still novel enough to be considered worthy of note. An early battlefield casualty was recorded in 1548 when an English officer called Christopher Ellerkar was shot in the neck by a French pistoleer outside Haddington. The injured Ellerkar had carried a lance and had killed his assailant before he could reload.[52] Indeed, in combat between cavalry, experienced soldiers such as the Elizabethan veteran Roger Williams continued to believe that the lancer had the advantage.[53] Contrary to Roberts' contention that the lance was abandoned, most armies continued to maintain some units of lancers. This suggests a continued belief in the potential of shock action and the usefulness of the weapon well into the latter half of the sixteenth century. With armour offering little protection from guns, these lancers adapted their equipment, seeking safety in mobility. Horse armour was largely abandoned by 1550, and many riders themselves chose stout leather boots over leg armour. Whilst retaining the lance, they adopted the pistol as their favoured secondary weapon, replacing the mace or war axe, for use in the mêlée. In English parlance these troopers were demi-lancers. Faster, cheaper and more agile than the traditional man-at-arms, the lancer still offered the potential of decisive shock action on the battlefield. The psychological impact of the lancers' advance was far greater than that of the pistoleer. Williams observed in the wars in France and the Low Countries that 'the charge of the [lancers] is terrible and resolute, being in carier to break; the enemies perceive their resolution is to enter, and not wheel about like unto pistolers'.[54] Lowered lances and thundering hoofs were far more likely to send a nervous infantryman fleeing for cover than trotting pistoleers, who he knew would wheel away once their pistols were fired.

For Williams this problem was compounded by the lack of skill of some troops who carried the pistol. He singles out the German *Reiter* as particularly likely to misuse his weapon, either loading it incorrectly so it failed to discharge, or firing it too soon, before reaching effective range. Pistol-armed cavalry abandoned the charge *en haye* (in line) favoured by the lance-armed *gendarmerie*. In its place they perfected the caracole, whereby cavalry attacked in column, with successive ranks riding up to the enemy line, discharging their pistols and wheeling off to left or right, reloading and rejoining the rear of the column. The caracole was merely the mounted equivalent of the infantry counter-march. By this means the cavalry could maintain an almost constant barrage of fire. The manoeuvre required skill, discipline and nerve, for pistol ranges were short, accurate only at point blank.

The inability of some cavalry to perform this manoeuvre well has led to the

---

[52] *Calendar of State Papers Relating to Scotland, Vol. 1, 1547–63* (Edinburgh, 1898), 257.
[53] John X. Evans (ed.), 'A Brief Discourse of Warre', in *The Works of Sir Roger Williams* (Oxford, 1972), pp. 28–35.
[54] Evans (ed.), p. 34.

caracole being dismissed as entirely ineffectual.[55] Yet capable troopers scored some notable successes, using their pistols to devastating effect and then charging home with the sword against shaken opponents. Their close order could give them an advantage over traditionally armed men-at-arms. The French Huguenot commander François de la Noue, despite reservations about the efficacy of the caracole, actually praised the *Reiters* for their well disciplined formations:

> Herein wee must say that the Germaines exceed all other nations, because they seeme to bee not onlye close but even glewed each to other . . . whensoever they be broken, in their retire and flight they still remaine unseparate and joyned together: which the speares [lancers] do not.[56]

Heavy cavalry, whether armed primarily with lance or pistol, continued to be an essential arm of sixteenth-century armies. Not only useful against rival cavalry, mounted troops threatened disordered or manoeuvring infantry. Against a broken enemy they were irresistible, and could annihilate a fleeing army. David Eltis lists a number of occasions in the sixteenth century when heavy cavalry played a pivotal role on the battlefield: the Battle of the Spurs (1513), Moncontour (1561), Mouk (1574), Gembloux (1578), Courtrai (1587), Ivry (1590), Tournhout (1597) and Nieuport (1600).[57] Although cavalry formed a smaller proportion of armies than in previous centuries the mounted arm was still a potent one. This was also reflected in the development of the light cavalry.

The mounted arm: light cavalry

The development of an effective light cavalry arm, capable of independent action was one of the most important developments of fifteenth- and sixteenth-century warfare. The French commander Martin du Bellay distinguished between four different classes of cavalry in his *Discipline militaire* of 1548. The man-at-arms and the *chevaux légers* (demi-lance) were the shock troops of the mounted arm. They were complemented by two classes of light cavalry, the stradiot or genitor and the mounted arquebusier.[58] The stradiots were recruited in the Balkans, primarily Albania. They appeared in Venetian armies from 1463 onwards and, veterans of the wars against the Turks, were a formidable foe. They rode unarmoured horses and were armed primarily with javelin, scimitar and sword. Faster and more mobile than men-at-arms, the stradiot was still capable of fighting effectively from horseback. Michael Mallet comments:

> clearly the possession of organised units of such troops gave an army much greater manoeuvrability and flexibility in battle . . . both in the mounted crossbowmen [also a feature of Italian armies] and the Stradiot units, the Ital-

55 See, for example, Howard, p. 34.
56 Eltis, *Military Revolution in Sixteenth-Century Europe*, p. 65.
57 Eltis, pp. 21–24.
58 Delbrück, *The Dawn of Modern War*, p. 118.

ians had seen the way forward in cavalry development and the light horse was to become increasingly significant during the Italian wars.[59]

In Italy the stradiots had enjoyed some early successes in skirmishes with the cumbersome and less agile French men-at-arms of Charles VIII, who initially lacked a comparable force of light cavalry.[60] The French, like the Italians and Spanish, went on to employ large numbers of stradiots themselves, investing a considerable amount of money in what was clearly regarded as a valuable arm.

The Spanish also had their own native light cavalry, the genitors. The genitors had developed from contact with Granadine and Moorish light cavalry and proved useful troops in Italy. Armed, like the stradiot, in light armour with sword, shield and javelin, they fought with similar tactics. Using speed and agility to evade charging heavy cavalry, they would hang on to a formation's flanks, hurling their javelins, tempting their opponents to charge, harrying them, wearing them down. When the enemy grew tired or disordered the light horsemen would charge home.[61] In the Burgundian army of the late fifteenth century the *coustillier*, armed with javelin and sword, provided the independent light cavalry arm. Across the Channel, Yorkist and Lancastrian forces had their complements of scourers and prickers, similarly equipped.[62] The possession of lightly armoured horse armed with light lance, spear or javelin gave commanders a long-range strike force, substantially enlarging the battlefield. Williams, who had commanded cavalry himself in the Low Countries, sums up the duties expected of the arm:

> . . . the service of all light horsemen, consists chiefly in marching of great marches . . . to surprise Companies a farre off in their lodgings, or marches, likewise to defeat convoys . . . Also to scout and discover, to spare the . . . Lancers and other horsemen; likewise both to spoil and conduct foragers.[63]

During Williams' service during the latter half of the sixteenth century, the spear- or javelin-armed light cavalry was being supplanted by the mounted arquebusier. The arquebus, at 2.5 to 3 feet long, was a cumbersome weapon to use from horseback. Nevertheless, mounted companies using the weapon had been organised by the Italian *condottiere* Camillo Vitelli as early as 1496.[64] Like the mounted archers of English and Burgundian armies of the fifteenth century, the mounted arquebusier could act as mounted infantry, soldiers who in later centuries would be termed dragoons. Yet they did use their guns from horseback too, however inaccurate their fire must have been. They could even act in close support of lancers, forming wings or a skirmish line to formations of heavier cavalry, mirroring infantry tactics. It is this versatility that, for Williams, made

---

[59] Mallett, *Mercenaries and their Masters*, p. 152.
[60] Taylor, *The Art of War in Italy 1494–1529*, pp. 69–77.
[61] Taylor, pp. 72–73.
[62] Anthony Goodman, *The Wars of The Roses* (London, 1991), pp. 177–178.
[63] Evans (ed.), 'A Brief Discourse of Warre', pp. 30–31.
[64] Delbrück, p. 118.

the mounted arquebusier a more effective soldier than the spear-armed light horseman.[65]

The growth and sophistication of the light cavalry arm is highly significant. It demonstrates again the continued utility of mounted troops in early modern armies, and decisively influenced the manner in which war was waged. An out-scouted commander would be unable either to force a battle on a reluctant opponent or to refuse battle if held at a disadvantage.

However, many of those involved in the military revolution debate seem not to have recognised the importance of light cavalry. It would seem that the absence of discussion of the light cavalry is a consequence of their tactical role. They have rarely been the decisive factor actually on the battlefield. Thus their impact on the ability of armies to fight decisive battles has been obscured. Since the issue of decisive battles has been a crucial one in the debate, the apparently irrelevant light cavalry arm has been neglected. This is an example of how the military revolution debate has restricted thought on early modern military history. The debate has focused attention on specific areas (logistics, infantry, heavy cavalry, siege warfare), to the exclusion of others. This lack of thoroughness when dealing with the preserve of the military historian has inevitably led to mistakes. David Eltis, for example, cites the success of firearm-armed cavalry at Pinkie in 1547 as evidence of the value of heavy cavalry armed with pistols performing the caracole manoeuvre.[66] Yet the contemporary accounts are quite clear. The mercenary firearm cavalry who fought for the English at Pinkie were light cavalry. They were mounted arquebusiers, 'hackbutters on horseback' as the English called them. They did not carry pistols, and there is no evidence that they utilised the caracole.[67] Despite the scant attention that has been paid to light cavalry, they were an influential factor in early modern warfare. In reconnaissance, screening and raiding, an effective independent light cavalry arm added a new dimension to warfare.

They even had an impact on siege warfare, another crucial area in the military revolution debate. Light cavalry could seriously disrupt the logistical arrangements of besieging armies and, conversely, a besieging army's own light cavalry was vital for foraging, raiding and detecting the advance of relief forces. The importance of light cavalry on the peripheries of siege warfare is frequently indicated by Elis Gruffydd, a Welsh soldier who served during the 'Enterprise of Paris and Boulogne' in 1544. As the campaign bogged down, the English force besieging Montreuil became dependent on victualling from Boulogne. Indeed, the danger of starvation became a very real one. The battles to feed the starving besiegers were largely fought by light cavalry, although even some of the King's Burgundian mercenaries, heavily armoured men-at-arms, found themselves engaged on the loathsome task of escorting convoys. Gruffydd gives

[65] Evans (ed.), 'A Brief Discourse of Warre', pp. 31–32.
[66] Eltis, *Military Revolution in Sixteenth-Century Europe*, p. 114.
[67] William Patten, *The Expedition into Scotland, 1547*, in A.F.Pollard (ed.), *Tudor Tracts* (Westminster, 1903), pp. 78, 123.

a typical account of one encounter in which light cavalry featured prominently. An inexperienced English captain has led a disordered and unprepared convoy into a French ambush:

> There Captain Hussey could see the evidence of his folly, for from there he could see the French appearing on the top of the brow a mile and a half away, to the south of which the French killed as many of the victuallers as came over the brow. From there some fled back to seek the safety of the main body, which the French light horse realised and followed them over the hill. There the flock of English horsemen struck them and forced them to recoil a little . . . At this moment the French burst on the English horsemen who turned their backs and as fast as their horses could carry them rode straight on the front of the battle, as if they intended to ride through the footmen . . . but when they came within a stick's throw of the bowmen they turned their horses' heads to the side of the line . . . so as to lead the French within range of the bows and handguns which the English host let fly as soon as they saw the French . . .[68]

The success or failure of a siege could depend on the outcome of such well conducted skirmishes. Gruffydd's description of the clash between French and English light cavalry also gives an indication of the sophistication of their methods. This is an example of classic light cavalry tactics, a feigned retreat drawing an impetuous adversary into the range of missile-armed troops. It is worth noting how well the English light cavalry co-operated with its infantry support, evidence of an effective combined arms approach and tactical competence.

Artillery

In a prepared position, fire from missile troops could be supplemented by cannon. The use of cannon on the battlefield remained problematic, given their slow rate of fire and relative lack of mobility. It was, consequently, much harder to integrate them into the tactical system of armies in the field than to get the component arms of infantry and cavalry to work together. Machiavelli, in his *Art of War* (Florence, 1521), is altogether dismissive of field artillery's potential. In his description of the ideal battle, it is able to fire off only one or two inaccurate shots before being overrun by light cavalry or skirmishers. For sturdy troops, he believed, cannon held little terror. He cites as a worthy example in this respect the Swiss: 'they never decline an engagement out of fear of artillery, but always give the death penalty to those who would stir from the ranks, or those who show the least sign of being frightened by it'.[69] Yet it was the bold tactics of the impetuous Swiss that allowed for an awesome demonstration of how effective cannon could be in the field, if properly supported. At Bicocca in 1522, an

---

[68] M.B.Davies (ed.), 'The "Enterprise" of Paris and Boulogne', *Fouad I University, Bulletin of the Faculty of Arts*, vol. 11, part 1 (1949), pp. 62–64.
[69] Niccoló Machiavelli, *The Art of War* (New York, 1990), pp. 92–97.

assault by the Swiss on Spanish artillery and arquebusiers sheltering behind a sunken road ended in disaster for the attackers. The defeat severely dented Swiss confidence in their ability to seize victory unaided by other arms. There was a growing appreciation, despite Machiavelli's reservations, of the importance of artillery as an offensive arm on the battlefield.

Indeed, this had been evident during the final stages of the Hundred Years War. At Castillon (1453), French cannon had bombarded the English out of a strong defensive position, forcing them to take the offensive. In the ensuing assault the roles of Agincourt and Crécy were effectively reversed, with the English destroyed by missile fire as they struggled to advance. Fifty-five years later the Spanish had a similar experience, but on a far greater scale, at Ravenna. Here the Spanish had occupied a well entrenched position, and their infantry and artillery had been able to keep the French pike at bay. Their cavalry, however, held in reserve behind the trenches, had been unable to withstand a heavy bombardment and had abandoned their position guarding the infantry's flanks. French cavalry was then able to ride through the gaps created by the artillery and attack the Spanish from the rear. At the forefront of those using artillery as an offensive arm were the Portuguese. They had carried cannon with them to Morocco in 1415, for the assault on Ceuta that marked the beginning of the Iberian state's imperial adventure. By the 1440s they had taken advantage of technical innovation in cannon construction, using powerful bronze guns served by German and Flemish mercenaries. They also perfected the shore bombardment, using ship mounted guns to support land forces, as at Qasr-s-Saghir in 1458. The use of delayed action fuses and canister shot was also part of the Portuguese gunner's repertoire in North Africa, long before they became common on European battlefields.[70]

Siege warfare

Much of the Portuguese expertise in the use of cannon was devoted to siege warfare, both in the attack on Moroccan cities and in defence of their own footholds in North Africa. The European use of cannon in sieges was no less significant in Europe. Siege craft and fortifications have become, perhaps, the most important elements of recent debates surrounding the military revolution. The impact of gunpowder weapons on castles and defensive fortifications generally was profound, although not immediate.

In the early fourteenth century early cannon had lined up alongside some of the older, but technically ingenious, siege engines of the middle ages. Rock throwing devices, usually grouped under the generic name of trebuchet, were

[70] John Vogt, 'Saint Barbara's Legion: Portuguese Artillery in the Struggle for Morocco, 1415–1578', *Military Affairs*, vol. 41 (1977), pp. 176–182. Weston F. Cook, 'Warfare and Firearms in Fifteenth-Century Morocco, 1400–1492', *War and Society*, vol. 11, no. 2 (1993), pp. 25–40.

used to hurl missiles of startling weight at besieged castles and towns. These missiles might be hurled into the castle to destroy buildings, kill defenders and terrify the garrison into surrender, or they might be used to batter down high walls and towers.[71] The first cannon were probably less effective than these awesome devices, but they were cheaper (a gun weighing 40 pounds was purchased for 13s 6d in 1353) and, belching flame and smoke as they discharged with a fearsome crash, were a powerful inducement to surrender. The earliest function of cannon in sieges certainly seems to have been as a terror weapon. The walls of fortifications were seldom their target. More normally cannon were used to destroy buildings within those walls, as Henry V used his twelve great guns at Harfleur in 1415.[72]

Over the course of the fifteenth century, gunpowder artillery grew in size and destructive capability, the most important development being the lengthening of the barrel, allowing more accurate firing at greater velocity. With these changes came new opportunities in their tactical deployment. Walls themselves were now to be their targets, through which they could blast breaches for infantry to storm through. Lofty walls that once might have held a besieger at bay for months, or defied him completely, could now be shattered in days. Non-gunpowder artillery such as trebuchets soldiered on, but increasingly as the secondary partner to gunpowder weapons. As France drove the English from Normandy, mangonels (a type of trebuchet) were deployed in assaults on English strongholds, as at the Tour Grise at Verneuil. As late as the 1460s, French inventories list trebuchet-type artillery, and elsewhere they continued to be deployed into the latter decades of the century. During the 1480 siege of Rhodes, the Knights of St John bombarded the Turkish siege lines from within the city with a stone-throwing engine of traditional design.[73]

The French campaign in Normandy is, however, seen as a watershed in the fortunes of gunpowder artillery. Castles and cities that had once been regarded as formidable bastions crumbled before France's all conquering cannon. One hundred English strong points fell in 1450 alone. A year later Guyenne's steadfast loyalty to England was not strong enough to resist the might of the French artillery train.[74]

The architecture of castles had reflected the growing presence of gunpowder weapons for some time. Since the early fourteenth century defenders themselves had hoisted cannon onto walls and towers. Thin medieval walls were, however, unsatisfactory emplacements. The size of cannon, and their recoil, meant that wider, stable gun platforms were needed. Gunports were cut through existing walls at ground level, or in towers which were lowered and reinforced with earth

[71] Philippe Contamine, *War in the Middle Ages* (Oxford, 1984), pp. 104–105. Kelly DeVries, *Medieval Military Technology* (Ontario, 1992), pp. 127–142.
[72] Clifford J. Rogers, 'The Military Revolutions of the Hundred Years War', in Rogers (ed.), *The Military Revolution Debate*, pp. 64–65.
[73] Contamine, pp. 195–196.
[74] Rogers, p. 67.

and timber. In the late fifteenth century the power of artillery gave an added urgency to the modification of aging castles. In Italy and France, particularly, considerable ingenuity was applied to strengthening existing positions. Walls were thickened with earth or masonry, not just to provide a gun platform but to make them more resistant to bombardment. Sometimes this scarping of walls would take the form of a glacis, a sloping surface off which shot might glance. The tops of walls might be stripped of their crenellations because exposed blocks of masonry could shatter dangerously under cannon fire. Round and semi-circular multi-storey bastions, bristling with cannon on every floor, were grafted onto existing walls. Protective ditches, impervious to bombardment, might also be considerably enlarged. Deep ditches were vital to artillery fortifications. Gunpowder had given sappers a new and terrible means of bringing walls crashing down. In 1495 a Sienese architect, Francesco di Giorgio, had exploded a mine under the barbican of the Castel Nuovo in Naples. The effect on the French garrison had been devastating and the castle had fallen soon after. Explosive mines became one more horror of siege warfare, but deep ditches were an obstacle that forced the sapper deeper still.

Medieval castles could thus be reinforced to meet the challenges of fifteenth-century artillery, but these were extemporised solutions that gave no guarantee of success in the face of a large and competently handled siege train. New earthworks, on which defensive artillery would be positioned, might be added to particularly vulnerable points of a fortification. Earth absorbed the impact of shot far better than stone. One method of rendering an old and vulnerable castle more defensible was by adding a *fausse-bray*. This was a low rampart of earth, perhaps faced with masonry, wide enough for cannon to be fired from it. It would be defended by a ditch of sufficient depth to deter storming parties, and so designed to achieve the minimum of dead ground over which enemies might approach unseen and unscathed. Another way of providing support for sections of wall that might be attacked was by building outlying casements. These were detached gun chambers, often built on the floors of dry ditches. They were provided with perhaps half a dozen embrasures, gun ports through which light cannon could pour flanking fire onto attackers as they approached the wall. Besides being used to reinforce the defences of existing castles, such features became standard in the design of new fortifications.

Newly built fortifications were designed around both the threat posed by gunpowder artillery and the need to incorporate cannon into the fortification's defence. In some instances angular towers were abandoned in favour of deep round artillery towers linked by thick high curtain walls pierced with gunports, defended by deep ditches. This style of artillery fortification reached its apogee in the coastal defence fortifications built by England's Henry VIII in the wake of the invasion scare of 1538. Yet it was in Italy that engineers and architects perfected the most effective combination of resilience to offensive artillery and maximisation of defensive fire power. An early exponent of what became known as the *trace italienne* was Leon Battista Alberti, author of *De re aedificatoria*, written in the 1440s, but not published until 1485. Alberti stressed the following principals in the design of fortifications. Walls should be low-lying and wide. Artillery towers should project at an angle beyond the walls, to cover dead ground, and provide a platform for the defender's artillery to bombard the besieger. Similarly angled bastions should also project from the walls, to provide mutually supporting flanking fire in the event of assault. The besiegers should be faced by deep, wide ditches and outlying works: casements, detached bastions and ravelins. These formidable mini-fortifications would have to be tackled before the main defences could be approached. Any assault that merely tried to by-pass them would be subject to devastating flanking fire as it passed. Particular points of strategic value that lay outside the fort, for example a jetty or bridge, could be defended by detached bastions, or by a hornwork, a fortified tentacle reaching out from the castle or city.

In practice the *trace italienne* grew even more elaborate and complex. Ditches became so massive that whole fortifications could be sunk into them. This protected the bottom half of the walls and gave artillery fortifications a menacing low profile in contrast to the soaring walls of the older castle. Defenders as well as besiegers burrowed and dug. Passageways and tunnels connected ravelins and casements to the main fortifications. In 1509 the armies of the League of Cambrai turned on Venice, attacking its possession Padua. The Venetians had reinforced the fortifications of the city, building some powerful outlying bastions. After hard fighting the League managed to capture one of these bastions. Before they even had time to pause for breath, the whole structure, and its victorious captors, were consumed in a massive explosion. The Venetians had mined their own position and destroyed it when it fell. The attackers made no further headway, and the siege was raised soon afterwards. In siege warfare the balance of power was tipping back towards the defender.[75]

Fortification and strategy

Both the new style fortifications and the up-dating of older works had an effect on the strategic planning of military operations. Siege became a lengthy and inordinately expensive business, but an absolutely necessary one for the successful conduct of a campaign. Subduing an enemy meant subduing his fortifications. Open battle, always wasteful and often indecisive, was to be avoided where possible by commanders of talent. For Geoffrey Parker this represents a strategic change that lies at the heart of the military revolution.[76] After the end of the first phase of the Italian Wars in 1529, it was very rare for a commander to actively seek battle unless he had an overwhelming advantage. Ceresoles in

---

[75] For the development of fortifications in the early modern world, see Christopher Duffy, *Siege Warfare: The Fortress in the Early Modern World* (London, 1979), Nicholas Adams and Simon Pepper, *Firearms and Fortifications* (Chicago, 1986), Kelly DeVries, *Medieval Military Technology* (Ontario, 1992), pp. 263–270.

[76] Parker, *The Military Revolution*, pp. 15–16.

1544 was one of the few engagements where both armies actually marched out to meet each other. More usually, where engagements did take place, it was often the consequence of poor generalship, such as the lax reconnaissance that resulted in an outnumbered Huguenot force blundering into a Catholic army at Dreux in 1562. Alternatively, battles might be fought in close connection to sieges if a relief force tried to break through the besieging army, as at St Quentin in 1557.

On the whole pitched battles fought away from siege lines became increasingly rare. Whilst not wholly denying the significant effect of the *trace italienne*, this situation is still not without precedent. Medieval commanders had also sought to avoid battle where possible. That, after all, was a central tenet of Vegetius, the most widely read of the classical authorities in medieval Europe. From 1369 until his death in 1380 the French constable, Bertrand du Guesclin, had confounded English ambitions in France by steadfastly refusing battle, even when he held a numerical advantage. Instead the French defended their cities, towns and castles. If the English by-passed them, the French would sally out to cut off their foragers or lay ambushes. This was not an untypical strategy in medieval Europe. In the fifteenth century artillery had, temporarily, made this strategy of avoidance less viable. With cannon making short work of fortifications, commanders were often forced to fight battles rather than hide behind castle walls. From 1450 to 1529, Europe witnessed an unusually large number of pitched battles. Over the same period, military architects adapted castles and developed the new styles of artillery fortifications. Ultimately they met the challenge of cannon. The *trace italienne* did not create a new balance of power; it restored an old one.

Just as avoiding battle was not a new strategy, neither was the attritional strategy of destruction with which it is often associated. As du Guesclin had artfully avoided the English in the field, they had practised the *chevauchée*, the fast moving destructive raid. Its intention was not to fight battles, but to destroy crops, burn towns, steal cattle and generally inflict enough misery on the populace that their authorities would be forced to negotiate. The Scottish practised the same tactic in the north of England. The avoidance of battle, the importance of siege warfare, the strategy of destruction of resources, all have been cited as features of the military revolution, yet all had long been features of medieval warfare.[77]

Tactical synthesis and military competence

What made it possible for commanders to adopt these strategies was the competence of their officers and the tactical effectiveness of their armies. Without a skilled light cavalry commanders might blunder unexpectedly into their

[77] Prestwich, *Armies and Warfare in the Middle Ages: The English Experience*, pp. 185–218, 281–333.

enemies. The *chevauchée* required mobility, not just of cavalry but from accompanying artillery and infantry too. The possibility of ambush and raid called for a high degree of proficiency in small unit tactics. Nowhere was this more true than during sieges, when the *camisado* (surprise attack) by relatively small numbers of men was widely used by both besieged and besieger. Whether in skirmish, siege or pitched battle, the successful implementation of a wider strategy depended on the combined efficiency of horse, foot and gunner. This synthesis of cavalry, artillery and infantry on the battlefield and in the siege lines should counter any lingering notion that late fifteenth- and early sixteenth-century warfare was simply a case of blundering masses engaging in grim contests of attrition. Many armies were showing considerable sophistication in their organisation.

In particular, Europeans had long admired, and feared, the discipline of Ottoman armies, especially their household cavalry, the *sipahi of the porte*, and their standing force of permanent infantry, the janissaries. The pressed sons of Christian families, the janissaries were rigorously trained from early boyhood. Unswervingly loyal to both Sultan and Islam, theirs was a highly professional corps. Promotion was by merit, not by birth. A well developed bureaucracy and careful logistical arrangements allowed the Ottomans to field massive armies. At Mohacs in 1526 the doomed Hungarians faced an awesome seventy thousand of the Sultan's soldiers, with only twenty-five thousand men of their own. Their discipline and order were a revelation to European observers: 'The Turks surpass our own soldiers for three reasons; they obey their commanders promptly; they never show the least concern for their lives in battle; they can live for a long time without bread and wine, being content with barley and water', wrote Paolo Giovio in 1530.[78]

The Turkish system, which remained dominated by cavalry, had its weaknesses. Lacking pike or halberd the jannisary often had to be protected by linked waggons in action, as at Chaldiran in Persia in 1514. They had, however, adopted gunpowder weapons early, handguns being the standard weapon of the jannisary by the final decade of the fifteenth century. Western historians have tended to assume that they adopted firearms after encountering European troops armed with handguns in the Balkans. In particular, at the Second Battle of Kossova in 1448 John Hunyadi's Hungarian forces, which included large numbers of Bohemian handgunners, have been identified as influencing the Ottomans.[79] Yet the Ottomans were not merely imitating Europeans. The geographical location of the Ottoman Empire exposed the Sultan's armies to a range of differing military practices: Persian horse-centred forces to the east, galley warfare in the Mediterranean, European firearms in the Balkans. Tactically and

---

[78] Quoted in J.R.Hale, 'Armies, Navies and the Art of War', in G.R.Elton (ed.), *The New Cambridge Modern History* (Cambridge, 1962), vol. 2, p. 485.
[79] Djurdjica Petrovic, 'Fire-Arms in the Balkans on the Eve of and after the Ottoman Conquests of the Fourteenth and Fifteenth Centuries', in V.J.Parry and M.E.Yapp (eds), *War, Technology and Society in the Middle East* (London, 1975), pp. 164–194.

technologically the Turks learned much from various foes, including their co-religionists to the east, for the Islamic lands were almost certainly the conduit through which gunpowder originally reached the West.[80] They favoured long and heavy calibre firearms, which, although slow to load, often gave them the edge over European soldiers. This superiority was clear to the Knights of St John defending Malta in 1565. Although ultimately they were able to hold the island fortress, Turkish snipers firing at longer ranges than were normal took a steady toll of the garrison.[81] This professionalism and technical expertise should make us wary of Eurocentric claims that the Ottomans were, as Geoffrey Parker claims, 'expert imitators, but poor innovators'.[82] In the development of a professional permanent standing force, the Ottoman Empire was ahead of Europe.

That the Ottomans failed to keep pace with sixteenth-century developments in Western European infantry tactics is hardly surprising. Following their victory at Mohacs in 1526, the Ottomans in Europe concentrated on siege operations and raiding. In these circumstances they had little incentive to develop a more mobile field artillery or expand their infantry corps. Other than the Austrian Hapsburgs, their major opponents throughout the sixteenth century (Mamelukes in Egypt, Persians in Asia, Hungarians and Poles in eastern Europe) fielded armies based around cavalry, not pike and shot units.

When war came with the Austrians in 1593 the Ottomans found themselves confronted by an army that made sophisticated use of cavalry, infantry and artillery in synthesis.[83] Where west European armies had forged ahead of the Ottomans was in this effective combination of arms on the battlefield. The origins of this approach were evident in the early decades of the fifteenth century. Commanders could recruit their forces according to their specific needs, recruiting bowmen, arquebusiers, gunners, men-at-arms, light cavalry as necessary. Armies were thus composed of specialist units and were best deployed to take advantage of the complementary skills of their component parts.

Amongst the most proficient builders of effective combined arms forces was fifteenth-century Burgundy. In 1417 Duke John the Fearless deployed dismounted men-at-arms with archers and crossbowmen to meet the main thrust of an enemy attack, with mounted archers and men-at-arms guarding their flanks. In the 1476 ordinance of Lausanne Charles the Bold 'prescribed an even more complex battle plan, integrating longbowmen and crossbowmen, men-at-arms, pikemen and gunners into eight "battles", each with its own carefully considered structure, and with systematic provision for liaison and cooperation among the different arms'.[84] Close examination of this ordinance reveals, as Philippe Contamine notes, 'the degree of complexity which a professional soldier could

---

80 DeVries, *Medieval Military Technology*, p. 143.
81 Ernle Bradford, *The Great Siege, Malta 1565* (Harmondsworth, 1964), p. 66.
82 Parker, *The Military Revolution*, pp. 126–127.
83 V.J.Parry, 'La manière de combattre', in V.J.Parry and M.E.Yapp (eds), pp. 218–256.
84 Showalter, 'Caste, Skill, and Training: The Evolution of Cohesion in European Armies from the Middle Ages to the Sixteenth Century', p. 422.

achieve at the end of the fifteenth century'.[85] The first battle lined up from left to right. On the left flank were one hundred men-at-arms, then three hundred archers. In the centre seventeen hundred infantry armed with pike, crossbow and handgun deployed three ranks deep. To their right another three hundred archers, and beyond them another one hundred men-at-arms. The second battle comprised the household troops, arranged from left to right in three groups of men-at-arms, alternated with three archer formations and three pike and shot formations. The remaining six battles deployed in the same manner as the first. To achieve optimum co-operation the eight battles could be brigaded two by two, under the command of four senior captains. This refined deployment allowed for the effective integration of the components of Charles' army.

The Burgundian duke was careful to employ the best available specialists, English, Welsh and Picard archers, Flemish pikemen, German gunners, Italian men-at-arms. It was due to Charles' rash and impulsive nature that this formidable and innovative instrument of war was broken in a disastrous series of battles against the Swiss. The multi-national Burgundian force lacked the cohesion and self-confidence of their opponents. Charles did not allow his troops enough time to develop mutual confidence, leading them into battle prematurely, often against superior numbers. At Granson in 1476 Burgundian infantry units in the centre of the line were ordered to withdraw in an attempt to draw the Swiss forward into a position in which they could be enveloped. However, as soon as these units of infantry began to fall back, their neighbours assumed the worst and broke and fled. Only the Swiss's lack of cavalry prevented them from annihilating the retreating army. In later battles, especially at Nancy in 1477, when the Swiss were supported by allied men-at-arms, the Burgundians were not so fortunate.[86] Nevertheless, the Burgundians' ultimate failure on the battlefield should not obscure the achievement of their military organisation. Most of the innovations that Michael Roberts credits to Gustav Adolphus had been anticipated by the Burgundians, 150 years earlier.

In a series of remarkable ordinances issued between 1468 and 1476, Charles the Bold created a recognisably modern force, comprehensively regulating the equipping, training and organising his armies. The lowest level of organisation was the *lance*. This was a nine-strong unit, comprising a man-at-arms, his page, a *coustillier* (light cavalryman), three mounted archers, a culverineer (handgunner), a crossbowman and a pikeman. The men of the lance were to be uniformed in the blue and white livery of the Duke of Burgandy, emblazoned with a red cross of St Andrew. A clear and effective chain of command was also established. According to the ordinance of 1473, one hundred men-at-arms, each the leader of a nine-man lance, were organised into a company of ordnance. This company was commanded by a *conducteur*. It was sub-divided into four squadrons of equal size. Each squadron was captained by a *chef d'escadre*. Each squadron was further sub-divided into four *chambres* of five men, commanded

---

[85] Contamine, *War in the Middle Ages*, p. 233.
[86] Oman, *The Art of War in the Middle Ages*, vol. 2, pp. 265–272.

by a *chef de chambre*. To ease identification on the battlefield and keep order on the march, each squadron would have its own colours, an ensign for the *conducteur* and cornets for each squadron. Individuals would wear their squadron colours on *bannerols*, attached to their *sallets* (helmets).

The provision of uniforms, standardisation of equipment, sophisticated unit organisation and the establishment of a clear hierarchy of command were features of the Burgundian army long before the military revolution. Even more significantly, Charles ensured that his army was highly trained. The *chef d'escadre* and the *chef de chambre* were instructed to exercise regularly their men-at-arms and the men of the lances. The men-at-arms were to practise charging in close formation, withdrawing on command, rallying, supporting each other in combat and withstanding the enemy's charges. Mounted archers were to learn how to dismount and bring their bows into action quickly. They were to be able 'to march briskly forwards and to fire without breaking rank'. What is more, they were to do this in concert with pike. If threatened by cavalry they were to form squares or circles, with the bows firing over a front rank of pikes.[87]

The Burgundians' emphasis on practical training long precedes the reforms of Maurice of Nassau or Gustav Adolphus. Yet, whilst acknowledging the existence of the Burgundian precedent, David Eltis simply dismisses it as 'a primitive discipline'. This is because, he argues, medieval soldiers lacked 'the complicated mathematical tables later used to draw men up in formation'.[88] Many of those complicated sixteenth-century mathematical tables were in fact entirely impractical as guides for infantry formations. However sophisticated they look on the page they could not have been achieved on the battlefield. The 1562 Captain's Handbook of Henry Barrett contains an eminently practical guide to training for a militia captain, followed by some eminently unpractical mathematical tables. There are few clear guidelines as to which direction the formations are supposed to be facing, and Barrett fails to recognise that a square of men cannot occupy a square of ground.[89] Many of the more theoretical works cited by Eltis were written by men who had never commanded troops in action. Thomas Digges wrote his *An Arithmeticall Militare Treatise Named Stratioticos* in 1579 whilst still a civilian.[90] Even experienced soldiers who turned their hand to writing recommended the most bizarre of formations. Thomas Gerrard, a veteran of fourteen years service in the Spanish army, urged captains to arrange their men in the 'double bissa', a 'convoluted formation not unlike the human intestinal tract'.[91] The French theorist Raimond Fourquevaux designed a series of meticulous formations, based on the most pedantic and exact measurements. The slightest deviation in terrain, not to mention the effects of enemy fire,

---

[87] Vaughan, *Charles the Bold*, pp. 197–229.
[88] Eltis, *Military Revolution in Sixteenth-Century Europe*, p. 59.
[89] Hale, *Renaissance War Studies*, p. 268.
[90] Henry Webb, *Elizabethan Military Science: The Books and the Practice* (London, 1965), pp. 17–27.
[91] Evans (ed.), *The Works of Sir Roger Williams*, p. lxxx.

would render them all valueless in the field. As John Evans has commented, 'the more one reads the more one realises that most of the military writers actually were to varying degrees arithmeticians who thought in terms of symbols that even the most skilful captain could not transform into soldiers prepared for battle'.[92]

The military literature of the late sixteenth and early seventeenth centuries that supposedly diffused the ideas of the military revolution contained a host of fanciful mathematical abstractions which can have been of little practical value to the serving soldier. If these formations were inappropriate for the battlefield, they would have been ludicrous in siege work, which was by then the normal occupation of west European troops. The field training of the Burgundians was surely far more geared to the realities of the battlefield. One cannot help but conclude that the more practical late sixteenth-century soldier would have seen more value in the Burgundian model than in the 'double bissa'. However primitive their discipline, medieval infantry at least had a fair idea of which direction they were supposed to be facing on the battlefield.

Indeed, the level of skill required by even a simple pikeman was far higher than is normally assumed, for his weapon, as John Evans emphasises, 'required deft and resolute manipulation in synchronization with the motions of other soldiers in the column'.[93] Burgundian practice in organisation and practical training in the field was not unique. The Swiss pike column was not simply a human battering ram. It was a fast and well co-ordinated tactical unit that required high levels of skill from individuals working in concert. To achieve this speed and cohesion they developed a sophisticated drill, marching in step to the beat of a drum. Their success led to imitation, for, as Hans Delbrück has noted, 'the creation of the infantry which became the model for all countries was the contribution of the Swiss to world history'.[94]

One of the first to recognise the value of infantry on the Swiss model was the Emperor Maximilian. In 1487 he raised the first units of *Landsknechte*, German halberdiers, pikemen and handgunners, who became Europe's universal soldiers serving as mercenaries from the Balkans to the British Isles. Trained to act in concert on the Swiss model and well organised into *Fähnleinen* (companies) of four hundred men, each with its own staff of officers and veteran *doppelsoldner*, the *Landsknechte* regiments are clear evidence of the professionalism of the late fifteenth-century soldier.[95] Most successful armies of the next century would mirror that organisation, and use arms, cavalry, infantry and artillery, in a complex synthesis.

---

[92] Evans (ed.), p. lxxxi.

[93] Evans (ed.), p. cxx.

[94] Delbrück, *The Dawn of Modern Warfare*, pp. 86, 157. Showalter, 'Caste, Skill, and Training: The Evolution of Cohesion in European Armies from the Middle Ages to the Sixteenth Century', pp. 407–430. John F. Guilmartin, 'The Military Revolution: Origins and First Tests Abroad', in Rogers (ed.), *Military Revolution Debate*, pp. 304, 325–326.

[95] For a brief history of the *Landsknechte* see Douglas Miller, *The Landsknechts* (London, 1976).

Conclusions

The architectural and tactical response to the increasing use of gunpowder weapons is indicative of the adaptive pattern of military development in early modern Europe. Technical innovation was countered, change was gradual, largely a matter of response and counter-response. There remained strong connections with the tactical practice of preceding centuries. Thus the interspersed ranks of pike and archers found in Burgundian armies gave way to the interspersed ranks of pike and arquebusiers that fought at Ceresoles. The solid blocks of men-at-arms flanked by herces of archers, seen on the fields of Crécy and Agincourt, gave way to a solid core of pike flanked by sleeves of arquebusiers on the sixteenth-century battlefield. The effective tactical synthesis of infantry, cavalry and artillery achieved in the Great Italian Wars of 1494–1529 was contingent on the organisation and sophistication of the combined arms approach of fifteenth-century armies, most strikingly the Burgundians. Cavalry, although faced once more with infantry with the will and ability to stand its ground, proved versatile and adaptable. Light cavalry gave early modern commanders a fast and mobile force with which to feint, scour, shield and pursue. Heavy cavalry continued to threaten all but the most sturdy infantry, and provided the most effective means to turn a favourable position on the battlefield into a strategic victory by riding down a broken enemy. Cannon and guns were refined, tactics were perfected. Old castles and city walls were up-graded or replaced by the new artillery fortifications. The temporary dominance enjoyed by the besieger was negated, warfare returned to the pattern of siege and destructive raid that had characterised medieval strategy.

These multifarious changes do not seem to have been the product of a military revolution. No consensus has emerged on when such a revolution might have occurred, and the emphasis on technological change has led to the idiosyncrasies of individual circumstance being ignored. Thus we have the crews of Venetian galleys clinging to their bows throughout the sixteenth century, to supplement their slow firing guns. The gun was initially utilised within the existing tactical framework. That framework, which was already more sophisticated than early modernists have generally realised, gradually developed alongside the gun. Social context, geography and historical circumstance governed those changes as much as technology. Eastern European armies clung to the horse because in that system lay their greatest prospect of success against the superlative and numerous cavalry of the Ottoman Empire. At the other end of Europe, on the western periphery, were the British Isles, where the rival armies of England and Scotland faced one another. Their military practices too were to develop in response to the unique circumstances that confronted them.

CHAPTER TWO

THE RIVAL ARMIES

British warfare: continental or insular?

AT FIRST SIGHT isolation from continental military practice might have seemed an inevitable consequence of the expulsion of the English from their possessions in France during the final stages of the Hundred Years War. In the latter half of the fifteenth century both England and Scotland were caught up in internecine conflicts which were, by their very nature, insular affairs. This, it has been argued, led to military retardation in the sixteenth century. The battles of the Wars of the Roses and Scotland's civil wars have largely been dismissed as peripheral to the mainstream of continental development. The emergence of standing forces, the renaissance of lance-armed cavalry, the growth of field artillery and the use of field fortifications were not reflected on British battle-fields where wars were fought by armies marshalled in the old style. These comprised large units of billmen, halberdiers and spearmen, flanked by archers. Sixteenth- century England and Scotland inherited essentially medieval military institutions, organisationally, tactically and technologically backward. England consequently became reliant on expensive foreign mercenaries to counter the inherent deficiencies of native troops. The smaller and less wealthy Scottish kingdom was almost inevitably doomed to medievalism in military matters, with the implication that medieval always equated with inefficiency.[1]

There can be little doubt but that the nature of civil warfare in fifteenth-century Britain, and the peculiar features of insular conflict, did lead to some distinctive military characteristics in the sixteenth century. However, it would be a mistake to overemphasise both the isolation from continental practice and the retardation of English and Scottish military institutions. The island kingdoms were not entirely peripheral to European developments, even if their own adaptations of military patterns were often idiosyncratic. Britain's isolation from the continental mainstream was lessened by the influence of those mercenaries and auxiliaries who crossed the Channel and North Sea in both directions, and in considerable numbers, during the fifteenth and sixteenth centuries. Recent accounts of the Wars of the Roses have emphasised parallel developments on

---

[1] See, for example, Sir Charles Oman, *A History of the Art of War in the Sixteenth Century* (London, 1991), pp. 285–287 and Gilbert John Millar, *Tudor Mercenaries and Auxiliaries, 1485–1547* (Charlottesville, 1980), pp. 3–25.

continental and British battlefields. These developments were characterised by the growing synthesis between cavalry, infantry and artillery that lay at the heart of European military practice.

Anthony Goodman has commented that English armies of the late fifteenth century 'blended traditional and innovatory methods', establishing a precedent which Tudor armies followed.[2] The same could also be said of Scotland, which imported, or was lent, military talent from France, although in the grim race to modernise, the northern kingdom was always at a disadvantage compared to her wealthier southern neighbour. The years after 1513 saw considerable evolution in the military practices of both countries, in fields as diverse as organisation, tactics, weaponry and fortification. By the middle of the century, as Scotland fought to expel Protector Somerset's English garrisons, both nations were, within the peculiar limits set by the realities of British warfare, committed to the techniques, equipment and tactics of contemporary continental warfare.

Standing forces and military professionals

The occupation and garrisoning of Normandy from 1420 to 1450 might have given rise to the first English standing army. It was the household troops and permanent garrisons of many fifteenth-century states that ultimately laid the foundations for professional military forces. Such had been the case with the *provisionati* and *famiglia ducale* of the Italian city states, which by the sixteenth century had developed into standing armies. This opportunity had slipped past England. The forces in Normandy were raised and organised in the traditional manner, stressing the personal bonds of obligation between a noble commander and the soldiers of his own retinue, rather than developing a system whereby soldiers were employed directly by the state and organised by a professional military bureaucracy. Similarly, the civil wars of the latter half of the fifteenth century were fought largely by the retinues of individual lords and local levies.[3]

England's major continental rival, France, was able to gain an important lead in this area. The reforms initiated by Charles VII in 1439 and 1445 created companies of equal size, armed and equipped in a uniform manner. Both officers and common soldiery were employed directly by the state and the fifteen *compagnies d'ordonnance* existed on a permanent footing. However, a long-standing mercenary tradition ensured that some English soldiers did gain experience in such nascent professional forces. Large numbers of English archers had served with the Burgundian army of Charles the Bold. Two thousand of these were recruited from Edward IV's expeditionary force of 1475. Charles had commented, with one eye on the volatile situation in their own country, that they

2 Anthony Goodman, *The Wars of the Roses* (London, 1981), pp. 162–195.
3 Anne Curry, 'The First English Standing Army? – Military Organisation in Lancastrian Normandy, 1420–1450', in Charles Ross (ed.), *Patronage, Pedigree and Power in Later Medieval England* (Littlefield, 1979), pp. 193–214.

might as well stay with him and fight the French as massacre each other in England.[4] Yet with the need for garrison troops much reduced following the expulsion from Normandy, geography continued to militate against the establishment of large standing forces within England itself, even into the sixteenth century.

Unlike France, the island nation did not have the same long land frontiers neighbouring potentially hostile powers, which required permanent defences. The two most important English bastions were Calais, and its surrounding castles, and Berwick on the border with Scotland. These garrisons provided employment for a small number of men, for whom soldiering became a profession. The number of soldiers employed on a permanent or semi-permanent basis in garrison towns increased over the course of Henry VIII's reign, particularly as a result of his programmes of coastal defence fortification between 1539 and 1546. These small posts offered more opportunity to military professionals. By 1540 the stretch of coast land between Gravesend and Portland boasted twenty-six castles and bulwarks, housing more than 170 soldiers and gunners.[5]

The men of the garrisons were drawn from all the corners of the King of England's realm and beyond, the work attracting an unsavoury mix of mercenaries and adventurers alongside loyal subjects of the Crown. A large number of the garrison of Calais were Welsh, including the garrulous and outspoken veteran Elis Gruffydd. Gruffydd left a detailed chronicle of his service and describes his fellow soldiers in the garrisons of the Calais Pale: 'there were many depraved and brutish foreign soldiers from all nations under the sun – Welsh, English, Cornish, Irish, Manx, Scots, Gascons, Portingals, Italians, Arbonnoises, Greeks, Turks, Tartars, Almains, Germans, Burgundians, Flemings'.[6] Employment in the garrisons may have been transitory for many men, so there must be some question mark over the efficiency of these soldiers in time of war. Berwick seems to have had a particularly rapid turnover of personnel. In 1544 the garrison of the castle was recorded as comprising 40 soldiers, 2 porters, 3 watchmen, 1 priest, 1 cook and 10 gunners, under the command of Sir Cuthbert Radcliffe. It was noted at the same time that there were no less than 50 gunners resident in the town itself.[7] The need to provide these garrisons with effective artillery was a further incentive for the Crown to concern itself with military requirements. The King was in direct charge of artillery, appointing a Master Gunner of his choice, recognising the importance of the new arm.[8]

Besides the hard-bitten men of the garrisons, the King also raised bodies of

4　Richard Vaughan, *Charles the Bold: The Last Valois Duke of Burgundy* (London, 1973), p. 217.

5　Jeremy Goring, 'The Military Obligations of the English People, 1511–1558' (London University Ph.D., 1955), pp. 244–249.

6　M.B.Davies (ed.), 'Boulogne and Calais from 1545 to 1550', *Fouad I University, Bulletin of the Faculty of Arts*, vol. 12 (1950), pp. 14–15.

7　Goring, 'Military Obligations', pp. 242–243.

8　J.D.Mackie, 'The English Army at Flodden', *Miscellany of the Scottish History Society*, vol. 8 (1951), p. 49.

heavy cavalry on a permanent or semi-permanent footing. One of the first acts of Henry VIII after his coronation was the establishment of an elite corps of young nobles, the King's Spears, to act as a personal bodyguard. This was to comprise fifty fully equipped men-at-arms, each accompanied by two mounted archers and a custrell (light cavalryman) armed with a light lance or javelin.[9] Although the King's Spears were disbanded after six years, a similar body, the Gentlemen Pensioners, was raised in 1539. This corps remained in existence into the reign of Edward VI, serving with Somerset's army in Scotland in 1547. Whilst the Pensioners could serve as a unit in their own right, they also provided a pool of experienced officers who could be assigned to other commands, and provided a leavening of experience and professionalism throughout the whole army. For the 1547 campaign in Scotland they were joined by the Bulleners, heavy cavalry permanently employed as part of the garrison of recently captured Boulogne.[10]

England's tentative progress towards the creation of standing forces during the first half of the sixteenth century, did, at the least, outstrip that of Scotland. Scotland had few professional soldiers, although a small pool of experienced soldiers did exist. Many Highlanders and Islesmen served as mercenaries in Ireland. Indeed this was an ancient tradition. Warriors from the Norse kingdoms of Argyll and the Hebrides had first taken service in Ireland in the twelfth century. These *gallóglaigh* (foreign soldiers) and their descendants maintained close links with Scotland. In the sixteenth century a fresh wave of Highland mercenaries, the New Scots, had also learned their trade in Ireland.[11]

In Scotland itself a few men may have found employment in the garrisons of mighty lords, particularly if they possessed specialist knowledge, such as the four gunners employed by David Beaton at St Andrews in 1545.[12] There was a limited tradition of the Crown employing professional soldiers, particularly in times of crisis. For example, in 1482 James III had maintained a garrison of five hundred men at his own expense in Berwick whilst instructing the captains of six border castles to raise forces of a hundred men each, whose wages would also be paid by the King.[13] The cost of employing such 'men of weir' was not always borne by the Crown or the Regent. In 1547 the Abbot of Inchcolm was ordered to pay the Regent Arran £500 to cover the wages of a body of troops raised specifically to recover the island from the English who had occupied it.[14]

[9] For details of the organisation of the King's Spears, see John Glas Sandeman (ed.), *Facsimiles of the Ordinances and Statutes of the Spears of Honour, 1509, and the Oath and Articles of the Gentlemen Pensioners, 1600* (Hayling Island, 1912).

[10] Goring, 'Military Obligations', pp. 232–239.

[11] See Andrew McKerral, 'West Highland Mercenaries in Ireland', *The Scottish Historical Review*, vol. 30 (1951), pp. 1–14.

[12] David Caldwell, 'A Sixteenth-Century Group of Gun Towers in Scotland', *Fort*, vol. 12 (1984), p. 18.

[13] Ranald Nicholson, *Scotland: The Later Middle Ages* (Edinburgh, 1974), p. 494.

[14] John Burton (ed.), *The Register of the Privy Council of Scotland*, vol. 1 (Edinburgh, 1877), p. 80.

Scotsmen could also follow the profession of arms in French service. In the fifteenth century Scottish auxiliaries had served against the English in France.[15] In the sixteenth century their descendants served France in the wars in Italy.[16] An elite served as halberdiers in the French King's guard, clad extravagantly in yellow, blue and crimson velvet.[17] The French also employed Scottish light horse, three companies of whom escorted the defeated English garrison of Calais to Gravelines in 1558. At this time France was seeking to build up its own light cavalry arm, and Scotland was clearly considered a valuable source of recruits. The sixteen hundred light horse stationed in Péronne in 1558 included six hundred Scotsmen, commanded by their own captains.[18] A few Scottish nobles would have served even further afield, in the English *langue* of the Knights of St John of Jerusalem in Rhodes and, later, Malta. The Knights had continued to attract adventurous young crusaders and enjoyed considerable influence with James IV, who himself preached the virtues of war against the Turk. These links with continental armies ensured that there were Scottish soldiers well-versed with the practice of warfare. In 1542 the vanguard of the Scottish army which fought at Haddon Rigg was commanded by an 'ancient lord of S.Johnne', Sir Walter Lyndsay, 'who was weill besene and practissit in weiris baitht in Itallie and had fouchin oft tymeis against the Turkis in defence of the Christieane men'. After appointing the Earl of Huntly as Lieutenant General, James V instructed him to do nothing without 'this nobill mans adwyse and consall'.[19]

Levies, retinues, musters and wappinshaws

Around these small corps of professional soldiers the English and Scottish crowns would build their field armies as and when they were required. There were two main methods by which troops were raised for military service. Firstly, in both countries, all able bodied men between the ages of sixteen and sixty were theoretically liable to serve in the levy, although certain groups, for example mariners, could be given exemptions, in time of war.[20] Secondly the

[15] Raymond Paterson, *My Wound is Deep: A History of the Later Anglo-Scots Wars 1380–1560* (Edinburgh, 1997), pp. 55–70.

[16] Ian Roy (ed.), *Blaise de Monluc, the Valois-Habsburg Wars and the French Wars of Religion* (London, 1971), pp. 72–76.

[17] A.F.Pollard (ed.), 'The Manner of the Triumph at Calais and Boulogne', in *Tudor Tracts 1523–1588* (London, 1903), p. 5.

[18] David Potter, *War and Government in the French Provinces* (Cambridge, 1993), pp. 166, 183.

[19] Pitscottie, *The Historie and Cronicles of Scotland*, vol. 1 (Edinburgh, 1899), pp. 396–397. For Scottish links with the Knights of St John see I.B.Cowan, P.H.R.Mackay and A.Macquarrie (eds), *The Knights of St John of Jerusalem in Scotland* (Edinburgh, 1983) and A.Macquarrie, *Scotland and the Crusades, 1095–1560* (Edinburgh, 1997), pp. 105–119.

[20] P.L.Hughes and J.F.Larkin (eds), *Tudor Royal Proclamations*, vol. 1 (New Haven, 1964) p. 322.

Crown could contract with individual nobles and gentlemen to raise bodies of troops for service in their retinues. Armies composed predominantly of retinue and levy troops could, however, be augmented considerably by the employment of mercenaries, auxiliaries (troops lent by a friendly power), volunteers and pressed men.

England's levy system was generally effective and well organised, Henry VIII benefiting from the legacy of administrative efficiency left by his father. In each shire commissioners of array, normally local gentlemen and justices of the peace, were charged with the responsibility of maintaining the levy, checking that individuals armed themselves according to their wealth and were trained and ready for service at short notice. The system owed much to the planning of Henry VII. The commissions established for each shire in 1488 were composed of a magnate, six gentlemen and a sheriff. They could quickly calculate the strength of their shire and raise a given number of troops when ordered to do so. When the troops were required for continuous service, as in France in 1492 – for the English shire levy was not restricted to home defence – 'a sort of professionalism arose'.[21]

Government statutes throughout the early sixteenth century encouraged military training, particularly with the longbow, and the commissioners of array were charged with enforcing these statutes. When crisis came it was they who selected the hardiest and most likely men for active service, since it would have been entirely impractical to mobilise the entire levy. Ideally the commissioners would have seen the archers shoot and would select them on the basis of their skill and fitness. If possible they would send unmarried men rather than those with families to war but they might perhaps take the opportunity of ridding their villages of the idle and the unemployed.[22]

The commissioners would also appoint captains and petty-captains to command their levies. These would be drawn from the local gentry and hopefully would have some prior military experience. The Dorset levy in 1546 was fortunate to find one Bartholomew Hussey, an elderly gentleman who had served with the Knights of St John in Rhodes, to serve as captain. In general the number of experienced officers available to the levy must have been quite low. The proportion of officers to men could consequently vary enormously. In 1544 the English army in France had about one captain for every fifteen men. In 1558, there was one captain for every 200 to 250 men. Ratios could vary even within a single small unit. A foot band of 341 Irish soldiers in English service who passed through Chester in 1550 was divided into eleven irregularly sized companies, numbering between 20 and 45 men, each commanded by a petty-captain.[23] The quality of officers could vary enormously too. By the middle of the century there was a growing recognition of the need for a meritocracious

21 Hughes and Larkin (eds), pp. 49–52.
22 Goring, 'Military Obligations', pp. 77–79.
23 Chester City Record Office, Mayors' Military Papers, MMP/1/1, MMP/1/2. Goring, 'Military Obligations', pp. 75–77.

system of appointment. Thomas Audley, writing in about 1550, noted that many a man 'was made a captaine before he was a soldier'.[24] However, the writing of handbooks and treatises by such individuals as Audley and Henry Barrett did at least ensure that the captains of the levy had some kind of guide to the handling of their men.

Broadly speaking, the levy was divided into two military districts. Those in the north country (traditionally the most heavily militarised zone in England), were responsible for defence against the Scots.[25] Those in the south faced the possible threat from France and the continent. The Border country was of particular concern and the levy system there had developed very distinct characteristics. In the latter years of the fifteenth century some clannish Border families held land in return for an obligation to serve the Crown in times of war. In 1498 Bishop Fox wrote a letter to the clergy of Tynedale and Redesdale which implied that their parishioners were expected to serve militarily against the Scots. The Northumberland musters of 1538 record the 'Northe Tyndell Theiffs' as a distinct unit, 391 tough reivers, 'able with horse and harness.'[26]

In the Marches, which were subject to sudden and violent commotion, the distinction between thief and soldier, as between war and peace, was very fine indeed.[27] Further south, where populations did not need to exist in such a permanent state of military readiness, the gap between peacetime occupation and serving soldier was altogether wider. The overall preparedness of the levy was clearly a matter of some concern during the reign of Henry VIII. He reissued the 1285 Statute of Winchester in 1511, to ensure that everyone owned arms, armour and horses according to their estate. In 1522 a new Domesday survey was undertaken, known as the General Proscription, in response to the worsening diplomatic situation. England's then ally, Charles V was preparing his invasion of France and was counting on English support. England was sure to be drawn into the conflict, particularly as Scottish forces, under the Duke of Albany, were menacing the English border. The General Proscription was both a military and fiscal survey of the nation as it teetered on the brink of war.[28] The survey revealed that few individuals owned the appropriate equipment and musters became more frequent as the commissioners of array sought to improve the quality of the levy. Certain administrative difficulties which the musters of 1522 highlighted were dealt with. For example, those able-bodied men who owned no arms were assigned equipment from those who owned arms but were unfit for service.

---

[24] Thomas Audley, 'A Treatise on the Art of Warre', *The Journal of the Society of Army Historical Research*, vol. 6 (1927), p. 69.
[25] Goring, 'Military Obligations', pp. 232–239.
[26] J.A.Tuck, 'War and Society in the Medieval North', *Journal of Northern History*, vol. 21 (1985), p. 51.
[27] Cynthia Neville, 'Local Sentiment and the "National" Enemy in Northern England in the Later Middle Ages', *Journal of British Studies*, vol. 35 (1996), pp. 420–421.
[28] Jeremy Goring, 'The General Proscription of 1522', *English Historical Review*, vol. 86 (1971), pp. 681–705.

The overall effects of the survey were probably beneficial, but it did highlight the extent to which the reissuing of the Statute of Winchester had thus far had a limited impact. There is evidence that the government's strenuous efforts to improve the quality of the levy were ultimately rewarded. In 1539, when the threat of invasion loomed again, the French ambassador, Marillac, reported:

> ... in Canterbury, and the other towns upon the road, I found every English subject in arms who was capable of serving. Boys of seventeen or eighteen have been called out, without exemption of place or person. . . . On the road I met a body of men, I was told there were six thousand of them, going as a garrison to Sandwich . . . Artillery and ammunition pass out incessantly from the Tower, and are dispatched to all points on the coast where a landing is likely to be attempted.

Everywhere Marillac travelled he encountered men mustering, practising at the butts and building fortifications. Whatever fears Englishmen voiced about the readiness of their levy, this Frenchman who witnessed their musters concluded that any invasion of the country was doomed. This conclusion might have been echoed by those of his countrymen who clashed with the English levy on the Isle of Wight six years later and were driven back into the sea. In that year, 1545, the English government kept a force of 120,000 men in the field for the whole summer in response to a renewed invasion threat.[29]

Whatever its imperfections, the levy system gave every indication of responding magnificently in the hour of crisis. The deficiencies of the system only really became apparent when militia men were called upon to serve outside the realm. The depths of desperation to which ordinary men sank when threatened with overseas service is poignantly demonstrated on a muster list of Glamorgan soldiers embarking for Ireland in Chester in 1596. This records that 'John Lewys runne away and found in a bushe and he cut his owne throte and so dead'.[30] The unhappy history of levied soldiers outside England, especially later in the century, should not, however, detract from the record of success of the Henrician levy as a defensive force.

A second method by which soldiers were raised for English armies was by indentures whereby the Crown contracted with the lords of the land for 'a definite number on a definite term'.[31] Throughout the wars with France and during the civil wars of the fifteenth-century troops had been raised by these agreements. Indentures were formal contracts by which nobles and gentlemen agreed to provide a fixed number of men for a fixed term, stipulating their pay, conditions and rewards for service.[32] The formal use of indentures appears to have

[29] Lindsay Boynton, *The Elizabethan Militia 1558–1638* (London, 1967), pp. 8–9.
[30] Chester City Records Office, Mayors' Military Papers, MMP/7/32. The sequence of documents MMP/7/1–35 contains a wealth of evidence that Elizabethan levies raised for service in Ireland contained a high proportion of poorly equipped, physically infirm and mutinous soldiers.
[31] Mackie, 'English Army at Flodden', p. 49.
[32] For an overview of their early development see N.B.Lewis, 'The Organisation of

fallen into disuse after 1512, but the principle remained whereby individual lords raised soldiers from amongst their tenants and servants by agreement with the Crown.[33] Nobles had been free to recruit for their individual retinues from wherever they pleased and any soldier who served a lord for any length of time would certainly have acquired a degree of professionalism in his trade.

Henry VIII chose to make an important modification to the indenture system. From 1511 onwards, indentured captains could recruit only from amongst their own tenants and dependants. Henry's system has therefore been described as semi-feudal, stressing the obligation of landholders to provide military service for their King, and in their turn, the obligation of tenants and servants to follow their lords to war. During the Pilgrimage of Grace, the northern rebellion of 1536, Henry raised most of his troops by letters under the Privy Seal to members of the landed gentry ordering them to raise troops.[34] Those individuals who received signet letters would also generally have been expected to lead their men in battle as captains and draw their petty-captains from the ranks of their kinsmen or friends.[35] Statutes passed in the reign of Edward VI reinforced this sense of military service as a bounden duty of subjects, as well as taking new measures to ensure efficiency, blending innovation with tradition. In 1549, whilst English troops were still heavily engaged in Scotland, Parliament offi-cially sanctioned the post of Lord Lieutenant. Lord Lieutenants were sent into the counties to assemble the commissioners of array and oversee the mustering of the levies, directly supervising military mobilisation on behalf of the Crown at a local level.

The English system of raising troops, therefore, was not entirely moribund, however archaic its continued emphasis on the bonds of personal obligation seemed. Nor was the English Crown entirely reliant on these semi-feudal mechanisms to raise troops. One alternative source of men was the large number, especially in London, of 'ruffians and vagabonds, to whom God hath given personage and strength apt and able to labor, work and do service for their living, yet be so wasted in mischief and idleness that they give themselves to no honest labor or honest kind of living'.[36] Such individuals were liable to be pressed for service if need be, and whilst they may have made poor fighting ma-terial, use could be found for them. A royal proclamation of 26 May 1545 sent 'all such ruffians, vagabonds, masterless men, common players, and evil-disposed persons' to the galleys and 'other like vessels'.[37] The social upheavals of the mid-century provided another source of recruits. In the aftermath of

Indentured Retinues in Fourteenth Century England', *Transactions of the Royal Historical Society*, 4th Series, vol. 27 (1945), pp. 29–39.

[33] Jeremy Goring, 'Social Change and Military Decline in Mid-Tudor England', *History*, vol. 60 (1975), p. 188, n. 29.

[34] Herman Hattaway, 'Some Aspects of Tudor Military History', *Army Quarterly*, vol. 8 (1969), pp. 53–63.

[35] Goring, 'Military Obligations', pp. 138–145.

[36] Hughes and Larkin (eds), *Tudor Royal Proclamations*, p. 352.

[37] Hughes and Larkin (eds), p. 352.

Kett's Rebellion of 1549 the ringleaders were forced into military service. Five years later, Arthur, Lord Grey of Wilton, requested that some of those sentenced to hang for their part in Thomas Wyatt's rebellion should join the garrison of Guines Castle in the Calais Pale.[38]

Yet not all the masterless men who found their way to the wars were pressed men. Campaigns attracted adventurers who attached themselves to armies but, being outside any official structure, operated essentially as freebooters. Lawless, ill-disciplined and seemingly under the command of the natural leaders drawn from amongst their own ranks, they were tolerated as useful scouts and irregulars. The most infamous of these adventurers were the 'crackers' or 'krekers'; the sobriquet was apparently given to them by the French, who arrived in Calais in 1522 hoping to join the Duke of Suffolk's invasion force. Denied acceptance into the army proper, the krekers looted, burned and plundered across the countryside. Buzzing around the flanks or vanguard of the English army as it marched into France, they acted as unofficial skirmishers, bringing in cattle and clashing with French cavalry and villagers. Since they received no pay they lived on what they stole and would fight desperately, and with horrible brutality, when they were hungry. Surrender was rarely an option for these men. A common soldier taken in battle could be ransomed for a month's wages. The krekers fought solely for plunder and received no wages and were thus valueless as prisoners.

Even after the invasion was abandoned, many of these adventurers remained in Calais and the chronicler Edward Hall recorded their eventual, and perhaps inevitable, fate. Preceded by only twenty-five scourers, a force of two hundred krekers had set out on a pillaging expedition 'to get som good botie, to make us merry with, in the cold wether'.[39] The raid had gone well and the ragged band were herding a good haul of cattle and oxen back towards Calais when the scourers stumbled into a force of fifteen hundred French cavalry. The twenty-five English horsemen had no choice but to turn tail and run, pursued by the vengeful French horse, who would give no quarter to the hated krekers. They soon came upon the English foot, catching them in the open and a desperate struggle ensued:

> The Frenchmen came on, on every syde, thenglishmen shot their arrowes, and defended them aswel as they could. The Frenchmen perceiving that the Englishmen kept them selfs so close, caused diverse of the horsemen to lyght a fote, and so they dyd, and fought wyth their speres against the pikes, and shote wyth crossebowes on every side. Alas, the while for while the Englyshmen had arrowes to shote, they were not broken, but close wythout peryl, but when their arrowes were spent, the Englyshmen fought valiauntly, and slew many Frenchmen that lyghted on foote, but in the conclusion the horsemen entered,

---

38 Goring, 'Military Obligations', pp. 77–81.
39 Edward Hall, *The Triumphant Reigne of Kyng Henry the VIII*, vol. 2 (London, 1904), p. 17.

and killed them all . . . This was thend of these compaignons, called the krekers . . . which were as hardie men, as ever served prince or captain.[40]

The reputation won by these 'hardie men' seems to have survived them, for similar bodies of troops would henceforth be formally raised to serve the King. In 1545, one John of Calais was licensed to recruit 'Soldier Adventurers' at the 'sign of the gun' in Billingsgate, London. The recruitment was signalled by the beating of drums, a method employed again by the Duke of Northumberland when raising troops for service in Ireland in 1551.[41]

Outside Britain the Crown made contracts with foreign captains, and mercenaries formed a significant part of all English armies of the period.[42] In 1544, Henry VIII had amassed 42,000 men for the enterprise of Boulogne, which included 4836 foreign horse and 5392 foreign infantry. For the most part these were specialists, men who bore arms and equipment not usually found in English armies. Whilst the English continued to struggle to raise large numbers of native heavy cavalry, Burgundian men-at-arms were hired in large numbers to make good the deficiency. German *Landsknecht* pikemen were another favoured type, as were Spanish and Italian arquebusiers. For his campaign in Scotland, Protector Somerset hired the services of a troop of mounted arquebusiers, under a Spanish captain, Pedro de Gamboa, who proved invaluable, both on the battlefield and in protecting the army on the march.

The fact that the English hired (or were lent as auxiliaries) so many men armed with the latest weapons of pike and shot formations has led naturally to the conclusion that this was a reflection on the technical and tactical backwardness of England's native soldiers.[43] Yet there was nothing unusual in this age of increasingly large armies in the hiring of large numbers of specialist troops, and few of the wealthier European states fielded nationally homogeneous armies. In 1542, the French amassed for service an army of seventy thousand men. It consisted of forty-three thousand Swiss and German pike, four to five thousand Italian cavalry, two thousand Clevelander horse, an assortment of Basque genitors and Albanian stradiots with the remainder native French. The primary concern seems to have been quantity not quality.

The unruly professionals hired by Henry VIII often proved to be unreliable, and occasionally treasonous. At the Battle of the Spurs in 1513, between a quarter and one fifth of the victorious English army was composed of foreign mercenaries.[44] Yet the flight of the French men-at-arms was precipitated

---

[40] Hall, pp. 17–18.
[41] Goring, 'Military Obligations', pp. 251–252.
[42] For a detailed account of the service of mercenaries and auxiliaries (troops lent to English armies by continental allies), see Gilbert John Millar, *Tudor Mercenaries and Auxiliaries, 1485–1547* (Charlottesville, 1980) and 'Henry VIII's Preliminary Letter of Retainer to Colonel Frederick Von Reiffenberg for the Raising of 1500 Men-At-Arms', *The Journal for the Society of Army Historical Research*, vol. 67 (1989), pp. 220–225.
[43] Millar, *Tudor Mercenaries*, pp. 3, 25, 48, 145.
[44] Millar, *Tudor Mercenaries*, p. 45.

entirely by English longbows; Henry's German infantry played no part in the battle at all. The expensive Burgundian heavy cavalry 'remained aloof in the early stages of the encounter, then hastened to join in when they saw how things were turning out'.[45] Nor was the search for troops confined to the continent. The English Crown also made widespread use of Irish and Scottish mercenaries, whom Gruffydd noticed amongst the garrison of Calais.[46] Again, since these men's equipment would be just as traditional as that of the English (bows, two-handed swords and javelins), the motivation for hiring them seems to have had far more to do with the need for manpower generally than with any perceived qualitative deficiency in the English ranks.

Scotland, lacking both Henry's wealth and continental ambitions, relied, for the most part, on native troops fulfilling their personal obligation to serve in either the retinues of the nobility or the national levy. Yet the system lacked the institutional efficiency that the Tudors had striven to establish in England. The bonds of manrent, formal contracts of mutual assistance and protection between laird and noble, would allow individual lords to raise considerable bodies of men for military service.[47] There is little evidence that the size of retinues or the exact terms of their service were in any way fixed. Nor was there any guarantee that nobles' retinues would not become private armies. Consequently, although the Scottish Crown could raise forces, as in England, by privy letters to individual magnates, far more reliance was placed on the levy.

Theoretically all men between the ages of sixteen and sixty were obliged to serve for a maximum of forty days in any one year if required. This forty days service would be at their own expense and they were expected to carry their own victuals, a factor which severely limited the ability of Scottish commanders to engage in prolonged campaigns. A French gentleman who served with the Scots in 1548 noted that they 'never would serve in a campaign more than forty days after leaving their homes'.[48] Individuals who ignored the calls to muster did so at their own peril, for the harshest penalties could result. In August 1547, as Scotland prepared to meet an English invasion, a proclamation was made in the market at Dumfries for the local men to hurry to the muster, on pain of death.[49] The summons to the muster could be even more dramatic, with riders bearing

45 Charles Cruickshank, *Henry VIII and the Invasion of France* (Stroud, 1990), pp. 93–107, p. 105.
46 See also D.G.White, 'Henry VIII's Irish Kerne in France and Scotland, 1544–1545', *The Irish Sword*, vol. 3 (1958), pp. 213–25, T.Blake Butler, 'King Henry VIII's Irish Army List', *The Irish Genealogist*, vol. 1 (1937), pp. 3–13, 36–38 and C.H.Dillon, 'Irish Troops at Boulogne in 1544', *Journal for the Society of Army Historical Research*, vol. 1 (1922), pp. 81–84.
47 For a full discussion of manrent, see Jenny Wormald, *Lords and Men: Bonds of Manrent, 1442–1603* (Edinburgh, 1985).
48 J.B.Brown, 'The French Troops in the Borders in 1548', *Transactions of Hawick Archaeological Society* (1905), p. 39.
49 *Calendar of State Papers Relating to Scotland, Vol. 1, 1547–63* (Edinburgh, 1898), p. 34.

'the fiery cross' galloping through villages and towns summoning their menfolk to arms.[50]

To ensure that all eligible men maintained the appropriate equipment, musters or wappinshaws were held in all parts of the realm between two and four times a year. As in England, the wappinshaw was a social event of some importance. Piper and drummer turned out, drinks were provided at public expense, and absentees were fined, as were those who turned out in borrowed gear.[51] In fact, for both nations, dealing with those individuals who were failing in their military obligations would become a central activity for sheriffs and commissioners of array. In an era of social and religious tensions, conflicting loyalties would undermine the sense of personal obligation owed to lord and even to the Crown, undermining the basis of both nations' military systems.

Military activity, discipline and social obligation

By the middle of the sixteenth century there was widespread concern that England's much vaunted military prowess was in decline. Insidious comparisons were drawn with the subjects of other lands. The unwillingness of country folk to practise with their arms was contrasted with the Swiss, whose martial exercises were 'the gretyst cause of theyr grete fame in dedys of armys'.[52] In a political tract entitled *A discourse on the Commonweal of this realm of England*, John Hales expressed grave doubts on the ability of the English to defend themselves in times of war.[53] Fear centred on a perceived decline in population. At the time contemporaries blamed land enclosure, with honest yeomen forced from the soil to make way for sheep, and it is clear that the social tensions of sixteenth-century England impacted on the military effectiveness of Tudor armies. The extent of population decline was perhaps exaggerated, although plague and the sweating sickness (probably influenza) do seem to have reduced the number of able bodied men available for muster in the 1540s.[54]

More worrying still though was the feeling that the quality of English soldiers was in decline. Early in the century an Italian diplomat had written of the English, 'they have a very high reputation in arms; and from the great fear the

---

[50] See, for example, the English report of the 'fyer crois' passing 'throwcht the realm' in *Cal. State Papers Scot.*, vol. 1, 40.

[51] Gladys Dickinson, 'Some Notes on the Scottish Army in the First Half of the Sixteenth Century', *The Scottish Historical Review*, vol. 28 (1949), p. 133.

[52] Sidney Heritage (ed.), *England in the Reign of King Henry the Eighth, Part 1, Starkey's Life and Letters* (London, 1878), pp. 152, 79, 161.

[53] Elizabeth Lamond (ed.), *A Discourse of the Commonweal of This Realm of England* (Cambridge, 1893).

[54] Goring, 'Social Change and Military Decline', pp. 184–197. On the sweating sickness, see Adam Patrick and R.S.Roberts, 'A Consideration of the Nature of the English Sweating Sickness', *Medical History*, vol. 9 (1965), pp. 272–278, 385–389.

French entertain of them, one must believe it to be justly acquired'.[55] In 1539 another foreign ambassador commented that Englishmen in the past 'have been of good hearts, courageous, bold, valiant in martial feats, but those Englishmen are dead'.[56] On campaign the Englishmen's old reputation could still precede them. In 1544, the Gascon captain, Blaise de Monluc, noted the repute that his English adversaries were held in by his countrymen, who whispered amongst themselves that 'one Englishman would always beat two Frenchmen, and that the English would never run away nor never yield'. Yet Monluc, in his skirmishes with English soldiers around Boulogne, had begun to have his doubts: 'I discovered them to be men of very little heart and believe them to be better at sea than by land.'[57]

Yet one should be wary of exaggerating the extent to which English armies had actually been enfeebled. The prophets of doom at home clearly had a political axe to grind, particularly over the issue of enclosure, which, they argued, robbed honest yeomen of the land on which they practised archery. In 1514 Edward Hall recorded that:

> ... the citizens of London, finding themselves greeved with inclosures of the common fields about Islington, Hoxton, Shoreditch, and other places neere to the citie, whereby they could not be suffered to exercise their bowes ... assembled themselves on a morning, and went with spades and shovels unto the same fields, and there (like diligent workmen) so bestrired themselves, that within a short space, all the hedges about the town were cast down, and the ditches filled.[58]

Much of the anxiety expressed about the state of the levy was probably thinly disguised commentary on the evils of enclosure. As for de Monluc, his attitude was soured by his experiences during the night attack on Boulogne on 6 October 1545, which had gone disastrously wrong for the French. The English clearly could fight with something of their old vigour on occasion.

Yet it is equally clear that cold, hungry English soldiers, on long drawn out campaigns, lapsed into apathy and could behave on the battlefield with a temerity that belied their reputation of old. Elis Gruffydd served with the force blockading Montreuil during the enterprise of Boulogne in 1544. Poorly victualled and unable to make any headway against the town, the performance of the soldiers in the field was disappointing. Gruffydd 'never saw Welshmen and Englishmen so badhearted or so unadventurous as I saw at this time. Not a

---

[55] Charlotte Sneyd (ed.), 'A Relation or rather a True Account of the Island of England', *Camden Society*, vol. 37 (1847), pp. 20–21, 23. See also C.H.Dillon, 'The English Soldier of the Sixteenth Century', *Journal for the Society of Army Historical Research*, vol. 1 (1921–22), pp. 200–204.

[56] Goring, 'Social Change and Military Decline', p. 187.

[57] Roy (ed.), *Blaise de Monluc*, pp. 127–131.

[58] Holinshed, *Chronicles of England*, vol. 3 (London, 1808), p. 599.

single one of them would dare to go near where the handguns were shooting at us.'[59]

It would appear that the malaises that were afflicting the Tudor realm were having a particular impact on the supply of hardy soldiers. The old ties of obligation were breaking down in an era of economic hardship and social conflict. The ageing dual system of recruitment relied both on individuals shouldering their responsibility to equip and maintain themselves in readiness for war, and on the strength of the quasi-feudal bonds that would allow individual lords to raise retinues of armed men. Those bonds now appeared to be breaking down. The prospect of military service outside England itself was particularly unwelcome. In 1542 tenants of a Derbyshire landlord, John Port, maintained that they had no obligation to serve him in the war with Scotland. Tenants, particularly those of some substance, were now possessed of the confidence to challenge archaic demands that they dutifully follow their lords to war. For their part, lords and gentlemen themselves were struggling to fulfil their military obligations. If their tenants were asserting their independence they should at least have been able to rely on their household servants. Yet in an age of chronic inflation and economic crisis, the size of gentry households was contracting. Fewer now could afford to employ, let alone arm and equip, large numbers of retainers.[60]

Just as the quasi-feudal system was beginning to shown signs of strain, so was the reliance on individuals fulfilling their own obligations in terms of maintaining their equipment and training at the butts. The decline in archery was of particular concern. To be effective a longbowman needed to train strenuously over a lifetime. The first threat to England's archery tradition came from new-fangled weapons, handguns and, surprisingly, crossbows. In 1526, a royal proclamation attacked the use of these weapons. Their use was restricted to persons 'having lands, tenements, fees, annuities or other yearly profits . . . to the yearly value of £100'. A few months later attempts were made to enforce statutes against unlawful games and to encourage practice at archery. 'Bowling, closh, quoiting, loggatting, playing at tennis, dice, cards, and tables' were picked out as being 'so continually used and exercised within this realm' that archery 'is almost utterly set apart and extremely decayed'. Such acts were repeated throughout the reign of Henry VIII, which may suggest that their implementation was ineffectual.[61]

For whatever reason, it has been calculated that between 1522 and 1557 the proportion of able-bodied Englishmen who could be designated as archers in the muster returns fell from one in three to one in four.[62] The English were not insensible to the utility of gunpowder small arms and whilst recognising that their chief strength lay in archery, the statutes against use of handguns were

---

[59] M.B.Davies (ed.), 'The "Enterprise" of Paris and Boulogne', *Fouad I University, Bulletin of the Faculty of Arts*, vol. 11 (1949), p. 71.
[60] Goring, 'Social Change and Military Decline', pp. 188–190.
[61] Hughes and Larkin, *Tudor Royal Proclamations*, pp. 151–153.
[62] Goring, 'Social Change and Military Decline', p. 193.

occasionally relaxed and, indeed, modernisers such as the Duke of Somerset sought to encourage the use of the weapon. Ironically this may have accelerated the decline in archery, for, by way of encouragement, arquebusiers were offered a higher rate of pay, 8d a day. On 16 February 1547, Lord Cobham wrote to Somerset on this matter, commenting that:

> this increase in wages to them will not only be a great hinderance and a decay to the archery of the nation, since all men covet the highest pay, but will be a means, as they have found by experience, that the able and tall men who receive for other weapons only 6d. a day shall be greatly discouraged when they see such weak personages entertained for the harquebuse, as besides that weapon, are apt nor meet for any other service of war, and yet very few of them skilful and expert of that weapon.[63]

The difficulties faced by the English Crown in securing sufficient numbers of able bodied, well equipped and skilled soldiers were compounded by disciplinary problems. The heady mix of nationalities serving the Tudor Crown made for a volatile situation in camp and garrison. Angry words frequently escalated into brawls with sometimes fatal consequences. This problem was so serious that attempts were made to regulate relations between the various nationalities. The royal proclamation providing for the regulations for Therouanne Camp in 1513 contained this section:

> Concerning relations between English and German soldiers. The King our sovereign lord straightly chargeth and commandeth that no Englishmen intermeddle or lodge themself within the ground assigned to the Almains for their lodgings, or to give them any reproach or unfitting language or words by which noise or debate might ensue, upon pain of imprisonment, and further to be punished as the case shall require. And in like wise, if that any Almain give any reproach or unfitting language to any Englishmen, that then the Englishmen to complain them to the captains of the Almains, which shall see and provide for remedy in that behalf. And over that, the King's highness commandeth that all Englishmen and other of his army friendly and courteously do treat the said Almains after like manner as though they were his proper subjects.[64]

Yet for all such efforts it was hard to stop soldiers fighting amongst themselves. Despite the above ordinance, Edward Hall notes that the King's Almains clashed with his English subjects in camp. The Germans reached for their pikes, the English for their bows and a number of men were killed before 'the captynes tooke such payne that the fray was appeased'.[65] In 1544 the Germans caused problems again, during the enterprise of Boulogne. This time their quarrel was with the Irish, one of whom was 'thrust through with a spear without provoca-

63 H.A.Dillon, 'Arms and Armour at Westminster, the Tower, and Greenwich, 1547', *Archaeologia*, vol. 51 (1888), p. 230.
64 Hughes and Larkin, p. 121.
65 Hall, *Henry the VIII*, vol. 1, p. 84.

tion'.[66] Notwithstanding the reputation of the Germans, Gruffydd believed that the Spaniards were the worst offenders, being by nature 'proud, unreasonable, quarrelsome, contentious, very scornful and haughty . . . not a day passed without one or two affrays in the market place contrary to the law and custom of [Calais]'. Gruffydd also suggests that English soldiers particularly resented the high wages received by the King's foreign hirelings. In 1545 a party of Spanish and Burgundian mercenaries under the command of a Flemish captain, John DeHaar, had attempted to desert the Calais garrison and the English soldiers who intercepted them had to be restrained from slaughtering them to a man. There had been trouble on the northern border too. Spaniards and Italians had been stationed in Newcastle and a seemingly timeless problem had quickly arisen. According to the outraged Gruffydd, 'it was a sad sight to see the ungodly beastly lives they led defiling and corrupting the purity of the girls and women of the town and country until the men of the town rose against them and killed them when any one of them was caught astray'.[67]

It would be unfair, however, not to recognise that English and Welsh troops could also be undisciplined. Collective indiscipline, or even collective apathy, were tools by which English soldiers registered their displeasure at material deprivation and the prolonging of campaigns into winter. Gruffydd gives this description of troop behaviour during the abortive campaign of 1523 under the Duke of Suffolk. The English army was held up outside the town of Bray. As darkness fell the men of the English rearward were drawn up on waterlogged ground. Cold, wet and miserable the soldiery began to grumble; if they could not go on, they would go back:

> Some Welshmen from South Wales who were under Lord Ferrers, among whom were many unruly men, heard this and these took the matter so seriously that they sent round word to cry all together 'On to the town', 'on to the town' which they did, while beginning to turn back. Lord Ferrers and the captains of that end of the host perceived this and had trouble enough to pacify the unruly ones, concerning which word went swiftly to the Duke of Suffolk and the other end of the host . . . This was explained to him in the worst possible way by saying that it was the Welshmen who were turning their faces towards England and saying they would not cross the river Somme. These tales created great discontent among the men on the south side of the river who put the whole blame on the Welshmen although there were twice as many Englishmen more eager to turn home than the Welshmen . . . At the time there was plenty of talk in the council, for some wanted to hang all the Welshmen there, others to kill them all, but as it happened the matter was settled when they turned round and came to the town . . .[68]

[66] C.H.Dillon, 'Irish Troops at Boulogne', p. 82.
[67] M.B.Davies (ed.), 'Boulogne and Calais from 1545 to 1550', *Fouad I University, Bulletin of the Faculty of Arts*, vol. 12 (1950), pp. 15, 17–18, 46.
[68] M.B.Davies (ed.), 'Suffolk's Expedition to Montdidier 1523', *Fouad I University, Bulletin of the Faculty of Arts*, vol. 7 (1944), pp. 35–36.

A marked sense of despondency soon began to characterise this abortive campaign. Low morale seemed a product of appalling material conditions rather than fear of battle or the enemy. The onset of winter saw tempers fray and the soldiery become apathetic and slovenly. The possibility of having to winter in France

> was well received by the gentlemen of England and those men of the common soldiers who had set their minds on being men of war, but those cowardly men with base hearts who would rather go home to their mothers and fathers, some to plough and thresh, others to follow the cart and hedge and dig and live niggardly, these were unwilling and were angry with anyone who talked about staying there during the winter.[69]

With morale so low, soldiers lost interest in taking care of themselves properly: 'there was no lack of food or drink or wood for fire or making huts, and plenty of straw to roof them and to lie on if they had only fetched it. But there was many a man weak in body who preferred from sheer laziness to lie under the hedge rather than take the trouble to make a snug warm hut to keep him from the frost and snow.'[70] It is small wonder that English soldiers of the day acquired a reputation for liking soft living. When the men of Essex and Suffolk struck up the cry 'Home! Home!' Gruffydd noted 'it is certain that the Duke and all captains who had any sense were amazed at this shouting, not only from the shame that the foreigners from Burgundy should see the shiftlessness and the unruliness of the English soldiers, but also for fear lest the enemy should get to know of this tumult and fall suddenly upon them'.[71]

Whilst this campaign was dogged by particularly acute disciplinary problems, such outbreaks were by no means infrequent in English armies throughout the first half of the sixteenth century. They appear to have been a common response to material deprivation, cold and hunger. However well English troops were capable of fighting at the onset of a campaign, they do appear to have lacked staying power on long campaigns. Essentially the English fielded peasant armies, of mercurial temperament. The Venetian ambassador, Sebastian Giustinian, summed them up thus: 'When they take the field, their arms consist of a breast plate, bow, arrows, sword . . . They insist on being paid monthly, and do not choose to suffer any hardship; but when they have their comforts they will do battle daily, with a courage, vigour and valour that defies exaggeration.'[72]

English armies were thus unpredictable instruments of policy: capable of fighting with stubborn courage on occasion but also given to indiscipline and outspoken demonstrations of grievance. The situation in Scotland was, if anything, even worse. The weakness of central authority, particularly during the long minorities of James V and Mary Queen of Scots, led to factionalism and

---

[69] Davies (ed.), 'Suffolk's Expedition to Montdidier 1523', p. 39.
[70] Davies (ed.), 'Suffolk's Expedition to Montdidier 1523', p. 40.
[71] Davies (ed.), 'Suffolk's Expedition to Montdidier 1523', p. 41.
[72] *Calendar of State Papers, Venice, Vol. 2, 1509–1519* (London, 1867), 1287.

internal rivalries that militated against the operation of a levy system that relied on a strong sense of personal loyalty. The tensions of a contested Reformation only served to exaggerate this trend.

The campaign in 1513 had seen a magnificent response from James IV's subjects, noble and commoner. However, as the century wore on there was an increasing reluctance to obey even the most insistent summonses. With religious and political loyalties deeply divided, this reluctance to serve became most obvious in the 1540s. In 1546 the Privy Council issued an insistent proclamation to 'all Scheriffis, Stewartis, Ballies, and their Deputis, alswele Regalite as Riate, Provistis, Aldermen, and Bailles of Burrowis' to organise wappinshaws to check that men were armed and equipped appropriately, since it was feared that many were forgetting their obligation.[73] Men of all ranks refused the summons to war, or absented themselves from the army at the first opportunity. At the height of the war with the English in 1549, the provosts and ballies of Edinburgh, Linlithgow and Stirling and other smaller towns launched night time raids on lodgings and stables to uncover deserters. On occasion whole towns were summoned to court for their negligence in sending their menfolk to the defence of their country.[74]

Prohibitions on the playing of golf and football to encourage practice at the butts suggests that the Scots had similar worries to the English about the efficiency of their levy system in the early sixteenth century. Yet Scotland could clearly assemble large and reasonably well equipped armies at little cost to the Crown. Keeping them in the field for any length of time was a different matter, a perennial problem with a levy system. In spite of this, foreign observers seem frequently to have been impressed by the appearance of Scottish troops in the field. Don Pedro de Ayala, Spanish ambassador to the court of James IV, commented both on the size and quality of his army.[75] Similarly, in 1547, William Patten, accompanying an English army, wrote of Scottish troops: 'They cum to the felde well furnished all with jak and skull, dagger, buckler, and swoordes all notably brode and thin, of excedinge good temper and universally so made to slyce, that I never sawe none so good . . . Hereto, every man his pike; and a great kercher wrapped twice or thrice about his neck; not for cold but [against] cutting.'[76]

---

[73] John Hill Burton (ed.), *The Register of the Privy Council of Scotland, Vol. 1, 1545–1569* (Edinburgh, 1877), p. 62.
[74] Dickinson, 'Some Notes on the Scottish Army in the First Half of the Sixteenth Century', p. 144, Mackie, 'The English Army at Flodden', p. 43.
[75] David Caldwell, 'Royal Patronage of Arms and Armour Making in Fifteenth- and Sixteenth-Century Scotland', in David Caldwell (ed.), *Scottish Weapons and Fortifications 1100–1800* (Edinburgh, 1981), p. 73.
[76] William Patten, 'The Expedition into Scotland, 1547', in A.F.Pollard (ed.), *Tudor Tracts 1532–1588* (Westminster, 1903), p. 112.

Arms, armour and equipment

In Scotland, as in England, individuals were obliged to equip themselves for war according to their estates. In 1318 individuals worth £10 in goods were to provide for themselves an acton (quilted armour not unlike the jack or brigandine), a basinet (steel helmet), or haubergon (neck and breast protection), a hat of iron, spear and sword. Those commoners whose wealth stretched to the ownership of a cow were to muster with a bow or spear. Over the next two centuries these provisions were consistently up-dated to reflect changing military realities. In 1456 a targe (round shield) was added to the accoutrements of men not designated as archers, and would continue to be carried by some Scottish troops into the eighteenth century. A larger type of shield, the pavise, also seems to have been retained in Scottish use, at least during the first half of the sixteenth century.[77] On the continent the pavise was generally used by missile troops, particularly crossbowmen, for protection as they loaded and aimed their weapons. These heavy, rectangular shields were sometimes large enough to shelter two men, one of whom would support it, the other fire from behind it. They offered reasonable protection from bows but would have become hopelessly cumbersome had they been made proof against gunpowder weapons. They were thus fast disappearing from Europe's battlefields.

Instructions given to the sheriffs in 1513 give a good indication of the kind of arms and armour carried during the sixteenth century. Gentlemen were now expected to muster in 'white harness' (plate armour), whilst common soldiers were to wear jacks and sallets. As in England, the Crown was taking increasing responsibility for the provision of equipment, and large quantities of munition armour, equivalent to the Almain rivet purchased in such quantity by Henry VIII, was acquired from France and the Low Countries.[78] Oddly enough, however, in the aftermath of Flodden there seems to have been a deliberate abandoning of plate armour even by the nobility. This could have stemmed from the vulnerability of heavily armoured pikemen in mêlée, with more agile English billmen wearing jacks and brigandines. Whatever the reason, by 1547 it was difficult to distinguish noble from commoner in the Scottish line of battle. Patten claimed that 'their armour among them so little differed and their apparel was so base and beggarly; wherein the Lurdein was, in a manner, all one with the Lord; and the Lound with the Laird; all clad alike in jacks covered with white leather; doublets of the same or of fustian; and most commonly all white hosen'.[79]

For offensive arms, various forms of axes and pole arms were acceptable at the wappinshaws. As with the English bill and halberd, these weapons were to provide a defence against cavalry. As late as the eighteenth century Highlanders

---

[77] G. Gregory Smith (ed.), *The Days of James IV* (London, 1900), p. 156.
[78] Caldwell, 'Royal Patronage of Arms and Armour Making', p. 84.
[79] Patten, p. 127.

in Jacobite armies were using Lochaber axes against mounted troops.[80] Other varieties of long shafted weapon included the Leith axe and the Jedburgh stave. It is difficult to distinguish precisely between these various forms of battle axe. By the eighteenth century the name Lochaber axe had become a generic description for all Scottish pole arms. In the sixteenth century, however, it would appear that the distinctions between the weapons, most notably the shape of the head, were of some importance.[81]

The weapons seem to share a common ancestry in the broad axes introduced into the British Isles by Scandinavian peoples. The Danish axe was usually short shafted, possibly for use one-handed in conjunction with a shield. Its use was widespread throughout Scotland as late as the fourteenth century and they were still being carried by some west Highlanders into the early 1500s. It is probable that sixteenth-century references to Lochaber axes refer to these single-edged weapons, which could by then be regarded as a distinctive arm of Highland troops. An Act of Parliament of 1574 ordering the holding of wappinshaws contains official recognition of the differences in arms and armour of the two regions of Scotland. This act almost certainly reflects a long standing tradition of Highland preference for axe and targe over the Lowland spear or pike.[82]

The distinctiveness of the Gaelic speaking 'wild Scots' of the Highlands and Isles was well noted by contemporaries. The Lothian born historian John Mair wrote of their costume: 'From the mid-leg to the foot they go uncovered; their dress is, for an over garment, a loose plaid, and a shirt saffron-dyed.' In battle Mair noted the contrast between the Lowland laird, who wore plate armour, and the Highland chieftain, who still wore a coat of mail. Likewise the common soldiery differed in protective clothing. The Lowlanders favoured the quilted jack and brigandine, whilst Highlanders wore an ample linen garment 'sewed together in patchwork, well daubed with wax or with pitch, and an overcoat of deer skin'.[83] A description of 1597 describes how Highlanders:

> delight in marbled cloths, especially that have long stripes of sundrie colours; they love chiefly purple and blue; their predecessors used short mantles, or plaids of divers colurs, sundrie ways divided, and among some the same custom is observed to this day; but, for the most part now, they are brown, most near to the colour of hadder, to the effect when they lye among the hadders, the bright colour of their plaids shall not beway them . . .[84]

The lightness of the clothing and the concern for camouflage reflect the requirements of warfare in the Highlands and Western Isles. The normal pattern

[80] David Stewart, *Sketches of the Character, Manners and Present State of the Highlanders of Scotland* (Edinburgh, 1977) p. 69.
[81] See David Caldwell, 'Some Notes on Scottish Axes and Long Shafted Weapons', in Caldwell (ed.), *Scottish Weapons and Fortifications 1100–1800*, pp. 253–314.
[82] Caldwell, 'Some Notes on Scottish Axes and Long Shafted Weapons', p. 275.
[83] Archibald Constable (ed.), *John Major's History of Greater Britain* (Edinburgh, 1892), pp. 49–50.
[84] Stewart, p. 76.

of clan conflict was ambush and skirmish. Battles rarely involved more than a few hundred combatants; opening with an exchange of missile fire from bows, the clansmen would come to handstrokes once they had exhausted their arrows.[85] Fighting tended to pit individual against individual, requiring a high degree of weapon skill but little unit cohesion. Highlanders were thus unsuited to use as shock troops in close order mass formations using the pike. Those who fought at the Battle of Loch Lochy in July 1544 are described as carrying the characteristic weapons of light infantry: bows, two-handed swords (the *claidheamh-mor*) and 'Dence' (Danish) axes.[86] Similarly, John Mair describes their arms as 'bow and arrows, broadsword and small halbert', the latter presumably being the one-handed Lochaber axe.[87]

Besides the Lochaber axe three other main forms of axe seemed to have developed by the sixteenth century. Firstly there was the long-shafted axe, combined with a spear point and a hammer head or fluke, virtually identical to the English halberd. Secondly there was the two-handed Leith axe with a long, heavy, curved cutting edge and a hook projecting from the top of the staff, behind the blade. The third form, the Jedburgh stave, was a weapon of the Border Marches, popular with English reivers as well as Scots. By tradition it was the smiths of Jedburgh who manufactured this lethal looking weapon, with long, thin steel blades, up to four feet in length, stretched to a sharp point, mounted on sturdy oak shafts. Several surviving examples have roundels, metal disks, fitted around the shafts, presumably to protect the hand and prevent the stave from slipping. Such devices are often associated with lances used from horseback, and there is good reason for supposing that the Jedburgh stave was most effective when used by mounted men. In 1515 attempts were made to ban the weapon, possibly because in the hands of dismounted soldiers at Flodden it had proved less effective than the heavy-bladed Leith and Lochaber axes. By 1546, however, the Jedburgh stave is once again included amongst arms acceptable at wappinshaws. It may well have been too versatile a weapon to abandon. Its long, thin, curved blade culminating in a sharp point allowed it to be used as a lance by mounted troops, and an axe once they dismounted. Less common than axes, but also apparently still carried by some sixteenth-century Scottish soldiers, were staff weapons combining spear head and mace, similar to the

---

[85] For example, at the Battle of Loch Lochy in July 1544 the Frasers numbered three hundred, the Clan Ranald, at the most, six hundred. See William Mackay (ed.), *The Wardlaw Manuscript Entitled 'Polichronicon Seu Policratica Temporum, Or The True Genealogy of the Frasers', 916–1674* (Edinburgh, 1905), p. 135. See also John Leslie's account of the same battle for evidence of Highland tactics, John Leslie, *The Historie of Scotland*, trans. James Dalrymple and ed. E.G.Cody and W.Murison (Edinburgh, 1895), pp. 281–282.

[86] Mackay (ed.), pp. 134–138. For another description of Highland troops' equipment in battle see Robert Lindesay of Pitscottie, *The Historie and Cronicles of Scotland*, vol. 1 (Edinburgh, 1899), p. 270. On the use of the word 'claymore' see Claude Blair, 'The Word Claymore', in Caldwell (ed.), *Scottish Weapons and Fortifications 1100–1800*, pp. 378–387.

[87] Constable (ed.), p. 49.

'morning star' or the Flemish *goedendag*. In 1500 the theft of one such 'broggit staff with a spere' was reported from Dunbeath castle.[88]

Despite the employment of this variety of staff weapons, the Scottish army in the field had in fact moved a long way towards standardisation of its weapons. The most widely used weapon of sixteenth-century Scottish armies was the pike. Whilst retaining a small proportion of axe-armed troops, formations of Lowland infantry would invariably consist of blocks of pikemen. There were sound tactical reasons for the utilisation of the pike. The Scottish had much in common with the Swiss. They had an established tradition of fighting on foot, and during the wars of independence had proved their ability to withstand cavalry charges by noble men-at-arms. Yet in the two hundred years since Bannockburn the greatest threat had come not from mounted English men-at-arms, but from English and Welsh longbows. The Scots had adopted the bow themselves, with some success, but they must have remained acutely aware of the need to close quickly with English troops, to bring them to mêlée and thus minimise the danger posed by English missile fire. Like the Swiss of the fifteenth century, the Scots also needed to conclude their campaigns swiftly, since their infantry could not afford to remain in the field for more than forty days. It was also the case that the majority of Scottish soldiers in the field would be equipped with only light armour. Thus, like the Swiss, the army of Scotland needed to advance swiftly upon their enemy, nullifying the English advantage in missile weapons and bringing battle to a rapid conclusion.

The pike, therefore, was a weapon ideally suited to their needs. It provided an effective defence against cavalry and it provided an offensive capability – the attack by a rapidly moving column – to overrun English bow and bill formations. These were novel tactics for the Scots. It is tempting to see the schiltrons of Bannockburn in the solid pike phalanxes of Flodden and Pinkie, but this is not the case. After the Battle of Flodden, the Bishop of Durham reported that the Scots had advanced 'in good order, after the Almayne's manner'.[89] The Scottish army had consciously adopted the tactics and equipment of the best infantry in Europe, infantry which won its victories by carrying the battle to its enemies, by attacking. The pike was, essentially, an offensive weapon, and it was the adoption of this modern weapon that determined Scottish tactics.

Whatever constraints existed on the development of a modern army in Scotland, the country's military arrangements were not hopelessly locked into archaic medieval practice. Nor were the Scots doomed by some inherited commitment to 'the tactical offensive – the attack against all reason, against all odds', that some have identified as the central tenet of a continuity in Celtic warfare stretching from the sack of Rome in AD 387 to the nineteenth century.[90]

---

[88] Caldwell, 'Some Notes on Scottish Axes and Long Shafted Weapons', pp. 290–299.
[89] *Letters and Papers [LandP], Henry VIII*, vol. 1 (London, 1862), p. 4461.
[90] For this thesis, see in particular James Michael Hill, *Celtic Warfare, 1595–1763* (Edinburgh, 1986), *passim*. It is worth noting that even the Gaelic Highlanders were influenced by mainstream developments in European warfare. The combination of sword and targe puts

Scottish armies in the first half of the sixteenth century deliberately took the pike-armed Swiss and German infantry of the day as their model. They fought in the aggressive manner that they did because modern tactics demanded that the pike be used that way, taking the battle to the enemy, sweeping his infantry from the field, defying his cavalry with a solid wall of pike points.

This desire to create an army that depended ultimately on shock tactics rather than firepower is further evidenced by the differential pay received by those few Scottish soldiers who actually received wages. Troops who could close with the enemy appeared to have been accorded the most value. In 1482 the spearmen raised by James III for defence of the Border were to receive 2s 6d per day, whilst his archers received just 2s daily.[91] The importance of soldiers armed with pole arms was even more evident during the reign of his son. As Norman MacDougall has noted, James IV would take the Swiss as his model and would endeavour to use their tactics against the English.[92]

Paradoxically it was to be a consequence of this attempt at modernisation that spelled danger for the Scots. For there were inherent weaknesses in this system, relying as it did wholly on rapid assault by close order infantry to the neglect of other arms. This lesson was already being learned on the continent. At Cerignola, in 1503, Swiss pike had floundered before Spanish entrenchments, well defended by cannon and arquebusiers. At Marignano, in 1515, a battle that was to have distinct echoes at Pinkie in 1547, a Swiss pike column was halted by a cavalry charge then decimated by artillery fire. The pike column was far from invincible, even in the hands of the Swiss.

Yet, where it had been beaten, entrenchments and prepared positions held by a disciplined infantry supported by gunpowder weapons had played a major part. Against an enemy manoeuvring for position in the open the pike was still formidable. The Scots, therefore, had reason to place their faith in the pike, so long as they could fight on fields of their own choice. Certainly, accusations of Scotland's military backwardness ignore sound evidence for Scottish competence in the use of the pike. From early in the sixteenth century, French officers had been present in Scotland training their soldiers. William Patten, who accompanied Somerset's invasion of Scotland in 1547, noted the effectiveness of Scottish pike formations:

> ... they thrust shoulders ... nigh together, the fore rank, well nigh to kneeling, stood low before their fellows behind holding their pikes in both hands, and

them in the same category as English, Spanish and Dutch sword and buckler troops. Hill claims that the 'Highland Charge', closing with the enemy, discharging their pieces and then charging home with the sword, was a novel tactic developed by Montrose's Highlanders in the seventeenth century. in fact European infantry had been utilising this tactic at least a hundred years earlier. See Roy (ed.), *Blaise de Monluc*, pp. 128–130 and Thomas Churchyard, *A Generall Rehearsall of Warres, Wherein is five hundred severall services of land and sea* (London, 1579), p. 56.

91 Ranald Nicholson, *Scotland: The Later Middle Ages* (Edinburgh, 1974), p. 494.
92 Norman MacDougall, *James IV* (Edinburgh, 1989), pp. 274–276.

herewith on their left [arm] their bucklers; the one end of the pike against their right foot, the other against the enemy breast high; their fellows crossing their pike points with them forward; and thus, each with other, so nigh as place and space will suffer, through the whole ward so thick, that as easily shall a bare finger pierce through the skin of an angry hedgehog, as any encounter the front of their pikes.[93]

Besides the adoption of the pike, Scotland had also developed a keen interest in the gunpowder revolution. The first gunpowder weapons to be used in Scotland probably came in the train of English armies. In 1327 Edward III brought 'crakys of wer' north of the border and the English deployed siege cannon at Berwick in 1333 and 1405.[94] The Scots themselves were using guns by the 1380s, if not earlier.[95] By the next century wrought iron guns were being manufactured, on a small scale, in Scotland itself.

The most formidable artillery of Scotland's siege train continued to be imported from aboard, particularly from the Low Countries, but was used to great effect by James II as he reconquered lost territory from England and suppressed the rebellion of the Black Douglases. At the siege of Threave Castle in 1455 the siege train included the giant bombard Mons Meg, capable of hurling a stone shot of over 500 pounds weight for two miles.[96] It must be admitted that Threave successfully defied James's guns and fell instead to bribery, but he had more luck elsewhere. In the same year James besieged Abercorn Castle, the most formidable of the Douglas strongholds. Here a French gunner in James's pay had wrought considerable destruction to the towers and curtain wall of the castle, forcing its surrender.[97] Ironically James II's interest in cannon cost him his life. He was killed by a burst barrel during the siege of Roxburgh in 1460. This did not, however, deter his successor from expanding Scotland's artillery train.

James III had acquired cast bronze guns from France. Impressed by their ruggedness and power he had made efforts to instigate their manufacture in Edinburgh, but apparently with little success. In 1481 he had taken steps to furnish several coastal and Border castles with artillery, but there is little evidence that he met with any more success in this area than he had with establishing an indigenous gun founding industry. Undeterred by the slow progress made by his father, James IV persevered, importing French gunners in 1505 and appointing a successful Scottish master gunner, Robert Borthwick, in about 1511. Guns continued to be imported, but at least some of the large artillery train which James commanded was manufactured in Scotland. Not only did this weight of ord-

[93] Patten, *The Expedition into Scotland, 1547*, p. 112.
[94] Alastair Maxwell-Irving, 'Early Firearms and their Influence on the Military and Domestic Architecture of the Borders', *Proceedings of the Society of Antiquaries of Scotland*, vol. 103 (1970–71), p. 193.
[95] For this section, see Caldwell, 'Royal Patronage of Arms and Armour Making', pp. 73–93.
[96] Maxwell-Irving, p. 194.
[97] Geoffrey Stell, 'Late Medieval Defences in Scotland', in Caldwell (ed.), p. 40.

nance cause the English considerable alarm in 1513, but James had already shown that he could employ it successfully, even in difficult country. Beginning in 1493, he had led a number of expeditions to enforce royal authority in the Highlands and Isles, and his artillery had made a considerable impression on his recalcitrant northern subjects.[98]

James's involvement with the Yorkist pretender Perkin Warbeck had also provided the Scots with valuable operational lessons, particularly in the transport of a siege train into England. It had also brought foreign expertise to Scotland, in the shape of a German captain, Roderick de Lalain, and his small band of *Landsknechte*, who pledged to serve James. The invasion of England which commenced in September 1496 was a logistical triumph. Cannon, covered carts, munitions, pavilions and other assorted equipment had been carried over the Tweed by 143 carters with 196 horses. The river had presented quite an obstacle, and James had had to enlist local labour to help when some of the pieces had stuck fast in the water. Once in England, the Scots had not penetrated far, concentrating on seizing and demolishing a few small Border towers, gathering booty, and trying out their siege train on the castle at Heaton, although without success. The artillery train was too precious to risk on a deeper incursion, and James withdrew when an English army approached. However, the expedition had demonstrated the possibility of transporting artillery all the way from Edinburgh, across the Lammermuir Hills and the River Tweed into England and safely back again. The following year he repeated this feat, besieging Norham Castle.[99]

By the sixteenth century, therefore, Scotland had an established tradition of using artillery, both at sieges and in the field. Fortifications and places of strength were also often well provided with defensive artillery. When Home Castle was taken by the English in 1547 they found it contained two bastard culverins, one saker, three bronze falconets and 'eight pieces of iron'.[100] Scottish gunners had, it must be admitted, an inconsistent record in action. The resistance of Tantallon Castle, held against James V by Archibald Douglas, 6th Earl of Angus, to a twenty day siege in 1528, and Regent Arran's failure to make any impression on the rebels holding St. Andrews in 1547, indicate that commitment to artillery did not always equate with skill in its handling. Unfortunately for Scotland the indigenous gun-founding industry was also slow to develop, and the country remained largely dependent on foreign imports.

This was true not just for the larger gunpowder weapons but for hand firearms too. Traditionally the Scots' chief infantry missile weapon was the bow. Scotland had its own bowyers, but English craftsmen of this art were highly prized and at least one English bowyer was operating under royal patronage in Edinburgh in the 1530s. Similarly, French crossbow makers were employed by the Scottish Crown. Like the French, the Scots retained the crossbow for ship-

98 R.L.Mackie, *King James IV of Scotland* (Edinburgh, 1958), pp. 72–78.
99 Goodman, *The Wars of the Roses*, pp. 111–113.
100 Patten, *The Expedition into Scotland, 1547*, p. 144.

board use well into the 1540s.[101] As in English armies, there was to be a long transitional period during which bows would be fielded alongside arquebuses. Highlanders were still using the longbow during the British Civil Wars of the 1640s, whilst Lowlanders retained the weapon into the middle decades of the sixteenth century. In 1548 John Erskine of Dun used archers to repel an English amphibious landing near Montrose.[102]

By that time the use of handguns was also widespread. Handguns appear to have been present in small numbers in Scottish armies from the late fifteenth century, but few guns were manufactured in Scotland itself. Handguns are mentioned in the treasurer's accounts for 1513 and from there on the weapon gradually becomes more common. By 1541 it was recorded that 413 arquebuses were held in stock in Edinburgh Castle. In 1545 an English force besieging Kelso found the abbey defended by a stout band of Scottish arquebusiers.[103] Nine years later Parliament stipulated that every Scottish Borderer was to arm himself with a 'hakbut', in addition to a sword, dagger, 18 foot pike, Jedburgh stave, buckler, jack and leg armour.[104] However much the Scots struggled to initiate a domestic gun-founding industry, they had clearly acquired enough guns to worry the English. One panicky estimate of 1522 spoke of the Duke of Albany's forces on the Border having a 'marvelous greate number of hand gonnes' and one thousand 'Arquebus à Croc', heavy arquebuses mounted on waggons.[105] There has been a tendency to assume that Scotland was unable to field significant numbers of arquebusiers on the battlefield, largely because of William Patten's remark on the Scots at Pinkie: 'hackbutters have they few or none'.[106] Yet Patten himself testifies to the use of arquebuses by Scottish skirmishers outside Prestonpans, before the battle.[107] Considerable numbers of arquebuses had been fielded in 1542, before Haddon Rig. The vanguard under Sir Walter Lyndsay had numbered two thousand, a thousand of whom carried spears, five hundred carried bows and five hundred were armed with 'hagbuttis'.[108]

Wherever possible, Scottish commanders aimed to achieve this equal division of foot between pike and shot. In response to the English seizure of Broughty in 1547, the Church, the local nobility and the inhabitants of Dundee were ordered to raise a force of three hundred men. A third of these were to be cavalry and the remaining two hundred foot were divided equally between 'speirmen' and 'hagbutmen'.[109] This indicates that the need to provide pikemen with adequate fire

101 Caldwell, 'Royal Patronage of Arms and Armour Making', p. 83.
102 George Buchanan, *The History of Scotland*, vol. 3 (Edinburgh, 1821), p. 62.
103 *LandP, Henry VIII*, vol. 20, part 1 (London, 1905), 347.
104 Maxwell-Irving, 'Early Firearms and their Influence', p. 201.
105 *Calendar of State Papers, Henry VIII*, vol., part 1 (London, 1831) p. lxi.
106 Patten, *The Expedition into Scotland, 1547*, p. 111.
107 Patten, p. 97.
108 Pitscottie, *The Historie and Cronicles of Scotland*, vol. 1, p. 397.
109 *The Register of the Privy Council of Scotland, Vol. 1, 1545–1569* (Edinburgh, 1877), p. 80.

support was now appreciated, even if was not always possible to achieve in the field.

The main conduit for the supply of gunpowder weapons was France. Three hundred arquebuses were given to the Scots in 1543, along with a large number of cannon, including eighty 'lyght peces for the feelde', when an English invasion seemed imminent.[110] Even more firearms were supplied during the English occupation of 1547 to 1550. At this stage the French seem to have made a very thorough job of re-equipping their allies, much to English alarm. In January 1548 English raiders near Dundee were pursued by a thousand Scottish mounted arquebusiers and were fortunate to extricate themselves after a sharp skirmish.[111] The English themselves were employing large numbers of Spanish mounted arquebusiers to considerable effect and it was important for the Scots to keep pace and raise comparable bodies of troops. Ironically, the English were also placing firearms in Scotland in this period, by equipping assured Scots, loyal to the English Crown, as arquebusiers. Many of the 'hackbutters' from the garrison of Wark sent to Broughty Craig in late 1547 were Scots.[112] The rising number of arquebusiers present in Scottish armies of the 1540s is indicative of the Scottish commitment to modernisation, despite the constant struggle against inadequate resources and a pervading atmosphere of political chaos.

The mounted arquebusiers are a particularly important development, for Scotland's cavalry arm was in general considerably weaker than England's. Scotland had fielded heavy cavalry in the past. From the twelfth century, at least, Scottish kings had recognised the desirability of including lance-armed, fully armoured men-at-arms in their armies. Yet the training and equipping of such a force was a considerable financial burden for a small country such as Scotland. More problematic still was the provision of suitable horses. Even Robert the Bruce possessed only one sturdy war horse, and he rode to Bannockburn on a palfrey to keep his destrier fresh for the battle. After 1314 heavy cavalry practically disappeared from Scottish armies. In the first half of the sixteenth century James V, with one eye perhaps on the growing strength of the English cavalry arm, imported great horses and mares from Denmark in an attempt to improve the breed, but progress must have been slow.[113] In 1548 the English were noting the advantage that their demi-lancers, some of whom had mounts sturdy enough to wear horse bard, gave them over the Scots and their 'few horsemen'.[114]

It may be that in the long term James V's efforts yielded some success. The Scottish brigade that served Holland in the latter years of the sixteenth century was to include lancers, mounted arquebusiers and *cuirassiers*, a designation

[110] *The Hamilton Papers, Vol. 2, 1543–1590* (Edinburgh, 1892), 61.
[111] *Cal. State Papers Scot.*, vol. 1, 142.
[112] *Cal. State Papers Scot.*, vol. 1, 129.
[113] David Caldwell, 'Some Notes on Scottish Axes and Long Shafted Weapons', pp. 255–256.
[114] *Cal. State Papers Scot.*, vol. 1, 266.

reserved for heavy cavalry wearing, at the very least, breastplate, back and helmet.[115] However, for the first half of the century Scotland could only field light cavalry. The vast majority came from the Borders, identical in equipment, skill and tactical role to their English equivalents. In 1551 a French visitor to Scotland, Estienne Perlin, was unimpressed by the reivers' rough and ready appearance:

> [They are] bold and gallant enough, but are not so well armed as the French, for they have very little well made, clean and polished armour, but use jackets of mail in exercising daily with the French, and have the custom of using little ambling nags and small horses; their lances are small and narrow, and they have scarce any large horses, and few are brought to them, except from France.[116]

The difficulties faced by the Scots in keeping pace with military innovation, particularly those techniques mastered by the English, should not overshadow the commitment to modern pike and shot formations. This commitment demonstrates that, in terms of tactics and equipment, the Scottish army was developing on the same lines as other European armies, but always within the constraints imposed by Scotland's limited resources. The presence of the French was a driving force in modernisation, from the forty captains in James IV's host at Flodden to the tough and experienced expeditionary force that spearheaded the war against Somerset's garrisons from 1548 to 1550. Scotland's kings had been aware of how important France was to them as a source of military expertise. Before Flodden James IV had asked Louis XII for two thousand soldiers used to campaigns and sieges, three hundred men-at-arms, artillery and gunners, all well versed in war.[117] Louis, of course, could not spare the men, but the request demonstrates a commitment to fielding a modern army.

English warfare was more heavily influenced by continental practice from an earlier date than was Scottish, largely because of the high number of foreign mercenaries serving in early Tudor armies. It was generally a case of borrowing new techniques and adapting old ones, with the traditional bow and bill combination remaining the mainstay of English infantry well into the sixteenth century. Yet this continuity should not obscure the extent to which English tactical thought was developing. Even with weaponry not considered typically English they developed their own tactics, and foreign troops who served alongside them noted their distinctiveness. The Italian mercenary captain, Giovacchio de Comiano, who served in the English army at Boulogne in 1544–46, was intrigued by English pike and shot formations. The arquebusiers stood behind the pikes, who stooped low to allow the shot to fire over their heads. He

---

115 James Ferguson (ed.), *Papers Illustrating the History of the Scots Brigade in the Service of the United Netherlands 1572–1782*, vol. 1 (Edinburgh, 1899), xii–xiii.

116 Caldwell, 'Some Notes on Scottish Axes and Long Shafted Weapons', p. 256.

117 Marguerite Wood (ed.), *Flodden Papers* (Edinburgh, 1933), xvi.

described how the English formed up in battle, archers and arquebusiers on the wings of blocks of pikemen and halberdiers, interspersed with more shot.[118]

This combination of arms was, for the period, a practical, pragmatic and sensible arrangement. There was no sudden technical innovation that rendered the longbow obsolete overnight, rather the traditional missile weapon of English troops was gradually supplanted for a variety of reasons. The continued refinement of the handgun, from the primitive mechanisms of the late fifteenth century to the musket in the sixteenth, eventually surpassed the longbow in terms of penetrative power, though never in terms of rate of fire. It is worth bearing in mind how marginal the improved performance of gunpowder small arms remained over the course of the late fifteenth and sixteenth centuries. The curved stock braced against the shoulder of the arquebus allowed for a larger powder charge and the larger calibre of the musket allowed for a heavier ball and consequently a slightly greater range and penetrative power. Yet the weapon's fundamental inaccuracy and slow rate of fire always limited its battlefield potential. Gunpowder small arms were most effectively used *en masse* in defensive formations, supported by staff weapons and defended by fortifications.

The English had been using bows in this fashion for centuries, so gunpowder weapons offered little that was tactically innovative in the British Isles and there was little chance of guns revolutionising British warfare. The debates that took place in the final decade of the sixteenth century between progressives who favoured the abandonment of the bow and traditionalists who urged its retention tell us much about the strengths and weaknesses of the bow as a weapon.

One point that was continually emphasised was the decline in the number of skilled archers available for service. Sir Roger Williams, a Low Countries veteran, maintained that of five thousand archers, only one thousand could shoot with sufficient force to be effective. Dependent on their physical strength, Williams also noted that after a few months on campaign the proportion of effective archers fell to one in ten. He acknowledged that horses were vulnerable to archery from well defended positions, but thought that combinations of well armoured cavalry and musket-armed troops would always best bowmen, whose effective battlefield range he calculated at only 12 or 14 score yards. Both he and another champion of the new discipline, Humphrey Barwick, believed that firearms would outrange bows in battle, and Barwick noted that bows were less effective against armour. He quoted a French soldier who, when he saw arrows coming, would lower his helmet to protect his face and allow the arrows to bounce harmlessly off his plate armour. Barwick does acknowledge the bowmen's high rate of fire, six arrows loosed in forty seconds, compared to one ball from an arquebus, but suggests that fire at such a rate was wildly inaccurate.[119]

---

118 J.R.Hale, *Renaissance War Studies* (London, 1983), p. 267.
119 See John X. Evans (ed.), *The Works of Sir Roger Williams* (Oxford, 1972), pp. 39–41, J.R.Hale (ed.), *Certain Discourses Military by Sir John Smyth* (Ithaca, 1964), *passim*, Humfrey Barwick, 'A Breefe Discourse, Concerning the force and effect of all manuall weapons of fire', in E.G.Heath (ed.), *Bow Versus Gun* (Wakefield, 1973), *passim*. A useful

However, even though fears of a decline in the value of archery were apparent during the reign of Henry VIII, there is a danger of placing the obsolescence of the weapon too early in the century. The size and power of longbows recently recovered from the *Mary Rose* suggest that well into the middle of the century there were still some English bowmen of incredible skill and dexterity. The smallest and lightest of these bows had a draw weight of 100 pounds. At the other end of the scale, the largest bows, it has been claimed, had a draw weight of 185 pounds.[120] It is difficult, if not impossible, to recreate the conditions of sixteenth-century battle and thus any claims for the range and penetrative power of such a weapon in action must remain tentative. Professor P.L.Pratt, a physicist at Imperial College, London, has tested two bows, one of 165 pounds draw weight, the other of 100 pounds, modern approximations of weapons taken from the *Mary Rose*. The larger bow achieved a maximum range of 320 yards with a heavy armour-piercing bodkin arrow and 350 yards with a lighter flight arrow. For the smaller weapon the range decreased by 100 yards for each arrow type.[121] The velocity of a bodkin arrow could, if it hit its target at an angle of about 50 degrees from the horizontal, penetrate plate armour up to about 1.5 millimetres thick.[122] Such a penetration, however, could only have been achieved at close range, about 10 metres, and the more glancing the shot the less effective it would have been.[123] Nor would the bow have fared as well against expensive plate armour as it would have done against the thin, poor quality munition armour worn by the common soldier. The utility of the bow therefore depended largely on conditions. For use on the Anglo-Scots border, for example, where fighting was conducted primarily by lightly armoured but highly mobile cavalry, its rapid rate of fire, light weight and accuracy made the bow the weapon of choice for northern levies until the end of the century.[124]

Although the relative merits of the bow and the firearm were clear by the end of the century, it is difficult to ascertain exactly when English archers began to

summary is Thomas Esper, 'The Replacement of the Longbow by Firearms in the English Army', *Technology and Culture*, vol. 6 (1965), pp. 382–393.

[120] Robert Hardy, *Longbow* (London, 1995), pp. 194–221. The largest bows have been the subject of much debate. It has been maintained that they are bow staves, rather than completed bows, but the team responsible for recovering them from the *Mary Rose* remain adamant that these were completed weapons, of awesome proportions. The longbows all had discoloured tips, evidence that they had once had horn 'nocks' fitted, which had since degraded. The 'nock' was the device by which the bow string was attached to the weapon, and a weapon with a bow string is a finished bow, ready to shoot, not a stave. The discovery of a surviving horn 'nock' in 1997 strengthens this case considerably. See Gareth Dupré, 'At Long Last! Research Concludes Longbow Mystery', *Mary Rose Newsbrief*, no. 54 (Autumn 1997), p. 1. For an assessment of the performance of the *Mary Rose* bows, see Gareth Rees, 'The Longbow's Deadly Secrets', *New Scientist*, vol. 18 (1993), pp. 24–25.

[121] P.L.Pratt, 'Testing the Bows', in Robert Hardy, *Longbow* (Sparkford, 1995), p. 217.

[122] Gareth Rees, 'The Longbow's Deadly Secrets', pp. 24–25.

[123] Peter Jones, 'The Metallography and Relative Effectiveness of Arrowheads and Armor during the Middle Ages', *Materials Characterisation*, vol. 29 (1992), pp. 111–117.

[124] George Macdonald Fraser, *The Steel Bonnets* (London, 1989), p. 88.

struggle when faced with rival bodies of shot armed with guns. It is only from the middle of the sixteenth century onwards that we begin to have evidence that English missile weapons were being seriously outranged in action. One such suggestion comes from the Gascon veteran, Blaise de Monluc, who commented during the Boulogne campaign of 1544: 'they [the English] all carried arms of little reach and therefore were necessitated to come up close to us to loose their arrows'.[125] Fourteen years later an English account of the siege of Calais details a skirmish in the outer defence works of the city between English ́shot (long-bowmen and arquebusiers) and their French counterparts. The French 'curriors', it was noted, 'assuredely shot very great bullets, and carry far'.[126] It would not be unreasonable to suppose that some of these French skirmishers were armed with the musket. Whether this is correct or not, the range of the French weapons was sufficient to startle the English. Evidently, therefore, it was a recent development.

In England itself rebel armies armed with the bow, and probably possessed of a fair degree of military skill and experience, had fared badly against troops armed with firearms. In 1549 Lord Protector Somerset had deliberately empha-sised the use of long-range arquebus fire against bow-armed peasants from the West Country. At the Battle of Fenny Bridges an army of Cornishmen were praised for their courage but were driven from the field by Somerset's Italian arquebusiers.[127] On the other hand, the bow's most outspoken champion, Sir John Smythe, claimed that two prominent foreign captains, the Italian Paolo Baptista Spinola and Philip Francis, Count of Salm, who had both faced English bowmen in the late 1540s, gave 'singular commendation to the archery of Eng-land'. Smythe also delights in recounting how twelve hundred *Landsknechte* were routed by Kett's bow-armed rebels before Norwich in 1549, although he somewhat glosses over their subsequent defeat.[128]

The evidence from the battlefields of the middle of the century is thus a little ambiguous. Tentatively one could argue that the firearm did not begin to fully assert an edge over the longbow on the battlefield until the latter half of the six-teenth century. The bow's rapid rate of fire still told in its favour but, from the 1540s onwards, English archers had to close to inside the range of enemy shot before they themselves could fire. In the first half of the sixteenth century the potential advantages then offered by firearms were offset by the continued viability of the tactical system the English had devised, which was centred around the bow.

This tactical system relied on two factors: the rapidity of fire possible with a

---

[125] Roy (ed.), *Blaise de Monluc*, p. 129.

[126] George Ferrers *et al.*, *The Winning of Calais by the French, January 1558 AD* (Tonbridge, Kent, 1991), pp. 308–311.

[127] Julian Cornwall, *Revolt of the Peasantry 1549* (London, 1977), pp. 160–167. On the mili-tary capabilities of peasant armies see Bob Scribner and Gerhard Benecke (eds), *The German Peasant War of 1525 – New Viewpoints* (London, 1979), pp. 98–108.

[128] Hale (ed.), *Certain Discourses Military by Sir John Smyth*, pp. 95–98.

longbow and the ability of the longbowman to defend himself in mêlée with a secondary weapon, usually the bill or maul.[129] The wholesale adoption of the arquebus in place of the longbow would have required the abandonment of a tactical system that evidently worked very well for a new missile weapon giving only marginal increases in range and penetrative power. In the event, the gradual integration of firearms into English armies meant that no such drastic action was necessary. As the proportion of arquebusiers in English armies rose so the bow was gradually moved to the peripheries of English infantry formations. The traditional centrality of the bow to English tactics was gradually displaced.

There was no sudden revolution in the arming and deployment of English soldiers. The Battle of Agincourt in 1415 provides a sound example of their traditional practice. Here the English had advanced to within range of the French men-at-arms and goaded them into a premature and disorderly assault by rapid discharge of arrows at long range. The arrows used for this long-range firing were light, designed not to kill but 'to gall and annoy the enimyes farder of them the usuall custom of the sheafe arrowes'.[130] This relied on the longbow's rapid fire. Once provoked, attacking troops would draw closer, into the range of the heavier bodkin arrows, and finally come to handstrokes where, as at Agincourt, archers armed with bills and mauls could settle the day.

Henry VIII's archers clearly fought in the same manner, relying on their rate of fire to disrupt and disorder the enemy formation but willing and able to come to handstrokes if necessary. The 1562 Captain's Handbook of Henry Barrett was still stressing the importance of arming bowmen with an effective mêlée weapon. He recommends 'a maule of leade with a pyke of five inches longe, well steiled, sett in a staffe of fyve foote of length'. Such a fearsome weapon would allow the bowman to 'mayntayne the fighte as oue elders have donn, by hand strokes'.[131] The maul itself performed a double function. Like their predecessors of the fifteenth century, English bowmen still carried staves, which were hammered into the ground with the archer's mauls. The Venetian ambassador Giustinian reported that each man carried two, 'with which they make their pallisadoes or stockades'.[132]

Such stockades were a feature of fifteenth-century warfare, but the tactical deployment of the longbow did develop to meet the realities of the sixteenth-century battlefield. There was a move away from the dense infantry formations of the past to smaller, more flexible units. In 1521 Wolsey and Henry discussed the deployment of the six thousand archers they were lending to the Emperor's army. Wolsey reminded Henry of 'the experience of your last war', which had demonstrated that six thousand archers could not function together effectively on the battlefield and would need to be dispersed into smaller units.[133]

[129] J.R.Hale (ed.), 'On a Tudor Parade Ground: The Captain's Handbook of Henry Barrett, 1562', in J.R.Hale, *Renaissance War Studies*, p. 277.
[130] Hale (ed.), p. 277.
[131] Hale (ed.), pp. 276–277.
[132] *Cal. State Papers Venice*, vol. 2, 1287.
[133] *Cal. State Papers, Henry VIII*, vol. 1, part 1, xxii.

The retention of the bow within these smaller units was not indicative of a rejection of gunpowder weapons; it shows the English continued to rely on the archer's rapid rate of fire. Henry Barrett, in his 1562 instructions to militia captains, notes that the 'longe bowes . . . sharpe and manyefolde hailshotte may not be indured . . .'. For Barrett, the main function of the bow was harassing the enemy either in small mobile groups or as part of mixed bow and arquebus units. As in Venetian service, the bows would cover the arquebusiers as they reloaded.[134] Hall recounts how French skirmishers issuing out of Therounne during the siege of 1513 were driven back behind the city walls by the speed with which the besiegers loosed off their arrows.[135] Arquebus-armed troops would have been unable to match this rapidity of fire, nor were they typically armed with the longbowman's secondary weapon, a pole arm, such as bill or maul, that would allow them to come to handstrokes in mêlée.[136]

Only slowly had the handheld firearm developed into the dominant infantry weapon, remaining for many years a subsidiary arm in the hands of skirmishers. The English themselves utilised a variety of gunpowder weapons of a bewildering array of calibres, as the ordnance recovered from the *Mary Rose* has indicated. They were, particularly during the reign of Henry VIII, very willing to experiment and innovate with gunpowder weapons. Naval tactics, especially, demonstrated sophistication and skill with ordnance. At Pinkie in 1547 the English army was supported by an off-shore bombardment which drove a portion of the Scots' army from the field.[137] Warcarts mounting several heavy arquebuses called shrimps, like those used by the Spanish at Ravenna in 1512, were to be found in the English army that invaded France in 1513, as were Organ guns, multi-barrelled pieces which were devastating anti-personnel weapons.[138]

Henry VIII was fascinated by artillery, importing not only guns but also gun founders themselves, such as the Frenchman Peter Baude and the Italian Arcanus brothers, who could both practice their trade and train Englishmen in their arcane art.[139] Soon there was a thriving English gun-founding industry which supplied Henry with iron and bronze pieces throughout his reign. The expansion of the artillery train began early in Henry's reign. In 1512 Hans Poppenruyter, the master gun founder of Malines, supplied Henry with forty-eight artillery pieces. Just one year later, as Henry prepared to invade France, Bavarin, the Venetian ambassador, reported to the Doge that the English had 'cannon enough to conquer Hell'.[140]

Henry augmented his artillery train not just through manufacturing new pieces but through the spoils of war. Victories in France or Scotland yielded

---

134 Hale (ed.), 'On a Tudor Parade Ground', p. 284.
135 Hall, *Henry the VIII*, vol. 1, pp. 62, 66.
136 Hale (ed.), 'On a Tudor Parade Ground', p. 277.
137 R.A.Konstan, 'Sixteenth-Century Naval Tactics and Gunnery', in Ruth R. Brown and R.D.Smith (eds), *Guns from the Sea* (London, 1986), pp. 17–23.
138 Cruickshank, *Henry VIII and the Invasion of France*, p. 65.
139 Adrain Caruana, *Tudor Artillery 1485–1603* (New York, 1992), pp. 3–15.
140 H.A.Dillon, 'Arms and Armour at Westminster, the Tower and Greenwich, 1547', p. 225.

cannon. Seventeen 'Skottishe gonnes of Brasse' were recorded in the inventory of the Tower taken in 1547. Less honestly won were the six valuable cannon seized from three Venetian galleys that Henry detained at Southampton in 1522 on the pretext that Venice might ally with France.[141] By the end of his reign Henry counted 64 bronze guns and 351 iron pieces at the Tower alone. Greenwich, Berwick, the Calais Pale and the ships of the royal fleet were also well provided with artillery. Whilst this was an impressive weight of ordnance, standardisation of artillery equipment came late. Henry had, by the time of his death, established sets of pattern models for guns. The most likely dates for the standardisation of calibres are either 1537, when the artillery charters were issued, or 1543, when the office of the ordnance was reconstituted. In either case, it is worth noting that English standardisation of calibres preceded that of the French, which was undertaken by Henri II in 1552.[142]

The English did not confine themselves to the heavier-calibre gunpowder weapons. Small arms had first made an appearance on English battlefields in significant numbers during the fifteenth century. When Edward IV landed at Holderness in 1471 from continental exile he was accompanied by 'three hundred . . . Flemings armed with hand-guns'.[143] The English thus had plenty of opportunity to study the equipment and techniques of the handgunner. If this did not cause an immediate revolution in their own military arrangements it is hardly surprising. They had little reason to be impressed by what they saw. The fifteenth-century handgun was a crude, clumsy and inaccurate weapon which compared poorly to the English longbow.[144] Pikemen too, although dominating continental battlefields, had little immediate impact in England. The German mercenary captain, Martin Schwarz, commanded two thousand *Landsknecht* pikemen, and possibly some Swiss, in the army of Lambert Simnel in 1487. They fought furiously to the last and, it was acknowledged, 'yield little to the English in valour' but with no answer to the longbow, they were slaughtered almost to a man.[145]

There was, therefore, little incentive for the English in the fifteenth century to abandon the bows and bills that had thus far served them so well. The adoption of new weapons could be gradual, with the Crown purchasing gunpowder weapons for its own arsenals and hiring specialists, such as *Landsknechte* or arquebusiers, as and when required. The inventory of the Tower in 1547 records that 6700 'demi-hakes or hand-gonnes' as well as 275 'shorte gonnes for horsemen' had been acquired by the end of Henry's reign.[146] Despite Henry's reputation as an archer and his desire that his countrymen practise with their bows, he

---

[141] Dillon, pp. 223–224.

[142] Caruana, pp. 7–8.

[143] John Warkworth, *A Chronicle of the first hirteen years of the reign of King Edward IV* (London, 1839), p. 13.

[144] Simon Pepper and Nicholas Adams, *Firearms and Fortifications: Military Architecture and Siege Warfare in Sixteenth-Century Siena* (Chicago, 1986), p. 15.

[145] Denys Hay (ed.), *The Anglia Historia of Polydore Vergil* (London, 1950), p. 23.

[146] Dillon, 'Arms and Armour at Westminster, the Tower and Greenwich, 1547', p. 228.

showed an early interest in acquiring handguns and arquebuses to supplement English missile strength. In March 1511 Lewis and Alex de Fava supplied 420 handguns at 8 shillings a piece. A year later Peter Corsy received 9 shillings a piece for 420 handguns with powder flasks. In 1530 Henry's master smith supplied 100 handguns, destined for the Dublin Palesmen, at 5 shillings each.

A careful eye was kept on the technical development of the handgun. In 1534 Henry was informed from the continent that 'arquebuses are now made here which give double the stroke of a hand-gun'.[147] As the role of the arquebus evolved on the battlefield it was being used in English armies, not instead of but in conjunction with the longbow. Giovacchio de Comiano has already been quoted, describing English formations flanked by both archers and arquebusiers. This kind of formation must have been a powerful combination of rapid firing longbows and hard hitting firearms. In September 1547 the Earl of Lennox, an ally of England, commanded such a force as he tackled the fortified 'steple of Anande' during Somerset's campaign in Scotland. Supported by six small artillery pieces, it was the responsibility of the archers and hackbutters to 'maik warre', as pioneers worked under the cover of a pavise to undermine the steeple.[148]

The English attachment to the bow, and their desire that the traditional skills of archery should not be allowed to decline, was not preventing them from experimenting with gunpowder weapons. The English were even developing early variants of the counter-march by the mid-sixteenth century. Arquebusiers might operate in pairs, one firing then falling back whilst his 'follower' discharged his piece, or in mutually supporting small groups, each taking turns to fire volleys. The arquebusiers were also drilled to pass through ranks of pike when pursued by cavalry, and then to turn to fire over their heads.[149]

In keeping with the development of gunpowder tactics in Europe, the English displayed an early appreciation of the utility of field fortifications. This was one of the lessons learned from defeat at the hands of the French. At the Battle of Northampton in 1460 the Lancastrians, to quote Oman, 'borrowing a leaf from the French in the late war',[150] dug entrenchments in which they positioned a substantial quantity of artillery. Ironically a sudden downpour drenched their gunpowder and the Yorkists stormed the stockade at little cost. It is surprising that weapons of such precarious reliability, however innovative, were persevered with but Anthony Goodman has noted that by 1485 'the use of a variety of guns had become a commonplace of warfare in England'.[151]

Just as the gun first augmented, then supplanted, the bow so the pike gradually replaced the bill, halberd, Boar spear and 'Holy Water sprinkler' (combined mace and spear) that had been the standard English mêlée weapons. Here the

---

147 Dillon, 'Arms and Armour at Westminster, the Tower and Greenwich, 1547', p. 230.
148 *Cal. State Papers Scot.*, vol. 1, 42.
149 Hale (ed.), 'On a Tudor Parade Ground', p. 257.
150 Sir Charles Oman, *Art of War in the Middle Ages*, vol. 2 (London, 1991), p. 409.
151 Anthony Goodman, *The Wars of the Roses*, p. 173.

tactical function of the weapons was more obviously interchangeable. The English clearly intended that men armed with pole arms such as the bill and halberd should be able to engage cavalry and infantry. A Venetian diplomat described English billmen as carrying 'a short thick staff with an iron like a peasant's hedging-bill, but much thicker, and heavier than what is used in the Venetian territories; with this they strike so heavily as to unhorse the cavalry, and it is made short because they like close quarters'.[152] In 1521, when it was planned to supply six thousand archers as auxiliaries to the Emperor's army, the number of halberdiers dispatched to accompany them was limited only because they were to be protected by Imperial cavalry in action.[153]

Alongside the graceful longbow, the bill has often been dismissed as the workman-like, extemporised weapon of the unskilled levy man. One historian has commented on English muster lists: 'those not listed as archers were normally designated "billmen" – which was another way of saying that they had no military skill whatsoever'.[154] This view is perhaps symptomatic of the tendency to regard any facet of medieval warfare as primitive, unskilled and unsophisticated. In fact the specific association of the bill with untrained men dates from the seventeenth century, following the widespread adoption of the pike, and was not necessarily the case a hundred years earlier.[155] The bill was undoubtedly a simple weapon, but the intention clearly was that Englishmen armed with staff weapons, like the Swiss at Laupen, should stand their ground even before charging horse. To topple a charging lancer from his steed would require not only lightning reflexes and phenomenal personal courage, but considerable skill in handling the bill or halberd. In must, therefore, also have required training. Anyone who attempted to learn this trick on the battlefield would have had a very short life expectancy indeed. We should be wary of dismissing billmen as unskilled soldiers compared to the pikemen who came after, whose efficiency depended on their discipline and cohesion. Billmen, too, would have to have been skilled practitioners with their weapon. Their lives, and the lives of the archers they supported, depended upon it.

The pike offered a longer reach than the bill or halberd and, in the hands of well drilled troops, could make blocks of infantry virtually impenetrable. Consequently it was rapidly becoming the standard infantry mêlée weapon of Western Europe. Its effectiveness depended on its being well handled. Disordered pike, or pikemen, caught in the press of a mêlée in constricted positions were vulnerable to handier weapons, as the Spanish sword and buckler men had demonstrated at Ravenna. The English, armed with the bill and halberd, were content to hire *Landsknechte* initially, but the number of native English infantry

---

[152] Dillon, 'Arms and Armour at Westminster, the Tower, and Greenwich, 1547', p. 235.
[153] *Cal. State Papers, Henry VIII*, vol. 1, part 1, xxii.
[154] Goring, 'Social Change and Military Decline', p. 193.
[155] Manchester Central Reference Library L1/40/1/2, Certificate of Muster for the County of Lancashire, 1639. None of the men of these Lancastrian 'Trained Bands' carried bills at this muster, but 413 of the untrained men did, whilst 481 carried pikes.

using the weapon grew steadily over the first half of the sixteenth century. There was a recognition that skilful pikemen had the advantage over billmen on the battlefield. In 1522 the Earl of Surrey, watching the build up of the Duke of Albany's Scottish forces, begged Henry for four thousand *Landsknechte* to counter Albany's French pikemen. He added that the English would learn the use of the pike from the 'Almains'.[156] Whilst the proportion of billmen would remain high in early Tudor armies, the inventory of 1547 reveals that the pike had by then surpassed the older staff weapon in importance. In the Tower 6700 bills were stored alongside 306 halberds and 52 halberd heads. Of pikes, usually referred to by the English as 'Morris [Moorish] pikes', there were 20,100.[157]

The other weapons which appear to have been common equipment for English infantry are swords and javelins, often referred to as darts. Early in the century the immense two-handed 'slahge sword' was a favourite of the whiffler, who performed the function of an NCO, 'to keep the people in array'. By the middle of the century the whifflers, in tune with continental practice, seem to have abandoned the two-handed sword in favour of the one-handed sword and buckler combination.[158] Javelins, augmenting the missile strength of English armies, were a favourite weapon of Irish soldiers. One hundred barbed darts are mentioned as being stored at Calais, presumably for the use of Irish mercenaries in the 1544 campaign. The Irish javelin is recorded as being lighter than its English counterpart and could be cast 'with wonderful facility and nearness'. Whilst having virtually no armour-piercing qualities, they could injure, and possibly kill, horses and unarmoured men.[159] The English used the javelin too, particularly it would seem for combat at sea where, as ships closed, it would be a less cumbersome weapon for shipboard use than a longbow or a gun. Edward Hall described the preparations for naval combat in 1513: 'every man prepared accordyng to his duetie, the archers to shote, the gonners to lose, the Men of Arms to fight, the Pages went to the toppe castle with dartes'.[160] Once again, that most martial of kings, Henry VIII, was noted for his skill at casting javelins. As with his riding and his archery, the young Henry was more than a match for any of his courtiers.[161]

The inventory of 1547 tells us much about the defensive armour of the English soldier. Shields, usually referred to as targets or bucklers, remained in common use by both light cavalry and infantry. A shipborne landing party of 308 soldiers included 20 sword and buckler men in 1548, but some archers, and even those who carried pole arms, may also have carried shields.[162] Body armour was not restricted to the privileged few. Whilst complete sets of plate

---

[156] J.W.Fortescue, *A History of the British Army* (London, 1899), p. 118.

[157] Dillon, 'Arms and Armour at Westminster, the Tower, and Greenwich, 1547', p. 235.

[158] *Cal. State Papers Scot.*, vol. 1, 172.

[159] G.A.Hayes-McCoy, *Irish Battles* (Belfast, 1989), p. 52.

[160] Hall, *Henry the VIII*, vol. 1, p. 55.

[161] Dillon, 'Arms and Armour at Westminster, the Tower, and Greenwich, 1547', p. 239.

[162] *Cal. State Papers Scot.*, vol. 1, 172.

were beyond the means of the common soldiery, the Crown purchased large quantities of Almain rivet, mass produced issue armour for distribution to the troops. Almost all would have worn head defences, from simple steel skull caps to visored sallets and, by mid-century, the distinctive high crested morion. Pikemen and troops armed with pole arms would ideally have worn back and breast plates and possibly tassets, armour for the thighs. Brigandines and jacks, padded canvas garments stiffened with metal plates, were also frequently worn. Although traditionally the armour of the common man, they were light and allowed freedom of movement whilst remaining effective in turning aside blows. They were thus sufficiently useful that even members of the nobility might take the field in richly decorated, high quality brigandines.

Over their armour soldiers might wear surcoats. For English soldiers traditionally these were white, bearing the red cross of St George. To a certain extent the move towards a standard national uniform was retarded by the quasi-feudal character of English armies. At a mustering of 'the gendarmery' in Greenwich Park in May 1552 it was noted that the men had 'ther cottes in brodery of yche lords colers'.[163] However, the appearance of many other English troops was now so uniform that by mid-century the term white coat was synonymous with soldier, in much the same way that red coat would be in later centuries.[164]

Despite the slow progress towards standardisation of uniform, the extent to which the Crown was taking responsibility for the distribution of standard issue equipment is striking. In spite of the number of minor gentry unable to support large household retinues and the growing reluctance of yeomen to bear the expense of arming themselves, English armies were not taking the field unequipped. Whilst the mass produced Almain rivet may have been of a generally poor quality, it is likely that a higher proportion of English soldiers were wearing plate armour in the sixteenth century than in the fifteenth. To a large extent, where individual gentlemen and yeomen were unable to provide arms and harness fit for war, the Crown was now filling the gap. Henry built up a reserve of munitions that would allow him to equip a large army at short notice. On the basis of the inventories of Westminster, Greenwich and the Tower in 1547, it has been calculated that the Crown could arm 44,500 men.[165] Additionally, the government was ready to intervene in the market to ensure that individuals could afford to arm themselves as required by law. In 1542 the King was informed that:

> . . . diverse covetous persons having harness, artillery, and other habiliments
> for the war to sell, hold them at such unreasonable and excessive prices that
> his loving and obedient subjects cannot buy nor provide the same at reason-

---

[163] Goring, 'Military Obligations', p. 92. For the appearance of English soldiers in the early sixteenth century, see P.Cornish and A.McBride, *Henry VIII's Army* (London, 1987) and K.Durham and A.McBride, *The Border Reivers* (London, 1995).

[164] See, for example, Thomas Churchyard, 'The Siege of Leith', in *The Firste Parte of Churchyardes Chippes* (London, 1575), p. 19.

[165] Dillon, 'Arms and Armour at Westminster, the Tower, and Greenwich, 1547', p. 234.

able and convenient prices to serve . . . as by the laws, statutes, and customs
. . . they are bounden to do.

Consequently royal proclamation set the prices for arms and armour. Bows were
to be available in three classes, costing from 2s to 3s 6d. Fighting bills were
priced at 12d, halberds at 16d to 20d, Almain rivet 'of the best sort' at 7s 6d,
javelins at 10d to 14d, horseman's swords at 2s 8d. Full equipment for a demi-
lancer (light lance with defensive armour of 'curase, vambrace, polren, head-
piece with a beaver'), was to be available at 45s 'and not above'. Efforts were
being strenuously made to keep equipment within the purchasing power of
common soldiers who, paid but 6d a day, were vulnerable to any kind of inflation or profiteering.[166] Yet these efforts often seemed to have been circumvented
by crafty merchants. Five years after this proclamation was issued, the problem
was recurring. In May 1547, shortly after Henry's death, Bishop Tunstall wrote
to Protector Somerset that:

> . . . We doo fynde in our countre greate lack of bowes and arrowes, and
> specially of bowes, whereof there is almost none in the countree of ewe. The
> cause is . . . that a merchaunte of Danske hath of late tyme engrossed up and
> gotten in to his hands alone, the byinge of all bow staves in Eastland, which
> were wont to be brought hyther by diverse merchauntes, and then they were
> plentye and good cheap, and nowe one man havinge theim alone, enhaunceth
> the prices as he lyste.

At this time the problem was worsened by the King's bowyers, who also seemed
to have been controlling the supply of bow staves to ordinary bowyers, high
prices being ultimately passed on to the King's subjects, 'poore men [who]
cannot attain the price of them'. Tunstall begged Somerset to take action, for he
warned that otherwise his army 'shall lacke furnyture of archers'.[167]

The decline in the number of archers was, however, being offset by the rising
number of English troops armed with arquebuses and pikes. These weapons
were being integrated into the existing tactical system, which, in turn, was
adapted to meet their growing importance. A great deal of emphasis has been
placed on the decisive break with the past that took place in the final decade of
the century, with the official abandonment of the bow (although it was to make
the occasional reappearance as late as the 1640s). Yet long before this the traditional centrality of the bow to the English tactical system had been challenged.
If not actually marginalised, the bow was being assigned battlefield roles in the
1540s that demonstrated that it was now giving way to the firearm as the principal missile weapon of English troops.

As has been stressed, this was a gradual development which could only take
place as the number of skilled bowmen available to English armies declined, and
the arquebus itself was adopted in greater numbers. It is clear throughout the
Scottish campaign of 1547 to 1550 that infantry armed with firearms was in

---

166 Hughes and Larkin, *Tudor Royal Proclamations*, p. 213.
167 *Hamilton Papers*, vol. 2, 440.

most demand, and bows, although often in integrated units, were the weapons of skirmish and support troops. This was a role to which the weapon was well suited, and which it had fulfilled to some extent in the past. Even in major engagements such as Crécy archers, it has been suggested, 'stood some distance apart, like modern skirmishers'.[168]

Once bodies of pike and shot appeared in large numbers in English armies, bowmen could flank them as once they had flanked dismounted men-at-arms. Details have survived of an English landing party operating from the garrison at Broughty Craig, near Dundee, in February 1548. The 308-strong force was under the command of an Italian mercenary captain called Tiberio and was a composite force of English and mercenary soldiers. Its equipment and organisation offers a few clues as to its formation and consequently to English infantry tactics of the mid-century.[169]

> For landing from the ships: –
> Skirmishers – 20 harquebusiers and 20 bowes
> For the Battle – 4 ranks of harquebusiers, 7 ranks of pikes, 4 ranks of bills
> For the wings of the battle – 40 archers, 20 sword and targets for wyfflers
> The whole number of Tiberio's company is 308

The bows are concentrated amongst the skirmishers who preceded the advance and on the wings of the battle. The battle itself is fifteen ranks deep, whilst each rank must have been about thirteen or fourteen men across. The formation, therefore, would appear essentially to be a column, suitable for moving along a track, preceded by a cloud of skirmishers armed with bows and arquebuses and flanked by wings of archers and sword and buckler men.

[168] Hereford B. George, 'The Archers at Crécy', *The English Historical Review*, vol. 10 (1895), p. 735. See also E.M.Lloyd, 'The "Herse" of Archers at Crécy', *EHR*, *ibid.*, pp. 538–541 and J.E.Morris, 'The Archers at Crécy', *EHR*, vol. 12 (1897), pp. 427–436.
[169] *Cal. State Papers Scot.*, vol. 1, 172.

```
A  H  A  H  A  H  A  H  A  H  A  H  A  H  A  H
   A  H  A  H  A  H  A  H  A  H  A  H  A  H  A
          H  A  H  A  H  A  H  A  H
```
(Skirmish Line)

```
A A A A A A A A A    HHHHHHHHHHHHHHH    A A A A A A A A A A
S S S S S S S S S    HHHHHHHHHHHHHHH    S S S S S S S S S
     (Wing)          HHHHHHHHHHHHHHH          (Wing)
                     HHHHHHHHHHHHHHH
                     PPPPPPPPPPPPPP
                     PPPPPPPPPPPPPP
                     PPPPPPPPPPPPPP
                     PPPPPPPPPPPPPP
                     PPPPPPPPPPPPPP
                     PPPPPPPPPPPPPP
                     PPPPPPPPPPPPPP
                      BBBBBBBBBBBB
                      BBBBBBBBBBBB
                      BBBBBBBBBBBB
                      BBBBBBBBBBBB
                        (Battle)
```

A: Archer
H: Harquebusier
S: Sword and buckler
P: Pike
B: Bill

Figure 1. English infantry formation, 1547

The battle here is clearly a pike and shot formation on the modern model. The bows continue to play an important role, though, providing flanking support for the battle and rapid fire from the skirmish line. Evidence would suggest that the bow was an effective weapon in the hands of skirmishers, not just because of its rapid rate of fire but because bowmen were highly mobile and could close, or withdraw if necessary, at speed. Additionally, they could defend themselves in mêlée, for they carried secondary arms that would allow them to come to hand-strokes if occasion demanded. This is a small and flexible unit, a far cry from the image of cumbersome battles usually associated with early Tudor English armies.

To an extent its size is dictated by its function. It was being landed from ships to pillage and burn, not fight major battles. However, the ability to operate effectively in small and flexible formations is a hallmark of well trained and disciplined infantry. The army led by the Earl of Shrewsbury into Scotland in August 1548 was composed of the traditional three battles, vanguard, main battle and rearward. Yet each battle was sub-divided into 100-strong companies, with some larger bands, under prominent nobles or captains, of 200 to 359 men.[170] The Venetian Daniel Barbaro reported in 1551 that English infantry was 'divided into companies of 100 men, who have their captain, lieutenant, ensign and sergeant. The cavalry is also divided into squadrons of 100, and officered in like manner. The cavalry use trumpets, the infantry use drums.'[171] That such companies and bands were capable of independent tactical action was amply demonstrated during the war of 1547 to 1550. A band of arquebusiers were the first English foot into action at Pinkie, advancing ahead of the vanguard to occupy a defensive position in the path of the Scottish advance. During the latter stages of the war much of the fighting was conducted by small units, in siege or raiding operations, of which Tiberio's company of 1548 is typical.

The high proportion of sword- and buckler-armed whifflers may well have had a significant bearing on its proficiency in small-unit tactics. During the 1513 invasion of France the Earl of Shrewsbury's vanguard of about twelve thousand men had included three whifflers, 'to keep the people in array'.[172] Tiberio's company of just 308 included twenty whifflers, suggesting an enhanced role, perhaps including exercising authority on the battlefield itself. The emergence of a kind of proto-NCO with authority in combat would explain the viability of small-unit tactics in early modern armies. It is worth noting, however, that such a development was not entirely without precedent. Since the reign of Edward I soldiers had been grouped into twenties under the authority of a double-pay vintener. The rank of vintener had survived into the sixteenth century. It appears, for example, on the muster roll of the garrison of Calais in 1533. The Captain's Handbook of Henry Barrett, written in 1562, advised that good captains 'chewse of his owne company, unto every hundreth, fyve honest and circumspect soldiers, placinge them in the office of vintaynes, that every of them have the leading of XX men, of whose weapons they have the best skill'.

The vintener of Barrett's day played a key part in training and supervising his allotted twenty men. He notes 'they shall ofte assemble their noumbers to see their furniture of armure and weaponns or any other things to them necessarie, practisinge them in the necessitie of the same'. The precise role of the vintener on the battlefield itself is not at all clear. The sixteenth-century whiffler, with his distinctive armament and allotted place in the tactical scheme of infantry formations, seems to have a far more clearly defined function in combat.[173]

The survival of the vintener, alongside the new rank of whiffler, in units utilising the modern pike- and shot-based tactics, indicates how English armies, like their continental counterparts, adapted existing practices as need dictated from the fifteenth to the sixteenth century. This pattern held true for mounted

---

[170] *Cal. State Papers Scot.*, vol. 1, 318.
[171] Dillon, 'The English Soldier of the Sixteenth Century', pp. 198–200.
[172] Cruickshank, *Henry VIII and the Invasion of France*, p. 30.
[173] John Gough Nichols (ed.), *The Chronicles of Calais in the Reigns of Henry VII and Henry VIII* (London, 1846), pp. 136–137, Michael Prestwich, *Armies and Warfare in the Middle Ages: The English Experience* (London, 1996), pp. 127–128. Hale (ed.), 'On a Tudor Parade Ground', p. 275.

warfare too, with Tudor soldiers building on the foundations lain by Yorkist and Lancastrian cavalries. Anthony Goodman in particular has pointed to the evidence for a revival in the use of cavalry in the fifteenth century. At Towton in 1461 Jehan De Waurin states that Edward concentrated horsemen on one wing of his army. These were engaged and chased from the battlefield by the Lancastrian vanguard who, as Goodman points out, must also have been mounted.[174] Two other instances of the use of cavalry on the battlefield can be cited with confidence in the reliability of the sources. The anonymous author of the *Historie of the Arrivall of King Edward IV AD 1471* describes events with an old soldier's informed eye for detail. He recounts how at the Battle of Tewkesbury the Lancastrian vanguard under the Duke of Somerset was charged in flank by Yorkist cavalry laying in ambush in a wood. Consequently the Lancastrians were driven back, eventually breaking and fleeing the field.[175] The effectiveness of the charge does not suggest that English knights were, as is often suggested, 'conditioned to fight on foot'.[176]

This renaissance in English cavalry warfare was sustained during the reigns of both Henry VIII and Edward VI who, as has been noted, raised bodies of mounted men-at-arms as household troops and employed foreign men-at-arms when necessity required. These men were true *gendarmes*, wearing full plate armour and still retaining horse-bard. However, in line with continental developments, English demi-lancers, such as the Bulleners, were adopting three-quarters armour, favouring stout thigh-length boots over leg armour. The provision of a sufficient number of effective cavalry, above and beyond those raised by the Crown, was a major priority. The burden naturally fell on the nobility. The passing of the War Horses Act of 1542 was indicative of this concern, obliging the wealthy not just to provide horses but also men able to serve as demi-lancers.[177] For the invasion of Scotland in 1547 the English amassed no less than four thousand men-at-arms and demi-lancers, in a force that numbered just over eighteen thousand in total.[178]

The reappearance of the mounted man-at-arms on English battlefields was accompanied by the growth of an independent light cavalry arm, again reflecting continental developments. *The Arrivall* details the use by Edward of prickers (also termed scourers and coureurs) to gather intelligence, to carry out feints and skirmish with their Lancastrian counterparts. Polydore Vergil, in his account of the Battle of Barnet in 1471, claims that light cavalry acted in support of Warwick's hard pressed infantry on the battlefield itself.[179] Once

---

174 W.Hardy and E.Hardy (eds), *Recueil des Croniques et Anchiennes Istories de la Grand Bretagne, à présent nommé Engleterre* (London, 1872), pp. 337–338.

175 J.Bruce (ed.), *Historie of the Arrivall of King Edward IV, AD 1471* (London, 1838), pp. 29–30.

176 Millar, *Tudor Mercenaries and Auxiliaries, 1485–1547*, p. 23.

177 Goring, 'Military Obligations', pp. 39–41.

178 Patten, *Expedition into Scotland 1547*, pp. 77–78.

179 Bruce (ed.), pp. 7–8, 18, 28, Henry Ellis (ed.), *Polydore Vergil's English History* (London, 1844), pp. 145–146.

again, the developments of the fifteenth century were sustained, and indeed amplified, in the sixteenth century.

In England the Northern or Border horse, recruited from amongst the cattle thieving reivers of the volatile Border country, mirrored the genitor and stradiot in tactics and equipment. They formed an important and successful component of English armies of the sixteenth century. Their exploits in the French campaign of 1513 were celebrated by the chronicler Edward Hall: 'diverse tymes the Northern light horsemen under the conduite of Sir Jhon Nevell skirmished with the stradiottes [in French service] and take diverse of them prisoners and brought them to the Kyng'.[180] The sophistication of the tactical system inherited from the English light cavalry of the Wars of the Roses is indicated by another passage from Hall:

> The Kyng continually sent forth his light horses to seke the country and to see yf anye apparance wer, and they ever brought tidings of such things as they saw , so that always it was forsene that the Kyng nor his people should be taken unprepared, nor the Frenchmen shoulde not come on them sodainly . . .[181]

By the sixteenth century it is clear that English light cavalry were also operating on the battlefield itself. At Flodden, in 1513, the life of the young Lord Edmund Howard, whose slender vanguard had fled before the onset of the Scottish attack, was saved by a timely charge of Northern horse under Lord Dacre and John the Bastard of Heron.[182] The reivers both scouted and fought on horseback during the King's campaigns in France: 'the French diverse times issued out on horseback and many a staffe [lance] was broken and manye a proper feat of arms done'.[183] It would seem, however, that both they and their French counterparts habitually carried missile weapons and could fight dismounted. There was, of course, an English tradition of including mounted archers in their armies dating back to the fourteenth century, but these had been genuine mounted infantry, who always dismounted to fight. Sixteenth-century light cavalry seem altogether more versatile. Edward Hall described a typical action in France in September 1524:

> . . . fyfty lyght horsemen of Calice . . . rode toward Bullein, and passed the water of Margison and came to the water of Sclakes nere Bullein where sodainly thei encountered Lx Frenchmen, of the garrison of Bullein, there was shotyng with long bowes and crosebowes, on every side strong was the fyght, but at the last the Frenchmen fled, the Englyshemen followed, and toke thre

---

180 Hall, *Henry the VIII*, vol. 1, pp. 72–73.
181 Hall, vol. 1, p. 83.
182 *Cal. State Papers, Venice*, vol. 2, 134, Henry James (ed.), 'Account of the Battle of Flodden', in *Facsimiles of National Manuscripts from William the Conqueror to Queen Anne*, Part 2 (Southampton, 1865) p. 2.
183 Hall, vol. 1, p. 66.

lyght horsemen, and when they perceyved the Alarme on every side, they put them selfes in array, and with their botie came to Calice.[184]

Yet despite their undoubted skill as 'scourers', the Northern horse shared many of the characteristic flaws of irregular light cavalry. Tough fighters though they were, they had a villainous reputation in the eyes of many of their country-men – a reputation founded on the kidnapping, cattle raiding and 'hot trod' pur-suits of the Border bred men, whose priority in time of war was the acquisition of booty and prisoners for ransom. Their behaviour was much criticised during the Flodden campaign of 1513, when an absconding party of Northern horse-men helped themselves to new mounts as they fled through the English baggage train during the opening stages of the battle. The Cheshire poet, Leigh of Bag-gerley, recorded that many men who had fought for hours had then to 'wander home on foot', doubtless with abiding memories of the behaviour of their com-patriots from the Marches.[185]

It was not just that they lived by thieving but, as Borderers, their loyalties were held to be suspect too. During the English campaign in Scotland in 1547 Protector Somerset's personal secretary, William Patten, wrote of the Northern horse:

> . . . some of their crosses [the identifying red cross of St George worn by English troops] were so narrow, and so singly set on, that a puff of wind might have blown them from their breasts; and that they were found, right often, talking with the Scottish prickers within less than their [spears] length asunder; and when they perceived they had been spied, they have begun to run at one another . . . they strike few strokes but by assent and appointment.[186]

There can be no doubt that the Borderers fought hard and well on many occa-sions and the accusations levelled against them seem often a reflection of a long standing southern prejudice against Northerners in general and Borderers in particular. Yet their constant quest for ransom and booty can only have added weight to their evil reputation. 'If their faults had been fewer, their infamy had been less', wrote Patten.[187] In the final analysis though, whatever the problems that such irregulars brought to English armies, they did at least provide a fight-ing arm that was the equal of any comparable force on the battlefields of conti-nental Europe. Those serving as auxiliaries with Imperial forces at Landrecy in 1543 won the admiration of the Emperor Charles V himself, as their proud captain, John Wallop, reported to the King.[188]

---

[184] Hall, vol. 2, p. 16.
[185] Leigh of Baggerley, 'Scotish Feilde', in Ian Baird (ed.), *Scotish Feilde and Flodden Feilde: Two Flodden Poems* (London, 1982), lines 415–417.
[186] Patten, *The Expedition into Scotland 1547*, p. 135.
[187] Patten, p. 135.
[188] *Cal. State Papers, Henry VIII*, vol. 9, part 5 (London, 1849) dcccxix.

Military theory: literature and practice

The pattern of continuity and adaptation in military practice from the fifteenth to the sixteenth century is also reflected in the development of a canon of published military theory and literature in England. The use by English troops of regular order, drill and response to words of command, all controlled by a hierarchy of military authority, has been associated with the spread of military literature of the Elizabethan period.[189] Yet just as there was already a hierarchy of authority on the battlefield, so there was already an established tradition of military literature in English, outlining developments in the art of war.

Shortly before Henry VIII's death Thomas Audley produced his *A Book of orders for the warre both by land and sea*. In about 1550 an undated version called *A Treatise on the Art Of Warre* was published. Audley's work, like the slightly later Captain's Handbook written by Henry Barrett, clearly drew on a common cluster of manuscript sources, now lost.[190] Although unrelated to Audley or Barrett, some earlier works can be more positively identified. Robert de Balsac's *La nef des batailles* was published in English in around 1525 and again in 1540.[191] Even in the fifteenth century, military manuals had been produced for an English audience. Most were based on classical works, particularly Vegetius's *De Re Militari*. The translators of these works adapted them, so that they were relevant to contemporary military practice. For example, the first English translation of Vegetius was commissioned by Thomas, Lord Berkeley, whilst he was besieging Owain Glyn Dŵr's forces in Aberystwyth Castle in 1408. His translator, with one eye on his patron's experience in Wales, introduced a section on the use of cannon into the text.[192] In 1489 William Caxton printed his translation of Christine de Pisan's *Fayttes of Armes*. Again, although the greater part of the book is compiled from the works of Vegetius, Frontius, Valerius Maximus and Honore Bonet, its authoress inserted numerous original passages to give the work a greater relevance to contemporary military practice.[193] Perhaps the most famous of these up-dated versions of Vegetius's original text is *Knyghthode and Bataile*, a paraphrase in verse of *De Re Militari*. This was written by a resident of Calais against the backdrop of England's expulsion from Normandy.[194] Perhaps this indicates that military failure in France stimulated English thought on warfare, rather than retarding it. As a corollary to this established literary tradition, there is also evidence for the systematic training of military professionals, particularly in the science of artillery,

---

189 David Eltis, *The Military Revolution in Sixteenth-Century Europe* (London, 1995), pp. 43–74.

190 Hale, *Renaissance War Studies*, p. 264.

191 John Bury, 'Early Writings on Fortifications and Siegecraft: 1502–1554', *Fort*, vol. 13 (1985), pp. 7–8.

192 Diane Bornstein, 'Military Manuals in Fifteenth-Century England', *Mediaeval Studies*, vol. 37 (1975), p. 470.

193 A.T.P.Byles (ed.), *The Book of Fayttes of Armes and of Chyvalrye* (London, 1934), xi.

194 Z.M.Arend and R.Dyboski (eds), *Knyghthode and Bataile* (London, 1935), xvi–xxiv.

before the Elizabethan period. The Servitor Gunners studying in the Office of Ordnance established in 1537 undertook a standard programme of instruction, and examples of the manuscripts they produced as part of their training have survived.[195]

Artillery fortifications in the British Isles

Of particular significance to both military theorists and practitioners was the importance of siegecraft and fortification. The gradual emergence of the *trace italienne* on the continent would be reflected in the British Isles but, once again, the response in England and Scotland was governed by the peculiar circumstances of insular warfare.

This is perhaps most clearly illustrated in the case of Henry VIII's coastal fortifications. This was not the first scheme to provide England with places of strength built, or modified, to take ordnance. Raiding from the sea had been common during phases of the Hundred Years War when English fortunes had been at a low ebb.[196] The threat to England's security, particularly during the reign of Richard II, saw the addition of gunports to both castles and city walls. At 1380 a particularly impressive gate was added to Canterbury's west wall. This was built specifically for gunpowder artillery defence and contained eighteen gunports to cover all approaches. In the majority of cases, gunports merely replaced arrowslits, and the architectural design remained essentially medieval, little changed since the thirteenth century.

Yet improvement could bring some dramatic additions to older castles, many of which were up-dated throughout the fourteenth, fifteenth and sixteenth centuries. In 1509 a new wall, well provided with casements for cannon, was added to the Bishop of Durham's castle at Norham in Northumberland, in the path of Scotland's chief invasion route into England. Following the castle's destruction in 1513 it was rebuilt essentially as a gunpowder fortification, with new gun embrasures and low angular towers in the curtain wall, and a solid internal bastion protecting the inner ward.[197]

Berwick-upon-Tweed, England's most important garrison town alongside Calais, also received much attention from military engineers. In 1522 Richard Candishe, Berwick's Master of Ordnance, added both earthen 'bulwarks' and new masonry towers to the town's defences. Existing towers were adapted for artillery. Their overall height was lowered, and their ground floor vaults converted into casements for cannon. Further work was undertaken between 1532 and 1535, when it was noted that many of the earlier defences were falling into

---

[195] Caruana, *Tudor Artillery*, pp. 4–5.
[196] Ian Friel, 'Winds of Change? Ships and the Hundred Years War', in A.Curry and M.Hughes (eds), *Arms, Armour and Fortifications in the Hundred Years War* (Woodbridge, 1994), pp. 183–193.
[197] Andrew Saunders, *Norham Castle* (London, 1998), pp. 24–26.

decay. The upper levels of some towers were filled with earth to better absorb
the shock of bombardment. Their parapets and roofs were adapted as gun platforms. On the whole, Berwick seems to have been extensively up-graded by the
adaptation of its medieval defences and the addition of new bulwarks constructed of earth.

England's other premier garrison, Calais, went through a similar process. The
main castle in Calais itself and the strongholds in the Pale, at Guines and
Hammes, were periodically strengthened to take into account the threat from
artillery, and to give them an artillery capability of their own. A string of
detached bulwarks was constructed around the frontier of the Pale. Elaborate
plans were laid to modernise these fortifications throughout the first half of the
century, but royal parsimony saw them shelved time and again. Calais had to be
content with piecemeal improvements to an essentially medieval defensive
system. Yet these improvements could not transform the high, thin walls of pre-
gunpowder-era castles into modern fortifications. Older strongholds remained
highly vulnerable to an efficiently handled siege train. Nowhere was this demonstrated more clearly than at Calais, which fell to the French after a short siege
in 1558.[198]

There were, however, portents of Henry's more sophisticated scheme. At
Portchester Castle on the Solent a new tower completed in 1385 was an early
attempt to provide all-round command of the approaches for gunfire. In
1420–22 Portsmouth harbour was provided with a solid masonry blockhouse,
'the round tower', whose function was to be mirrored by Henry VIII's later
works.[199] Henry's scheme was to be altogether more comprehensive.

The danger of invasion emerged strongly in 1538, when the Emperor Charles
V concluded peace with France. The King's 1533 divorce from Catherine of
Aragon and the subsequent rift with Rome made the militantly Catholic Charles
a potentially very dangerous enemy. Henry's response was a comprehensive
scheme of coastal defence, its founding document *The Device of the King* drawn
up in February 1539.[200] Agents of the Crown searched out suitable sites for fortification throughout the shires of England and South Wales. Building began
with forts to protect the Thames at Dartford and Woolwich, at Gravesend,
Milton and Tilbury. The Kent Downs were to be defended with works at
Sandown, Deal and Walmer. Elsewhere construction began at Camber, guarding
the entrance to Southampton. These schemes were the most visible manifesta-
tions of what was clearly regarded as something of a military emergency. An

---

[198] For the fortifications at Berwick, see Marcus Merriman and John Summerson, 'The Scottish Border' in H.M.Colvin (ed.), *The History of the King's Works*, vol. 4, part 2 (London,
1982), pp. 607–663. For the Calais Pale see H.M.Colvin, 'The King's Works in France', in
H.M.Colvin (ed.), *The History of the King's Works*, vol. 3, part 1 (London, 1973), pp.
337–394.

[199] On these early gunpowder fortifications, see J.R.Kenyon, 'Coastal Artillery in England in
the Late Fourteenth and Early Fifteenth Centuries', in Curry and Hughes (eds), pp. 146–149.

[200] For a full account, see J.R.Hale, 'The Defence of the Realm, 1485–1558', in H.M.Colvin
(ed.), *The History of the King's Works*, vol. 4, pp. 367–401.

early warning system of beacons around the coast was fuelled and manned. Ramparts and bulwarks of turf and earth were thrown up at Portsmouth, Hurst Beach, East and West Cowes and at Harwich. Women and children worked alongside men in the trenches, giving an indication of the sense of urgency that gripped the nation. Eventually a series of fortifications was established from Hull round the coast of southern Britain to Milford Haven.[201]

It was not just the scale of Henry's fortifications that was novel, but their design. The form of the self-standing fortresses of 1539 was most heavily influenced by a north European tradition of cylindrical artillery towers and semi-circular bastions rather than by the angled bastions and stress on flanking cover of the *trace italienne*. Amongst the most explicit statements of this tradition are the ideas of the German architect, Albrecht Dürer (1471–1528). In his *Etliche Underricht zur Befestigung der Stett Schloss und Flecken* (Nuremburg, 1527), Dürer advocated fortifications dominated by massive, squat semi-circular towers. These would have immensely thick walls bristling with gunports and artillery.[202]

Henry himself took an avid interest in military architecture and these designs reflected his own early preferences. He imported foreign talent to provide specialist knowledge. A Bohemian architect, Stefan Von Haschenperg, was associated particularly with Sandgate Castle and the citadel at Carlisle, but the most elaborate expression of this Germanic style was found at Deal and St Mawes.[203] The common features in their design are the circular plan, with from between three and six protruding semi-circular bastions, around a low central tower. Many of the forts were defended by a moat, covered at ground level by gunports for arquebuses. Indeed every floor of the forts carried a tier of guns. The designs were advanced in many respects. Embrasures for guns were adequately splayed and gun chambers were vented to clear them of smoke.[204] However, the extent to which these developments were the result of the presence of Von Haschenperg and the influence of Dürer should not be exaggerated. The most profound influence on the design of the forts seems to have been the King himself, and these works are, quite rightly, styled Henrician.

These Henrician forts have been much criticised for failing to incorporate the more advanced features of the *trace Italienne*.[205] Certainly the circular bastions of Henry's forts contained inherent vulnerabilities. Their thick walls were structurally weakened by the number of apertures for artillery that they contained. The arrangement of cannon on successive tiers meant that as an assault moved

---

201 Hale, 'The Defence of the Realm, 1485–1558', p. 370.
202 Christopher Duffy, *Siege Warfare: The Fortress in the Early Modern World 1494–1660* (London, 1979), p. 4.
203 B.H. St J. O'Neil, 'Stefan Von Haschenperg: An Engineer to King Henry VIII and his Work', *Archaeologia*, vol. 91 (1945), pp. 137–155.
204 For the fullest description of the architectural features of Henry's forts, see Martin Biddle, H.M.Colvin and John Summerson, 'The Defences in Detail', in Colvin (ed.), *The King's Works*, vol. 4, pp. 415–606.
205 Geoffrey Parker, *The Military Revolution* (Cambridge, 1992), pp. 26–28.

towards the fort successive layers of guns would become masked. The circular surface of the bastions left dead ground, where no flanking fire could be brought to bear. In this ground *camisados* could approach the walls, or miners could work unhindered by the defenders' guns. The profile of the forts was lower than that of a medieval castle but high enough to present guns with an easy target. Walls were thick, but roofs and floors were thin so that plunging artillery fire could have taken its toll.

In short, it could be argued, the forts retained too many essentially medieval characteristics. They were too tall, hollow, and rounded to be effective artillery fortifications. To an extent this argument neglects the precise purpose of these forts. These were coastal fortifications, housing a small permanent garrison. Their function was to protect anchorages or beat off raiders, not meet invasions. That remained the function of the levy, activated by the beacon and muster system. The little forts were unlikely to be the object of a formal siege. Their enemies were to be shipping, not sappers or a huge siege train. Nor was the circular design quite as anachronistic as it first appears. Circular bastions were still being built in Italy at this time at Assisi and Cortona for example.[206] The angled bastion of the *trace italienne* really only established itself in the 1530s. Even then the debate about the relative merits of angular and circular bastions lingered.

In the event, within a few years the English had been clearly convinced by the case for the *trace italienne*. Ultimately this was to have a considerable impact on the war in Scotland between 1547 and 1550. Crucial to the change in English attitudes was the experience gained on the continent in 1543 and 1544. These campaigns had seen English troops heavily involved in a series of operations based primarily around siege-works. The Catholic crusade against England led by Charles V had not materialised. Indeed, to pursue his long running quarrel with Francis I of France, Charles V had courted Henry VIII as an ally. Subsequently twelve thousand English auxiliaries had fought for him at the siege of Landrecy in the summer of 1543. The following March Henry had led a 40,000-strong invasion force against Boulogne and Montreuil. Boulogne had fallen after a hard fought siege on 14 September, but Montreuil had successfully defied the English. Henry was then thrown onto the defensive. Charles had concluded a separate peace with Francis, freeing France to concentrate on the English. Not only was recently captured Boulogne under threat but the possibility of raids on England itself re-emerged.

With the experience of recent months in trenches, breaches and siege-lines, the manner in which the English now approached the task of fortification, both in France and on the English coast, was largely a break from the past. The permanent fortifications now built on the English coast to some extent reflected Italian practice. Sandown on the Isle of Wight had a combination of styles, comprising one square, one round and one angled bastion. Southsea Castle owed

---

[206] Hale, 'The Defence of the Realm, 1485–1558', pp. 381–382.

more to the Italian style, protected by two triangular bastions. Early design flaws at Southsea, where the bastions initially lacked flanking batteries, were corrected by the intervention of the King himself. This demonstrates the extent to which Henry himself was keeping pace with the science of fortification.

Yet in other respects the coastal forts remained conservative in design. They represented a considerable financial investment and therefore perhaps Henry was not prepared to take too many risks in their construction. At Boulogne the experiment was being conducted in earth. This presented a major advantage over the stone built fortification. It required considerable manpower for the construction teams, but these could be composed of unskilled labour, particularly soldiers. Grumble as these reluctant labourers might, they were cheaper than masons. If necessary, ramparts and bulwarks could be faced in stone later, for it was not unknown for earthworks to be washed away by heavy rain. Overall the form these earthworks took was altogether more innovative than Henry's coastal forts. Around Boulogne both the English and the French burrowed feverishly, fighting, in essence, a war of emplacement.

The works they threw up were clearly on the Italian model. Angled bastions, flanking batteries, fosse brays and bulwarks characterised some formidable works built on the most modern of principles. Around the Tour d'Ordre, an old Roman lighthouse known to the English as 'the Old Man', a polygonal fort defended by a ditch and Italianate bastions dominated the estuary of the River Liane. This was connected to Boulogne by a long trench, guarded by a smaller fort built of brick and dubbed 'the Young Man'. When the trench reached Basse Boulogne it ran to the walls of a citadel, a strong point completed in 1547. The existing enceinte walls of Boulogne were strengthened by the addition of new bastions and fosse brays.

On the opposite bank of the Liane estuary the French were busy constructing forts of their own, the Fort d'Outreau and the mighty Fort de Châtillon. The English building programme escalated to meet this threat. Outlying forts were built on Boulemberg, a hill overlooking the town. Additionally, two important works were built to the north of Boulogne, at Ambleteuse and Blackness. These works were built during an on-going conflict. The French and English still clashed with sword as well as spade until the Treaty of Camp, June 1546, officially ended hostilities. By the terms of this treaty Boulogne was to be returned to France in 1554 on the payment of 2,000,000 crowns. The terms also stipulated that no new fortifications were to be built. This stipulation was ignored by both sides, a fact which caused open hostilities to flare up during the remaining years of English occupation. French construction north of Le Portel provoked an English raid under Sir Thomas Palmer in September 1546. Two years later a French assault disrupted work on a new mole, clearly intended to mount guns, which the English were building in Boulogne harbour.[207]

---

[207] For a complete account of English fortifications around Boulogne, see H.M.Colvin, 'The King's Works in France', in Colvin (ed.), *The King's Works*, vol. 3, pp. 383–393.

This frantic activity around Boulogne from 1544 until 1550 is worthy of note. Here the English received a fast, and occasionally brutal, lesson in field fortification and siege warfare. The conversion to the Italianate style was led, surprisingly, by English architects, most notably the master masons John Rogers and Richard Lee. They were responsible for much of the works at Boulogne. The English certainly employed Italian mercenaries, chiefly as soldiers, occasionally as military engineers, but Rogers, Lee and indeed the King himself, took the initiative in the design and implementation of the new forts. In fact Rogers proved himself not just a skilled engineer but an excellent surveyor or 'platmaker'.[208]

The lessons learned at Boulogne were carried back to Britain by veterans of the fighting around the Liane estuary. Prominent amongst these was Sir Edward Seymour, Earl of Hertford, who had commanded at Boulogne in 1546. In 1547 Seymour, by then created Duke of Somerset, would lead an army into Scotland with the express purpose of establishing garrisons, protected by modern fortifications, to hold what he had conquered. The lessons of Boulogne were to be applied north of the Tweed.

In Scotland, the use of artillery over the preceding century had had little effect on defensive fortifications. The most common characteristic associated with the use of gunpowder weapons was the provision of gun loops in the walls of otherwise traditional structures. Ravenscraig Castle, completed in the period 1460–1463, was liberally provided with gun loops as well as some exceptionally thick walls, up to 4.4 metres, a clear response to the threat of bombardment.[209]

Elsewhere walls remained thin and high, only occasionally demonstrating an awareness of the state of the art on the continent. Threave Castle, which had done so well against James II's artillery train, included a gun-looped curtain wall and circular artillery towers, which were probably in place by 1450.[210] Drum towers, existing within that north European tradition that gave rise to some English artillery fortifications, were also constructed. Work began in 1513 on a blockhouse to protect Aberdeen harbour. This blockhouse was maintained throughout the sixteenth century. In common with many early modern fortifications, it was strengthened by the addition of an earthen rampart.

A blockhouse was also constructed at Dunbar Castle, at the command of the Duke of Albany around 1520. This work boasted a sophisticated design, incorporating features particularly associated with French fortification, especially the wide-mouthed gun loops which were subsequently copied extensively in Scotland. In places the masonry rampart of the blockhouse was up to 6.5 metres thick, making Dunbar a tough proposition for any would-be besieger. In 1523,

[208] For the career of John Rogers, see L.R.Shelby, *John Rogers, Tudor Military Engineer* (Oxford, 1967).

[209] Iain MacIvor, 'Artillery and Major Places of Strength in the Lothians and the East Border, 1513–1542', in Caldwell (ed.), *Scottish Weapons and Fortifications 1100–1800*, p. 101.

[210] See Christopher J. Tabraham and George L. Good, 'The Artillery Fortification at Threave Castle, Galloway', in Caldwell (ed.), pp. 55–72.

Cardinal Wolsey received this report on Dunbar Castle from Lord Dacre, the Warden of the English Marches:

> And finally touching the state and strenth of the castell of Dunbar whereof your grace is desirous to be advised, I assure your grace it is a thing in maner unprenable for I have bene in it. It standith upon a crag and there is no waye to go to it but one which is strongly and substantially made with a new bulwark and sett with ordinance as can be devised by the Duke of Albany for in the said castell is all the said Dukes trust. And if the said Bulwerk could be won I think there is no doubt but the castell might be won semblably be reason that the said castell stands low upon a crag and the erth without it is hygh about it, and so there could nothing stirr within it but the ordinance that were without the castell shulde bete it.[211]

In other words, the modern fortification was the key to the whole castle. Those lords who were able would follow Albany's example at Dunbar.

The influence of the Dunbar blockhouse could soon be seen at St Andrews. Here, sometime between 1523 and 1537, Archbishop James Beaton enhanced the castle with two massive round towers, furnished with gun loops constructed in the distinctive French style. His nephew, Cardinal David Beaton, added a sturdy 1.7 metre thick curtain wall, giving St Andrews a, perhaps deceptively, formidable appearance. Tantallon Castle went through a similar process of improvement after coming under royal authority in 1528, having already proved itself a formidable bastion. Here existing fourteenth-century towers were extensively remodelled to cope with a potential bombardment. Towers were given flat roofs and pierced with gun loops for the siting of the defenders' artillery.[212]

At Craignethan Castle, in Lanarkshire, Sir James Hamilton introduced the caponier (a covered passage built across a defensive ditch and pierced with gun loops) to the British Isles in the 1530s. Earthworks, too, became a cost effective way of upgrading ageing strong points. One of the most successful examples was at Cessford Castle near the Border. Seat of Sir Andrew Kerr, Warden of the Scottish East March, Cessford defied a small English army under the Earl of Surrey in 1523. Surrey brought with him eleven heavy guns and numerous lesser pieces that had battered down a number of smaller towers on the path to Kerr's castle. Yet at Cessford he found that the castle's outer 'barmkin' wall had been strengthened with a rampire, a sloping earthwork raised against the wall, to absorb the impact of shot. To complete this rampart, the rear of the wall had an earthen countermure, giving even greater resilience to cannon fire. Beyond this rampart, the tower's own stone walls proved thick enough to resist shot. Bombardment and repeated assaults failed to dislodge a resolute garrison. Two of the English culverines managed to blast open a blocked up window, but the storming parties were beaten back by gunfire from within the tower. Those who managed to position their scaling ladders by the castle walls were repulsed by

211 MacIvor, pp. 94–118.
212 David Caldwell, 'A Sixteenth-Century Group of Gun Towers in Scotland', *Fort*, vol. 12 (1984), pp. 15–24.

the old fashioned, yet effective, measure of large stones cast down from the roof. Surrey, compelled ultimately to negotiate for the castle, reported afterwards that he doubted that it could be taken by force.[213]

Provision for cannon can also be found at the Hermitage, 'the chief strength of Liddesdale'. This squat, brooding fortress, of evil legend, was a vital stronghold of the Scottish Middle March. In 1540, with the Marches perched on the edge of the abyss of war, the Hermitage's thick walls were augmented with gun loops large enough to house carriage-mounted cannon. Probably contemporary with these was the earthwork gun-mount built to command the approach to the castle.[214]

Doubtless provisions for cannon were made on a smaller scale elsewhere, although they have often left little trace. In the Marches, particularly, the architectural characteristics of typical defensive towers were slow to develop to meet the challenge of gunpowder weapons. One might have assumed that these towers, being effectively in the front line of war with England, might have adapted more quickly. Yet the particular circumstances of Border warfare militated against this. With so many of the Marcher population living by brigandage, all but the poorest chose to dwell in some kind of fortified house, such as the solid-looking bastle houses. Normally these were built to take advantage of natural defensive features, morasses or defiles that might keep cannon at a safe distance anyway. In general though, against a background of constant alarms and sudden eruptions of violence, families of no great substance were not in a position to experiment with artillery or to radically restructure their homes. The thick walls of older structures had few windows near ground level that might be adapted as gun loops. Such openings would only have offered a route for fire brands and torches. Instead the wall bases were sometimes strengthened by the addition of a splayed plinth, seemingly designed to deflect cannon shot. Most towers would have been defended from the parapet of the roof, a precarious position for a gun. Where gun loops are found on surviving Border strongholds they are often badly positioned, with poor fields of fire, suggesting a lack of confidence in their utility.[215]

Logistics and their influence on strategy

Nevertheless the significance of fortifications in the Border country was particularly marked. In strategic terms the Scots and English had radically different attitudes towards permanent defensive works. In the late fourteenth and early fifteenth centuries the English had held much territory in the south of Scotland, their presence secured by their possession of the castles at Lochmaben and Roxburgh. The reduction of such garrisons was so problematic that it would have

---

[213] Alastair Maxwell-Irving, 'Early Firearms and their Influence', p. 198.
[214] Maxwell-Irving, p. 202.
[215] Maxwell-Irving, pp. 195–196, 218.

been better for Scotland had such fortifications not existed. As John Mair wrote in 1521, 'The Scots do not fortify their strongholds and cities by entrenchments, because, were these to be held at any time by the enemy, they would simply serve him as a shelter: and thus it would in no way profit the Scots, especially within the marches . . . to possess fortified cities or even strongholds.'[216]

Although this exaggerates the actual situation to an extent, the Scots did place less emphasis on the construction of fortifications than the English. They were also quick to demolish some castles which had been held by the English, such as Roxburgh in 1460. The English appreciated this same point. If a Scottish army refused battle and retreated leaving 'scorched earth' in its wake, there was little a commander invading Scotland could achieve. The seizure, garrisoning and maintenance of a castle offered a clear objective. The Scots could either tolerate its presence, or be forced to lay siege. Such a task was fraught with major operational difficulties.

The reduction or capture of any defended location required considerable expenditure of resources and thus frequently exposed the inadequacies of contemporary logistical arrangements. The tenuous sinews of supply did not just limit the length of a campaign, they often dictated the nature of the fighting. One reason why the destructive raid, the *chevauchée*, was favoured as an instrument of strategy by both England and Scotland was that it allowed a force to live off the enemy's land whilst destroying those resources that an opposing army required to operate. Simultaneously, the acquisition of booty and plunder would help motivate the common soldiery.[217]

Yet fortifications commanding fords or roads, or protecting habitations, posed raiders a serious challenge. They rarely had the time to starve garrisons into submission. Defended locations, therefore, had to be tackled fairly directly, by bombardment and assault, as with James IV's attacks on Norham in 1497 and 1513, or the Earl of Surrey at Cessford in 1523. If, as was often the case, a garrison was able to resist an assault for long enough then the attacking army would have to retire once it had exhausted its own supplies and consumed all those gathered locally by its foragers. Castles, tower houses, even abbeys and large churches, thus assumed a tremendous strategic importance in Border warfare. A small but determined garrison could utterly frustrate the purpose of a *chevauchée* merely by delaying progress for a matter of a few days. In these circumstances, supply became a crucial determinant of military effectiveness.

In practice, for England, war with Scotland posed the most serious of difficulties, for the Marches were scarcely able to support their own population, let alone an army of several thousand. Most of the grain to feed the troops was shipped north from East Anglia. Cheese (a staple of the soldiers' diet), came from Suffolk. Cattle was driven from the Midlands to the slaughter houses of Berwick. If winds were unfavourable or roads muddy then the poor soldiers went hungry. With no professional commissariat corps in existence responsibil-

216 Constable (ed.), *John Major's History of Greater Britain*, p. 30.
217 Nicholson, *Scotland: The Later Middle Ages*, pp. 48–49.

ity for raising supplies rested with individuals, usually members of the royal household, with experience of feeding large numbers. Their competence was by no means guaranteed.

Victuals were bought by commissioned 'purveyors'. The price they paid was fixed by royal proclamation in an effort to combat profiteering. Naturally this aroused the frequent fury of farmers who failed to receive even a fair price for the products of their labour. The grain, hops, oxen and assorted raw material necessary to feed an army were then conveyed to one of the major bases of operation. For the campaigns against Scotland this generally meant Berwick. Here bakers, brewers and butchers laboured to prepare victuals for the campaign. They would also accompany the army into the field. Travelling breweries, mills and bakeries would accompany the army on the march. The supplies would be actually distributed by the company victualler. They were paid for on credit, the money eventually deducted from the men's wages, or by the company captain, who would in turn recover the money from his men's pay. If the men's pay was not forthcoming then war could become a ruinously expensive business for captains. The whole system was ad hoc, vulnerable to incompetence, corruption or simply the enormous obstacles posed by the transportation of such a bulk of foodstuffs over land and sea.[218]

All too often Tudor armies were dependent on what they could carry, or forage from the land which they crossed. This was true of Scottish armies to an even greater extent. De Beaugué, one of the French officers who served in Scotland in the 1540s, recalled that:

> it was quite a new thing to the seven or eight hundred Scottish horsemen who accompanied us to see 'Vivandier' [victuallers] following the army. The Scots never would serve in a campaign more than forty days after leaving their homes, and the poorest among them always had with him a horse or strong servant to carry his baggage; by this means carrying enough food with him to last while he was in the field.[219]

De Beaugué's observations may well have been true for the fast moving Border horsemen who led the majority of Scottish incursions into England. There is some evidence, however, that larger Scottish forces had slightly more elaborate arrangements for the provisioning of troops in the field. When the English overran the Scottish encampment at Flodden they found large quantities of 'wyne, bere, aill, beiff, multon, salt fisshe, cheis and other vitailles necessarye and convenyent for such a great army'.[220] Thomas Ruthal, Bishop of Durham, informed Wolsey that:

[218] C.S.L.Davies, 'Provisions for Armies, 1509–50: A Study in the Effectiveness of Early Tudor Government', *The Economic History Review*, 2nd ser., vol. 17 (1964–65), pp. 234–248.
[219] J.B.Brown, 'The French Troops in the Borders in 1548', *Transactions of Hawick Archaeological Society* (1905), p. 39.
[220] David Laing (ed.), 'The Trewe Encountre or Batayle don betwene England and Scotlande', *Proceedings of the Society of Antiquaries of Scotland*, vol. 7 (1866–68), p. 151.

the Scottes lackyd no thyng necessary for the warrys but oonly the grace of God, for of elect men, harneys, ordinaunce and vitaylis thay had suche plentie that never the lyke hathe ben harde of in this parties, and I assure you alle England cowd not have vitaylid our host as thay wer vitaylid, every thing consideryd.[221]

These provisions were probably a combination of foodstuffs and livestock gathered in from English farms by James's foragers, and victuals transported with the army's baggage train from Scotland. The successful transportation of such bulky cargo by waggon was in itself no small achievement but this fact should not disguise the inherent fragility of both English and Scottish logistical arrangements. Supply would ultimately set limits to strategic possibilities and, consequently, to the potential for waging decisive military campaigns.

Medical services

The limitations imposed by supply were reinforced by high mortality rates due to sickness and injury. Disease claimed far more casualties than battle and struck armies with a depressing inevitability. A commander who deliberately avoided giving battle to a superior force could usually count on his opponent's army soon dwindling as sickness took its toll. Disease, like logistics, was thus a major factor in strategic calculations. It is therefore worth looking at the nascent medical services which accompanied English and Scottish armies into the field.

Traditionally men too sick or injured to fight had been discharged on the spot, ceasing to be of any concern to the army. During the Hundred Years War the wounded and ill had been evacuated as far as England, but once they had reached port the Crown's obligations were felt to be at an end, and the invalids were expected to make their own way home. Sadly, little had changed by the sixteenth century. In the winter of 1548–1549 Captain John Brende noted that many of the sick and injured evacuated from the garrison of Haddington were soon 'dying of want' in the streets of Berwick.[222] Not until the final years of Elizabeth I's reign would the government pay the travel expenses of discharged soldiers and make their home parishes responsible for the welfare of the injured.[223]

During the Henrician campaigns the government's major concern was that fit men should not be able to evade further service by feigning illness. In 1544 large

---

[221] 'Thomas Rythall, Bishop of Durham, To Almoner Wolsey, September 20, 1513', in Henry James (ed.), *Facsimiles of National Manuscripts from William the Conqueror to Queen Anne* (Southampton, 1865), p. 7.

[222] *Calendar of State Papers, Domestic, Elizabeth, 1601–1603, with Addenda, 1547–1565* (London, 1870), p. 394.

[223] An example of the Elizabethan legislation in action can be found in Manchester Central Reference Library, Manuscript M35/7/4, A Book of Rates for the Countie Palatine of Lancashire, which provides details of parish responsibilities for 'the reliefe of the maymed souldiers'.

numbers of healthy soldiers were being shipped home to England from France. Indeed the problem was so acute that Henry accused the English commander, the Duke of Norfolk, of facilitating the passage of malingerers in an attempt to undermine a campaign to which he was not genuinely committed. In response a committee was established to oversee the process of evacuation. From a bureaucratic point of view this was an innovative reform, although the four gentlemen who were duly appointed had no medical training and do not appear to have pursued their task with any vigour.[224]

In spite of this general lack of long-term provision for discharged invalids, injured and sick soldiers might receive some treatment from qualified medical practitioners whilst in the field. English and, in particular, Welsh troops had been accompanied in the field by *medici* since at least the thirteenth century.[225] By the sixteenth century expeditionary forces always included barber-surgeons who had served a seven- or nine-year apprenticeship followed by a qualifying examination. The Duke of Suffolk's expeditionary force of 1523 included a Master Surgeon, paid 2 shillings a day, and eight other surgeons, paid 10 pence. A Master Surgeon was also attached to the ordnance of Suffolk's army and he was assisted by two other surgeons.[226] In 1541 English surgeons were exempted from 'bearing arms or being put on watches', thus allowing them to concentrate on tending the injured.[227]

Unfortunately the small number of qualified surgeons serving in the field was usually augmented by assorted quacks and itinerant healers, particularly after the liberalisation of laws governing the practice of medicine in 1543. In 1544, during the campaign around Boulogne, the Duke of Norfolk became concerned at the high proportion of English soldiers who were dying of 'small wounds'. He requested that Thomas Gale, one of the qualified surgeons accompanying his force, investigate. The cause was soon found to be a 'great rabblement' of 'sowe gelders . . . horse gelders . . . tinkers and cobblers' who 'toke upon them to be Chirugions'. Indeed they took 'not onlie the name but the wages also'. They had been treating wounds with 'such trumpery as they did use to grease horses' heels, and laid upon scabbed horses' backs'. Others had concocted 'noble salves' from shoemaker's wax mixed with the rust scraped off old pans.[228] Eventually these 'Dogge Leeches', as Norfolk called them, were 'committed to the Marshalrie', threatened with execution, and driven from the

---

224 David Stewart, 'Disposal of the Sick and Wounded of the English Army during the Sixteenth Century', *Journal of the Royal Army Medical Corps* [*JRAMC*], vol. 15 (1948), pp. 31–32.
225 H.A.L.Howell, 'An Historical Retrospective of the Army Surgeon in Britain, prior to the Sixteenth Century', *JRAMC*, vol. 1 (1903), pp. 118–119.
226 David Stewart, 'The English Army Surgeon in the Sixteenth Century', *JRAMC*, vol. 88 (1947), p. 240.
227 H.A.L.Howell, 'The Army Surgeon and the Care of the Sick and Wounded in British Campaigns During the Tudor and Early Stuart Period', *JRAMC*, vol. 2 (1904), p. 607.
228 Howell, 'The Army Surgeon', pp. 607–608.

English camp.[229] Yet all too often the shortage of qualified barber-surgeons meant that armies in the field had to recruit fairly indiscriminately. Some individual bands were well provided for in terms of medical personnel. In 1550 a 341-strong company of Irish mercenaries passing through Chester had three surgeons attached to it.[230] Yet three years earlier in 1547 the whole of the Berwick garrison had but one surgeon, and there were severe doubts about his competence.[231]

So long as a barber-surgeon had been properly trained, an ill or wounded soldier could expect fairly sophisticated, and not ineffectual, treatment. On expeditions surgeons practised as 'physics' and apothecaries, treating sickness as well as performing operations. In this respect their science was not yet sufficiently advanced to combat serious disease, and plagues would sweep through camps and garrisons unchecked.[232] However, the barber-surgeons could cope well with injuries. They had a wealth of experience with various dressings for closing wounds. This was a vital skill because of the widespread use of edged-weapons in close combat. Richard Wisemen, a seventeenth-century military surgeon, observed that soldiers hurt by bills, halberds or swords in mêlée tended to have multiple injuries, the wounds being 'large, transverse, yea and oblique, at the same time'. In particular, infantrymen from formations broken by cavalry could be 'most cruelly mangled' around the head and arms.[233] With many sixteenth-century battles involving prolonged fighting at close quarters, the barber-surgeons would have had to deal with large numbers of such casualties as well as those affected by missile weapons.

Their tool kit included specialised instruments for the extraction of arrow-heads, crossbow bolts and arquebus balls, such as the Alphonsinum bullet extractor and the goose-billed bullet forceps, controlled by arrangements of transverse screws of sophisticated design. Indeed the whole development of surgical instruments had been stimulated to a great extent by the challenge posed by gunshot wounds.[234]

Such injuries posed particular problems. In the early sixteenth century, and probably in a break with earlier traditions, it had become the normal practice on the continent to cauterise gunshot wounds by pouring boiling oil onto them.

---

[229] Thomas Gale, *Certaine Workes of Galens, Called Methodus Medendi, with a briefe Declaration of the Worthie Art of Medicine, the Office of a Chirurgion, and an Epitome of the third booke of Galen, of Natural Faculties* (London, 1586), p. 27, James Watt, 'Surgeons of the *Mary Rose*: The Practice of Surgery in Tudor England', *Mariner's Mirror*, vol. 69 (1983), p. 5.

[230] Chester City Records Office, Mayors' Military Papers, 1/1–2.

[231] *Cal. State Papers Scot.*, vol. 1, 73.

[232] David Stewart, 'Sickness and Mortality Rates of the English Army in the Sixteenth Century', *JRAMC*, vol. 91 (1948), pp. 23–35 and 'The Causes of Disease in the Sixteenth-Century Army', *JRAMC*, vol. 92 (1949), pp. 35–41.

[233] John Comrie, *History of Scottish Medicine*, vol. 1 (London, 1932), p. 233.

[234] J.R.Kirkup, 'The History and Evolution of Surgical Instruments', *Annals of the Royal College of Surgeons of England*, vol. 63 (1981), p. 282. R.M.Downes, 'What Medicine Owes to War and War Owes to Medicine', *JRAMC*, vol. 67 (1936), p. 385.

This method had been advocated by the military surgeon Giovanni da Vigo and was popularised by his widely read texts, which were published in more than forty editions in Italian, French, Spanish, German and English. It was da Vigo's opinion that cauterisation was necessary to eliminate the residue of gunpowder in the wound, which he believed to be poisonous. This conclusion was eventually challenged by the French military surgeon Ambroise Paré, following his experiences at the siege of Turin in 1536, and the dangerous practice of cauterising victims of gunshot wounds thereafter fell into disfavour.[235]

It seems likely that English surgeons had practised cauterisation sparingly anyway. Heavily influenced by the Italian Bologna school, English surgeons favoured clean, non-traumatic surgery. Wounds would be thoroughly cleansed and irrigated with wine, which had antiseptic qualities. Missiles and splinters were carefully removed and wounds were closed by stitching and with balsam dressings. Techniques had long been developed to aid in the knitting of broken and fractured bones. Amputations of smashed, infected or diseased limbs could be carried out with a reasonable chance of the patient surviving. A soporific sponge, impregnated with opium, hyoscyamus, hemlock, mandragora, lettuce, mulberry and ivy would be held for inhalation until the patient became unconscious, a form of anaesthetic used in England since 1200.[236]

Scottish armies, too, benefited from the services of some skilled military surgeons. Medical affairs held a special fascination for James IV, and he himself undertook to perform surgical operations and tooth extractions, although not always with success. His treasurer's accounts record the payment of 14 shillings to a blind woman whose cataracts the King had failed to couch. James did prove a generous patron of professional surgeons and physicians, and they were the frequent recipients of royal grants. In 1505 the surgeons and barbers of Edinburgh, along with the various other guilds of the city, were incorporated under the 'Seal of Cause' from the town council. This act conferred useful privileges, such as the provision of corpses for dissection, on the city's medical practitioners. The members of the new college were required to be able 'to read and write, to know anatomie, nature and complexion of every bodie of the human bodie, and lykwys to know all the vayns of the samyn that he may make flewbothomie in due time, together with a perfect knowledge of shaving beards'.[237]

Their activities included undertaking military service when required. Later in the century, in 1567, Mary Queen of Scots was to emulate the English and specifically exempt surgeons from bearing arms, but up until that point Scottish

---

[235] Kelly DeVries, 'Military Surgical Practice and the Advent of Gunpowder Weaponry', *Canadian Bulletin of Medical History*, vol. 7 (1990), pp. 131–146. Owen Wangensteen, Sarah Wangensteen and Charles Klinger, 'Wound Management of Ambroise Paré and Dominique Larrey, Great French Military Surgeons of the 16th and 19th Centuries', *Bulletin of the History of Medicine*, vol. 46 (1972), pp. 207–218.

[236] Watt, 'Surgeons of the *Mary Rose*', pp. 9–10. Henry Webb, 'English Military Surgery during the Age of Elizabeth', *Bulletin of the History of Medicine*, vol. 15 (1944), pp. 261–275.

[237] Howell, 'The Army Surgeon', p. 607.

military surgeons presumably combined their medical role with that of combatant. Certainly the apprentices of the guild were well represented amongst the forces raised by Edinburgh for the defence of the city during the first half of the century. In Scotland, therefore, developments in surgical practice had a peculiarly close relationship with military conflict. Indeed an articulated prosthesis dating from the sixteenth century, the 'Iron Hand of Clephane', would appear to be the work of an armourer, made for a laird of Carslogie who had lost his own hand in battle.[238]

Notwithstanding the individual skill of the trained barber-surgeon, the provision of systematic medical care to soldiers in both English and Scottish armies, particularly ordinary soldiers, remained rudimentary in the extreme. It is unlikely that there were ever sufficient trained surgeons present to cope with the aftermath of a major engagement, and the efforts of those who were available were probably concentrated on injured officers and nobles. For the common soldier, if he received treatment at all, it would most probably be at the hands of an apprentice barber-surgeon taking the opportunity to learn his trade, or an impressed common, and untrained, 'healer'.[239]

[238] Comrie, *History of Scottish Medicine*, vol. 1, pp. 143–191.
[239] See also Richard Gabriel and Karen Metz, *A History of Military Medicine*, vol. 2 (New York, 1992), pp. 45–72. Richard D. Forrest, 'Development of Wound Therapy from the Dark Ages to the Present', *Journal of the Royal Society of Medicine*, vol. 75 (1982), pp. 268–273.

CHAPTER THREE

THE WARS OF JAMES IV, 1496–1513

Anglo-Scots conflict and the Border Marches

EVER SINCE the onset of war in 1296 Anglo-Scottish relations had been characterised by near permanent hostility. Open conflict alternated with uneasy peace, with the border country becoming a scene of constant tension, and a simmering 'low intensity' conflict of raid and counter-raid. This country was to be the main arena for Anglo-Scots warfare and, because of this accident of geography, it developed its own unique social and legal institutions which, in turn, impacted on military operations.

Both sides of the Border were divided into three administrative areas: the East, Middle and West Marches. The Scottish East March comprised the coastal plain of the Merse, bordering the English East March roughly from Lamberton to Birgham. Its most important strong point was Home Castle, but there were numerous fortified 'piles', such as the tower at Ayton, to guard against English incursions. The English East March comprised of the extreme north of Northumberland. It bordered the Scottish East March along the length of the River Tweed from the North Sea to Carham opposite Birgham, at which point the border swung south, and from there on it bordered the Scottish Middle March from Carham down to the Cheviot. The Tweed formed a natural border between the two countries although Berwick-upon-Tweed itself, which was north of the river, changed hands no fewer than six times between 1174 and 1482. In 1482 the English finally gained, and retained, its possession. Berwick was to be England's strongest garrison in the Marches. The two other most important posts defending the English East March were the castles at Wark and Norham, traditionally the most dangerous place in England, stormed by the Scots on four occasions (1136, 1138, 1322 and 1513) and unsuccessfully besieged on a further five occasions (1215, 1318, 1319, 1327 and 1497).

Norham's peculiarly violent history arose from its location on a major invasion route. The Tweed, fed by the streams of the Cheviots and Lammermuirs, tended to rise and swell unexpectedly, but usually did not present an impassable obstacle to an army. It could be crossed at many places, but one of the best fords was hard by Norham Castle. In the east the English could strike north across the flat coastal plain towards Lothian and Edinburgh, whilst the Scots could cross easily into England and penetrate into Northumberland. The East Marches thus witnessed the passage of the majority of cross border invasions by large armies.

On the whole, however, the East Marches of both England and Scotland were less prone to the anarchic lawlessness and raiding that often typified the Middle and West Marches. In the East Marches the fertile, low-lying land supported arable farming. Furthermore, there were strong economic links between the English and Scottish East Marches, and their populations seemed more settled than the cattle-rearing and horse-breeding peoples of the upland Middle and West Marches.

The geography of the Middle Marches contrasted sharply with those of the East. Where the Border leaves the Tweed and runs south from Carham down to Cheviot there is no natural line of demarcation between England and Scotland. The Border then swings to the west and for forty miles passes through the Cheviots and their neighbouring mountains. These desolate heights offered few viable routes to an army with cannon and baggage, but had many passes suitable for the purposes of the reivers, the cattle thieves and raiders who gave the Marches their unwholesome reputation. Thus, on both sides of the Border, the Middle March was dotted with pele towers and bastle houses. In the English Middle March the people of both Tynedale and Redesdale were notorious for their unruly and lawless conduct. North of the Border, the populations of Teviotdale and Liddesdale had a similar reputation. Indeed in Liddesdale the Scottish Crown appointed a 'Keeper' based at Hermitage Castle specifically to maintain law and order in the valley, although in practice most of the Keepers tended to be less than scrupulous in their pursuit of justice. Militarily the Scottish Middle March saw some of the most destructive *chevauchées* launched by the English into Scotland. There were many tempting targets within striking distance, such as Kelso, Jedburgh, Hawick, Melrose and Dryburgh. These *chevauchées* were generally launched from the English East March, since it was easier to get cannon and baggage across the Border before it rose into the Cheviots.

The Border of the English West March ran through the head lands of the River Lyne, a desolate area known as the Cumberland Waste, through Kershopefoot along the Liddel Water to the River Esk and down to the Solway Firth. The March itself comprised Cumberland and Westmorland and was dominated by the fortifications of Carlisle, with important secondary posts for English Border officials guarding the wastes at Askerton, Naworth, Bewcastle and Scaleby. Lying between the English and Scottish West Marches was a small stretch of territory, measuring about twelve miles long and three to five miles wide, bounded by the rivers Lyne, Sark and Liddel Water. This was the 'Debatable Land' whose ownership had been contested for the past 240 years. Since neither Scotland nor England could establish jurisdiction over the ground, it naturally became the refuge of the Border's most notorious 'broken men' (outlaws), vagabonds and fugitives from justice. In particular the Debatable Land became the home territory of the Grahams, a notorious Anglo-Scots reiver clan who plundered north and south of the Border with equal vigour.

The Scottish West March lay to the north of the Debatable Land, comprising Eskdale, Dumfriesshire, Annandale and the valley of the River Nith. Like the English West March, it was heavily fortified with major strongholds at Caerlaverock, Lochmaben, Langholm and Lochwood, whilst the larger churches, such as that in Annan, also served as defensive bastions when necessary.

The administration of the Border Marches was the responsibility of the wardens appointed by the Crown. In peacetime English and Scottish wardens were expected to work together to control lawlessness on the Border. They met on designated truce days to settle grievances ranging from complaints of murder and kidnap to theft and the extortion of money for protection, the practice known as 'blackmail'. The settlement of these complaints was a complicated business. Much of the actual violence in the Marches was not a question of national conflict. English and Scottish 'riding' families feuded amongst themselves and forged cross-border alliances. Wardens were often Borderers themselves, and thus they, and their subordinate land sergeants, keepers and deputies, were frequently involved in criminal activity and the pursuit of their own blood feuds. The usefulness of such men in wartime meant that the Crowns generally turned a blind eye to their deprivations. Efforts to pacify the Border were usually half-hearted, since it served the purposes of both England and Scotland to have a certain level of discord in the Marches, which could be escalated when necessary in pursuit of political or diplomatic objectives.[1]

The invasions of 1496 and 1497

The Marches did not exist in a permanent state of open hostilities and it would be wrong to exaggerate the extent to which conflict shaped the Border region's economic and social development.[2] However, the potential for conflict was always great and the usefulness of the Marches as an arena in which to pursue political objectives through acts of war is clearly illustrated by the two invasions of England launched by James IV in 1496 and 1497.

James needed to demonstrate, both at home and abroad, that he was now in personal control of his government. The invasion of England was a spectacular means of announcing his arrival on the European stage, of gaining international prestige and winning for himself a reputation as a warrior king. By acting as a patron to the Yorkist pretender Perkin Warbeck, James involved Scotland in the diplomatic manoeuvring of the major powers of continental Europe. The Emperor Maximilian, Ferdinand and Isabella of Spain, Archduke Philip and Margaret of Burgundy, had all been involved with the man who claimed to be Richard of York. Besides which, Henry VII regarded Warbeck as a genuine

---

[1]   On the development of Border society, see George MacDonald Fraser, *The Steel Bonnets: The Story of the Anglo-Scottish Border Reivers* (London, 1989), Thomas Hodgkin, *The Wardens of the Northern Marches* (London, 1908) and Ralph Robson, *The English Highland Clans: Tudor Responses to a Medieval Problem* (Edinburgh, 1989).
[2]   See Richard Lomas, 'The Impact of Border Warfare: The Scots and South Tweedside, c.1290–1520', *The Scottish Historical Review*, vol. 75 (1996), pp. 143–167.

threat, and the possibility of re-igniting England's civil wars and profiting from the consequent chaos must have been an attractive one to James.

In the event, the two invasions became merely large-scale forays, but profitable ones nevertheless. In September 1496 James plundered Northumberland for a fortnight, harrying the population to such an extent that Warbeck complained about the treatment of 'his people', only to be sent back to Scotland in disgrace. Besides making a tidy profit on the raid James also destroyed the fortifications at Twizel, Tillmouth, Duddo, Branxton and Howtel, thus easing the passage for a second invasion along the same route of the Till valley. He withdrew on news that an army under the Earl of Surrey was leaving Newcastle to meet him in the field, but James, having violated the truce that was then current, had now initiated open war with England.

Henry VII certainly intended to retaliate but his arrangements for a counterinvasion were frustrated by the rebellion in the West Country and his army was needed at Blackheath to crush the Cornish rebels. Scottish forces continued to raid into the English Marches and James himself reappeared on the Border in August 1497, accompanied by a large siege train, including Mons Meg, which was used in an assault on Norham Castle. Although he failed to take the castle and quickly withdrew back into Scotland, James had done well in strategic terms. An English army crossed into Scotland and took Ayton but Henry could not afford to prosecute the war further.

James, on the other hand, had amassed a considerable amount of plunder, stolen from the homes of Northumberland, had weakened English fortifications in the Till valley leaving open a useful invasion route into England, and had forced Henry to negotiate with him. That process of negotiation would ultimately end in a marriage to Henry's daughter Margaret in 1503. James's military ventures therefore, although quite limited in terms of their immediate objectives, had reaped considerable political dividends.[3] The same was true of the King's experience of using military force within his own realm. He had led expeditions to the Highlands in 1494, 1495 and 1498–99 to assert royal authority and suppress revolt in the wake of the forfeiture of the possessions of John, the last Lord of the Isles. His success can only have reinforced his sense that military action secured positive political results.[4]

Henry VIII and his early campaigns

The parsimonious Henry VII, whilst not afraid to fight when absolutely necessary, was less inclined to view war as a useful instrument of policy. His son and successor, Henry VIII, however, shared with James a desire to use war as a means of achieving status on the international stage. From the moment of his

3   Norman MacDougall, *James IV* (Edinburgh, 1989), pp. 112–145.
4   Donald Gregory, *The History of the Western Highlands and Isles of Scotland, AD1493–AD1625* (Glasgow, 1881), pp. 86–113.

coronation in 1509 Henry was, according to the chronicler Edward Hall, 'ever desirous to serve Mars'.[5] Even when he himself could not lead them in person, he was quick to commit his subjects to battle. The earliest expedition had proved inauspicious.

In 1511, sixteen hundred English soldiers arrived in Spain in preparation for a crusade against 'the Moores of Barbary'. English crusaders had served Spain valiantly during the *Reconquista* and their record augured well for those who planned to serve in North Africa. However, this was not to be. The small force was immediately beset by disciplinary problems. Hall recounts a lamentable tale: 'the Englyshmen whiche went a lande, fell to drinking of hot wines and were scarce masters of theim selfes, some ran to the stewes, some brake hedges, and spolyed orchards and vyneyards, and orynges before they were ripe, and did many outrageous dedes'. Nor did their behaviour improve much once they had sobered up. Several Spaniards were killed in brawls, and the English were confined to their ships. In June they finally sailed, not for North Africa, but for Plymouth.[6]

Henry had better luck with the fifteen hundred bowmen he sent as auxiliaries to fight for Margaret of Savoy against the rebellious Duke of Guelders. This small force had fought well, enhancing England's military repute. Encouraged by this success, a larger force, five thousand strong, was dispatched to Biscay under the command of the Marquis of Dorset. Dorset was to co-operate with Henry's father-in-law, Ferdinand of Aragon, in his campaign against France. Simultaneously Henry initiated naval war with France, sending the Lord Admiral, Edward Howard, and the fleet to raid and burn in Brittany. The ultimate prize for the English was to be Guinne, the old English possession lost in the final stages of the Hundred Years War. Yet this hope was to be frustrated. The naval campaign soon went badly awry. An encounter with the French fleet off Brest saw the 1000 ton *Regant*, the pride of Henry's navy, catch fire when grappled to a French warship and subsequently sink with practically all hands. On land, a combined Anglo-Spanish force occupied Navarre without difficulty, and with that the Spanish were well satisfied. The promised support for an English invasion of south-west France did not materialise.

The English soldiery garrisoned at Fuentarrabia wilted and sickened in the heat, and had no beer to cool their thirst. Resentment against the Spanish grew. The English bows had put French horse to flight in several skirmishes, but without cavalry, which the Spanish had promised but not provided, there could be no pursuit. The level of discontent teetered on the verge of mutiny. Dorset was left with little choice but to embark his sick and discontented troops on ships and sail home to an angry and humiliated King. Worse news was to follow for Henry. Howard again attacked the French fleet in Brest. Stealing into the harbour by night on small barges, Howard attempted to board a French galley

---

[5] Edward Hall, *The Triumphant Reigne of Kyng Henry the VIII*, vol. 1 (London, 1904), p. 30.
[6] Hall, pp. 30–33.

but was pitched overboard by a pike thrust and drowned. Having lost its admiral, the English fleet was thrown onto the defensive and the war was carried into English waters. All in all, 1512 had been a bad year for English arms, but this only seemed to strengthen the King's resolve to win glory on the field of battle. For now he planned to lead personally a great expedition against France which would wipe out the memory of these setbacks.[7]

The invasion of France, 1513

England was to join the papacy, Venice, Spain and the Empire in an alliance designed to counter the growing French hegemony in Europe. Yet the Pope's Holy League against the schismatic French King Louis XII was far less unified than it first appeared. A grandiose strategy was devised. Henry, the Emperor Maximilian and Ferdinand of Aragon were to wage a three-fronted war against France. However, the duplicitous and secretive Ferdinand had already come to terms with Louis. Furious as this betrayal left Henry, he remained determined to carry through his grand designs on French soil, even if it meant fighting alone.[8]

In June 1513 the English Army arrived in Calais. Divided into the traditional three battles, the first to arrive were the 8000-strong vanguard and the 6000-strong rearward, commanded respectively by George Talbot, Earl of Shrewsbury, and Charles Somerset, Lord Herbert. Henry himself arrived with much pageantry and the main battle, comprising around 9000 men, on 30 June. Perhaps three thousand of this force were mounted northern horse, mounted archers and one thousand demi-lancers under the experienced Welsh captain, Sir Rees Ap Thomas. Over the next three weeks the army was augmented by foreign mercenaries, chiefly *Landsknecht* pike and Burgundian men-at-arms.

By the 21 July it was ready to move, although early progress was painfully slow as the weather broke and the carters and gunners toiled in heavy rain and mud. The first objective was the small Artois town of Thérouanne, where elements of Shrewsbury's vanguard were already fighting. It would take the Army Royal eleven days to reinforce them. As it approached it was harried by the French. On 25 July a French force drawn from the garrisons of Boulogne and Montreuil was held at bay by the King's artillery. Hurrying on from this skirmish, which seems to have unnerved the King, some of this same, much prized, artillery was allowed to fall behind on the march. Two cannons, 'The Red Gonne' and 'St John the Evangelist', were subsequently captured by the French

---

[7]   Jasper Ridley, *Henry VIII* (London, 1984), p. 60. For an account of the disastrous expedition to Biscay and the naval war around Brittany, see Hall, pp. 42–61, and Sir James Marshall-Cornwall, 'An Expedition to Aquitaine, 1512', *History Today*, vol. 23 (1973), pp. 640–647.

[8]   For a full discussion of the motivation behind Henry's French wars, see Steven Gunn, 'The French Wars of Henry VIII', in Jeremy Black (ed.), *The Origins of War in Early Modern Europe* (Edinburgh, 1987), pp. 28–51.

as they struggled across a swollen river. Rees Ap Thomas's cavalry was able to rescue 'St John' from under the noses of a large French force, but the 'Red Gonne' was lost for good.

On 27 July the entire army had to be drawn up in battle array near Tournehem as French cavalry threatened to attack again. Now the sun blazed down on the armoured men, who stood to arms in the open from six o'clock in the morning until three in the afternoon. The threatened attack did not materialise but, lacking both shade and water, the unfortunate English soldiery had ample cause to remember the 'Dry Wednesday' with some displeasure.

Despite these mishaps, the advance continued. By 4 August Henry was finally able to invest Thérouanne. Here he was joined by the Emperor Maximilian. The Emperor managed to divert attention from his own failure to launch a serious campaign against France by flattering Henry, offering to serve in his army, and wearing the cross of St George prominently on his armour. On 11 August Henry received a less welcome visitor. Lyon Herald, sent by his royal master James IV of Scotland, arrived in the English camp. Undeterred by papal threats of excommunication, James had chosen to honour his alliance obligations to France.

The treaty and marriage alliance of 1502 had brought peace between England and Scotland. The wedding of James to Henry's sister Margaret had, in the early years of the new century, even offered the possibility of a peaceful union of the crowns. The prospects for friendly relations between the two nations had been very favourable indeed, despite the nagging friction on the Border and a vigorous rivalry between their merchant fleets. But James had allowed himself to be pulled into the orbit of Louis XII's expansionist ambitions. Having reactivated the Auld Alliance, Louis called insistently on James's support in the face of English aggression and James stirred to France's defence.

At least it was his obligations to his ally that James stressed in his declaration of war. He also catalogued a string of lesser English misdemeanours, chiefly the withholding of Henry VII's legacy from James's wife Margaret, the failure of the English authorities to punish John the Bastard of Heron for the recent murder of Sir Robert Kerr, Warden of the Scottish Middle March, and the death of Andrew Barton, a Scottish sailor and alleged pirate, killed in 1511 by Thomas Howard, England's Lord Admiral. Besides these *causa belli*, there are grounds for believing that James genuinely coveted the English throne. With Henry and his Army Royal on the other side of the Channel, the threat to England's security was very real. Certainly Louis encouraged James to regard himself as the rightful King of England by virtue of his descent from St Margaret, Queen of Scotland, and through his wife, eldest daughter of Henry VII.[9]

His declaration of war delivered, Lyon Herald departed, leaving Henry trusting that he had made adequate provision for the defence of his own realm as he assaulted another's. Any doubts that he had must have been pushed to the back

[9] Marguerite Wood (ed.), *Flodden Papers* (Edinburgh, 1933), xv, xvi, xvii.

of his mind by the appearance of an 8000-strong French force sent to raise the siege. Their presence was reported to Henry on the morning of 16 August, in his pavilion at Guinegatte. Moving out to meet the threat, the English main battle clashed with the lead elements of the French force near the village of Bomy. The sudden storm of arrows seems to have taken the French by surprise, for they had misjudged the position of the English army. With their path blocked by well positioned infantry, supported by artillery, the French suddenly became aware that English cavalry on their flank was in a position to envelope them completely. A hasty retreat was hotly pursued by English and Burgundian men-at-arms. Six French standards and a large number of noble prisoners, including a duke, a marquis, the Vice Admiral of France and the famous Chevalier Bayard were captured.

This, the 'Battle of the Spurs', was the high point of Henry's campaign. The besieged town of Thérouanne, now denied hope of succour, surrendered within a week. Maximilian, who had played the rather naive young Henry very well indeed, was given possession of the English prize, which he then had razed to the ground. Henry moved swiftly on to a second siege, at Tournai. Hammered by English guns and mindful of the flames that had consumed Thérouanne, this citadel surrendered after just eight days, on 24 September. The King might have revelled in this his moment of glory, yet England had gained little from his triumph.[10]

The Scottish challenge and the English response

As Henry waged his war in France his realm lay in real peril from its northern neighbour. Pledged to France's aid, James IV had begun his preparations for war long before Lyon Herald had arrived at Henry's camp. English agents reported his purchases in Flanders of pikes, guns and armour.[11] In the Border country the people tensed themselves for the coming storm as raiding and foraying escalated. In May of 1513 forty French veterans landed at Dunbar, under the command of a captain called D'Aussi, to train the Scots in the use of their new arms.[12] On 16 July James drafted the declaration of war, which was delivered to Henry in his camp outside Thérouanne by Lyon Herald on 11 August. At the same time James dispatched his fleet to his ally's aid, attacking the English garrison at Carrickfergus *en route*. The first notices had already been sent out to the furthest reaches of the Highlands and Isles summoning the clan chieftains and their men to their King's banner. Over the next few days such summonses were

---

10 The best account of the war of 1513 is Charles Cruickshank, *Henry VIII and the Invasion of France* (Stroud, 1990).

11 Hall, *Henry the VIII*, pp. 95–96.

12 *Calendar of State Papers, Venice, Vol. 1, 1509–1519* (London, 1867), 316.

sent throughout Scotland, calling the levies to Borough Muir, outside Edinburgh, for the mustering on 13 August.[13]

South of the Tweed, the defence of England had been left in the capable
hands of an experienced old soldier, Thomas Howard, Earl of Surrey. Surrey
was now in his seventieth year. As a young man he had supported Edward IV
during the turbulent years of 1469–71. Following Edward's death, he had gone
on to serve his brother, Richard III. At Bosworth in 1485 he and his father, the
Duke of Norfolk, had followed their King to defeat. The Duke had been killed
on the field. Thomas Howard had been captured, attainted and imprisoned in the
Tower. Released after three years' incarceration, Howard became a loyal and
trusted servant of the new Tudor dynasty. He was raised successively to the
posts of Lieutenant of the North, Lord Treasurer and Earl Marshall of England,
although his father's title remained forfeited.

In his capacity as Lieutenant of the North he had come close to crossing
swords with James already, chasing him back across the Tweed after the Scottish
incursions into England in 1496 and 1497. Indeed, if James had had his way, the
two men would literally have crossed swords in 1497. In that year the Scottish
King challenged the Earl to single combat, with Berwick as the prize. Surrey
regretfully informed James that he had no commission to fight for Berwick, but
that once he had dealt with the Scottish army he would gladly fight the King, on
horseback or on foot, at His Majesty's pleasure.[14] Once the Scottish army was
safely back north of the Tweed, the combat was apparently forgotten, but this
was not the last time that these two men would exchange such chivalrous
defiances.

Their next meeting had been peaceful, when Surrey had escorted Margaret
Tudor to meet her royal groom James in 1502. Yet that was but a brief interlude
in a relationship which seemed characterised by a degree of genuine animosity.
By 1513, against the broader background of Anglo-Scots conflict, an altogether
more personal rivalry had arisen between the Scottish king and the Howards.
Surrey, as a young man, had grown up in an England still smarting from expulsion from France. Now a youthful, strong and warlike King of England campaigned once more on the continent. Surrey felt his place was at his king's side.
Instead he found himself left behind to guard the Border and for this he held
James personally responsible. Now it was his singular hope that James should be
made 'as sorry as he is for letting him from the French war'.[15]

During his years of service in the North, Surrey had proved himself a capable
soldier and administrator, frustrating Yorkist hopes for insurrection, and guard-

---

[13] Charles Oman, *A History of the Art of War in the Sixteenth Century* (London, 1991), pp.
298–299.
[14] Thomas Howard, 'The Early Career of the 3rd Duke of Norfolk' (University of West Virginia Ph.D., 1984), pp. 29, 42–43.
[15] Thomas Hodgkin, 'The Battle of Flodden', *Archaeologia Aeliana*, vol. 16 (1894), p. 10.

ing the Border well.[16] With Scottish preparations hardly shrouded in secrecy, Surrey had not waited long to begin his advance to the north country. Setting out from London on 22 July, he was accompanied by his own personal retinue of five hundred professional soldiers. He reached Doncaster by 1 August and immediately sent missives to the sheriffs and gentry of the northern counties to stand in readiness. Sir William Bulmer, sheriff of the bishopric of Durham, was dispatched with two hundred mounted archers to patrol the Marches.[17]

On 13 August the storm broke. A massive foray, perhaps eight thousand strong, under Alexander Home, the Lord Chamberlain and Warden General of the Scottish Marches, burst across the Border. Burning seven villages, looting as they went, the raiders rounded up an impressive haul of livestock and turned back from Northumberland, riding hard for Scotland. With the warning beacons along the Border ablaze, Bulmer's two hundred mounted archers, joined by about eight hundred Borderers, were soon in 'hot trod' pursuit. Loaded down with plunder and driving their stolen livestock before them, the raiders were out paced by their pursuers, who were able to circle ahead of them.

At Millfield the English halted and lay in wait for their quarry. Still outnumbered, Bulmer was to offset his numerical disadvantage with a carefully staged ambush, into which Home obligingly rode. As the raiders drove their stolen livestock incautiously northwards they passed between two concealed bodies of dismounted English archers who loosed their arrows at close range, the arrows enfilading their victims. The ensuing arrow storm cut down about five hundred of Home's men with the opening volleys. A precipitous flight ensued as the raiders scattered for cover, again hotly pursued. A further three hundred Scots were captured, one of them Home's own standard bearer. Home himself was amongst the more fortunate survivors who fled home, but now empty handed.[18]

Home's disastrous venture across the Tweed, quickly dubbed the 'Ill Raid', was, although large, nothing too unusual in the cut and thrust of Border warfare. The two massive armies that were now gathering, however, presaged an altogether bloodier clash. Surrey was mustering the levy of the northern shires, his expanding army forming around the nucleus of his ordnance, under Sir Nicholas Appleyard at Newcastle. Surrey was himself proceeding northwards, gathering in troops as he did so. On 25 August he collected the levies of Yorkshire in their county town. The following day the indomitable seventy-year-old Earl set out towards Newcastle, his army lashed by fierce winds and driving rain, and trudging through deep mud, 'the fowlest night and day there could be', as the chronicler Edward Hall commented. On 30 August, Surrey's weather-beaten army reached Durham to be joined by the men of the bishopric. Here they collected the ancient banner of St Cuthbert, which was to be the chief standard of the English during the coming campaign.

---

[16] Anthony Goodman, *The Wars of the Roses* (London, 1981), pp. 89, 91, 106, 108–109, 113, 212.
[17] Hall, *Henry the VIII*, vol. 1, p. 96.
[18] Hall, p. 97.

Here, too, Surrey received ill-tidings from the Border. James, with a massive army, was across the Tweed. Scourers reported him to be in the vicinity of the Till valley, familiar countryside from the campaigns of 1496 and 1497. James had set off for the Border with his army divided into three battles on 18 August. With the benefit of the experience gained in 1496 and 1497, his army was accompanied by a truly formidable artillery train. The pride of this collection of ordnance were seven heavy guns taken from Edinburgh Castle and named, collectively, 'the Seven Sisters'.[19] In all probability these had been manufactured by James's Master Gunner, Robert Borthwick, who now accompanied James to serve his guns in battle.

The King picked up more levies as he moved south, particularly in the Scottish Marches. The precise strength of his army as it crossed the Tweed was disputed by contemporaries, but all believed it to be large. Polydore Vergil's figure of sixty thousand was amongst the more cautious estimates. Hall claimed the army numbered a staggering one hundred thousand. Even granting the chroniclers' tendency to exaggerate, it would certainly not seem improbable to estimate that the King's army numbered at least forty thousand as he crossed the Border.[20]

The first target of this mighty force was Norham Castle, besieged by James in 1497. He had enjoyed little success on that occasion, and since then Norham had been strengthened by its owner, Thomas Ruthal, Bishop of Durham, who had added a wall with casements for guns. The castle was in a state of watchfulness and, forewarned being forearmed, was reckoned a tough obstacle. 'Impregnable if well furnished', thought Hall.[21] Besides the architectural improvements he had made, Ruthal had reinforced the garrison, supplying its captain, John Ainslie, with munitions and victuals, hoping to stall James before the castle's high walls.

Yet Norham was still vulnerable, even with its cannon and casements. The Scottish siege train gave a convincing display of its destructive power, hammering the castle into submission in just six days, a far more impressive performance than it had managed in 1497. Hall claims that Ainslie was too profligate in Norham's defence, repulsing three assaults on the castle walls, but, in so doing, 'he spent vaynely so much of his ordinaunce, bowes and arrowes and other munitions that at last he lacked . . .'.[22] It is far more likely that the ageing castle was simply battered into surrender and, once surrendered, looted and cast utterly to the ground. Ruthal was distraught at the news of Norham's loss, and wrote bitterly to Wolsey of the disaster, 'which . . . touched me so near with

[19] Robert Lindesay of Pitscottie, *The Historie and Cronicles of Scotland*, vol. 1 (Edinburgh, 1899), p. 259.
[20] For a full discussion of the relative strengths of the two armies, see Fitzwilliam Elliot, *The Battle of Flodden and the Raids of 1513* (Tonbridge, 1991), Appendix II, pp. 196–204.
[21] Hall, *Henry the VIII*, vol. 1, p. 97.
[22] Hall, p. 99.

inward sorrow that I had lever to have been out of the world than in it'.[23] When he finally recovered the castle, he discovered that the Scots had made a thorough job of its destruction, leaving only the dungeon and part of the wall still standing.[24]

The first success of James's huge and destructive foray was ample testimony to the capabilities of the army he had brought over the Border and, in particular, to the power of his artillery. James was to make similarly short work of the nearby castles at Etal, Chillingham and Ford. Ford Castle, however, was spared from complete destruction. Here the chivalrously inclined James encountered the disarming lady of the house, Elizabeth Heron, whose husband Sir William Heron was a prisoner of the Scots, held in Fast Castle. In characteristic Border fashion the resourceful Lady Heron now bargained hard for her husband and her home.

She arranged both the exchange of her spouse and the preservation of Ford Castle. In return she offered the release of two Scottish nobles, Lord Johnstone and Sir Alexander Home, taken prisoner at Millfield when Bulmer's men ambushed 'the Ill Raid'.[25] Accusations that James now dallied amorously with Elizabeth and forgot his purpose are unfounded.[26] However enchanting she may have been, James surely had other things on his mind. His scourers galloped hard through the country and cannot have failed to report the proximity of Surrey and his army of Northerners, closing quickly on the invaders. Many of the King's nobles were now advising him to withdraw to Scotland. He had, they argued, already done France a great service by diverting so many English troops to the Border. If the English were now determined to give battle, it would be to the King's advantage to meet them on his own ground. James, however, would not be persuaded. After exchanging harsh words with the King, Archibald Douglas, 5th Earl of Angus, withdrew from the army and the case for caution was no longer pressed with any real vigour.[27] James's confidence may well have stemmed from the successful outcome of his previous military expeditions, both in the Till valley and the Highlands. Although he had never fought a battle, war had served him well as an instrument of policy in the past. Furthermore, the King of England himself now campaigned in France with his expensive mercenaries, his household troops and the retinues of the major nobility. If James did face an English army, it would be composed predominantly of the shire levy, led by the experienced, but aged, Earl of Surrey. To James the situation must have looked like one of opportunity, and the voices urging caution have sounded unduly timid.

23 *Letters and Papers [LandP], Foreign and Domestic, Henry VIII*, vol. 1, 4457.
24 *LandP, Henry VIII*, vol. 1, 4461.
25 Hall, *Henry the VIII*, vol. 1, p. 101.
26 For a full discussion of the unreliability of this tradition, see Hodgkin, 'The Battle of Flodden', pp. 39–44.
27 George Ridpath, *The Border History of England and Scotland* (Berwick, 1848), pp. 336–337.

Yet the whole of the north of England now stood at the ready. Surrey had sent riders to 'all Lords spirituall and temporall, Knyghts, gentlemen or others which had tenants, or were rulers of Tounes . . . to certify what number of able men horsed and harnessed they were able to make within an houres warnynge'. From the Marches of Scotland to the Marches of North Wales the levies mustered, the commissioners deliberated and the most suitable men of war were equipped, 'horsed and harnessed', and sent northwards to join Surrey.[28] The merits of the national levy system were now made evident. Surrey's army grew rapidly and moved quickly. If Hall is correct, many, possibly most, of the shire levy were horsed, effectively mounted infantry. Here was an effective militia army, whose soldiers marched out to defend their homes and placed their faith in God, for, according to the Italian ambassador, Di Favri, there were few English soldiers who failed daily to recite the 'Office' and 'Our Lady's Rosary'.[29]

This disciplined force showed the potential strength of the shire levy in the event of an actual invasion. By careful selection, the commissioners of array had mobilised a highly efficient army. Selection of likely individuals for service, rather than reliance on a *levée en masse*, meant that the English army was to be out-numbered by the invader. Most contemporary authorities agree that Surrey's army numbered about twenty-six thousand four days before Flodden, with some contingents still to arrive.[30] Clearly a *levée en masse* of the North, perhaps drawing troops from as far south as Derbyshire and North Wales, would have raised a much larger army. It would, however, have included large numbers of half-equipped men, most of whom would have been on foot. In the event, the actual response to an invasion was a smaller (although by no means inconsiderable) force which was both mobile and well-equipped. A larger force would not only have been less efficient, but would probably have proved impossible to victual. Even as it was, the English were to fight the battle on empty stomachs.

From Durham, Surrey had advanced to Newcastle on 30 August. Here he joined Thomas, Lord Dacre, with the men of the West March. Dacre was an important figure in the north country: Warden of the West March, a veteran of countless Border skirmishes and frequently the representative of the English Crown at the Stuart court. Here, too, was the vanquisher of 'the Ill Raid', Sir William Bulmer. Having proved his mettle at Millfield, Bulmer was given command of the men of the bishopric of Durham. They would fight under the banner of St Cuthbert, whose honour had been affronted by the sacking of Norham, property of their bishop. Further reinforcements arrived with Sir Edward Stanley, who brought the levy of Cheshire and Lancashire.

Sir Edward Stanley's presence had a peculiar irony. His father was Thomas, Lord Stanley, whose mid-battle conversion to the cause of Henry Tudor had sealed Richard III's fate at Bosworth. With Richard had died Surrey's father. Now Surrey was to lead a Stanley into battle. Any lingering ill feeling did not

---

[28] Hall, *Henry the VIII*, vol. 1, pp. 97–98.
[29] *Cal. State Papers, Venice*, vol. 2, 333.
[30] Elliot, *The Battle of Flodden*, pp. 197–198.

manifest itself during the actual campaign. Although the old rivalry colours at least one of the subsequent accounts of Flodden, Stanley served Surrey well enough on the field of battle.[31]

Newcastle was now bursting with soldiers eating the townsfolk out of house and home. To relieve this pressure Surrey pressed on to Alnwick on 2 September. There he joined Henry Percy, Earl of Northumberland. New contingents were still arriving in Newcastle, but the atrocious weather conditions were causing further delay. Thus, Surrey paused at Alnwick to wait for late arrivals and to organise the mass of levies into one army whilst hopefully the storms would abate. On 4 September he received another welcome addition to his army. His son, Sir Thomas Howard, the Lord Admiral of England, arrived 'with a compaignye of valyaunt Captaines and able souldiers and maryners' from the fleet, a reminder of the versatility of the sixteenth-century navy.[32]

Howard was already a veteran of war with Scotland, having campaigned with his father in 1497, and being knighted for his services in the same year. He had been appointed Lord Admiral following the death of his younger brother, Edward, at Brest in 1512. Having slowly rebuilt the confidence of his navy, the new Lord Admiral had scoured the narrow seas to avenge his brother and was soon acquiring a fearsome reputation. Hall refers to him as 'wyse, hardy, and of great credence and experience' and it is likely that he made a major contribution to his father's plans for the coming battle as well as providing steadfast command on the field itself, once fighting had been joined. As his father's most trusted lieutenant, the Lord Admiral was given command of the English vanguard.

The manoeuvre for position

Arriving at Bolton in Glendale on 5 September, Surrey and his council 'wyth great deliberacion appoynted his battyles in order with wynges and riders necessarie'.[33] The riders referred to here would have been the light cavalry appointed to scour the land ahead of the advancing army. Following in the path they reconnoitred would come the main body of the army. Surrey did not divide this army

---

[31] The only suggestion of a feud between the Howards and the Stanleys influencing the course of the campaign comes from the Cheshire bard, Leigh of Baggerley, whose *Scotish Feilde* was a blatant piece of pro-Stanley propaganda. After the battle Surrey had commented unfavourably on the behaviour of a small contingent of Cheshire men placed under the command of his younger son, Edmund Howard. These men had fled the field early in the battle. Leigh blames their flight on the inexperience of the young Howard, and accuses the Earl of slandering Stanley's contingent because 'synce Kynge Richard's feyhte he never loved them'. It would seem more plausible that Surrey did not love them because when they fled they had left his youngest son alone in the path of about six thousand heavily armed Scottish Borderers.

[32] Hall, *Henry the VIII*, vol. 1, p. 100.

[33] Hall, p. 100.

into the traditional three battles that the King, for example, had deployed in France. Instead he chose to divide the army into two divisions, each flanked by wings, smaller and more flexible tactical units. The vanguard was about nine thousand strong, comprised largely of the men of the Durham bishopric and the soldiers and mariners from the fleet. The Admiral had with him a number of nobles who were to fight on foot amongst their own retinues, the Lords Clyfford, Conyers, Latimer, Scrope, Egle and Lomley, and a large number of knights, including the proven Border commander, Sir William Bulmer.

The smaller units flanking the vanguard were similarly officered. The right-hand wing was under the command of the Lord Admiral's younger brother, Edmund Howard, and with him an assortment of knights, esquires and gentlemen. The wing comprised a total of about three thousand soldiers, drawn from the levy of Hull, and also a 1500-strong contingent of men detached from the retinue of Sir Edward Stanley. The left-hand wing was considerably smaller, just one thousand Lancashire men under the ageing Marmaduke Constable, accompanied by an assortment of his sons and kinsmen and Sir William Percy.

The main battle was the Earl of Surrey's own command. It would appear that Surrey was expecting the main brunt of the fighting to fall on his son's vanguard, for his own battle was slightly smaller, about five thousand strong. This battle was flanked by two wings of roughly equal size. Lord Dacre and three thousand Marchmen were on the right, Stanley, with his three thousand Lancashire and Cheshire men to the left.[34]

With battle looming, Surrey, not forgetting the courtesies of war, dispatched Rouge Croix, pursuivant of arms, to issue a challenge to James. The herald soon found the King of Scots, his army now camped above Ford Castle, on a long ridge called Flodden Edge. By now James's army had been somewhat depleted by sickness and desertion to around thirty-four thousand men. This, combined with the awful weather, may have persuaded him to modify any grandiose designs and simply to wait instead for Surrey to show his hand. Surrey's challenge began with an acceptance of Lady Heron's proposals for a prisoner exchange, but moved quickly on to grimmer business. James stood accused:

> unaturally agaynste all reason and conscience, hath he entered and invaded this hys brothers realme of Englande, and done great hurte to the same, in castying doune Castelles, Towres, and houses, brenninge, spoylynge and destroiynge of the same, and cruelly murderynge the Kynge of Englande hys brothers subjects. Wherefore the sayde Earle wyll be readye to trye the righfulness of the matter wyth the Kynge in battaill by Frydaye next.

According to Hall, Surrey's son, the Lord Admiral, gave Rouge Croix an additional message to pass on to the Scottish King. The Lord Admiral now intended that the unresolved matter of redress for the death of the Scottish sailor Andrew Barton be settled on the field of battle. He informed James that he

---

34 Hall, pp. 100–101.

would be found in the English vanguard and that when the armies clashed he would neither give, nor expect, quarter.[35]

Behind these archaic courtesies and challenges, both Surrey and James were playing a canny game. The English suspected that the Scots would detain their herald, Rouge Croix, and dispatch one of their own with a reply, who would take the opportunity to make a full assessment of the English force. Doubtless they hoped that Rouge Croix would perform the same mission for themselves, but they were determined to prevent James from spying out their camp. Rouge Croix was indeed detained after he had delivered Surrey's challenge to James, and a Scottish herald, Islay, was sent in his place on 5 September. Islay was kept as clear of the English army as possible. He was met by another English herald, York, and entertained in a village two miles from the English camp.

On 6 September, Surrey, with the lords, knights and gentlemen of the English host, rode to meet Islay and hear the Scottish King's reply. Couched in the most courteous terms, James accepted the challenge to battle, leaving Surrey 'righte joyous and [he] muche praysed the honourable agreement of the sayde Royall Kynge'. With these pleasantries exchanged, Islay was held, pending the release of Rouge Croix, in the company of the herald York and Sir Humphrey Lysle and together they made 'good chere'.[36]

Surrey could have used some good cheer himself. However joyous he had been at the news that James had accepted his challenge, the report Rouge Croix now brought him must have changed his mood. The English were encamped three miles from the Scots at Wooler Haugh, offering battle on an adjacent open field of corn. Yet the Scots gave no indication of advancing to meet them. Indeed they had little reason to, for the Scottish army had been expertly positioned. The naturally strong defensive position along the crest of Flodden Edge was enhanced by field fortifications, in which was located the powerful Scottish artillery. These cannon had already lobbed some speculative long-range shots at incautious Englishmen who had ventured too close. The flanks of the Scottish position were protected by treacherous, broken ground, a marsh to one side, steep slopes on the other.

The only viable approach to the Scottish position was across a narrow field to the front of Flodden Edge. But any assault by that route would have been delivered straight into the teeth of the Scottish artillery. James's French officers clearly knew their job, and the Scottish King had every reason to welcome the English advance. His demonstration on behalf of France could now be brought to an even more satisfying climax than the mere burning and pillaging of some sorry and defenceless Border hamlets, and the slighting of some ageing fortresses. Surrey, it appeared, had only two options. He could assault the Scottish position, which would surely result in a repulse with heavy loss of life. If, instead, he chose not to fight, he could not stay in the field, for his army was

35 Hall, p. 102.
36 Hall, pp. 103–105.

hungry and out of beer. In this situation, with an invading army firmly planted on English soil, avoiding battle was tantamount to admitting defeat.

The first possible solution to this quandary that presented itself to Surrey seems to have rested upon James's reputation for chivalry. Rouge Croix was dispatched once more to the Scottish King. His message now hinted at surprise that the Scottish had not advanced to give battle, as they had agreed, and inquired whether the King 'of his noble courage would discende the hyll, where he laye and too give battayll', for his present position was 'no indifferent ground for twoo armyes too fighte'. But Surrey had misjudged his man. His sense of chivalry was tempered now with good sense and he would not throw away the advantage his position gave him in the name of fair play. Indeed, he would not even hear the words of Rouge Croix, sending a servant in his place, who told the English herald 'it besemed not an Earle, after that maner to handle a kynge'.[37]

Having failed to talk James out of his natural fortress, Surrey was in desperate straits. To withdraw was to hand James a painless but impressive victory: to have burned and looted at will, and then to have faced down the English army sent to defend the North. To attack was to invite destruction. If Surrey himself were to survive such a disaster, he would face the (possibly homicidal) wrath of his angry King. Yet the seventy-year-old veteran was not beaten yet; he had lived too long and fought too many battles for that. James had offered him two options. So he chose the third. James could still be manoeuvred from his position, if the English were to appear to his rear. Such a strategy required the English to march round the flank of the Scottish army. In doing so they would of course present their own flank to the Scots, and the army would be strung out over miles of countryside, fording a swollen river at one point. It was, to say the least, a risky venture.[38]

After conferring with his commanders, the Earl executed his daring plan. His army was to outflank the Scottish position, crossing the River Till, keeping James to their left. Having moved around the invader, the English army would cut behind it, placing twenty-six thousand men with bows and bills between the Scots and their homes. Of course this manoeuvre cut both ways, for Scotland, and the Tweed, would now lie to the English rear. Withdrawal would no longer be an option for either side. Surrey would force the Scots to fight, if not exactly on the ground of his choice, then at least not at the same disadvantage he would face if the English had had to try and carry Flodden Edge.

This was the plan in outline, but the manoeuvre was fraught with danger. It was a dismal, cold, drizzly day, with wet ground underfoot. The English had eaten the last of their rations for breakfast, washed down with water, for they had drunk the last of their beer two days before. It was five in the morning when

---

[37] Hall, p. 105.
[38] The plan may have been suggested to Surrey by his son, the Lord Admiral. Several historians have credited him with the strategy, although on what grounds is not altogether clear. See Howard, 'The Early Career of the 3rd Duke of Norfolk', p. 74.

they set out northwards. They would not eat again before battle was joined around four o'clock that afternoon.[39]

From his camp at Wooler Haugh, Surrey moved cautiously to Barmoor Wood, about two miles east of the Scottish field fortifications. Poor as the weather was, the English could not hide from the eyes of Scottish scourers. The best they could hope for was to disguise their motives. Where possible Surrey used the terrain to shield his force, at least partially, from view. As the English moved to Barmoor Wood they filed behind a low range of hills, whilst the Scots, straining their eyes through the steady drizzle, guessed at their destination. Scotland might have been the English objective, retaliation for the damage wrought by James's army. Alternatively, the English could have been heading for Berwick to revictual, a route which would have left James well content. If the English did not pick up the gauntlet he had thrown down, he could return to Scotland having fulfilled his duty to France and the victory would have been his, perhaps even the more satisfying for being almost bloodless.

He may have allowed the prospect of such a satisfactory outcome to his campaign to cloud his judgement as the English army lay strung out before him. Why provoke them to fight when quiescence might guarantee a victory? Had he known the Earl's intentions he may have acted sooner. The Admiral, with the vanguard and the artillery, was to proceed northwards, east of the Till, skirting Barmoor Wood. Passing both Ford and Etal castles, he was then to swing round westward and turn south, crossing the Till at Twizel Bridge, shortly before the confluence with the Tweed. From there he would march south, through an area of marsh, then onto Branxton Hill. Possession of that hill would place him directly to the rear of the Scottish army, which would have to abandon its trenches to meet the threat to its rear.

Surrey himself would be making for Branxton too, by a shorter, but more difficult, route. He, and Stanley's rearward, would be following his son's vanguard northwards, along the edge of Barmoor Wood, but would ford the Till south of Twizel Bridge. A westerly march through a boggy stretch of ground would place him on his son's right flank, hopefully as he crested Branxton Hill.

Unsure as to English intentions, the Scots initially watched, waited, but did little else. James was sure now that the English intended to burn and foray in the Scottish Marches. He sent his own Borderers out from Flodden Edge again, to put more English villages to the torch, but they steered clear of the English army. Doubtless the rival scourers of each army patrolled widely, and their paths must have crossed, but they seem to have kept each other at arm's length. Watching intently from the east end of Flodden Edge, it must have been about mid-morning that James learned that the Admiral had crossed Twizel Bridge immediately to the north of his position. Now the English objective must have been clearer. If James was still in any doubt. the danger he was in was now spelt out to him by one Giles Musgrave.

[39] Hall, *Henry the VIII*, vol. 1, p. 107.

Musgrave was an Englishman, a Border outlaw, one of that breed whose fluc-
tuating loyalties could be relied upon to provide an invading army with local
knowledge and intelligence. He guessed that the English were going to seize
Branxton, to cut James off from Scotland and 'to draw the scotis fra the hill'.[40]
Were the English to gain the summit of Branxton Hill they would have advantage of ground. So it now became imperative for the Scots to abandon their
present positions on Flodden Edge, to face about and occupy Branxton Hill
themselves. With the English vanguard still facing a lengthy trek over the
marshy ground of Palin's Burn, the Scots still had time on their side, and the
English might have found themselves fighting uphill yet.

The entire Scottish army was to about face and move onto Branxton Hill. The
artillery pieces were a priority. They would have to be dragged from their
entrenchments, over rough ground to a position from which they could dominate
the English advance. In the wake of the gunners and fighting men, the servants,
carters and teamsters also struck camp. The pavilions and tents came down and
the assorted detritus of the long occupation of Flodden Edge was piled up and
set alight. The primitive wood and branch huts which had housed the ordinary
Scottish soldiers were also torched at this time, for this was the custom of Highlanders and Borderers alike.[41] Despite the wet weather, the flames were soon
leaping high and the smoke from the fires would have been clearly visible to the
Admiral and his men, all of whom were now across Twizel Bridge, and moving
south in order of battle.

The Admiral's younger brother, Edmund Howard, led the way, followed by
the mass of the Admiral's battle, which was in turn shadowed by Marmaduke
Constable's wing. Behind them the gunners and their draught horses laboured to
keep up, hauling guns and munitions over some treacherous terrain. Ahead of
them figures could be seen forming up on Branxton Hill, but a fierce wind now
took hold of the smoke from the fires burning on Flodden Edge. A dense, black
billowing cloud rolled across Branxton and down the slope into the faces of the
English. Branxton was obscured from English view, but the Scottish scourers
fared no better; the smoke was equally impenetrable from their positions so that
'the one host could not perceyve the other'.[42] For half an hour the two armies
lost sight of each other.

Hidden from view, whether by accident or design, the Scots formed their
array of battle on Branxton Hill. There is here some disagreement amongst the
major sources over Scottish dispositions. All agree that the Scots did not form
up into the traditional three battles, vanguard, main battle and rearward. Instead,
like Surrey's army, and in line with recent continental practice, they formed into
a larger number of smaller units. Hall claims there were six Scottish battles, two
of which never came to handstrokes. This may have been because large numbers

---

[40] John Leslie, *The Historie of Scotland*, trans. James Dalrymple and ed. E.G.Cody and
W.Murison (Edinburgh, 1895), p. 145.
[41] Hall, *Henry the VIII*, vol. 1, p. 107, Elliot, *The Battle of Flodden*, pp. 49–50.
[42] Hall, p. 107, Holinshed, *Historie of Scotland*, p. 480.

of men (carters, gunners, servants, perhaps some of the less enthusiastic soldiery), continued to hover on Branxton Hill as battle was joined.[43] These may have looked like an unengaged battle, but there is little evidence that a formed body of Scottish troops failed to close with the English.

Most authorities follow the account of the Earl of Surrey, which speaks of five Scottish battles. On the extreme left of the Scottish line was a mixed battle of Borderers, armed with pikes, and Highlanders, armed with two-handed swords and axes. These were under the command of Lord Home and Alexander Gordon, Earl of Huntly. Some sources suggest that some of the Scottish Borderers remained on horseback here but they can only have been a very few.[44] To the right of Home and Huntly's battle was a second column of pikemen from Fife, Angus and Perthshire. This was led by William Hay, Earl of Errol, David Lindsey, Earl of Crawford, and William Graham, Earl of Montrose. In the centre of the Scottish line was the King's main battle. Here the monarch would lead his personal retinue with the levies of the western Lowlands. With them would be a large portion of the Scottish nobility, including the earls of Cassilis and Glencairn, Lords Herries and Maxwell and the King's own illegitimate son, Alexander Stuart, the 21-year-old Archbishop of St Andrews.

To the King's right Adam Hepburn, Earl of Bothwell, commanded the levies of Lothian. To their right, on the extreme right of the Scottish line, was the main body of Highlanders under Matthew Stewart, Earl of Lennox, and Archibald Campbell, Earl of Argyll. The whole army now numbered around thirty thousand, having continued to lose men to desertion. The battles each comprised about four or five thousand men with the exception of the King's main battle, which was perhaps nine thousand strong. Whilst still obscured by the smoke, the whole line must have extended right across Branxton Hill as they advanced.

The advance to battle

When the two armies regained contact at a distance of about a quarter of a mile the English vanguard was quick to recognise that it was in a perilous situation. With the Scottish battles drawn up along Branxton Hill, their line extended far beyond the left flank of the Admiral's battle, protected only by Constable's little wing. Aware that he might be enveloped by a Scottish advance, the Admiral desperately needed his father's battle to cover his left flank. To urge the Earl to the greatest possible urgency, the Admiral tore off the *Agnus Dei* badge that he wore on his breast and pressed it into the hands of a scourer, who galloped hard for Surrey's battle.

The English line of march was now forming into line of battle. On the right, opposite Home and Huntly's column was the young Edmund Howard, his little wing clearly outnumbered. Coming up on his left was the much larger vanguard

---

[43] Elliot, *The Battle of Flodden*, p. 102.
[44] Holinshed, *Historie of Scotland*, p. 481.

under the command of his older brother, the Admiral. Beyond that was Marmaduke Constable's wing. The force of mounted Borderers under Lord Dacre were spurring their sturdy hobblers on, riding to the support of the English right. The Earl of Surrey's main battle was squaring up to James's massive column and Bothwell's smaller unit to its flank. Away on the English left, pushing up towards Branxton Hill, were the levies of Lancashire and Cheshire under Stanley.

Having gained the crest of Branxton Hill and seeing the English still trooping into position below them the Scots hardly paused in their advance. With the wet ground slippery under foot many of the pikemen took off their shoes and 'faught in the vampis of their hoses' to keep their purchase.[45] Surrey later reported that the five Scottish battles were 'in grete plumpes, part of them quadrant', each 'an arrowe shotte from the othre'. They came on 'in good ordre, after the Almayns maner withoute spekyng of eny worde'.[46] In *La Rotta de Scocesi*, the battles are described as 'square' and 'shaped like pikes'. In this regular order and disciplined advance can be seen the influence of D'Aussi and his little corps of French officers, now distributed amongst the Scottish battles.[47]

With the English army still arriving piecemeal onto the field before him, James resolved to throw his powerful columns at their still unformed line, with he himself taking a prominent position in the front ranks. His decision to personally shoulder a pike and lead his battle against the English did not meet with universal approval:

> His capteins did what they could by words to remove him from his purpose, declaring to him the dutie of a prince: which is not rashlie to enter the fight, but to provide and see that evreie thing be doone in order: and whereas comming to trie the matter by hand blowes, he can doo no more than another man; yet keeping his place as apperteineth to his person, he may be worth manie thousands of others.[48]

Yet James was unmoved by such words. He knew full well where a King's place in battle was, at the head of his subjects.[49] The Spanish ambassador to Scotland, Pedro De Ayala, had recognised this tendency in 1497:

---

[45] David Laing (ed.), 'The Trewe Encountre or Batayle Lately Don Betwene Englande and Scotlande: In Which Batayle The Scotsshe Kynge was Slayne', *Proceedings of the Society of Antiquaries of Scotland*, vol. 7 (1866–68), p. 150.

[46] Henry James (ed.), 'Articules of the bataille bitwix the Kynge of Scottes and therle of Surrey in Brankstone felde the 9 day of September', in Henry James (ed.), *Facsimiles of National Manuscripts from William the Conqueror to Queen Anne*, Part 2 (Southampton, 1865), p. 2.

[47] *LandP, Henry VIII*, vol. 1, 4441, *La Rotta de Scocesi*, in William Mackay MacKenzie, *The Secret of Flodden* (Edinburgh, 1931) p. 29.

[48] Holinshed, *Historie of Scotland*, p. 481.

[49] At the Battle of the Spurs, Henry VIII 'woulde fayne have been afore wyth the horssemen, but hys counsayll perswaded hym the contrarye, and so he taryed wyth the footmen', Hall, *Henry the VIII*, vol. 1, p. 85.

He is courageous, even more than a king should be. I have seen him often undertake most dangerous things in the last wars . . . He is not a good captain, because he begins to fight before he has given his orders. He said to me that his subjects serve him with their persons and goods, in just and unjust quarrel, exactly as he likes, and that therefore he does not think it right to begin any warlike undertaking without being the first in danger.[50]

Now James took his own place in the leading rank of his battle once again. 'O what a noble and triumphant courage was thys for a kynge to fyghte in a battayl as a meane souldier', wrote the admiring Edward Hall.

As the infantry advanced, 'oute brast the ordinaunce on bothe sydes wyth fyre flamme and hydeous noise'.[51] At the first shot of the Scottish guns a number of Tynmouth and Bamboroughshire Borderers assigned to Dacre's command fled the field, but this was Borthwick's only success.[52] Attempting to fire downhill, the Scottish guns appear to have done little real damage. According to the Scottish historian John Leslie, 'our bullets . . . did thame na hurt, bot flewe ouer thair heidis'.[53] English cannon balls, on the other hand, smashed into the Scottish pike columns. The effect of this fire was 'to breke and constreyn the Scottisshe great army', compelling them to hasten their advance and disrupting the order of their pike formations.[54]

The battle at handstrokes would be joined sequentially, west to east, the vanguards engaging first, then the main battles, then the rearwards. Home and Huntly's column led the Scottish onslaught, plunging down the slope of Branxton Hill. In their path was Edmund Howard and fifteen hundred Cheshire and Lancashire men who, although wont to follow a Stanley to war, now found themselves under the command of a Howard and in the path of a ferocious assault.

The English line began to waver. Anxious eyes cast around, from the sight of the oncoming Scottish column to that of Dacre's Bamboroughshire Borderers, with their horses' hooves flying and their backs to the enemy. Leigh of Baggerley, writing to exonerate the behaviour of his Cheshire fellows, is quick to blame the unfortunate young Edmund Howard for the ensuing débâcle, claiming his men lacked trust in him and broke 'for wante of their captayne'.[55] It was not the young nobleman, however, who lacked courage. Edmund Howard stood his ground, whilst those about him turned and fled. Wielding his pole-axe with furious desperation, he was soon alone apart from his standard bearer and two faithful servants. The standard bearer was the first to die, 'betten and hewed to peces'.[56] A tempting prize for the man who could capture him and secure his

---

50 R.L.Mackie, *King James IV of Scotland* (Edinburgh, 1958), p. 84.
51 Hall, *Henry the VIII*, vol. 1, p. 108.
52 *LandP, Henry VIII*, vol. 1, 4520
53 Leslie, *Historie of Scotland*, p. 145.
54 'Trewe Encountre', pp. 147–148, Holinshed, *Historie of Scotland*, p. 481.
55 Leigh of Baggerley, 'Scotish Feilde', in Ian Baird (ed.), *Scotish Feilde and Flodden Feilde, Two Flodden Poems* (London, 1982), lines 265–271, 331–332, 336.
56 'Trewe Encountre', p. 148.

ransom, Howard was quickly surrounded. Three times he was knocked to the ground and three times he fought his way back to his feet. And then, at the head of Dacre's charging Border horse, came salvation in the shape of John the Bastard of Heron.[57]

The timely arrival of Dacre's light horse undoubtedly stabilised the right wing of the English army and prevented it from being outflanked. Fifteen hundred strong, the Borderers had charged with sufficient force to halt the Scottish advance, many of whom had broken off the fight to search for plunder.[58] Heron, at some point 'sore wounded' and pitched from his horse, fought his way through to Edmund Howard, announcing that 'never noble mans sone so lyke too be loste as you be this day, for all my hurtes I shall here lyve and dye wyth you'. Shoulder to shoulder, 'in great daunger and jeopardy of lyfe', they hacked their way to the Admiral's battle and safety. Sir David Home, the Scottish Chamberlain's brother, made one last attempt to capture the young English noble, but Howard struck him dead as he blocked his path.[59] The young noble was safe, and the English flank was now secure. Dacre, 'like a good and hardy knight', had saved the English from disaster.[60]

Whilst the fighting on the extreme right wing died down, Montrose and Crawford's column now smashed into the Admiral's battle. The clash here was bloody and hard. A grim and merciless slogging match developed, for the Admiral seemed determined to make good his promise. He did not ask for, and he did not give, quarter. Not content with merely holding his ground, the Admiral had his men beat down the outstretched pikes and fought their way into the Scottish column. The blades of English bills rose and fell as they hacked their way forward. The Scots, including both Montrose and Crawford, died rather than yield ground:

> You saw so many weapons lowered that it seemed as if a wood were falling down; more folk at once move downwards than the leaves scattered in October. And already so much blood flowed that the air and not the plain only was stained. Great pity indeed it was to see so much blood and so many men falling.[61]

---

[57] The Bastard Heron was the half brother of William Heron, Lord of Ford Castle. He and two others had murdered Sir Robert Kerr, the Warden of the Scottish Middle March, in 1508. Fleeing justice, Heron had disappeared. Anxious to preserve the precarious peace in the North, Henry VII had John's unfortunate brother William surrendered to the Scots in his stead. He languished in an undeserved captivity until, as noted above, his wife negotiated his release. Rumour had it that John had died of the plague in 1511, but James IV was not convinced. Indeed he made the unsettled business one of his *causa belli* in 1513. Since appeasing Scotland was no longer an English priority, John had emerged from hiding and offered his expert services to a grateful Earl of Surrey. See Hodgkin, 'The Battle of Flodden', pp. 15–16.
[58] The Lord Admiral gives Dacre's strength as fifteen hundred men in his 'Gazette of the Battle of Flodden', reprinted in Appendix 1 in Elliot, *The Battle of Flodden*. Elliot himself suggests that Dacre's whole wing, three thousand strong, might have charged.
[59] Hall, *Henry the VIII*, vol. 1, p. 108.
[60] 'Trewe Encountre', p. 148.
[61] *La Rotta de Scocesi*, p. 34.

In the close press of the mêlée the bill-armed English had a distinct advantage over the Scots armed with the unwieldy pike. Once the pike columns failed to break their enemies with their first shock of impact they became locked in close combat against men armed with a lighter and handier weapon.[62] Many of the Scots chose to cast their cumbersome weapons aside. A Northumbrian in the English ranks recalled 'when thair speres failed and wer spent, then they fought with great and sharp swerdes . . .', yet this, ironically, would leave them outreached by the long-shafted English bill.[63] Wherever English and Scot came to handstrokes on this day, the pikemen would consequently be held at a fatal disadvantage.

Nowhere would this situation be clearer than on the Admiral's left, where now Surrey's battle collided with the King's. For James found 'the Englishmen not fleeing, but manfullie standing at resistance, so that there was a right hard incounter'.[64] Once again they would rely on their bills, for their bows had failed to stop the Scottish advance. There is ample testimony to the volume of arrows loosed by English archers as the Scots advanced towards them, but they seem to have had little effect. A flurry of rain had soaked their bow strings and they were now firing into the wind, both factors which must have seriously impaired the performance of the longbow in action.[65] Nevertheless, many arrows struck their targets, but the heavily armoured front ranks of the Scottish formations seemed largely impervious. According to Hall, the Scottish front ranks were; 'all chosen men with speres on foote . . . the most assuredlyest harnesed that hath bene sene' and they 'abode the most dangerous shot of arrowes, which sore them noyed, and yet it hit them in some bare place it dyd them no hurt'.[66] Bishop Ruthal noted the same thing: 'the said Scotes wer so surely harnessed with complete harneys, jackes, almayn ryvettes, splents, pavices and other habilments that shote of arrowes in regarde did thaim no harme'.[67]

The leading ranks of the King's battle, including James himself, fought ferociously, almost pushing their way to within striking distance of the banners that marked the centre of the English line. Here the fight was joined with bill, pike, sword, maul and two-handed axe. The fighting escalated as Bothwell's Lothian levies charged into the fray. Surrey's Englishmen, centred on the five hundred tough soldiers of his personal retinue, clung tenaciously to their ground, rallying to the cry of 'St Cuthbert!' Bill heads rose and fell, swords and pikes thrust forward, the battle hung in the balance. A Northumbrian soldier remembered:

> It is not to be doubted, but the Scotts faught manly, and were determynned outthir to wynne the ffield or to dye, they wer also as well appointed as was

62 *LandP, Henry VIII*, vol. 1, 4461.
63 'Trewe Encountre', p. 151.
64 Holinshed, *Historie of Scotland*, p. 481.
65 'Trewe Encountre', p. 150.
66 Hall, *Henry the VIII*, vol. 1, p. 109.
67 'Thomas Ruthal, Bishop of Durham, To Almoner Wolsey', in James (ed.), *Facsimiles of National Manuscripts*, Part 2, pp. 3–8, *LandP, Henry VIII*, vol. 1, 4461.

possible at all points with armes and harnes, soe that few of thaim wer slaine
with arrowes, how be it the billes did beat and hew thaim downe with some
paine and daunger to Englisshmen.[68]

The scales were tipping slowly against the Scottish King. The Admiral's
battle had continued its remorseless advance. The last remnants of Crawford and
Montrose's column were hacked down. Having pushed their way forward, the
Admiral's battle fell on the now exposed left flank of the King's battle. Some
even worked their way behind James's formation, enveloping the main Scottish
force. The mass of Scottish soldiers must have been compressed by the fresh
onslaught on their flank and rear. Those at the back of the column may have
chosen to make their escape as they saw the Admiral's men closing on them, but
most were caught between the anvil of Surrey's battle, and the hammer of the
Admiral's onslaught. The tightly packed ranks of heavily armoured men would
have found it increasingly hard to thrust or swing their weapons, whilst two or
three English billmen might have been able to take it in turns to strike at individual men-at-arms. Yet it was a slow, grim business. 'Whenne it comme to hande
strokes of billes and halberds they wer so myghtie, large, strong and grete men
that they wolde not fall whenne 4 or 5 billes strake on oon of thaym at oonys',
wrote Ruthal.[69] There could be no escape though, and the end, even for the
strongest, was inevitable. 'We blanked them with billes through all their bright
armor', sang the Cheshire balladeer, Leigh of Baggerley.[70]

Succour might have come from the Scottish forces on the flanks. But on the
right Home's column was curiously inactive. Pitscottie claims that Huntly tried
to persuade Home to move to rescue the King, but Home refused, saying 'He
dois well that dois for him self; we have faught our vanguard alreddie and win
the samin thairfore lat the laif do thair part as we.'[71] However accurate Pitscottie's allegations may be, it is unlikely that Home could have rallied all of his
scattered men, even had he wanted to. Once they had routed Edmund Howard's
command, many had turned their attention to gathering booty. Furthermore,
Dacre and his mounted Borderers continued to hover nearby, covering the
Admiral's flank.

Hall, with a characteristic southern prejudice, alleges that Dacre took no part
in the fighting at all.[72] This ignores his decisive contribution early in the fighting, following the collapse of Edmund Howard's wing. After that, however, a
stand-off seems to have developed on the English right flank between Home's
battle, depleted by those who had deserted in search of plunder, but still largely
intact, and Dacre's Border horse. Whatever slurs were later cast on Dacre's
conduct, his role was vital. By shielding the Admiral's battle he allowed it first

[68] 'Trewe Encountre', p. 150.
[69] 'Thomas Ruthal, Bishop of Durham, To Almoner Wolsey', in James (ed.), *Facsimiles of National Manuscripts*, Part 2, p. 6, *LandP, Henry VIII*, vol. 1, 4461.
[70] *Scotish Feilde*, lines 329–330.
[71] Pitscottie, *Historie*, pp. 271–272.
[72] Hall, *Henry the VIII*, vol. 1, p. 112.

to sweep Montrose and Crawford from the field and then to envelop the King's column.

Away on the east of the battlefield were Lennox and Argyle's Highlanders. They, too, might have moved to support the King if their advance had not been blocked by the Lancastrian and Cheshire levies of the English rearward: 'Sir Edward Stanley . . . seing the fourth batelles redy to releiff the said King of Scottes batell, coragiously and like a lusty and an hardy knyght, did sett upon the same'.[73] Their engagement was to be the final stage of the fighting. The Highlanders had not followed the lead of their King in a headlong charge against the English. Their advance had been altogether more cautious and they were still on Branxton Hill when Stanley's men began to scramble up the slope towards them. It was a difficult, slippery climb, but the Northerners hauled themselves up to the crest of the hill. The Highlanders appear to have been in some disorder, with their leaders once again to the fore, once again the first to fall. It has been suggested that, in contrast to the pike columns, the lightly armoured Highlanders were very vulnerable to Cheshire and Lancashire bows. For whatever reason, they put up little resistance.[74] Stanley's battle swept quickly forward, killing those who stood their ground before them. Argyll, Lennox and their most prominent chiefs dead, the Highlanders scattered, pursued by the victorious Northerners.

The pursuit did not last long. The battle had not begun until four in the afternoon. It was dark now, and the English were weary and hungry. They fell to plundering the dead and looting the Scottish camp. The author of the *Trewe Encounter* recalled finding 'mych good stuff . . . plenty of wyne, bere, aill, beiff, multon, salt fissh, cheis and other vitailles necessary and counvenyent for such a great army'. But he and his fellows would not touch it, believing that 'the said vitailles had bene poisonned for thair destruction'. Others were less cautious. The soldiers of Bishop Ruthal's Durham contingent found Scottish beer to be surprisingly good, and it was drunk 'by our folks to their great refreshing'.[75] Stanley's men began to move across the battlefield from the former Scottish positions on Branxton Hill, rifling the dead as they went.[76]

In the darkness the outcome of the battle remained a mystery, and the English do not appear to have realised that the field was theirs for some time. There was no pursuit, nor sense of triumph. James's fate was unknown and Surrey's troops remained on their feet all night, unsure whether the Scots had retired completely or lurked somewhere in the darkness. Home, commanding the only unbroken

---

73 'Trewe Encountre', pp. 148–149. The anonymous author, who was certainly present at the battle, counts four Scottish battles rather than the five claimed by Surrey. This may be because, once the battle was joined, the King's and Bothwell's battles fought effectively as one.

74 Oman, *Art of War in the Sixteenth Century*, p. 316.

75 *LandP, Henry VIII*, vol. 1, 4461.

76 'Ms. Batayle', in G. Gregory Smith (ed.), *The Days of James IV, 1488–1513* (London, 1900), pp. 158–160.

body of Scottish troops left on the field, seems to have retreated carefully under cover of darkness, although elements of his command remained in the immediate vicinity, still searching for plunder.

It must have been a terrifying night. The main body of the English arranged around their Earl, weapons poised, lashed by wind and rain, eyes and ears straining, whilst scattered groups of men, English and Scots, roamed the field, robbing the dead and finishing off the wounded. In the grey half light of dawn, a scene of quite unimaginable horror presented itself to the survivors. The slopes of Branxton were carpeted with Scottish dead. At the point of their furthest penetration into the English position, just yards from where the Earl of Surrey had stood, Thomas Lord Dacre found the body of the Scottish King, wounded by longbow arrows, killed by bill strokes.[77] Nearby lay the body of his son, the scholarly, short-sighted Alexander, Erasmus's favourite and most gifted pupil, all his promise now wasted. The English could not doubt the scale of their victory. To crown it all was the sight of James's magnificent artillery train on Branxton Edge, muzzles pointing defiantly towards the English, but silent, unguarded and abandoned.[78]

Aftermath

Most of the survivors had fled north across the Tweed, covered by Home's still intact battle, which was now Scotland's main guardian against English invasion. The survivors do not appear to have left the battlefield in rout or flight. Most had filed away from Branxton Edge some time between nightfall and the early hours of the morning. Some had been able to take with them booty from the looted English baggage train, or even prisoners from Edmund Howard's unfortunate command. This suggests that the retreat was orderly and not pressured.

Later the English were to claim that only lack of horses had prevented them

[77] Hall, *Henry the VIII*, vol. 1, p. 112. For the identification of Thomas, Lord Dacre, as the man who found the King's body, see *LandP, Henry VIII*, vol. 1, 5090. A shocked Scotland was slow to come to terms with the death of their 'stout, just and devout King', and many rumours circulated that he had escaped the field. John Leslie wrote that 'our King was seine that nycht in Kelso hail and sound' and had ended his days a simple pilgrim in the Holy Land. He acknowledges, though, that similar tales were told of Frederic Barbarossa in Germany and of King Arthur amongst the Welsh. Perhaps the tale that is most indicative of the Scottish mood after the battle was the widespread rumour that James had escaped the English only to be murdered by Alexander Home. See Leslie, *Historie of Scotland*, p. 146.

[78] Most of the English sources maintain that the Scots were routed from the field the previous evening and that this was known to the English. Scottish sources, such as Pitscottie, tend to suggest that the outcome of the battle was not known until the following morning. On this point they seem the more reliable, for the English would certainly have noticed the abandoned guns if the field had been won before sunset on the evening of the battle. For a good discussion of this point see Elliot, *Battle of Flodden*, pp. 105–111.

from pursuing and decimating the Scottish army as it left the field.[79] Yet the English did have horses. Not all of them could have been stolen from the horse lines, and Dacre's command on the battlefield itself had been mounted. The truth would seem to be that by the time the English realised that the field was theirs, their quarry had already slipped away.[80] Even then, the English must have been cold, hungry and exhausted, in no condition to follow up their victory. Ruthal saw the opportunity 'but suche capitayns and souldiers as wer at this businesse in mervoulous fowle wethyre, lackyng mete and drynke, which have also lost thayr horses and goodes, had lever dye then to cumme theyr agayn'.[81]

The morning after the battle, as the Admiral surveyed the field, a body of Scots reappeared, probably originally from Home's undefeated battle, perhaps looking to recover their guns or avenge their King. Their appearance seems to have caught the English by surprise, for Hall says that the Admiral's life was momentarily in jeopardy. Yet the battle did not recommence. English artillery fired on the die-hard band and the last remnants of the Scottish army withdrew from the field. The remnants of the Scottish army were greeted with reproach and anger as they struggled north. 'At their comming home, everie man spake evill of them, for that as cowards and naughtie persons, they neither sought to revenge the death of their noble king, nor yet to succour their fellowes that were beaten downe and slaine before their faces.'

The object of most reproof was Lord Home, whose battle had failed to come to the aid of his King, 'which behaved himselfe not as a capteine, but as a traitor or enimie to his countrie'.[82] In retrospect there can be little doubt but that Home had acted wisely. Had he thrown his battle into the fray again, it would undoubtedly have suffered the same fate as the rest of the army. As it was it was probably only nightfall that had allowed him to retreat in order. Alive, his Borderers could defend their homes; dead they would only have increased the magnitude of Scotland's losses.

The most conservative estimate of Scottish dead was around five thousand, the true figure was probably closer to ten thousand. The men who had stood in the front ranks had invariably paid the highest price. Of the twenty-one earls on the Scottish peerage roll of 1513, eleven fought at Flodden. Only one, the Earl of Huntly, escaped with his life. Similarly, thirteen barons died that day and a host of masters (eldest sons) of prominent houses and their younger brothers and cousins. Little thought had been given to ransom. Ruthal noted that:

Our folkes entending to make all thing sure, toke little regarde in taking of prisoners, but rid all that came to hande, bothe King, bisshopes, lordes, knyghtes, nobles, or others what so ever came which wer not so soon slayn but

---

[79] 'Articules of the bataille bitwix the Kynge of Scottes and therle of Surrey in Brankstone felde the 9 day of September', p. 4.
[80] William Murray, 'Flodden: Before and After', *Transactions of the Hawick Archaeological Society* (1913), p. 41.
[81] 'Thomas Ruthal, Bishop of Durham, To Almoner Wolsey', p. 8.
[82] Holinshed, *Historie of Scotland*, p. 482.

forthewith dispoiled out of their harnais and array and lefte lying naked in the feld.[83]

In fact just four hundred Scots were taken alive. Presumably they had been fortunate enough not to be in the path of the Admiral's battle. The intensity of the fighting had left few inclined to mercy. As the author of the *Trewe Encountre* put it:

> Many othir Scotissh presoners couth and myght have been taken but thay wer soe vengeable and cruell in thair feightyng that when Englisshmen had the better of thaim thay wold not save thaim, though it soe wer that dyvers Scottes offerd great somes of money for thair lyves.[84]

Despite the prolonged engagement at handstrokes, the victorious army had suffered far less than the Scots. Between 100 and 120 Englishmen were captured when Edmund Howard's wing collapsed at the outset of the battle.[85] Hall, basing his estimate on the 'book of wages by which the soldiours were paid', suggested that the total of English dead was fifteen hundred. Given the advantage the bill enjoyed over the pike, once the initial shock of impact had been withstood, and the fact that the main body of the Scottish army had been enveloped, this is a not unlikely figure. Spanish sword and bucklers, it will be remembered, inflicted similar carnage on *Landsknecht* pike at Ravenna.

Besides their dead, the Scots had suffered a considerable material loss as well. Their fine train of ordnance, abandoned forlornly on Branxton Hill, now fell into English hands. Hall records the capture of 'fyve great Curtalls, twoo great culverynges, foure sacres, and syxe Serpentynes as fayre ordinaunce as hathe bene beside other small peces'. The captured artillery was conveyed first to the slighted castle at Etal, where it remained for several days. On 20 September Ruthal expressed fears that the Scots might actually recover their lost guns. This would indicate that, despite the magnitude of their defeat, there were still Scottish forces at large in the Till valley.[86] In all probability these forces were composed of Home's Borderers, monitoring the movements of Surrey's army and looking for a chance to commit some mischief to keep the English off balance. Recapturing the lost guns would have been quite a stroke and one can imagine shadowy horsemen tailing nervous English carters and their escort as the trophies were finally hauled to Berwick.

The capture of these trophies, much trumpeted by the English, and the loss of life on the Scottish side, particularly the death of the King and many leading nobles, seems to have been victory enough for Surrey. He chose not to follow up his success with an invasion of Scotland and instead disbanded his weary army. The weather was worsening and it would have proved impossible to victual a

---

[83] 'Thomas Ruthal, Bishop of Durham, To Almoner Wolsey', p. 6, *LandP, Henry VIII*, vol. 1, 4461.
[84] 'Trewe Encountre', p. 150.
[85] 'Thomas Ruthal, Bishop of Durham, To Almoner Wolsey', p. 6.
[86] Elliot, *Battle of Flodden*, p. 135.

large army in the field for much longer. Yet the war was not yet over. Scotland had every reason to fear that the English might invade, and steps were hastily taken to meet the expected onslaught. Whilst Home covered the passage into Scotland at Coldstream, one of his able adherents, Andrew Kerr of Ferniehurst, garrisoned Kelso Abbey, commanding an important bridge across the Tweed.[87] Further north, the citizens of Edinburgh itself prepared to defend their city, building a new defensive wall, well provided with gun loops. Everywhere the population stood to arms, relaxing only gradually as it became apparent that the threatened invasion would not materialise.

The raids of 1513–1514

The English had decided instead to pursue a policy of large destructive raids into Scotland to capitalise on their victory, and the main burden of defence would fall on Home and his Borderers. On the English side, Lord Dacre was entrusted with taking fire and sword to the Scottish Marches. In the wake of their victory the English might have expected to dominate the ensuing Border war, but there is much evidence to suggest that the Scots held their own. They certainly had not been cowed by defeat. Several Englishmen had fallen into Scottish hands when Edmund Howard's little vanguard had broken in the opening stages of the battle. Dacre had been negotiating with Home for their release but found himself 'sore chafed and encumbered with the Scots', who demanded extravagant ransoms for their prisoners. His plans were further hampered by the weather, heavy rain frustrating his desire to foray across the Border in late September.[88]

Dacre's own preference was for small raids, fast moving forays against farms and towers, burning crops, driving off livestock, seizing hostages. This kind of conflict was second nature to most Borderers, but Henry, now back in England, wanted altogether larger operations. Dacre agreed to launch two large raids, one into the West March, another into the Middle March, as soon as the weather allowed. These were to be co-ordinated with a third raid into the East March by the men of the Durham bishopric. The raids were to be, at least partly, financed by the Crown, Dacre receiving 1000 marks for his services. Yet the cost of waging continuing war would fall most heavily on individual lords and the counties recently wasted by the fighting. Preparations for the larger raids were therefore hesitant.

In the meantime, between 10 and 15 October, four smaller forays were run into Teviotdale and three into Annandale, apparently the first English incursions into Scotland in the wake of their victory at Flodden. Dacre remained uneasy about the execution of large-scale raids, and about the burden of responsibility

---

[87] Elliot, pp. 133–134.
[88] *LandP, Henry VIII*, vol. 1, 4497.

that was being placed upon him personally. Particularly, he felt unable to command effectively raids made from the East March, and he reminded the King of how badly he had been served by the Tynemouth and Bamboroughshire Borderers at Flodden. He suggested instead that Lord Darcy, the King's officer in Bamboroughshire, would be better placed to lead these men in the planned foray in the east.[89]

In fact Darcy seems never to have carried out this raid at all and Dacre's own 'Great Raid', finally crossing the Border on 10 November, met with mixed fortunes. Two English forces were involved. Lord Dacre himself led one thousand horsemen across the Border at Gallespeth in Northumberland. To the west his brother, Sir Christopher Dacre, led a larger force, two thousand horse and four thousand bows, to Kershopefoot and from there into the Scottish Middle March through Liddesdale. The main objective of this giant pincer movement seems to have been Jedburgh, with the raiders to burn and foray as they went. Two parties of three hundred men, under Philip Dacre and Roger Fenwick, briefly detached from Lord Dacre's force to torch Ruecastle and Lanton.

Yet Dacre was already aware that his force was too small to execute his planned designs on Jedburgh. He had been badly let down by some of the gentlemen of the North. Prominent amongst these was Lord Ogle, the Constable of Alnwick, who had promised support but had not arrived at the muster. Indeed, Dacre had been advised at this point to abandon his raid altogether, but he had no time to warn his brother to call off his foray. So, for his brother's sake, he had ventured north with an undersized force. Such trepidation suggests the Scottish Border country was still well capable of defending itself, and this soon proved to be the case.

The night they crossed the Border the English had seen the Scottish warning beacons burning brightly and knew that Home and the men he had saved at Flodden would be quick to respond. After burning Ruecastle and Lanton, Dacre soon found himself heavily engaged, pursued south to the Scalter Ford on the water of Bowset, where the English and Scots 'bickered' at handstrokes. Whilst the mêlée was in progress, seven hundred more Scottish reinforcements arrived under the command of David Kerr of Ferniehurst, the Laird of Bonjedward and Sheriff of Teviotdale. With the defenders converging their forces so quickly, the English raiders were hard-pressed to make their escape.

Now outnumbered, Dacre's horse would have been in desperate straits but for a timely stroke of luck: 'And so we came forward where we saw my brother, Sir Christopher Dacre, with his host arrayed at a place called the Bellyng, which was to us no little comfort and to him a great gladness seeing the small power we were of at that time.'[90] Sir Christopher had so far met less resistance than his brother. Two large forays of five hundred men had broken off from his command and, led by Sir John Ratclif and Nicholas Haryngton, had gathered in a consider-

---

[89] *LandP, Henry VIII*, vol. 1, 4497, 4518, 4520.
[90] Henry Ellis (ed.), *Original Letters Illustrative of English History*, 1st series, vol. 1 (London, 1824), p. 94.

able amount of booty and lifted livestock. The raiding parties having rejoined Sir Christopher at Dykeraw, the whole force had then met with Dacre's beleaguered command. This had momentarily tipped the balance of forces in favour of the English. Relief, however, was short lived, for Home himself now arrived, bringing with him another two thousand men. The English renewed their retreat, driving their stolen livestock before them. They were pursued back into England by Home and his Borderers, who had conducted an admirable defence of their country.[91]

The most important lesson of the failure of the 'Great Raid' was that Flodden had not left the Scottish Borderers prostrate before the victorious English. Despite the accusations of treachery that were levelled at Home by his countrymen, his good sense at Flodden had saved the lives of the men who had now chased Dacre out of Scotland. The accusations about Home's suspect loyalties continued to fly. For example, he was held to account for failing to stop the English refortifying Norham. Finally these charges, and the even more ludicrous allegation that he himself had murdered James IV in the aftermath of Flodden, were used to justify Home's execution in October 1516 by Scotland's Regent, the Duke of Albany.

Yet it is clear that Home continued to pose a real threat to the English Marches in the months after Flodden, preventing the English from capitalising on their victory. Reporting to the King after his return from the 'Great Raid', Dacre wrote, 'I dare not be absent of this Middle March during this light for fere the Scotts schold distroye and burne the countrie in myn absence.'[92] In the spring of 1514 there were fears for the security of Berwick itself, with extra gunners and soldiers being dispatched to make up for a shortfall in its garrison.[93] Dacre himself was becoming increasingly discouraged. Like Home in Scotland, he was the subject of ill founded rumours about his loyalty. It would seem that both English and Scots held their compatriots from the Border country in low esteem and Dacre, for all his service, was not spared their malice.

Although the Crown was paying him a pitifully small wage for his services as Warden, Dacre had not shirked in his duty, and now, prompted by Ruthal and Wolsey, the King sent him letters of personal encouragement and support.[94] Dacre could now at least pursue his own favoured policy of small, fast moving raids into Scotland, which he believed to be the most effective means of waging war in the Marches. Yet he was still not able to assert any kind of ascendancy over the Scottish Borderers themselves. By May 1514 he found himself having to defend his record, both of taking the war to the Scots and of preventing the Scots themselves from raiding into England. Revealingly, he does not deny the presence of Scottish raiders south of the Tweed, but argues that his own meagre

[91] Ellis, pp. 92–99. Elliot, *Battle of Flodden*, pp. 143–166.

[92] Ellis, p. 97.

[93] *LandP, Henry VIII*, vol. 1, 4868.

[94] *LandP, Henry VIII*, vol. 1, 4523, Steven Ellis, 'A Border Baron and the Tudor State: The Rise and Fall of Lord Dacre of the North', *The Historical Journal*, vol. 35 (1992), p. 260.

resources as a 'poor baron' had prevented him from guarding the frontier as effectively as might have been wished and that others had been loathe to contribute to the defence of the country.

War of raid and counter-raid seems to have raged on both sides of the Border throughout 1514. Dacre claimed in his defence that he had done far more damage to the Scots than they had to England:

> for oone cattell taken by the Scotts, we have takyn, won, and brought awey out of Scotland 100; and for oone shepe, 200 of a surity . . . I assure your Lordships for truthe that I have, and hes caused to be, burnt and distroyed sex times moo townys and howsys, within the West and Middill Marchies of Scotland, in the same season then is done to us.[95]

Whatever the balance sheet of stolen livestock and burnt homes really was, the on-going conflict brought misery to both sides of the Border and no clear-cut advantage to either nation.

Conclusions

The invader had been crushed at Flodden, but the English had not been able to convert this victory into even the most fleeting dominance in the Border country. The single most important factor seems to have been the successful withdrawal by Lord Home of his battle from the field and his subsequent organisation of the defence of the Scottish Marches. In the small-scale Border war that followed Flodden the Scots held their own, either riding south themselves to steal and burn or catching English raiding parties and putting them to flight. Such considerations should not be allowed to downplay the significance of the English victory at Flodden. England had been defended successfully but, even in the face of disaster, Scotland had proved remarkably resilient and would prove so again.

In military terms, James IV's attempts to modernise his army had been to no avail. His ordnance had been disadvantaged by terrain, denied its opportunity to dominate the battle by Surrey's clever manoeuvring to Branxton. This point emphasises the limitations inherent in the use of artillery in the field in the early sixteenth century. Used *en masse*, in a prepared and defensible position, such as James had established initially on Flodden Edge, gunpowder artillery was a potent weapon. However, once James was forced to abandon his prepared position and fight what was essentially an offensive battle, his cannon were too clumsy and too awkward to have a major influence on the outcome of the engagement. Indeed the experience of the Scottish gunners at Flodden mirrors closely Machiavelli's expectations of gunpowder artillery's limited effectiveness in open battle.

---

[95] Elliot, *Battle of Flodden*, p. 219.

Once he was manoeuvred from his prepared position, and could no longer rely on a defence based around the fire-power of his cannon, James was forced to alter his tactics dramatically, from a defensive posture to an aggressive one. His army was composed primarily of pike-armed infantry and contemporary tactical thought required that pike columns be used offensively. The infantry columns seem to have begun their advance with discipline and order but, having failed to break the English on first impact, could make no headway against a stubborn defence. The Scottish adoption of pike columns on the continental model had not yet provided them with an answer to the challenge posed by English bows and bills.

The Scottish had not been particularly disorganised or foolish at Flodden. They had merely employed a tactical system which had worked well on many continental battlefields, but which fared less well against the English, who were armed with staff-weapons of their own and who had a strong tradition of standing their ground in battle. Some culpability for the defeat, though, must be attached to James IV, particularly to his decision to take his place in the front rank of the assault. This may have been a suitable station for a warrior king, but it was no place for a commander. Once committed to the attack, the Scottish army was effectively leaderless, far less able to respond to changing circumstance than the English. When disaster had threatened the English right early in the battle, Dacre's swift intervention had stabilised the situation. When the Admiral's battle ploughed forward, the bulk of the Scottish army allowed itself to be first outflanked and then enveloped. There was no systematic attempt to manoeuvre or redeploy in the face of this danger. There was nobody in a position to give the commands necessary to attempt such a feat. The Scottish pikemen merely stood their ground and were hacked down where they stood. The Scots, however, would not give up on the experiment. They were now committed to the pike and would once again seek instruction from French officers, experienced in continental wars, and to rebuild their lost artillery train.

Future English developments would follow the precedents set by the modern army that accompanied Henry to France, rather than the bow and bill formations which had won at Flodden. This, though, was no discredit to the northern levies of 1513. Whatever imperfections marred the shire levy, it had performed admirably in the crisis. Responding quickly to invasion, it had mustered with speed and efficiency. Cold, hungry and wet, it had faced a formidable invading army and won a complete victory. For all the vain young King's posturing in France, for all his expensive mercenaries and fearsome artillery, the most important battle of his reign was fought and won by a seventy-year-old veteran of the Wars of the Roses and his army of northern yeomen.

CHAPTER FOUR

WAR ON THE BORDER, 1520–1547

Anglo-Scots relations during the regency of Albany

THE DEATH OF James IV at Flodden had left Scotland with a 17-month-old King, James V. The nation faced the prospect of a long and turbulent minority, the competition for power commencing almost immediately. The King's 24-year-old widow, Queen Margaret, chose an ill considered union with the ambitious Archibald Douglas, 6th Earl of Angus. Their marriage on 6 August 1514 precipitated a crisis, for the Douglases had many enemies. In an effort to wrest power from Angus, Scotland's nobility turned to the heir presumptive, the dead King's cousin, and invited him to take up the position of Governor.

John Stuart, Duke of Albany, had lived in France for over thirty years, since the age of three. He spoke little Scots or English and was reluctant to return to his native land. He went only at the behest of his King, Francis I, in order to oust the pro-English faction of Queen Margaret and Angus. With the initial support of the majority of Scotland's nobility, Albany quickly gained custody of Margaret's children and drove her, and Angus, from the kingdom. He faced a brief, but serious, challenge for his position from the powerful James Hamilton, 1st Earl of Arran, in alliance with Alexander Home. Albany weathered the storm, and was remarkably magnanimous in victory to all his political opponents. Arran and Home were pardoned and even Margaret and Angus were allowed to return to Scotland. Albany's lingering fear of Alexander Home eventually sent the unfortunate Border lord to the executioner's block, yet on the whole Albany behaved with restraint.

In 1517 he returned to France, leaving Scotland under the control of a commission of regency, comprising Scotland's two archbishops, the Earls of Angus, Huntly, Arran and Argyll, and Albany's French agent Anthony Darcy, Sieur de la Bastie. The Frenchman, supported by small garrisons of his compatriots in Dunbar, Dumbarton and Inchgarvie, was a steadying influence on this volatile group. However, as Albany's lieutenant he had dangerous enemies. Whilst acting in his capacity of Warden of the Scottish East March, he was ambushed and murdered by the Homes. Without his stewardship the commission quickly fell apart. Angus plotted with the Homes, and clashed with Arran. Order was restored only by the return of Albany in 1521. The Duke now had a new mission in addition to stabilising Scotland. With the onset of the hostilities between France and England, Albany was to encourage his countrymen to take up the sword on France's behalf once more. This was to be the pattern of Anglo-Scots warfare over the course of the rest of Henry's reign. Fighting on the Border would wax and wane in time with the English King's fruitless onslaughts on France.

The primacy of Henry VIII's continental ambitions over his concerns for Scotland had been clearly evident since the beginning of his reign. Whilst he had claimed the ancient English suzerainty over Scotland in 1512, his limited imagination (and treasury) militated against the formulation of a genuinely constructive policy of union between the kingdoms. Scotland was a threat, a hostile power in the north, whose armies might once again spill across the Border if England were unwise enough to become preoccupied by events on the continent. If Henry were to wage war on France, and such thoughts were seldom far from his mind, then he would have to guard against the danger of possible Scottish intervention. To bully and cajole Scotland into acquiescence, or even to rule by proxy through a pro-English faction of the nobility, were the favoured policies of the English King. His main foreign policy objective remained the securing of a central role in the mainstream of European politics.[1]

The war with France was renewed in 1522, when Thomas Howard, the Lord Admiral, now himself Earl of Surrey, led a *chevauchée* into France, besieging Hesdin but with little success. A larger effort was made the following year when Charles Brandon, the Duke of Suffolk, led a 12,000-strong army deep into France. He stormed Bray and Roye before battering Montdidier into submission in late October. He halted just fifty miles short of Paris. Henry scented victory, urging Suffolk to hold on for reinforcements, but his army, which had not been paid, had already begun to disintegrate. It was late in the season, the army was cold and hungry. The French were gathering in strength before them. Discontent turned quickly to indiscipline; Suffolk had no choice but to lead his troops back to the English Pale in an inglorious and undignified retreat.[2]

The war on England's second front, the Border with Scotland, proved similarly inconclusive. Peace had not returned to the Border after Flodden. The normal course of raid, counter-raid, kidnap, blackmail and murder was deliberately escalated, particularly by the Warden of the English West March, Lord Dacre. Establishing a precedent for events later in the century, Dacre had taken to employing large numbers of Scottish 'broken men' to stir up trouble in their own country. Personal animosities, family feuds and the search for plunder had caused much bloodshed on both sides of the Border. Albany, during his first period as Governor, had sought to curb the aggression of his Scottish compatriots. Indeed he had negotiated an uneasy truce with England, always threatened by the mayhem endemic in the Marches. On his return to Scotland in 1521, however, Albany was determined to use his power to aid France, the nation

1 David Head, 'Henry VIII's Scottish Policy: A Reassessment', *The Scottish Historical Review*, vol. 61 (1982), pp. 1–24.
2 S.J.Gunn, 'The Duke of Suffolk's March on Paris in 1523', *The English Historical Review*, vol. 400 (1986), pp. 596–634.

where his first loyalties had always lain. To answer English deprivations across the Channel, Albany planned to lead a Franco-Scottish army into the north country, diverting English forces from France.

His preparations for war were duly noted in England. Indeed the danger was magnified out of all proportion, Wolsey warning Henry that Albany had eighty thousand men at his disposal, with forty-five pieces of artillery, one thousand *arquebuses à croc* and 'a mervellous greate nombre of hand gunnys'.[3] To meet this threat Henry despatched George Talbot, Earl of Shrewsbury. According to Wolsey, Shrewsbury was as 'active a captain as can be chosen within your realm, mete, convenable and necessary to be appointed for the ledinge of an armye ageinst Scotlande'.[4] Certainly, with Surrey then in France, Shrewsbury was the most capable English commander available. He marshalled his own forces at York, but Albany moved against the English West March, threatening Carlisle. There the Earl of Westmorland waited for him, with twenty-eight thousand men. With Albany halted at the Esk, just north of the Border, it seemed as if battle was imminent.

Yet Albany never crossed the Border. Resentment towards overbearing French officials had been simmering for some time, and Scotland's nobles baulked at the idea of risking another Flodden for the sake of the French King. Once more, in the hour of crisis, the English levy system had worked well. The Scots could see the forces opposed to them growing stronger by the day. And even if they defeated Westmorland, Shrewsbury, with his army, would be upon them quickly.[5] At this point Dacre, a canny politician as well as soldier, offered Albany an extension of the truce. At the head of a reluctant army Albany had little choice but to accept. Dacre's actions provoked his King to fury, he had given no consent to such a truce and for a while he blustered and threatened, claiming he would personally lead an army to Edinburgh. In the meantime he sent Surrey back to the North as his Lieutenant General. Soon, however, Henry's attention became mesmerised by events on the continent and Scotland was spared invasion.

The prospect of Scotland launching an invasion of England seemed even more remote. Scots would defend their own country, and their Borderers were enthusiastic raiders, but now seemed to lack the will to mount any kind of serious offensive against England. When widespread fighting resumed in the autumn of 1523, it was the English who took the initiative, hoping to cause enough distress in Scotland to discredit Albany.

---

[3] *Calendar of State Papers, Henry VIII*, vol. 1, part 1 (London, 1831), lxi.
[4] G.W.Bernard, *The Power of the Early Tudor Nobility: A Study of the Fourth and Fifth Earls of Shrewsbury* (Brighton, 1985), pp. 105–136.
[5] Edward Hall, *The Triumphant Reigne of Kyng Henry the VIII*, vol. 1 (London, 1904), pp. 271–273.

The raids and sieges of 1523: stalemate in the Borders

Typically, the English operations bore all the characteristics of the *chevauchée*. The strategy of destruction would destabilise the Scottish government and give Albany's opponents the opportunity to stage a *coup d'état*. The subsequent removal of French influence from the Scottish court would be clearly to England's advantage. Dacre and Surrey raided widely in the Scottish Marches to achieve this aim. Yet again, the overall pattern that emerges resembles that of the military status quo in the period immediately following Flodden. The English had little to fear from Scottish armies, but small raiding parties could slip almost at will into England. England's own raiders, sometimes in bands of several thousand, could wreak terrible destruction on the inhabitants of the Scottish Marches, burning villages and towns, lifting cattle and destroying crops, but could not establish a permanent military ascendancy.

The ordinary Borderer had little interest beyond short-term gain, and, as a later Warden of the West March noted, they preferred the 'Wardnes roode, which is to goo and cum in a daye ande night', to prolonged campaigning.[6] Defences, too, could be stubborn and militate against a prolonged stay in hostile territory. Even the largest raiding forces found themselves bogged down in tough and bloody fighting, and often returned from north of the Tweed battered and bruised. These skirmishes were not merely rough-and-tumble clashes between rival bands of ill-disciplined cattle thieves. Warfare in the Marches was a serious and practical business, conducted by experienced soldiers, well equipped and well organised.

In May of 1523 Surrey led a highly mobile, but hard hitting, column of light cavalry and cannon against a series of Scottish strong points. His artillery comprised of 'a very good cortowte, one very good colverin, one demi colverin, four lizards and four fawcons'. This train was manoeuvred over some difficult country and brought into action to good effect against a succession of smaller Border towers. Its limitations only became apparent when Surrey attempted to take Cessford Castle which, as has been noted, had been up-graded with earthworks to meet the threat posed by cannon. Surrey thought it the strongest work in Scotland, with the exceptions of Dunbar and Fast castles, and found it 'vawmewred with earth of the best sort I have seen'.

His smaller pieces made little impression on the earthwork defences and his heavy calibre 'cortowte' broke its axle early in the bombardment. The piece was remounted, but after a further three shots the new axle showed signs of weakening and Surrey dared not fire it again. He had no other spare gun-carriage and, were the new one to break, he would have been forced to abandon the gun. This suggests that a play-off had been made between the mobility afforded by light gun-carriages and the weight needed to cope with the recoil of a heavy piece in action. The heavier guns required to batter thick walled fortresses into submis-

---

6   *Calendar of State Papers Relating to Scotland, Vol. 1, 1547–63* (Edinburgh, 1898), 44.

sion were too cumbersome for Border warfare, whilst the lighter, more mobile, pieces lacked the necessary punch to end sieges unaided by more traditional means of assault. Surrey's experience at Cessford does at least emphasise the English commitment to the use of gunpowder artillery, operating within those constraints. From the 1523 campaign onwards, trains of what can legitimately be described as field artillery accompanied many large-scale English raiding forces into Scotland.

In action they usually played a supporting role, as the lighter pieces did at Cessford after the 'cowtowte' was withdrawn. Here Surrey had to resort to infantry assault with scaling ladders, led by a forlorn hope of gentlemen and knights. Whilst the assault was delivered the English cannon and bows did their best to provide covering fire against the defenders on the earthworks and at the gun loops. Under cover of this fire the English fought their way into the barbican, but were quickly driven out by the fire of Scottish guns and rocks hurled at them from the dongeon. Surrey now tried to use his guns again, concentrating fire at an old window, about six feet above the ground in the dongeon wall. Too light to blast a breach in the wall, the guns did at least do enough damage to convince Surrey that he could create an opening by laying a charge against the weakened masonry.

This was a dangerous task and it took the promise of a hefty financial reward to induce the gunners to undertake it. Their fears proved well founded. They struggled to the wall with four barrels of powder and set to work with shovels to place the charge. Spotting the danger, the defenders hurled some simple incendiary device at the powder barrels, igniting the charge prematurely and severely injuring the unfortunate gunners. Surrey was doubting that he could take Cessford at all, when he had a enormous stroke of luck. The owner of the castle, Andrew Kerr, Warden of the Scottish Middle March, who had been absent, stumbled unexpectedly on the siege. In return for being allowed to withdraw with all his possessions intact, he surrendered the castle. The success that the English might have felt at the eventual capture of Cessford and the damage done to other towers was more than offset by the upset to their schedule caused by the spirited opposition they had met. Surrey's force was now exhausted and hungry, having exhausted the victuals they had carried with them.[7] Even though able to cross the Border with impunity and inflict serious damage, these *chevauchée*-style forays were failing to establish a permanent English military ascendancy on the Border.

These mixed fortunes were made particularly evident later that year, during Surrey and Dacre's second massive foray into Scotland in September. At the head of a force of six thousand men, Surrey achieved what Dacre had been unable to manage in 1514. Jedburgh, a fair sized town, was taken, sacked and burnt. Yet the town was won only after the stiffest of fights, house to house, street to street, with bow, axe, sword and lance. It was a grim business that left

---

[7] *Letters and Papers Foreign and Domestic [LandP], Henry VIII*, vol. 3, part 2, 3039.

Surrey convinced that the defenders of Jedburgh were the bravest men he had ever seen. Surrey camped amongst the smoking ruins for three days, from 22 to 25 September. From this base he despatched Lord Dacre to seize the castle of Andrew 'Dan' Kerr, at Ferniehurst.

Again the English found themselves contending with a spirited defence. The castle was surrounded by thick woodland, which the English had to occupy before they could place their guns. Dacre had to dismount his entire force for the difficult and confused fighting amongst the foliage. Once the woods had been won, the English cannon had to establish their own ascendancy over the Scottish ordnance in the castle itself. There was a protracted artillery duel before Kerr finally admitted defeat. The Scots had fought most valiantly, as even that most prejudiced of chroniclers, Edward Hall, acknowledged, and Dacre, an old man now, much troubled with gout, grew weary and careless. That night, an alarm broke out in his camp and three hundred valuable horses fled into the night. The exasperated Dacre swore that the Devil himself was responsible, but there can be little doubt that Scottish knives had cut the tethers. The success of the English foray notwithstanding, the Scottish Borderers fought on. Surrey returned to England, leaving the Scottish March despoiled but still defiant.[8]

Albany, now having gathered more French troops and money, hoped to capitalise on that defiance. He also raised the spectre of England's recent civil conflicts. Surrey informed Wolsey that 'He doth make grete boost off the londyng off Ricard de la Pole in Scotlond assewryng the Lords off Scotland that he shall have gret help in this realm.'[9] Richard de la Pole, Earl of Suffolk, 'the White Rose', was the Yorkist claimant to the English throne. He was a talented soldier, commanding a company of *Landsknechte* in French service. His presence in the North would have been a very real threat. Yorkist sentiment lingered in Yorkshire and the Marches. Although James IV's attempts to exploit this sentiment in 1496 had failed, Albany may have reasoned that the presence of a genuine representative of the house of York could stir up dissension in Surrey's army. Indeed, were he to win a significant victory over Surrey, it was not beyond the realms of possibility that he could reignite the English dynastic struggle. Albany could have done no greater service to France or Scotland than plunging England back into civil war.[10]

By 23 October English spies were reporting that he had mobilised an army of sixty thousand men, three thousand of them French, outside Edinburgh, and, despite the lateness of the season, was making for the Border. Not expecting an attack so late in the year, the English were taken somewhat by surprise. Yet now it was their turn to be defiant. Albany sent a herald to Surrey, assuring him that if he were taken in battle he would be safe and held for ransom. Surrey's

---

8 Hall, *Kyng Henry the VIII*, vol. 1, pp. 300–301.
9 Henry Ellis (ed.), *Original Letters Illustrative of English History*, 1st series, vol. 1 (London, 1824), p. 231.
10 In fact Richard de la Pole was never able to play a significant role in English politics. He was killed whilst leading his *Landsknechte* at Pavia in 1525.

response had shades of his message to James IV eleven years earlier, on the eve of Flodden. If Albany was taken prisoner, Surrey informed the herald, 'he would strike off his head and send it to the Kyng of England'.[11]

The threatened battle did not materialise. Once again, Albany was unable to persuade his Scottish troops to cross the Tweed. Resentment against the over-bearing French and lingering memories of Flodden seem to have been the twin obstacles to invasion, and a frustrated Albany was forced to alter his plans drastically. He despatched a predominantly French force, three to four thousand strong, with artillery to besiege the Border castle of Wark. The commander of the garrison, Sir William Lyle had but one hundred men and was unable to prevent the French from storming first the barmkin, the outer ward of the castle, and then the fosse-bray.

Confined to the inner ward, the defenders were convinced that their time had come and resolved to sally out against their assailants 'for more shall our honor be to dye in fight, than to be murthered with gunnes'.[12] In the narrow confines within the castle walls the ferocity of the desperate English counter-attack swept all before it, and drove the French back beyond the barmkin wall. The besiegers' artillery might then have turned the tide of battle once more in favour of the French, but the Scottish gunners were already loading their carts and harnessing their guns to oxen, ready for a speedy withdrawal. The Earl of Surrey, with five thousand horsemen, was closing fast, the rest of his army not far behind.

The campaign ended in anti-climax. Surrey found three hundred French dead around Wark Castle and praised Lyle for his heroic defence, but the rest of the besiegers got away. Scottish Border horse shielded their retreat, covering the fords over the Tweed, preventing pursuit. Despite the successful relief of Wark, the outcome of the campaign was a serious disappointment to Surrey. 'And grete pitie it were that the Kingis Highnes shuld spend thus moche money withoute batayle', he lamented to Wolsey. Furthermore, Albany had escaped. Surrey's army had consumed all their victuals and now he feared 'it shall not be possible for me to kepe this Army no longer togidder; for suche as come oute of the bisshopriche, this contre, and other places, at their own costs, have spent all that they have; and with moche difficulte and faire words have kepte theym here thus long'. The danger was that Albany would slip back across the Border once Surrey's army was discharged. Holding his army together as best he could, Surrey lingered at Wark for several days. Perhaps remembering his experiences at Cessford, he took the opportunity to strengthen the castle by building earthworks.[13]

His precautions proved unnecessary. Once it was safely back in Scotland, Albany's army quickly dissolved. Frustrated and disillusioned, Albany himself soon departed for France, never to return. Once more a Scottish invasion had been parried, yet the military situation remained largely unchanged. The English could foray into, but not dominate, the Scottish Marches. For all his

11 Hall, *Kyng Henry the VIII*, vol. 1, p. 304.
12 Hall, pp. 304–305.
13 Ellis, *Original Letters*, pp. 231, 234.

efforts, Surrey had failed to satisfy his royal master, and in November he was recalled from the Border, ostensibly on grounds of ill-health. Shortly afterwards his father, the victor of Flodden, died and he succeeded to his title, becoming the 3rd Duke of Norfolk and Lord High Treasurer, but with his political power severely curtailed.[14]

Thomas Dacre fared similarly. As acting Warden of all three English Marches, charged not only with their defence but also with pursuing a strategy of destruction in Scotland, Dacre could not be too scrupulous about whom he chose as allies. He relied heavily on the support of some of the most notorious 'broken men' of the Borders, the reiver clans of Tynedale, Redesdale, Bewcastledale and Gilsland, predominantly Charltons and Milburns. These hardened thieves from the hungry Border highlands were the backbone of Dacre's personal retinues. They knew little of national loyalties. Happy enough to plunder in Scotland, they were equally quick to foray into Northumberland when pickings looked rich. With justice coming a poor second to defence in national priorities, the King turned a blind eye to their deprivations, so long as the war with Scotland dragged on. Once a truce was agreed in January 1525, Henry was altogether more receptive to the incessant complaints of the Northumbrian gentry that Dacre was negligent in the pursuit of criminals. Dacre was summoned before Wolsey and the Star Chamber. Fined and stripped of all three wardenships he was detained until September, when he was sent back north to arrange an extension of the truce with Scotland. Less than a month later he was thrown from his horse and killed.[15]

The fragile peace, 1523–1542

Surrey's withdrawal from the North and Dacre's fall from grace are indicative of a temporary shift in emphasis in the King's planning. With French influence in Edinburgh curtailed, Henry could now look for a diplomatic rather than a military means of securing his northern Border. This diplomatic approach centred initially on the Earl of Angus. With Albany back in France, Angus might now take his place at the helm of Scottish government. England's King was effectively his patron, for Angus had sworn to serve him against any prince except his own. The Earl could be relied upon to keep Scotland acquiescent whilst Henry pursued his continental designs. The main obstacle to this satisfactory arrangement was the Earl of Arran and the young King James himself, who heartily loathed Angus and his family.

Yet, with English support and powerful allies in Scotland, Angus was able to seize Edinburgh, overawe the Scottish Council, and control the young King.

---

[14] Thomas Howard, 'The Early Career of the 3rd Duke of Norfolk' (University of West Virginia Ph.D., 1984), pp. 116–120.
[15] Steven Ellis, 'A Border Baron and the Tudor State: The Rise and Fall of Lord Dacre of the North', *The Historical Journal*, vol. 35 (1992), pp. 266–267.

Angus would dominate Scottish politics until 1528, and under his direction a series of truces, ostensibly preparing the ground for a permanent peace, brought some measure of quiet to the tormented Borders. It was not to last. In 1528 the young James V asserted his ability to rule in his own right, and the Douglases were forced to flee Scotland. Henry sheltered Angus and worked hard to promote a reconciliation between the Earl and Scotland's King. This was difficult, for James was deeply suspicious of his uncle and deeply hostile towards his stepfather, Angus. For a time he trod a careful path, signing another truce in December 1528 agreeing to arbitration of disputes on the Border and paving the way for the negotiation of a permanent peace treaty within five years.

This allowed James to concentrate his efforts against his rebellious subjects in the Highlands and Western Isles, which had been in a state of unrest since May 1528. The young King was of the opinion, as he wrote to Francis I, that the best way to deal with the Highlanders was to use cannon to blow them out of their boats and strongholds.[16] Whilst James worked to pacify the Highlands, he struggled to maintain the peace with England. In 1531 another truce was signed, once more agreeing to the amicable settlement of the seemingly endless disputes arising on the Border. Yet these treaties masked mutual suspicion and hostility. The truces did nothing to halt the steady slide of the Marches into a return to chaos. Raiding grew more frequent and more savage. Attempts at mediation proved fruitless, and in 1532 the Border exploded once more.

After a series of large and destructive Scottish raids, Berwick itself seemed threatened and the King sent Sir Arthur Darcy, with 'thre hundred tall menne', to strengthen its garrison. By way of welcoming him to his new command, a powerful force of Scottish raiders pushed into the English Middle March, carrying out the normal acts of robbery and destruction as they went. Darcy and the exiled Angus, now resident in Berwick, led four hundred English reivers in pursuit. They were able to exact a measure of vengeance by torching several Scottish villages and successfully ambushing a large force of Scots sent to meet them.[17] The potential for conflict soon extended beyond the Anglo-Scots Border. James sent over five hundred archers to assist rebels fighting the English Crown in Ireland. In July 1533 Alexander MacDonald and Hector Maclean raided the Isle of Man, capturing an English ship, the *Mary Willoughby*, which James V claimed as a prize. This led the Earl of Derby to despatch a force of Cheshire archers to help the Manx defend themselves.[18]

The two nations seemed now to be poised on the brink of all out war. Henry threatened to lead an army to Edinburgh to personally reinstate Angus. James, with one eye on the domestic crisis then facing Henry, hinted that should Henry

[16] James S. Cameron, 'Crown Magnate Relations in the Personal Rule of James V, 1528–1542' (St Andrews University Ph.D., 1994), pp. 397–401.

[17] Hall, *Kyng Henry the VIII*, vol. 1, pp. 222–223.

[18] B.Coward, 'The Lieutenancy of Lancashire and Cheshire in the Sixteenth and Early Seventeenth Centuries', *Transactions of the Historical Society of Lancashire and Cheshire*, vol. 119 (1967), p. 51.

be deposed by the Pope he would assert his own claim to the English throne. Oddly enough, in the event, it was the circumstances of Henry's domestic crisis that headed off the incipient war. Henry's marriage to Ann Boleyn and his subsequent break from Rome brought him into direct conflict with the Emperor Charles V. Tentative negotiations with France for a united military front against the Empire heralded a nominal improvement in Anglo-Scots relations, mediated by Francis I. By a treaty signed in May 1534, Henry withdrew his support for Angus and James agreed not to wage war on England, whatever pretext the papacy might provide. Suspicions were not entirely allayed. The machinations of Europe's diplomats soon saw France making peace with the Empire.

The prospect of a joint crusade against the schismatic King of England was sufficiently real to set the English building coastal forts and preparing for invasion. James V spent long months in France at this time but studiously evaded Henry's attempts to negotiate a personal meeting. James's own intense distaste for the Reformation and the growing influence of David Beaton, Archbishop of St Andrews, made him wholly resistant to further English overtures. Events now seemed to take on a momentum guaranteed to escalate English fears. James's links to France were reinforced by his marriage to Mary of Guise, a bride whom Henry himself had once hoped to wed. Beaton was raised to Cardinal and pledged to guide his King in the confrontation with heresy. England itself seemed frighteningly vulnerable. The northern rebels of the Pilgrimage of Grace might have called on James's support in a civil war fought on Rome's behalf.

Yet the threatened joint onslaught from France, Scotland and the Empire never materialised. Francis I and Charles V soon quarrelled and, once again, England allied with the Empire against France. If, overall, this represented an improvement in England's diplomatic situation, it also made the prospect of war with Scotland more likely. James was still fervent in his opposition to the forces of the Reformation and in his commitment to the Auld Alliance. Throughout the summer of 1541, Henry was still hopeful of detaching James from his French connection. He sought once more to arrange a personal meeting, and sent Ralph Sadler, an experienced diplomat, to Edinburgh to make arrangements. Henry, it would appear, was convinced that James had agreed to a meeting in York and made elaborate preparations for his nephew's arrival. For two weeks he waited before recognising that James was not coming. Furious and humiliated, he ordered all Scots expelled from the North and ordered the Borders into a state of readiness for war. His own ambitions on the continent had now been reignited, and he faced the same problem that had confronted him in 1513 and 1521. Before he could campaign in France he must secure the northern Border. If the Scots could not be brought to truce, the issue would now be resolved by force.

Haddon Rigg and the return to war

In effect, the war had already begun on the Border. The Scots won an early triumph at Haddon Rigg in 1542, the credit belonging to George Gordon, Earl of Huntly. On 24 August a large English raiding force of about three thousand men had descended on Teviotdale under the East March Warden Robert Bowes accompanied by England's ally, the Earl of Angus. This operation appears to have been intended to be the opening of a protracted campaign of large-scale raids into the Scottish Marches. Once in enemy territory, Bowes's force committed the usual deprivations, burning Heiton of the Hill, Maxwell Heugh and other small hamlets.

Yet Bowes had made a serious tactical error. Establishing Haddon as a base for operations, Bowes had divided his force, sending out sorties to the surrounding countryside to burn and plunder. This was a standard procedure on the larger raids, designed to maximise the havoc the raiders could wreak in the shortest possible time. Yet this division of force in the face of a quick-witted and mobile enemy 'laid bare the cardinal weakness of the big raid technique'.[19] The Scots had concentrated their forces into two battles. The 2000-strong vanguard was led by Sir Walter Lyndsay, a veteran Knight of St John. Huntly followed with the main battle of six thousand. Lyndsay advanced quickly, cutting off the isolated sorties from their base, and catching the main body of the English unprepared.[20] A desperate retreat ensued with Huntly's Borderers in hot pursuit, inflicting perhaps a thousand casualties on the fugitives. Taken utterly by surprise by the swiftness of Huntly's attack, the English Borderers had made a feeble defence. Sir William Eure reported to the Privy Council:

> Scots prickers with showttinge and crying pursued and overthrew them . . . George Bowes, nephew to Sir Robert, and the captain of Norham who were there, say that Riddisdale with Sir Cuthbert Ratcliffe's company were the first to fly, and my Lord of Angus lighted like a nobleman, with the said Sir Robert . . . and gat away with great debate of himself, and the rest of his company did naught.[21]

The routing of Bowes's raiders at Haddon Rigg was a salutary reminder that the English could not yet operate in Scotland with impunity. Whilst in itself the defeat was of little consequence, it reinforced Henry's desire to render the Scottish Lowlands incapable of military activity. In the wake of their victory the Scots, according to Angus, grew prouder, and he urged the King to 'send a power to give them ane gryt snap'.[22]

---

[19] George MacDonald Fraser, *The Steel Bonnets* (London, 1989), p. 248.
[20] Robert Lindesay of Pitscottie, *The Historie and Cronicles of Scotland*, vol. 1 (Edinburgh, 1899), pp. 397–398.
[21] Gainsford Bruce, 'The English Expedition into Scotland in 1542', *Archaeologia Aeliana*, 3rd series, vol. 3 (1907), p. 195.
[22] Bruce, p. 197.

An altogether larger operation was therefore planned, still based on the premise that Scotland could be overawed by a display of military might into acquiesence. England's foremost soldier, Thomas Howard, Duke of Norfolk, was to command once more in the North. He was given authority to negotiate with the Scots, but the terms he offered demanded little short of total capitulation. All English prisoners were to be freed, Scotland was to relinquish its claim on the Debatable Land and deliver bishops and earls as hostages to England. These terms were unacceptable to Scotland and, although talks dragged on until October, the eventual outcome was inevitable. Despite the lateness in the year, Norfolk prepared his invasion.

From the beginning his plans were hampered by foul weather and problems with the provision of victuals. Indeed the whole campaign, the first English incursion large enough to merit the title invasion since the expedition to Jedburgh in 1523, graphically illustrated the vulnerability of Tudor armies to poor logistical arrangements. Throughout October Norfolk struggled to feed his men. From York to Newcastle and then on to Berwick his men trudged wearily on empty stomachs. The shortages were made worse by the lack of suitable waggons and carts, a recurring and seemingly insoluble problem for English armies in the North. Most distressing of all was the lack of beer. On the march north the man drank water. Even when they crossed the Border they were restricted to just a quart of beer a day. With pressing logistic problems clear from the outset, Norfolk quickly abandoned the King's ambitious schemes for the capture of Edinburgh, citing in particular the acute shortage of waggons. His hungry army was able to undertake little more than a large Border raid.

The invasion began on 23 October, the English camping that night at Banningburn. The first weapon employed by the defenders was guile. A small force of Scots stole into the English camp, but the alarm was raised before they reached the horse lines. Four were taken and hanged as spies the next morning before Norfolk resumed his advance. Progress was slowed, but not seriously impeded, by a series of skirmishes with small parties of Scots. When night fell, four more Scots were taken trying to spy on the English, and met the same grisly fate as their unfortunate compatriots of the night before. On 25 October the English approached Kelso, but found the surrounding area well defended. The skirmishes continued, with Norfolk's artillery gradually clearing the defenders from the high ground and opening the path into the town. Kelso and its surrounding villages was burned, and Roxburgh bombarded, but this marked the end of the campaign. After six days the army had consumed its entire supply of victuals and was forced to return to England, its achievements having fallen well short of Henry's hopes.

Norfolk, aware of the King's displeasure, made much of the destruction he had wrought, but it is clear that the whole expedition was held to be a failure. Far from being intimidated, the Scots were already preparing to retaliate. A large force had been mustered to meet Norfolk's army, were it to advance on Edinburgh. In early November Norfolk received news that a 12,000-strong Scottish army had gathered at Fala Muir, a plateau between the Lammermuir and Moorfoot hills. From here it could either defend Edinburgh or cross the Border.[23] James had successfully raised a considerable force with the support of the Scottish nobility. So long as the role of this army was defensive, James could count on its co-operation. Yet hampered by worsening weather conditions and lack of food, the King's army did not move quickly enough to intercept Norfolk north of the Border. Once the English had withdrawn from Scotland, James had to rethink his strategy.

The reluctance to cross the Border that had manifested itself in 1522 and 1523 had now hardened into established custom, and the levy-based force at Fala Muir was disbanded. James, however, was determined to catch the English off guard and set about raising another army. Again the leading magnates supported their King, who was able to raise a well-equipped and mobile force composed wholly of the retinues of the nobility. The English now found themselves wrong-footed. Whilst they had rampaged in the east, James V, mustering his new army in the west, was poised to strike towards Carlisle. His intention was probably that this should form a preliminary raid, the first in a series of *chevauchées* along the length of the Border which would devastate the English Marches and throw England onto the defensive.[24] This campaign would reach its conclusion in one of the most extraordinary battles ever fought between English and Scot.

The Battle of Solway Moss

James V had assembled a force of perhaps eighteen thousand men and on 24 November it had crossed the Border into the English West March. James, ailing and weak, did not accompany it, apparently giving command to Robert, Lord Maxwell, the Warden of the West March. The army made an impressive show; although predominantly an infantry force, its artillery train bristled with cannon and it advanced with confidence under a host of brighi standards. With English forces still concentrated in the East March, the opportunity for Scotland to settle old scores and establish military ascendancy in the Borders looked very good indeed.

The size of the force facing him was well known to Sir Thomas Wharton, Warden of the West March, for there was no shortage of good spies and scourers on the Border. With just three thousand men at his disposal, he might have been expected to wait for the invaders behind the strong walls of Carlisle, risking siege until relief arrived or until James's supplies ran out and his army melted away. Certainly, on the continent one would not have expected a commander

23 Bruce, pp. 191–212.
24 Cameron, 'Crown Magnate Relations', pp. 494–529.

faced with such a disparity of forces to meet his enemy in the field. But Wharton was a Borderer. He fought best on horseback with lance or sword and trusted his country's defence more to walls of flesh and bone than stone. Despite the odds against him, the wily Wharton resolved to meet the invaders in battle.

The first moves were played out in the Debatable Lands, the lawless strip of territory claimed by both nations but beyond the effective jurisdiction of either. Home of outlaws, 'broken men' and the great reiver clan of the Grahams, the Debatable Lands were James's first objective. The muster beacons now burned brightly in the English West March, but it is probable that they need not have bothered. The flames that consumed the homes of the Grahams would have been warning enough of the Scottish approach. Cumberland's farms and villages would be next. The Scots were across the Esk shortly after dawn, burning Oakshaw Hill as they passed. Wharton was not content to stand idly by and watch while his whole wardenry was consigned to flames. His patrols were already out 'pricking', scouting and probing the Scottish advance. His campaign was to be a masterly example of light cavalry tactics.

One of his patrols had already penetrated well to the Scottish rear, burning Middleby, eight miles north of the Border. For Wharton was determined to take the offensive, meeting the Scottish bludgeon with an English rapier. The previous night his patrols had found the Scots organised into two large battles, one at Langholm the other at Mortonkirk. The patrols had been shadowing them ever since, clashing repeatedly with strong forays of Scottish Border horse.

Wharton himself soon left Carlisle at the head of three hundred Border horse. He paused for a while at the Lyne, watching the red horizon as the Scots moved south, burning as they went. The English light horse tried again to harry them as they advanced, but were driven off by gunfire from the Scottish cannon, their army being well equipped with light, mobile pieces. The outnumbered defenders maintained the skirmish, choosing their ground carefully amongst the hills and mosses but unable to stem the advance. From Oakshaw Hill the Scottish army moved inexorably along the bank of the Esk to Arthuret Howes.

Yet Wharton was not about to lose his nerve. His own forces were growing. He had now been joined by several prominent gentlemen of the West March, including his cousin, Walter Strikland, with two hundred Kendal archers and his own son, with two hundred more horsemen. This little force crossed the Lyne and moved swiftly on to Hopesike Hill, directly in the path of the Scottish advance from Arthuret Howes. Here they planted six standards, their appearance putting fresh heart into the English prickers. A speedy council of war was held on the hill. Wharton had seen an opportunity and resolved to take advantage of it. The Scots were moving through difficult territory, now entering a straight pass, with the River Esk and Solway Moss, deep and treacherous, to their right flank. As he regrouped his foot to meet the Scots head on, Wharton sent an able lieutenant, Sir William Musgrave, with seven hundred horse to 'prick' at the Scots as soon as they came within bow range of Hopesike Hill.

Musgrave's horse would wheel round from the right of the English position, hitting the left flank of the Scottish army, driving them back towards the river and Solway Moss beyond.[25] Struggling across the boggy ground, battling to get artillery pieces and baggage carts forward, the Scottish army was now deeply vulnerable to the fast moving horsemen. Moreover, Musgrave reported that the sight of English bows and bills ahead of them had already been enough to persuade some of the common soldiery to turn for home.[26] If a lack of confidence was beginning to infect the Scottish army it is hardly surprising, for a leadership crisis had been precipitated by Oliver Sinclair, the King's favourite. Just as the army had struggled through the bog and was confronted by Wharton's forces, Sinclair had announced that James wished him, not Maxwell, to command. Why he chose this extraordinary moment to press his claim is unclear, but the ensuing argument left the army effectively leaderless at precisely the moment that Musgrave's reivers struck from the mist.[27]

His tactics were classic hit-and-run, his light horse darting in close to the tightly packed ranks of Scottish infantry, spearing and hacking with lance and sword, wheeling away and then darting back, 'bickering' at the flanks, cutting off stragglers, harassing and terrifying the disordered footmen. 'Our prekers . . . gatt theym in a shake all the waye', reported an approving Wharton.[28] Indeed the Scottish ranks were 'in a shake'. They convulsed, impacting on each other, men scattered or floundered helplessly into the bog. From Hopesike Hill Wharton could see that the rear ranks of the Scottish army were the first to turn their backs and head north. The rest soon followed. The battle was now over, but the pursuit had begun. The English foot advanced to Arthuret Howes, but was outstripped by the pace of the Scottish retreat. The fleeing army was struggling across the Esk at Sandyford when Musgrave's horse caught up with them again.[29]

Some of the Scottish gunners managed to loose off a round or two from their cannon, but to no avail. Their army was disintegrating around them. More drowned than died fighting as they plunged into the water. Three days later fishermen on the Esk were still hauling bodies from the water in their nets. Musgrave generously suggests that the Scottish gentry held their ground the longest:

---

[25] *The Hamilton Papers, Vol. 1, 1532–1543* (Edinburgh, 1890), xvi. Wharton records his instructions to Musgrave's prickers thus: 'We adviced them as the Scotis came within our shote of arrowes, that their shulde sett upon theym at the side upon the right hande, for upon the left hande was a grete mosse.' Some secondary accounts of Solway Moss have interpreted this as meaning that the English horse were to attack the Scottish right; for an example see Keith Durham, *The Border Reivers* (London, 1995), p. 38. This surely cannot be correct, for the right of the Scottish line would have been hard by the Esk. Wharton's scheme was to drive the Scots into the bog, not away from it. His phrase 'upon the right hande' must refer to the English right. Indeed his horse would already have been on this side of his line, having been driven south from Oakshaw Hill.

[26] *Hamilton Papers*, vol. 1, 240.

[27] For a brave, if not altogether convincing, attempt to exonerate Sinclair from blame for the Solway Moss débâcle, see George Sinclair, 'The Scots at Solway Moss', *The Scottish Historical Review*, vol. 2 (1904), pp. 372–377.

[28] *Hamilton Papers*, vol. 1, xvi.

[29] *Hamilton Papers*, vol. 1, xvi.

'Lord Maxwell with many other noble men . . . lighted at the waters side and fought valiantly . . .', but this hardly compensates for their doleful leadership and the common soldiery cannot be blamed for what had quickly, and astonishingly, degenerated into total rout.[30] Pursued across the boggy expanse of Solway Moss by the English light horse, there was no opportunity to rally or regroup. Abandoning cannon, carts and waggons as they went, those who could fled north, where the vengeful Grahams were waiting for them amongst the smouldering ruins of their homes. The army that had crossed into England a few hours before had marched proudly under 'thirtie and mo standertis'. Soon every one had been captured by the English horse, 'none of theme was borne on hight over the water of the Sark which divideth Scotland and the Bateable grounde'.[31]

The number of slain on both sides was small, perhaps only seven Englishmen and twenty Scots (not counting those drowned), but twelve hundred Scots were made prisoner, including the Earl of Cassill, the Earl of Glencairn, Lord Fleming, Lord Maxwell, Lord Somervell, Lord Olivaunt, Lord Grey and the sorry figure of Oliver Sinclair himself, whose military ambitions had now come to a premature and inglorious end. Politically these captives were worth their weight in gold. Many of them were already displaying pro-English and pro-Reformation sentiments and now enjoyed lavish and generous hospitality as captives of the English King. It was not difficult to persuade the majority of them that their own best interest lay in furthering England's cause in Scotland. James's material losses were great too. Wharton reported that 'twentie carted peces of ordenaunce for the felde . . . sex score half hakkes and grete nombre of handgonnes was won'.[32] This was an abundance of expensive, modern ordnance which Scotland could ill afford to lose. Scots would feel the loss grievously over the next few years. As the English trained up their own gunners and augmented them with foreign specialists the Scots would consistently struggle to field effective quantities of gunpowder weapons in reply.

Yet the greatest loss of all came after the battle. On 14 December 1542, a mere three weeks after he received the news from Solway Moss, James V died. The exact cause of his death is unknown, for he had been ill for some time. Few doubt, though, that news of the débâcle on the Esk was the final blow to the weary and already ailing King. Exhaustion and despair killed James V as surely as English bills had killed his father.[33]

---

30 *Hamilton Papers*, vol. 1, 240.
31 *Hamilton Papers*, vol. 1, xvi.
32 *Hamilton Papers*, vol. 1, xvi.
33 It has been suggested that James's illness was responsible for the impulsive decision to launch an invasion. See Albert Makinson, 'Solway Moss and the Death of James V', *History Today*, vol. 10 (1960), pp. 106–115.

England's strategy: war with France, 'Rough Wooing' in Scotland

The military opportunity that now presented itself in the North was lost on King Henry. The inevitable return to conflict between the houses of Valois and Hapsburg had given him the opportunity to re-open his war with France. Once again, English military activity in Scotland would be subordinated to the conflict on the continent. In 1543 English auxiliaries were sent to join Charles V's army in the Netherlands, assisting at the siege of Landrecies. This was a mere preliminary to the joint onslaught planned for 1544. Charles entertained grand schemes, an 'Enterprise of Paris', a combined attack from the Calais Pale and the Hapsburg dominions that bordered France. This was a strategic vision on the grand scale. Yet neither the English nor the Imperialists had the will to see it through.

The English contented themselves with an expansion of the Calais Pale, aiming particularly at the capture of Boulogne. An army of forty-two thousand was assembled. Once again, the King would lead his army in person, commanding the main battle as he had in 1513. The vanguard was to be led by Thomas Howard, Earl of Norfolk, and the rearward by Lord Russell. The first objective was Montreuil, well south of Boulogne. Had the English intended to push deep into France, then forcing the large French garrison away from Montreuil would have made much sense. As it was, England's main objective remained Boulogne. They moved against Montreuil only on self-serving Imperialist advice. The siege was conducted in a half-hearted and timid manner. Well away from the main English operations against Boulogne, it proved difficult to victual the besiegers. Supply convoys ran the gauntlet of ambush laid by French light cavalry. Starvation and privation took a hefty toll of those who manned the flimsy siege-works around Montreuil until they were withdrawn following the capitulation of Boulogne on 18 September 1544.[34] The success against Boulogne had been the culmination of a far more effectively conducted siege. This had opened on 19 July and the English had quickly captured the lower town and the usefully sited Roman lighthouse known as 'the Old Man'. Throughout August the noose around Boulogne was tightened. An elaborate network of siege-works, trenches and raised gun positions was built up, and the upper town was hammered by the English artillery. On 1 September the fosse-bray of the upper town was stormed and only the citadel itself remained in French hands. The garrison continued to maintain a ferocious defence, frustrating English attempts to mine the walls of the castle and repulsing assaults with heavy losses. They could not, however, defy the English artillery indefinitely and agreed terms for surrender on 13 September. Victory brought the English few grounds for celebration. For the Emperor Charles V had made separate peace with Francis, and the Dauphin now led thirty-six thousand veterans of the war in Italy

---

[34] For a vivid first-hand description of the siege of Montreuil, see M.B.Davies (ed.), 'The Enterprise of Paris and Boulogne', *Fouad I University, Bulletin of the Faculty of Arts*, vol. 11, part 1 (1949), pp. 37–93.

against the English at Boulogne. Henry had already departed home to England, leaving Norfolk in command. Tired and old, Norfolk was no longer the ferocious warrior who had led the vanguard at Flodden. Leaving Boulogne with an inadequate garrison of just four thousand men, he retreated to Calais, where plague and desertion further weakened his army. A furious Henry ordered him to return to Boulogne, but the Dauphin arrived outside its battered walls first.

The English had adopted a leisurely and unhurried attitude to reorganising the city's defences. The walls of the lower town were battered and in places inviting breaches gaped at the French. The heavier pieces of artillery were still in the siege trenches, outside the tumbled-down walls. English sentries seemed lax and half-asleep. The famous Gascon captain Blaise de Monluc found, to his surprise, that it was possible to penetrate easily through the English lines and reconnoitre the city defences without even being challenged. Noting these weaknesses, the French resolved to re-take Boulogne by *camisado*, a surprise night attack. Twenty-three companies of French and Italian veterans led by Monluc conducted the assault. Initially all went well for the French. They broke easily into the lower town (an English sentry was later hung for his negligence), but then fell to looting and slaughtering hapless parties of isolated, and frequently unarmed, Englishmen.

Meanwhile a determined English counter-attack was launched from the citadel, which eventually drove the attackers back beyond the city walls. The fighting was confused, street to street, house to house. Small groups of men fought running battles through narrow, twisting alleyways in the darkness and rain, others barricaded themselves in the little houses waiting for relief. Gradually the French were chased back out of the breaches. Monluc, cursing his luck, with three arrows embedded in his buckler, and a fourth piercing the sleeve of his mail coat, was the last to leave, spitting defiance at any Englishman unwise enough to close with him and damning his own men for their unsoldierly conduct.

Warfare around Boulogne then settled into a conflict of sword and shovel. The town was invested and both sides dug and scraped entrenchments and gun emplacements. The war spread into the Calais Pale, with a major French success in the capture of a fort in the county of Oye, but little progress was made by either side elsewhere. French threats to take the war to England itself came to nothing, despite the sinking of the *Mary Rose* in the Solent in 1545. A token invasion of the Isle of Wight was a dismal failure. Several days' fighting had culminated in an inglorious evacuation, with the invaders pursued by the local levy which had organised quickly and efficiently and had fought well.[35] Meanwhile the doleful conflict around Boulogne dragged on. The English command passed to Norfolk's son Henry Howard, Earl of Surrey, in September 1545.

Surrey, however, enjoyed little success. An attack on a French supply convoy badly misfired, with heavy losses, and Surrey was quickly replaced by Edward

---

35 Alexander McKee, 'Henry VIII as Military Commander', *History Today*, vol. 41 (1991), pp. 22–29.

Seymour, Earl of Hertford. Fighting became concentrated amongst the earth-works along the Lianne estuary. The two armies were held immobile by the rival bastions. The incessant cannonade and skirmishing could give neither side the advantage; negotiation was the only viable course of action. By the Treaty of Camp, 7 June 1546, it was agreed that Boulogne be returned to France after an eight-year period in return for a substantial indemnity.[36]

Throughout the course of the campaign in France the English had applied military pressure to Scotland. A suspension of hostilities negotiated in the wake of Solway Moss proved to be short lived.[37] Again Henry had adopted the strat-egy of destruction, intending to intimidate Scotland into acquiescence. Chronic political instability north of the Border made the task that much easier. A French diplomat, Jacques de la Brosse, found the whole nation under arms, not in preparation for national defence but because:

> all the friends of one faction mistrust all those of the other faction. So much so that not merely is the nobility in arms, but churchmen, friars and the country people only travel through the countryside in large companies all armed with pikes, swords and bucklers and a half pike in their hands.[38]

James V's successor to the throne was his baby daughter, Mary, then just one week old. The realm faced the prospect of another long and turbulent minority.[39] It was not just the extreme youth of the new monarch – Mary's coronation was held when she was barely nine months old – but her sex that created tension. This royal bride would include the kingdom in her dowry. If she were to marry a foreign prince, the best Scotland could hope for would be the subordinate role in an unequal partnership. At worst, Scotland's very independence might be at stake. There were, of course, plenty of suitors amongst the noble houses of Scot-land itself. Yet these rivals for Mary's hand were rivals for the power that the marriage would bring. Bitter and divisive factionalism, exacerbated by the impact of the Reformation, now permeated Scotland's politics.

Cardinal David Beaton was Catholicism's greatest champion, waging a battle against the spread of Lutheran ideas. Protestantism had taken hold in Scotland with remarkable speed and tenacity amongst a minority of dedicated reformers. One of the most striking political consequences of this religious conflict was the challenge it posed to the traditional orientation of Scotland's foreign policy. Scottish Catholics may have clung to the security offered by the Auld Alliance

---

[36] For contemporary accounts of the 'Enterprise of Boulogne' see Davies (ed.), 'The Enter-prise of Paris and Boulogne', in Ian Roy (ed.), *Blaise de Monluc: The Valois-Habsburg Wars and the French Wars of Religion* (London, 1971), pp. 117–131, and the anonymous diary of an English soldier, 'The Siege and Capture of Boulogne 1544', *The Journal of the Society of Army Historical Research*, vol. 1 (1922), pp. 188–199.

[37] British Library Additional MS 32648, F.224.

[38] Gladys Dickinson (ed.), *Two Missions of Jaques De La Brosse* (Edinburgh, 1942), pp. 2–3.

[39] For the political background to Mary's minority, see Gordon Donaldson, *Scotland, James V – James VII* (Edinburgh, 1965), chapter 5, and Jenny Wormald, *Mary Queen of Scots: A Study in Failure* (London, 1988), chapter 3.

with France but their Protestant compatriots naturally looked increasingly to England for aid and protection. There was now an influential faction within Scotland amenable to friendship, even union, with England.

The struggle for power during the Queen's fractious minority ebbed and flowed from the moment that Cardinal Beaton took the dead King's hand and traced his signature on a document purporting to be the royal will. This will named four 'protectors': Beaton himself, and the earls of Moray, Argyll and Huntly, the victor of Haddon Rigg. James Hamilton, Earl of Arran and Beaton's leading political rival, was to be excluded from authority. Arran, however, was quick to mobilise his own supporters. By his descent from the daughter of James II, he was the next in line to the throne after Mary and this gave him an authority which Beaton lacked.

In early January 1543 Arran was proclaimed Regent, having successfully excluded, at least for the time being, not only Beaton from government, but also his ally the Queen Dowager, Mary of Guise. Henry VIII was able to take advantage of this marginalisation of the pro-French faction in Scotland. Many of the powerful nobles taken prisoner at Solway Moss were now returned to Scotland. The earls of Glencairn and Cassillis, the lords Fleming, Maxwell and Somerville and other prominent individuals were to act as agents of Henry's interests in Scotland. Their initial action was to request that the English King should take the infant Queen into his protection and that she should, in time, be betrothed to his son Edward, the Prince of Wales.

This was the preferred means of achieving a union of the Crowns, but there remained the possibility that Mary might die in infancy. In this event Henry's supporters in Scotland were secretly pledged to support him in a bid to seize the Scottish throne anyway. The prisoners of Solway Moss were not Henry's only allies. The Douglases, Archibald Earl of Angus and his brother George, chased from Scotland by James V, now returned. It seemed that Henry's fortunes were in the ascendant. In March the Scottish Parliament met and Arran's position was secured. This Parliament agreed to open negotiations for the marriage of Mary and Edward. Parallel to this political leaning towards England were the religious inclinations of this Parliament, which authorised the reading of the scriptures in the vernacular. Arran seemed to be steering a steady course towards an alliance with England.

This gave Henry a confidence that he controlled events which proved to be unwarranted. He demanded that Mary be delivered into his hands immediately, tactlessly ignoring Scottish sensibilities and fears for the country's independence. The lingering fears at the price England might exact once Mary was safely in London were ultimately to doom the drift towards an Anglo-Scottish alliance. For the time being, all still seemed to be going well. On 1 July 1543 treaties of peace and marriage were agreed by both parties at Greenwich, guaranteeing Scotland's independence and keeping Mary in her native land until she was ten. Despite Henry's continued lack of tact (for example he offered English auxiliaries to Arran to crush internal dissent), the treaties of Greenwich were ratified at Holyrood Abbey on 25 August.

The opposition to closer ties to England, however, was now gathering in force, led inevitably by Beaton. Henry's actions only served to strengthen their hand. He demanded that English garrisons be based in Scottish castles south of the Forth, he seized Scottish shipping, he continued to demand that Mary be placed in his care immediately. Worse still was his printed 'Declaration', in which he claimed 'the true and right title that the King's most Royal Majesty hath to the sovereignty of Scotland'.[40] These actions seemed to pose a real and imminent threat to Scotland's independence and the pro-French faction, taking advantage of the fears about English intentions which were developing, orchestrated an impressive coup.

Their most striking triumph was the defection of Arran himself to their camp. Within one month of ratifying the treaties of Greenwich, Arran was hearing Mass and receiving the Sacrament from Cardinal Beaton. The illusion of Arran's strength of purpose was utterly torn way, revealing a weak, vacillating and unpredictable individual whose loyalties fluctuated with bewildering inconsistency. December 1543 saw the Auld Alliance renewed, Beaton raised to the position of Chancellor and a reaffirmation of the laws against heresy passed in the reign of James V.

The pro-English faction survived Arran's defection and continued to negotiate with Henry, but with scant reward. Little caring that it had been his own blundering lack of tact that had enabled Beaton to regain influence, the English King resolved that if he could not secure his son's bride by negotiation he would do so with the sword. Scotland would remember this war as the Rough Wooing.[41] Norfolk, his part in the triumph at Flodden now long forgotten, had been supplanted as England's foremost soldier by the King's brother-in-law, Edward Seymour, Earl of Hertford. It was to him that the task of terrifying Scotland into submission was now entrusted.

Hertford was a keen moderniser in military matters. He was quick to employ foreign specialists, arquebusiers, pikes and light cavalry. He admired the Spanish for their courage and the Germans for their discipline, regarding the latter as the most dependable troops for garrison duty on the dreary northern Border of England. He also worked hard at improving the quality of other troops. Towards the end of 1543 Henry's Lord Deputy in Ireland had begun to enrol Irish kern light infantry to serve the King. One thousand of these were dispatched to the Border under the command of Callough O'Bryne, to release Border horse for service in France. Although noted for their hardiness, Hertford was initially disappointed, complaining to the King in May 1544 that 'the Irishe Kerne are very unruly, their weapons are swords and darts . . . few can shoot in

---

[40] R.B.Wernham, *Before the Armada* (London, 1966), p. 155.

[41] The phrase is derived from a comment made by George Gordon, Earl of Huntly. Captured at the Battle of Pinkie in 1547, he had been asked by his captors how he felt about the proposed royal wedding. He replied that he 'haud weil with the marriage: but I like not this wooing'. See William Patten, 'The Expedition into Scotland, 1547', in A.F.Pollard (ed.), *Tudor Tracts 1532–1588* (Westminster, 1903), p. 77.

hackbuts'. He resolved to train them up, instructing some in the use of the arquebus, and within three weeks was able to report that 'the Irish did good service, are dreaded by the Scots as they take no prisoners after the Border custom but say that the King gives them money to live on'.[42]

Beyond the training and equipping of individual soldiers, Hertford was an able field commander. His armies marched with discipline and order, artillery was brought into action quickly and with good effect. Cavalry and flank guards secured his line of march. Logistics, too, received careful attention. In this Hertford was fortunate to benefit from the planning and forethought of Charles Brandon, Duke of Suffolk and Lieutenant of the North from January 1543 to March 1544. Confronted by the problem of victualling large armies in the North, Suffolk had searched long and hard for a solution. To overcome the lack of carts he had at first suggested carrying small barrels of beer on the soldiers' horses themselves. This was a not altogether satisfactory solution, although Hertford himself was later to convert soldiers to teamsters. Suffolk had instead taken up a suggestion of the King's to make greater use of ships. Suffolk gathered suitable shipping in Newcastle and kept tight control over the supply of victuals throughout the North. He laid the plans for an amphibious assault on Scotland and Hertford wisely built on those foundations when he took over Suffolk's command.[43]

Since Flodden, English incursions into Scotland had been little more than glorified forays, traditional forces of bow and bill, occasionally supplemented by cannon, living off what they could carry, stealing cattle and burning crops, but often stalled by determined resistance. Expeditions under Hertford were to be very different. His forces were true armies, a balanced synthesis of infantry, artillery, light and heavy horse, supported by pioneers and military engineers. He would take full advantage of England's naval might, recognising the potential of amphibious operations. He showed an appreciation of the need to establish garrisons inside Scotland to offer practical support to England's allies, his strategic vision going beyond the narrow objective of simply brutalising Scotland into submission. He was, in short, a tough and professional soldier and Scotland had good cause to fear him.

In conjunction with the military campaign, Henry adopted a series of familiar tactics to win support in Scotland. He offered handsome pensions to disaffected members of the nobility, he encouraged rival claimants to the regency to plot and intrigue. He enjoyed a particular success by re-establishing the old alliance between England and dissident Highlanders. The heir to the extinguished title of Lord of the Isles, Donald Dubh MacDonald, had led an insurrection against James IV between 1501 and 1506. Following the collapse of this rebellion he had been incarcerated in Edinburgh Castle until he had finally gained his

---

[42] T. Blake Butler, 'King Henry VIII's Irish Army List', *The Irish Genealogist*, vol. 1 (1937), p. 3. See also Dean Gunther White, 'Henry VIII's Irish Kerne in France and Scotland, 1544–1545', in *Irish Sword*, vol. 3 (1958), pp. 213–225.

[43] S.J.Gunn, *Charles Brandon, Duke of Suffolk c.1485–1545* (London, 1988), pp. 183–191.

freedom, thirty-seven years later, in 1543. With the financial backing of the English King, Donald of the Isles raised an army from his still loyal followers in the Highlands.

He was able to co-operate actively with England's ally, Matthew Stewart, Earl of Lennox, who in 1545 commanded a small sea-borne force of English and Highland troops in a series of raids into Bute, Arran and Argyll. The determination of the Scottish government to suppress revolt in the Highlands made these Gaelic rebels useful allies for Henry VIII. Scottish troops were diverted away from the Border, out of the path of English forays. In November 1545 an attempt to reinforce Donald's army with troops from Ireland, four hundred gallowglass and fifteen hundred kern, was only frustrated by bad weather.[44] Donald himself then travelled to Drogheda in Ireland to raise troops and discuss strategy with Lennox, but died soon after of a fever.[45] The Highlands, however, were far from pacified. The earls of Huntly and Argyll were forced to mobilise their own retinues in the Highlands in an on-going struggle to bring dissident clans to heel.

England had other allies in Scotland too, whom Henry was quick to finance. There were those who saw a compelling wisdom in the union of the Crowns. During the minority of James V the Scottish historian John Mair had written, 'I venture to think that the English and Scots consult the interests of their monarchs badly, if they do not always arrange marriages among them, seeing that from both kingdoms they might make one realm of Britain.'[46] There were Protestant rebels, most famously the Castilians, who seized St Andrews Castle and held it against Arran from May 1546 to July 1547. The most significant of England's allies were the assured Scots.

The 'assurance' was a common device on the Border. Contracting parties entered into a formal agreement to maintain a truce for a specific length of time, for example when English and Scottish wardens of the Marches met to arbitrate disputes and settle claims. The English now adapted the concept of assurance in an effort to create a body of Scottish allies who would not just maintain a truce but would actively co-operate with the English. This might involve feeding, supplying and acting as guides to English soldiers, turning over strong points to English garrisons and even bearing arms and fighting for England. These assured Scots were not just nobles, many of whom flirted with England, but lairds, gentlemen, burgesses and ordinary folk.

Their motives for assuring differed. Some had genuine Protestant sympathies, such as James Henrisoun, an Edinburgh merchant who worked tirelessly for union from 1544 to 1550, to free Scotland from 'the devil, the pope, and his rabble of religious men'.[47] Others merely appreciated where power lay in their

---

44 White, 'Henry VIII's Irish Kerne', pp. 222–224.
45 Donald Gregory, *The History of the Western Highlands and Isles of Scotland AD1493–AD1625* (Glasgow, 1881), p. 176.
46 G. Gregory Smith (ed.), *The Days of James IIII 1488–1513* (London, 1900), pp. 180–181.
47 Marcus Merriman, 'James Henrisoun and "Great Britain": British Union and the Scottish

own locality and took the opportunity to protect themselves and line their own pockets at the same time. This was particularly true on the Border. Wharton quickly took several leading Scottish reiver clans into English service, taking advantage of their propensity to feud. Thus in 1543 the Armstrongs were easily induced to spoil their old enemies, the Kerrs and the Scotts. In February 1544 Wharton bought the services of the great families of the Middle March, the Davidsons, Pringles, Taits, Youngs, Turnballs and Rutherfords. In the East March he recruited the Dixons, Trotters and Redpaths, who now pursued their long-standing vendetta against the Homes with official backing from England.[48]

For many assured Scots, though, the decision to serve England was taken reluctantly. Assurance offered protection, both from the English themselves and, supposedly, from other Scots who might regard the act as treason. If, militarily, the balance of power favoured England then many Scots were left with little choice but to assure or see their homes go up in smoke, their possessions stolen, and their families possibly put to the sword. Assurance could, thus, be a temporary and fleeting measure born of expediency, or it could represent a genuine commitment to the concept of union with Protestant England in preference to alliance with Catholic France. Assured Scots were to become a central feature of future English military operations in Scotland and the English actively sought such allies, usually assuming that it was best to win over such men by a show of force. The velvet glove would always contain a mailed fist, as Hertford's first campaign was to illustrate clearly.[49]

Hertford's first campaigns: old strategy, new tactics

Edward Seymour, Earl of Hertford, conducted his campaigns of 1544 and 1545 effectively and with the utmost brutality. Henry's instructions to his Lieutenant of the North made plain what kind of war this was to be, reaffirming the principles of the *chevauchée*:

> put all to fire and sword, burn Edinburgh town . . . and as many towns and villages about Edinburgh as ye may conveniently, sack Leith and burn and subvert it and all the rest, putting man, woman and child to fire and sword, without exception where any resistance shall be made against you.[50]

Despite personal reservations about the long term effectiveness of this strategy of destruction, echoed also by the Duke of Suffolk, Hertford determined to carry out his King's wishes to the best of his ability. Favourable winds on 1 May

Commonweal', in Roger A. Mason (ed.), *Scotland and England 1286–1815* (Edinburgh, 1987), pp. 85–112.

[48] Fraser, *The Steel Bonnets*, pp. 256–257.

[49] Marcus Merriman, 'The Assured Scots', *The Scottish Historical Review*, vol. 47 (1968), pp. 10–34.

[50] *The Hamilton Papers, Vol. II, 1543–1590* (Edinburgh, 1892), 207.

1544 carried a 200-ship armada, bearing a 16,000-strong army, from Newcastle northwards.[51] Although at the mercy of the weather, the mobility afforded by an amphibious operation gave the English a striking advantage. The traditional defensive strong points on the Border could be by-passed. Artillery and victuals would not have to be dragged over muddy roads or negotiate treacherous river fords.

The English had used ships before in their campaigns in Scotland. John Lord Howard, had raided the Firth of Forth during Richard Duke of Gloucester's campaign of 1480. Earlier than that, both William I in 1072 and Edward I in 1296 had been resupplied by sea during their invasions.[52] Yet Hertford was to make more sophisticated use of the naval arm's offensive capability. In these campaigns the English were to develop a particular expertise in combined land–sea operations. The army could strike from the sea almost at will, wrong-footing defenders, who would have to watch a whole coastline as well as the land border.

A sea-borne army moved quickly, too, outpacing Scottish mobilisation. On 21 April Arran had ordered that 'all manner of men baith to burgh and land to be ready upon twenty four hours warning baith to pass upon the Englishmen'. Instructions had also been issued to the inhabitants of Fife 'to mak fowseis (earthworks) for resisting the Englishe mennis navye under the paine of tinsall of all their gudis'. Yet besides these preparations Arran needed to muster a field army at a point convenient to meet the English, wherever they might land. Summonses were sent throughout Fife, Forfar, Kincardine, Stirling, Clackmannan and Kinross, 'charging all manner of men between sixty and sixteen to meet my lord Governor upon the Burgh Muir of Edinburgh the fifth day of May, to pas upon the Englishe men'.[53] Here Arran had miscalculated, for 5 May would prove too late to oppose Hertford's landing.

Complicating the process of mobilisation further was the inability to unite in the face of invasion. Arran's attempts to raise troops in the Highlands had been hampered by clan rivalry and the activities of Donald Dubh MacDonald. The danger of discontented Highlanders choosing this moment to exploit Scotland's difficulties had not been lost on either the Regent or the Council. Both had feared that the Highlanders might take the opportunity of renewed Anglo-Scots conflict to 'make a strong party and stand neuters [neutral] or join with either [side]'.[54] The inability of the government to control the clans had been manifest for some time. Law and order had completely broken down in the Highlands in

---

[51] The following account of the 1544 campaign is based on Hertford's communications with the government contained in *LandP, Henry VIII*, vol. 19, part 1, and the anonymous narrative by a soldier in his army, 'The Late Expedition in Scotland', in A.F.Pollard (ed.), *Tudor Tracts 1532–1588* (Westminster, 1903), pp. 39–51.

[52] Michael Prestwich, *Armies and Warfare in the Middle Ages: The English Experience* (London, 1996), pp. 195–197, Charles Ross, *Richard III* (London, 1992), p. 45.

[53] Sir J. Paul Balfour, 'Edinburgh in 1544 and Hertford's Invasion', *The Scottish Historical Review*, vol. 8 (1911), p. 121.

[54] William Mackay (ed.), *The Wardlaw Manuscript Entitled 'Polichronicon Seu Policratica Temporum, Or The True Genealogy of the Frasers', 916–1674* (Edinburgh, 1905), p. 133.

the wake of James V's death. 'The Scotis that duelt in the mountainis and Iles of Irland [the Hebrides], now began to schaw taknes of thair inconstancie and gret wildnes.'[55] Both Huntly and Argyll were periodically diverted from the business of defending the Borders and Lowlands for the purpose of subjugating the Highlands.

Huntly had been forced to intervene in a long-running feud between the Frasers and the Clanranald. He had supported Hugh Fraser, Lord Lovat, in driving the Clanranald from land they had illegally occupied in Abertarf and Stratherrick. In July 1544 Lovat was killed in a Clanranald ambush beside Loch Lochy, the so-called *Blar-ne-leine*, or Field of the Shirts, where the summer heat had caused the combatants to cast off their coats. Huntly then pursued the leaders of the Clanranald, who were active supporters of Donald of the Isles, throwing 'the princes of the clans' into prison and punishing the rest of their people 'with severitie of the law'.[56]

Re-establishing, to a certain extent, Edinburgh's authority in the Highlands, Huntly and Argyll made possible the raising of Highland levies for service in the Lowlands, but not in time for service against Hertford in the spring of 1544. With on-going factional fighting in the Highlands and levies arriving slowly and piecemeal in Edinburgh, Arran's defensive preparations were wholly inadequate.

With favourable tides the English arrived in the Firth of Forth on 3 May. A raiding party immediately rowed into St Mynettes, on the northern coast of the Firth. Finding the town undefended, the raiders began their grim duty, burning the town and stealing the boats in the harbour, which were needed for the main English landing. That night the fleet rested at anchor off Inchkeith, three miles from its intended target, Leith. Capture of this port was vital if the English were to land their larger pieces of artillery and find a secure haven for their fleet.

The following morning the invaders landed two miles west of the town. Once again, the English were surprised to meet no opposition as they undertook the difficult task of getting men and cannon ashore. Fearing attack at any moment, the whole army was speedily disembarked, the operation completed in a mere four hours. Still the defending army did not appear and the English began their march on Leith in confident mood. John Dudley, the Lord Admiral, led the vanguard, Hertford himself the main battle, and Francis Talbot, Earl of Shrewsbury, the rearguard. The army was accompanied by some of the smaller pieces of artillery, manhandled forward by gunners and pioneers, for it was impossible to disembark the draught animals without proper harbour facilities.

As the army closed on Leith they finally encountered the defending force, and with it Arran, Beaton and the Earls of Huntly, Moray and Bothwell. Gathering those who had arrived piecemeal in Edinburgh, the Governor had finally taken the field. About six thousand men, horse and infantry, with well sited

---

55 John Leslie, *The Historie of Scotland*, trans. J.Dalrymple, ed. E.G.Cody and W.Murison (Edinburgh, 1895), vol. 2, p. 280.
56 Leslie, p. 282, Gregory, *The History of the Western Highlands*, pp. 159–163.

artillery, blocked the approaches to Leith.[57] There was a brief exchange of artillery fire before the English, with the advantage of numbers, delivered an assault. This was led by a company of arquebusiers under a captain called Peter Mewtys, who pressed forward with vigour. Casualties do not seem to have been heavy, but Hertford commented that the fight was 'right sharply handled on both parts'.

Nevertheless, within half an hour the English had gained possession of the field, Mewtys's arquebusiers having overrun the Scottish artillery. A second, smaller, force still blocked the path to Leith, and the English took some casualties from artillery fire as they approached its position. Yet the English pressed on rapidly, closing quickly to bow range and firing on the Scottish gun crews. Three gunners were killed and the rest driven away, 'sharply assailed' by the archers. The key to the English success seems to have been the combination of mobility and firepower. Their forward impetus carried them quickly over Scottish positions, whilst arquebusiers and archers laid down a withering fire, driving gunners from their pieces and sending infantry scurrying for cover.

The English had, at this stage, no cavalry of their own, but the Scottish horse made no move to take advantage of their local superiority. If threatened by horse, the English skirmishers could have quickly fled for the cover of the thousands of outstretched pikes and bills of the three battles. Against those, the light Scottish cavalry could have made little impression. The Scots' confidence seems now to have wilted completely, whilst the mood of the invaders became increasingly buoyant.

The people of Leith had taken some measures for their own protection, and the English found the town defended by some hastily erected earthworks. A deep trench constituted the main defence, again strengthened with well placed artillery. One might have expected some pause in the remorseless progress of the invaders at this point, but the impetus of their rapid advance swept the English onwards. An immediate assault on Leith was delivered and, for all the effort that had been made in preparing the earthworks, the town was carried before nightfall. A handful of the attackers were killed as they approached the trenches, but the garrison, after an irresolute defence, quickly fled. That night the English rested, securely protected by those same trenches that had been dug to defy them.

On 5 May Hertford was able to take stock of his prize. Leith proved richer that the English had expected, and a considerable amount of plunder was gathered as the town was looted. A number of ships were also captured, including 'two of notable fairness', the French built *Salamander* and James V's *Unicorn*. Captured 'row barges' were pressed into service to help the English disembark victuals, draught animals and their heavier pieces of artillery. Again the operation progressed with speed and efficiency. Leith was garrisoned with fifteen

---

[57] The author of 'The Late Expedition into Scotland' claims the force numbered five to six thousand horse plus 'a good number of footmen', but Hertford claims only six thousand in total, *LandP, Henry VIII*, vol. 9, part 1, 472.

hundred men under the command of Lord Sturton, and the remainder of the army prepared to move inland against Edinburgh.

The population of the capital had noted with trepidation the ease with which the English had stormed Leith, and now the invaders had landed a larger siege train. Hertford spoke of offers of assurance from the town at this point, and suggested that if Edinburgh were garrisoned, Henry could count on the loyalty of all Scotland south of the Forth. The establishment of strong English garrisons in well fortified positions was Hertford's own preference for ensuring Scottish support for a union of the Crowns, but he would brook no negotiation or compromise in pursuit of his master's goals. When Edinburgh's Provost, accompanied by some prominent citizens, arrived in the English camp to parley he found the King's lieutenant in stubborn mood. Granted an audience with Hertford, the Provost offered 'that the keys of the town should be delivered unto his Lordship; conditionally, that they might go with bag and baggage, and the town to be saved from fire'. The English commander replied 'that unless they would yeild up their town unto him frankly and without condition, and cause man, woman, and child to issue into the fields, submitting themselves to his will and pleasure; he would put them to the sword, and their town to the fire'. Gloomy as this prospect was, the Provost could not bring himself to agree to such complete capitulation – 'better for them to stand to their defence than to yield to that condition'.[58]

On 6 May the English moved against Edinburgh. This time the defences were altogether tougher than those they had faced at Leith. The recently up-graded city walls were well provided with gun loops and embrasures and the gates were particularly well defended. The castle was on an immensely strong natural defensive site and was well garrisoned by two thousand soldiers under Patrick Hepburn, Earl of Bothwell, and Sir George Home. The English approached the city towards Canongate, the vanguard being accompanied by Sir Christopher Morris, Lieutenant of the Ordnance. The intention was to manhandle a number of battery guns (multi-barrelled cannon) forward, and blast the gate down. Yet the broad street up which the gunners pushed their guns was overlooked by many buildings and they soon found themselves under heavy fire from the defenders within.

Several of the gunners were killed and the supporting infantry wavered. Unable to get the guns into position and fearing that their men might bolt, a forlorn hope comprising captains from the vanguard attempted to storm the gate. A fierce skirmish ensued, the ferocity of the assault driving the Scottish gunners away from their pieces. One of the smaller Scottish guns was captured, actually dragged bodily by its barrel through its embrasure. Encouraged by their captains' heroics at the wall, the archers and arquebusiers followed them into the assault, shooting 'so hotly to the battlements of the gate and wall, that no man durst show himself'.[59] Under cover of this fire, the gunners managed to bring

58 'The Late Expedition into Scotland', pp. 41–42, *LandP, Henry VIII*, vol. 9, part 1, 472.
59 'The Late Expedition into Scotland', p. 42.

their battery cannon into action, hard by the gate. It took three or four shots to break this down, but as soon as it was smashed the infantry forced entry into the city. Those defenders who stood their ground were killed, the rest retreated into the castle.

Before Hertford could restrain them, the English pursued their quarry, pushing and pulling their artillery forward through High Street. Immediately they came under heavy and accurate artillery fire from the castle, which overlooked the town and whose gunners commanded all approaches. The English casualties mounted but once in range of the castle their own gunners opened fire. For almost two hours Morris battered away at the castle, with no discernible effect whatsoever. The castle's guns continued to reply, to much more effect, dismounting one of the English guns. Hertford now sought the advice of the military engineer Sir Richard Lee who had accompanied his force. His opinion that the castle was impregnable can not have come as a surprise. There was little or no cover to shelter any assault. The ground was solid rock and could not be trenched. Morris was unable to make any impression at all, whilst the Scottish gunfire was taking a steady toll of the attackers. The assault on the castle was therefore abandoned. The artillery was withdrawn to safety, except the dismounted piece which could not be remounted under the fire from the Scottish cannon, and was deliberately burst instead.

The town had to bear the brunt of English frustration and fires were started in several districts. The conflagration took hold so quickly that the English had to make a somewhat panicky exit through Canongate, with twenty men killed in the crush to escape. The burning and pillaging was renewed early the following morning, and sustained for several hours. The local people had made a hasty and ill-advised attempt to re-occupy Edinburgh and plug the breach at Canongate with earth and rubble, but to no avail. The battery guns blasted the makeshift rampart aside and the town was won again, for the second time in two days. With the garrison of the castle secure, but shut away, the whole of Edinburgh was now put to the torch, including the Palace and Holyrood House. What could not be carried away was consumed by the flames.

The English ability to wreak destruction was considerably enhanced by the arrival of four thousand Border horse. These carried the sword and the torch to the countryside around the capital, sparing neither the laird's house nor the peasant's rudest hovel. Burning crops, stealing cattle and pursuing refugees from Edinburgh, the Borderers devastated the country, seemingly without meeting any organised resistance. The devastation was even carried north of the Forth by Sir Nicholas Poyntz, who stormed and burned Kinghorn and its surrounding villages.

As a finale to the 1544 campaign, Hertford resolved to march the main body of his army home to Berwick, cutting another swath of destruction southwards as he did so. The larger artillery pieces were re-embarked to be shipped to Holy Island along with the assorted plunder and booty gathered in the course of the campaign. The more mobile pieces of artillery were retained for use in the field. To convert his amphibious force into a field army, Hertford gathered up captured carts and converted one thousand of his Border horse into teamsters to pull them. Each captain drew six days' victuals for his company, to be conveyed, with the army's tents and other necessaries, in the stolen carts.

Just two weeks after having set out, the English began their homeward journey. Before leaving Leith they demolished its pier and burnt the town to the ground. As the army moved southwards it destroyed everything in its path, including Lord Seaton's 'chief castle . . . which was right fair' and his orchards 'the fairest and best we saw in all that country'. The fleet continued to play its part in this ugly campaign too:

> our ships upon the sea were not idle; for they left neither ship, crayer, nor boat belonging to either village, town, creek or haven of either side of the Firth between Stirling and the mouth of the river, unburnt or not brought away; which containeth in length fifty miles. Continuing of time, they also burnt a great number of towns and villages on both sides the said water; and won a fortress situated on a strong island called Inchgarve, which they razed and destroyed.

One ship, the *Galie Subtile*, was even sent northwards to raid the towns and villages around St Andrews.[60]

Moving south, the army burned Haddington, including its monastic houses, and then pressed on to Dunbar, camping near to the town on the night of the sixteenth. The townsfolk, convinced that the English would launch an immediate assault, resolved to take the initiative. An attempt was made to storm the English camp, but the attackers were driven away by the watch. As the English camp settled, the Scots maintained their vigil from a distance through the night. In the morning they watched the English break camp and depart southwards.

Believing their town to have been spared, the population of Dunbar returned to their homes and many retired to their beds after a sleepless night. Yet five hundred of Mewtys's arquebusiers and five hundred Border horse had slipped away from the main body of the English army and now fell on the hapless and unwary town. The assault was, characteristically of this campaign, brutal and pitiless. Many of the victims were caught 'in their first sleeps closed in with fire – the men, women and children were suffocated and burnt'.[61]

Scottish forces were now beginning to gather, shadowing the English army. Yet Hertford's force kept such well ordered array that no opportunity to attack presented itself. The day after Dunbar was burnt, the Scots attempted to head off the English line of march, taking up a strong defensive position in the deep gorge of Cockburnspath, known as 'the Pease'. The morning of 17 May was foggy, men strained to see 20 yards into the gloom, and the prickers of both armies clashed in the mist. One party of Scottish Border horse infiltrated the English line of march, working its way between the vanguard and the main

[60] 'The Late Expedition into Scotland', pp. 44–45. *LandP, Henry VIII*, vol. 9, part 1, 510.
[61] 'The Late Expedition into Scotland', p. 45.

battle. Their sudden appearance, just 200 yards from Hertford himself, caused a considerable alarm before they were driven off by the English horse.

The attack unnerved the English. Alert that some danger lurked in the Pease and with reconnaissance confounded by fog, their march slowed. Reluctant to risk falling victim to ambush, Hertford toyed with the idea of halting and encamping. Yet at two o'clock the fog lifted and in clear weather the English approached the Pease. Home, Seaton and Bothwell commanded a force of some two thousand horse and six thousand foot in a strong position. Hertford estimated that a force of just three thousand should have been sufficient to hold his army in this narrow defile. Yet the humiliations and miseries inflicted on their land over the preceding two weeks seem to have taken all the heart out of the Scots. A ragged volley from their falcons opened the fight but, seeing the English neither hesitate in their advance nor break their order, the Scots simply scattered, clambering up the steep slopes on hands and knees to get out of the path of Hertford's oncoming array.

Even unopposed, the passage through the Pease took three hours. The English were still eight miles short of the Border when they made camp that night close to the 'pile' of Ranton, a fortified Border tower. Inevitably, the demolition of Ranton, 'an ill neighbour to the garrison of Berwick', was rapidly accomplished, and the following day Hertford's *chevauchée* came to an end as his army passed over the Tweed. Raiding parties great and small continued to rampage through the Border country, killing, burning and looting as they went. In June, Sir Ralph Eure attacked Jedburgh. Defended by just eight or nine pieces of artillery, the town was subjected to a three-pronged assault spearheaded by the mercenary Irish kern, stormed and sacked. Some Scottish Borderers retaliated in kind. As Eure's men headed back to the Border they saw the smoke rising from English villages put to the torch, and Eure led two hundred of his horsemen to chase the raiders.[62]

In order to frustrate Scottish attempts to carry the war back into England, a small garrison had been placed in the abbey at Coldingham, north of Eyemouth. Arran eventually led an 8000-strong army against the handful of English soldiers occupying the building, who stubbornly refused to surrender. The Governor's cannons bombarded the abbey for a day and a night without effect. When rumours of an English counter-attack from Berwick reached Arran's ears he abandoned his army and rode for Dunbar. This counter-attack turned out to be a relatively small relief force of Border horse which Arran could surely have met in the field. Yet the now leaderless Scottish army at Coldingham simply disbanded itself as the Borderers approached, leaving the English unscathed, astonished and still in possession of the abbey.[63]

Hertford's first campaign had some political repercussions in Scotland. To an extent it discredited both Arran and Beaton, whose efforts to meet the English in

---

[62] 'The Late Expedition into Scotland', p. 46.
[63] George Ridpath, *The Border History of England and Scotland* (Berwick, 1848), pp. 379–380.

the field had been little short of feeble. Others began now to reconsider the advisability of their opposition to the union of the Crowns or their persecution of heretics in the face of a ground swell of support for the Reformation. In the summer of 1544 a broad grouping of aggrieved nobles attempted to replace Arran with Mary of Guise. Angus led the pro-English nobles and was joined by Huntly, Moray and Argyll in their support for the Dowager.

Angus, however, was not altogether trusted south of the Border. He had actually been serving in the field against his erstwhile allies since November 1543. When Arran had deserted his army at Coldingham it had been Angus who had organised the withdrawal of the siege train, which would otherwise have been abandoned to the English.[64] He was now in receipt of a large pension from the Scottish Parliament, which did much to secure his continuing loyalties. For all his years as an ally of England, Angus had never been prepared to sacrifice his own political interest and, for the time being at least, he played the loyal Scot.[65] Henry had more faith in the pro-English faction led by the Earl of Lennox, who forayed on England's behalf throughout August and September. Denied English backing, the Dowager's faction eventually reconciled with Beaton in November 1544. The Cardinal now presided over a council on which both Mary and Arran sat and, with a timely call for unity, was able to win support for the administration from some of the pro-English faction.

The material damage aside, the political storm caused by Hertford's first campaign had been weathered. The lesson, which Hertford was beginning to appreciate, was clear. Once an English army withdrew from Scotland, no matter how successful its campaign had been, England was left with little or no political leverage north of the Border. With Arran and Beaton still firmly in power, the prospect of the union of the Crowns seemed as distant as ever and the incessant war on the Border dragged on and on.

Scotland on the defensive: Ancrum Moor and the raid of 1545

The continuing horrors inflicted upon the Scottish people alienated many former members of the pro-English faction north of the Tweed. Military resistance stiffened in response to English deprivations in the Marches, particularly those committed by Sir Ralph Eure, Sir Brian Laiton and Sir George Bowes. They had laid waste to practically the whole of the Merse and Teviotdale. Jedburgh, Kelso and Dryburg were burned to the ground. Smaller villages, churches, bastle houses and isolated towers were seized and destroyed. Thousands of sheep, cattle, goats and horses were rounded up and driven south. Over eight hundred of the inhabitants themselves were taken prisoner, four hundred were killed.[66]

---

[64] Ridpath, p. 380.
[65] Donaldson, *Scotland, James V – James VII*, p. 73.
[66] Robert Borland, *Border Raids and Reivers* (Dalbeattie, 1899), pp. 64–69.

King Henry was so pleased with this reign of terror that he granted Eure and Laiton possession of all the lands they had conquered. Much of this land was owned by England's former ally Angus, who now grimly resolved that he would personally write his *sasine*, or instrument of possession, on the skins of Eure and Laiton, 'with a sharp pen and bloody ink'.[67] He was soon to make good his words. Early in 1545 the two nobles once more crossed the Border to enforce their claim to the land. They were accompanied by a sizable force including fifteen hundred English Borderers, seven hundred assured Scots, including a contingent of Highlanders under Neil MacNeill of Gigha, and three thousand foreign mercenaries.[68]

To face them Angus, accompanied by the Governor Arran, led a small army which, even when reinforced by a contingent of seven hundred lances from Fife and a body of reivers under Sir Walter Scott, probably numbered no more than 2500. Angus, though, was not about to let discretion be the better part of valour. His country had been devastated, his own lands were under threat and now, to add insult to injury, an English raiding force had desecrated the tombs of his ancestors in Melrose Abbey.

On 17 February the English had returned to Teviotdale. Crossing the Teviot they headed along the causewayed Roman road, Dere Street, towards Lillards Edge. To their right was Peniel Heugh, a small hill from which suddenly a number of Scottish horse broke cover and galloped pell-mell along the Roman road, away from the English. Sensing an easy victory, the English horse gave pursuit, cantering down the narrow road, which was flanked on either side by marsh. Behind them, their infantry struggled to keep up. The ground rises and falls gently here and the view of the English cavalry must have been blocked until, gathering momentum as they went, they crested the last gentle ridge. They may have been in time to see their quarry veer away up Lillards Edge to safety.

In their place, standing astride the road and blocking the English pursuit, was a solid phalanx of pike. Angus and Scott had concocted and executed a classic ambush. Before they even hit the pikes, the leading ranks of English cavalry stumbled, their horses catching their legs in concealed pits dug by the Scots. The rear ranks, trying to avoid the traps, pitched off the road and into the bog. Those who turned back down Dere Street ran headlong into their own breathless infantry. The Scots levelled their pikes and advanced down the road after them. Mounted Scots, whose fleet-footed ponies somehow negotiated the treacherous bog, fell on the English flanks. Fearing that they, too, were about to be overwhelmed by this disaster, the assured Scots suddenly rediscovered their patriotism, tore off their flimsy red crosses and turned savagely on their erstwhile comrades.

Scattered pieces of arms and armour discovered in the nineteenth century suggest that some of the English horse fled south-westwards. A vengeful local population, however, was determined to block their escape, and those who made

---

[67] Pitscottie, *The Historie and Cronicles of Scotland*, vol. 2 (Edinburgh, 1899), p. 35.
[68] Gregory, *The History of the Western Highlands*, p. 168.

it safely across the Ale Water had to abandon their arms, armour and plunder in the process.[69] Scottish casualties were negligible, but perhaps eight hundred of Eure's men had been killed and a thousand more made prisoner.[70] The victory was complete. Indeed Arran even found time to express his pity for the dead. Standing over the prostrate body of Eure, who, like Laiton, had paid the price for his past brutality with his life, Arran had cried 'God have mercy on him for he was a fell cruel man and over cruel, which many a man and fatherless bairn might rue and, welaway that ever such slaughter and bloodshedding should be amongst Christian men.'[71]

Angus had made good his threat to Eure and Laiton, and the defeat sent shock waves into England. Unused to suffering such reverses at the hands of the Scots, Ancrum Moor severely dented English confidence. The Earl of Shrewsbury, the King's Lieutenant of the North since Hertford had taken command in Boulogne, had the whole Border stand in readiness in case of a Scottish incursion in the wake of their victory. The gentlemen of Yorkshire were warned to be ready at one hour's notice if summoned to the Border.[72]

Militarily, however, this was an overreaction. The battle had, in truth, been little more than a skirmish, it could not fundamentally alter the military balance of power in the Marches, or seriously impede the English onslaught. The French did see an opportunity in the victory to tie up English troops on the Border. Lorges de Montgomery was dispatched to Scotland with 3500 auxiliaries and for ten days led a series of destructive raids into England in the vicinity of Wark Castle. Yet he could not persuade the Regent and his council to sanction an actual invasion, which Arran feared would make no headway against English fortifications.[73] Nor were Montgomery's own troops able to stay in the Border country for any length of time. Elis Gruffydd, of the Calais garrison, later met one of them in France and was told that they had been repeatedly attacked by Scottish Borderers, 'chiefly for food and beasts of which there was a great scarcity, especially after the English burned Lothian'.[74]

They were soon withdrawn to Stirling, although Montgomery vainly continued to hope that the opportunity would arise for them to spearhead an invasion of England. Yet even if the military consequences of Ancrum Moor were slight, the victory still proved significant. It did enough in restoring Scottish

---

[69] The most spectacular of the nineteenth-century finds was a characteristic sixteenth-century peaked *burgonet* with a high 'comb' (crest), neck and cheek guards. It was found on a wooded slope which leads down to the Ale Water. Its unfortunate owner's escape must have been blocked by the brook, his pursuers catching him as he looked for a ford. For an illustration of the helmet, see Professor Duns, 'Notes on a Helmet found at Ancrum Moor', *Proceedings of the Society of Antiquaries of Scotland*, vol. 6, 3rd ser. (1895–96), pp. 317–322.

[70] Ridpath, *The Border History of England and Scotland*, p. 381.

[71] *LandP, Henry VIII*, vol. 20, part 2, 301.

[72] *Hamilton Papers*, vol. 2, 414.

[73] George Buchanan, *The History of Scotland*, vol. 3 (Edinburgh, 1821), pp. 31–32.

[74] M.B.Davies (ed.), 'Boulogne and Calais from 1545 to 1559', *Fouad I University, Bulletin of the Faculty of Arts*, vol. 12, part 1 (1950), pp. 43–44.

self-confidence that they felt able to reject new overtures from Henry, who wished to begin negotiations to resurrect the treaties of Greenwich. In the face of this rejection Henry could think of no other policy but an escalation of the military campaign.

In the spring of 1545 the English planned new and massive forays into Scotland. Twin thrusts were to be made through both the East and West Marches. Amphibious forces were to raid the coasts. Thirty-six thousand men were to be gathered, the promise of wages drawing even more blood-thirsty soldiers of fortune from all corners of Europe. Irish kern, Italians, Spaniards, *Landsknechte*, even Albanian stradiots, took service with the English Crown.[75] Yet the presence of the Seigneur de Montgomery and his French troops disrupted plans for offensive operations, for it was assumed that they would lead an invasion of northern England. Hertford had now returned from his brief spell of command in France and was soon confidently plotting how best to meet the Franco-Scottish threat.

Hertford had now firmly resolved that the best military policy for England was the seizure and garrisoning of strategic positions within Scotland, creating a Pale which could be policed by his light cavalry. His preference for this strategy had emerged clearly in 1544. He believed that there were many in the Scottish Lowlands who would serve Henry if he maintained a military presence in the region. His first thought had been to seize and fortify Edinburgh for that purpose, but he had been frustrated by the successful defence of the castle. Later, during the same campaign, he had regretted the destruction of the block-house at Inchgarvy, which if the 'first determination to fortify here had continued, had been worth the keeping'.[76]

More actual progress had been made in the West March. Here Thomas Wharton had planted English garrisons in Threave, Lochmaben and Caerlaverock castles by the end of 1544. Arran had to devote considerable time and expense to the reduction of these English outposts in sieges which he felt were important enough to warrant his personal supervision. Within a year these castles were back in Scottish hands. Yet the rapidity with which these garrisons had become the focus of conflict in the south-west of Scotland suggested that they had exerted considerable influence over the region.

The idea of establishing English garrisons in Scotland was not new. Henry had tried to do so in the aftermath of the signing of the treaties of Greenwich. Yet in Hertford's mind the vague and long-standing English notion that permanent garrisons in Scotland might serve some purpose was now hardening into the basis for his whole strategic vision. The garrisoning would be systematic, not isolated bastions in the midst of hostile territory, but centres of operations from which regions could be held under English authority. This authority would hearten and encourage those Scots sympathetic to the idea of union. Hertford

[75] Gilbert John Millar, *Tudor Mercenaries and Auxiliaries, 1485–1547* (Charlottesville, 1980), pp. 148–150.
[76] *LandP, Henry VIII*, vol. 19, part 1, 472.

had his gaze fixed on Kelso as his first target, which he intended to seize, possibly along with Home Castle, as a counter-stroke to Montgomery's invasion.[77]

Yet that invasion never came. Opposition to the operation had been led by Angus, his brother Sir George Douglas, the Earl Marshall of Scotland, and Gilbert Kennedy, the Earl of Cassillis. On 16 August they wrote to Hertford, claiming the credit for frustrating French plans and advising Hertford to strike against Scotland in September, at harvest time when the crops could be burned. Both Douglas and Angus had recently been rewarded for their services against England by France. Now it seems that their loyalties were wavering again, and their services could be secured by the highest bidder. Angus's fury at the insults done to his family and the threat to his lands seems to have died with Eure and Laiton at Ancrum Moor.[78] The continuing dissension amongst the Scottish nobility and the survival of the pro-English faction, even in the face of repeated English invasions, did not bode well for Scotland's hopes of effective military resistance.

Even so, steps were taken to organise some kind of defence. Five general musters were held in 1545, demonstrating the ability of the Scots to raise large armies, even though the will to lead them seemed so often to be lacking. On the Border a semi-permanent body of one thousand light cavalry was raised to guard the Merse and Teviotdale, funded by a special tax.[79] In September these preparations would be put to the test, as Hertford once more launched a *chevauchée* into south-east Scotland.

The total force numbered sixteen thousand, including four thousand horse. The vanguard was commanded by the Earl of Cumberland, the main battle by Hertford and the rearward by William, Lord Dacre. Each battle was accompanied by its own mounted contingent of a thousand English Border horse, whilst the main battle had a further one thousand men-at-arms in full armour and on barded horse. The General of the Horse, Sir Henry Knevet, also had charge of the 'strangers', the large mercenary contingent. This was divided into six wings, forming flank guards for each of the English battles. Added to this formidable array was the ordnance, under Sir Philip Hobbye.[80]

Most of this army crossed the Tweed two miles north of Wark on 9 September, but the rearward was cut off by a sudden rise in the water level and was compelled to seek a ford two miles further up river. Once the army was reunited it commenced a disciplined and well ordered march on Kelso. 'If Vegetius Frontius were present, which wrote the Stratigemes, Ordre and Policies of Civill Warres, he could not have mended our proceedings', boasted one of Hertford's soldiers.[81]

[77] *LandP, Henry VIII*, vol. 20, part 2, 96.
[78] *LandP, Henry VIII*, vol. 20, part 2, 144.
[79] Donaldson, *Scotland, James V – James VII*, p. 72, Ridpath, *The Border History of England and Scotland*, p. 382.
[80] *LandP, Henry VIII*, vol. 20, part 2, 533.
[81] *LandP, Henry VIII*, vol. 20, part 2, 533.

The town had little in the way of defences, only the abbey presenting a serious obstacle. This was immediately assailed by Hertford's Spanish arquebusiers, but they were met with a determined volley from the abbey's own garrison of arquebusiers, and were driven back leaving two dead. The English called on the occupants of the abbey to surrender, but its guardians yelled back their defiance, apparently unaware that the English had brought artillery. Hobbye had a demi-cannon, a culverin and two sakers wheeled into position and the gunners commenced a two-hour bombardment. English and Spanish arquebusiers provided covering fire for the gunners, concentrating their fire on doors and windows. Unable to return fire, the Scots were helpless as a breach was blasted in the abbey wall, through which the Spaniards quickly gained entry. The defenders retreated into the steeple.

At nightfall an uneasy stalemate developed, Hertford deferring the final assault until morning. Aware of how desperate their plight was, several of the men bottled up in the steeple effected a daring escape, climbing down ropes from high windows to the ground and fleeing into the night. Their less fortunate comrades, who stayed in the steeple, were killed when the English guns resumed their bombardment the next morning.[82]

This was the last serious fighting of Hertford's 1545 campaign. No defending army materialised and the English burned far and wide, outdoing in the scale of destruction even the expedition of 1544. Particular damage was done to the harvest, which had been gathered in quickly that year, but, tragically, not quickly enough to save it from destruction. The English still found the produce stacked neatly on the farms they put to the torch. The abbeys and towns of Melrose and Dryburgh were burnt, as were the hamlets and villages which surrounded them. Jedburgh and its neighbouring villages were sacked on 15 September. Sir Robert Bowes, Warden of the Middle March since Ralph Eure's death, took fifteen hundred Border horse to carry the devastation six or seven miles further north. Their victuals dwindling, the English now turned back for Wark, with Hertford satisfied that he had inflicted twice as much misery on the unfortunate people of the Scottish Border than he had achieved the previous year.[83]

Yet, in strategic terms, Hertford's achievements were limited. His clearest success had been in preventing Franco-Scottish forces from taking any serious offensive action against the English Marches. Beyond that he had wrought much destruction but this was largely confined to the Scottish Marches. Nor had the military effort been sustained long enough to represent a genuine threat to Arran's government. King Henry remained primarily concerned with the war in France, not Scotland, and Hertford's field armies, for all their tactical competence, had swiftly returned to England. In the final analysis, the political impact of the *chevauchées* of 1544 and 1545 was entirely counter-productive. The cause of the royal marriage had not been furthered but France had been given an

---

[82] *LandP, Henry VIII*, vol. 20, part 2, 347, 533.
[83] For a full catalogue of the destruction wrought by Hertford in this year, see *LandP, Henry VIII*, vol. 20, part 2, 533.

opportunity to intervene in Scotland. This active French support served ultimately to strengthen Arran's own grip on power.[84] Hertford recognised the consequences of failing to sustain military pressure in Scotland and this is reflected in his desire to plant permanent garrisons in an English Pale.

However, even though the impact of Hertford's military campaigns on Scottish politics was fleeting, an internal crisis was unfolding. The forces of Reformation were now impossible to contain and the continued, albeit inconsistent, persecution of heretics was only exasperating Scotland's deep divisions. On 1 March 1546 George Wishart, a prominent and influential preacher, was arrested and executed. Wishart's death only added to the list of Cardinal Beaton's enemies. Protestant reformers looked for vengeance. England's King was sponsoring shadowy plots to have the Cardinal assassinated. Many Scottish nobles had their own private feuds with Beaton. Just eight weeks after Wishart's death, a band of conspirators broke into St Andrews and put the Cardinal to the sword before dumping his body unceremoniously over the parapet. The Castilians who held St Andrews were later joined by others, including John Knox, the most formidable figure of the Scottish Reformation. Having committed themselves to the union of the Crowns, the rebels received moral, but not military, support from England.

The last years of Henry VIII

Beaton's death increased Arran's own authority, but he was ill-equipped to deal with the crisis. Just as St Andrews was now held by rebels, Dumbarton Castle was now taken by England's ally Lennox. Arran had conducted sieges before, against Scottish rebels, or small English garrisons, but his record was not impressive. He had struggled to subdue Dalkeith, Glasgow, Caerlaverock, Lochmaben and now Dumbarton. In July 1547 he had moved against an English garrison placed in Langholm by the enterprising Thomas Wharton. Langholm had proved difficult to fortify. The old castle was surrounded by ground too waterlogged or too stony to provide the material for earthworks. Yet the captain of the garrison, Michael Wharton, had done everything in his power to render his post more defensible. He lowered the profile of the tower, removing its uppermost battlements, converted the top floor into a gun platform, and countermured the stairs, windows and chimney.[85]

To deal with this handful of English soldiers in an ageing tower, Arran had to mobilise an army twenty thousand strong, with a considerable train of ordnance. One of Wharton's Scottish spies described it as 'the starkest host and the monest

---

[84] Marcus Merriman, 'The Struggle for the Marriage of Mary Queen of Scots: English and French Intervention in Scotland, 1543–1550' (London University Ph.D., 1974), p. 88.
[85] *Cal. State Papers, Domestic, Elizabeth 1601–1603, with Addenda 1547–1565 [Addenda]* (London, 1870), 22.

and wyth the best order that was sen Flodwn'.[86] This stark host had, eventually, succeeded against Langholm's crumbling, high walls but St Andrews defied Arran's ineffectual efforts at siege warfare entirely. It finally fell to the guns of his French allies, who arrived in July 1547 and took the castle for him. They were led by Leo Strozzi, a Knight of St John who demonstrated considerable ingenuity and professionalism, hoisting artillery onto a precarious platform on the church steeple of St Salvator's College. Other guns were pushed close to the wall, hammering the castle at short range. Soon the defensive ditch was filled with collapsed masonry and debris. At high tide, the French galleys could manoeuvre close enough to shore for their own guns to be able to join the bombardment. The surrender of the Castilians was an inevitability. For fourteen months Arran had been stalled before the castle. He had blustered and threatened the garrison, he had entreated and negotiated, he had bombarded and tunnelled, to no avail. The French reduced it in a mere six weeks.[87]

This was a telling reflection on the extent to which Scotland was falling behind in the arms race with England. The efforts to defend against Hertford's small, but modern, armies had been feeble. Scotland was not bereft of military talent; Ancrum Moor and Haddon Rigg had demonstrated that the experienced Border veterans could still turn the tables on the 'auld enemy' on occasion. Yet these engagements were little more than skirmishes; the record in larger engagements was dismal indeed. Scotland could muster great hosts, but they could not be persuaded to cross the Border to take the war into England.

Even in defence, whilst individuals might still fight with the stubborn courage of Bannockburn and Stirling Bridge, the will and ability to lead were sadly lacking. Why should ordinary Scots not choose to assure with England when so many members of their own nobility chose to ride under the banner of St George? What made Scotland's peril all the more great was that England clearly had absorbed the military lessons of continental warfare. In Hertford they had an experienced and capable commander, committed to the modern discipline of war. His armies bristled with pike and shot, effective field artillery and a powerful cavalry arm. His use of ships gave his expeditions not just an added mobility, but overcame many of the logistical problems that had faced earlier English armies in Scotland.

And the worst was yet to come for Scotland. On 28 January 1547 Henry VIII died. If the Scots hoped now for respite, they were to be sadly disappointed. The boy King Edward VI's Regent was to be his uncle, Hertford himself, now elevated to the title Duke of Somerset and Lord Protector. Somerset shared none of his former King's continental ambitions. For Somerset, France was the distraction and Scotland the prize. By July the scale of military preparations in the Marches was unmistakable. Berwick Bridge was starting to crumble under the weight of cannon and waggons laden with munitions that had rumbled across it.

---

[86] *Cal. State Papers Scot.*, vol. 1, 21.
[87] Holinshed, *The Description of Scotland* (London, 1805), p. 547, Leslie, *The Historie of Scotland*, p. 295.

Carlisle echoed to the sound of gunfire as Wharton trained a new company of arquebusiers, with new 'hackbuts' sent from Newcastle. In both cities, the stocks of victuals and munitions grew and grew whilst the fletchers and armourers toiled.[88] The Rough Wooing would now enter its next phase.

---

[88] *Addenda, 1547–1656*, 19, 22.

CHAPTER FIVE

THE CAMPAIGNS OF 1547, PINKIE CLEUGH AND THE OCCUPATION OF ANNANDALE

The Lord Protector and Scotland: a new strategic approach

EDWARD SEYMOUR, Duke of Somerset and the Lord Protector, uncle of the sickly boy King Edward VI, was a complicated figure. He combined deeply sincere religious principles with a genuine concern for the lot of the poor in an era of economic crisis. He was, however, far less resolute in his actions than in the conviction with which he held his principles. Veering between obstinacy and vacillation, he proved unequal to the political crisis, which manifested itself in numerous popular risings which ultimately engulfed him. Somerset's inability to restore domestic order was compounded by an almost obsessional desire to remove French (and Roman Catholic) influence from Scotland. He had long since recognised the futility of the policy of successive invasions, destructive and expensive both in men and materials but with little long term impact. Instead he focused upon the idea of creating a Pale in Scotland by establishing permanent garrisons north of the Border.

As the Border war had dragged on, Hertford himself had been temporarily removed to a very different theatre of operations, being appointed to command the English forces in Boulogne in 1546. Five months service in France was a valuable military education. Hertford fought no pitched battles with the French, but the two sides 'bickered' continually in the disputed ground around Boulogne. Fast moving raids, vicious skirmishes and ambushes were the order of the day. Here both the English and French were engaged in fortifying their positions, and Hertford would have seen the effectiveness of the modern, low-lying angled bastions of the *trace italienne*. It was fortifications of this type that Somerset hoped his pioneers would construct for him in Scotland.

Yet there was more to his strategy than the garrisoning of a series of isolated outposts. He wanted to create an English Pale in Scotland. The English had established garrisons in Scotland in the past and had, for long periods, occupied areas of southern Scotland. Somerset's strategy was, however, more sophisticated. The English Crown would win the loyalty of the Scottish population within this Pale through a mixture of intimidation and persuasion. Occupation would be accompanied by promises of religious reform and of the manifest benefits that would accrue from union of the crowns. Initially at least, Somerset envisaged not conquest but union, the creation of 'Greater Britain'.

For many Scottish Protestants such a union was divinely ordained and there was a real desire amongst them to advance the commonweal of their native land. Propagandists and pamphleteers stressed similarities in custom, language and descent between English and Scot, promoting the concept of 'Briton'. Individual preachers such as James Henrisoun worked tirelessly on Somerset's behalf to try to persuade their compatriots that the real threat to their country was a papist clergy and French intrigue.[1] In its initial conception, therefore, Somerset's strategy could rest on an assumption that his military action would receive support from some, perhaps most, of the population in the areas he chose to occupy. In this case the English would not have to contend with the scorched earth policy that had met previous invasions. The logistical problems that had always blighted English operations in Scotland could be overcome with the co-operation of a sympathetic local population. Somerset's strategy, therefore, initially rested on fundamentally different assumptions to previous English operations in Scotland. The opportunity for dynastic union, the ideological imperatives of the Reformation and the prospect of support in Scotland itself for the creation of a united Britain, underpinned an unprecedented strategic approach to English military activity in Scotland.

The final appeal would be entirely pragmatic. Military superiority implied that England offered individual Scots their best hope of receiving law, order and protection. Somerset's campaign therefore had two immediate objectives. Firstly, the government of Arran had to be militarily and politically discredited, a process in which some progress had been made during the *chevauchées* of 1544 and 1545. If the Scottish government continued to prove incapable of defending Scottish subjects, then those subjects may choose to seek the protection offered by the English Crown. This first objective would have to be achieved quickly. The time that an English army could spend on campaign would always be limited by the logistical problems inherent in supplying a large force in the devastated Marches. Calculations made in the spring of 1547 envisaged a campaign of twenty-eight to thirty days.[2] The second objective could be pursued once Scottish forces in the field had been dispersed. Somerset would establish a permanent and sustained presence in the new Pale by planting English garrisons at defendable sites within Scotland, which could be supplied by assured Scots.[3]

The greatest threat to the existence of these garrisons would be a French military intervention in force. Yet French intentions were hard to calculate. In the past their expeditionary forces to Scotland had been relatively small. Besides

---

1 Marcus Merriman, 'James Henrisoun and "Great Britain": British Union and the Scottish Commonweal', in Roger A. Mason (ed.), *Scotland and England 1286–1815* (Edinburgh, 1987), pp. 95–112.
2 W.K.Jordan, *Edward VI: The Young King* (London, 1968), pp. 250–251.
3 For Somerset's policy in Scotland see M.L.Bush, *The Government Policy of Protector Somerset* (London, 1975), chapter 2. Cf. A.F.Pollard, 'The Protector Somerset and Scotland', *The English Historical Review*, vol. 13 (1898), pp. 464–472.

which their priority now would surely be the recovery of Boulogne. Since Somerset did not share his late King's continental ambitions he could, if necessary, use the town to bargain for French acquiesence to the English presence in Scotland. The possible resumption of the Valois-Hapsburg conflict, and its military and financial demands, also militated against the possibility of France committing substantial forces to Scotland. Somerset thus had reasons to assume that any French intervention would not be on a scale sufficient to frustrate his strategy. Events would prove this to be a miscalculation but, initially at least, an understandable one.[4]

For the initial campaign a third of Somerset's troops would be mounted, a high proportion for an English army. Whilst he would show his willingness to use heavy men-at-arms on the battlefield itself, his light cavalry were, in the long term, accorded the most important role in his overall strategy. He seems to have envisaged a particularly novel and striking role for his light cavalry. Eighteen hundred of the Border horse were initially earmarked for service as garrison troops. The use of cavalry in this role has puzzled some.[5] Yet it would be a mistake to regard these men as mounted infantry; they were clearly intended to serve as true cavalry. Light horse continued to operate from the garrisons once they were established, either offering protection to assured Scots or else persuading others of the wisdom of taking assurance by burning their houses down. Thus we find, for example, 'bands of horsmen . . . readie to come foorth to skirmish abroad upon sight of the enimie' operating from Haddington in 1548 and 'fiftie light horsemen' based in Castle Milk responsible for the 'preseruation of the countrie thereabouts to the King of England's use'.[6]

The garrisons were designed to be more than isolated fortifications. They were to be bases for highly mobile forces of light cavalry which could police wide areas. Besides protecting assured Scots who swore allegiance to the English Crown, fast moving bands of light horse served an important defensive purpose. Somerset had seen how quickly the Scottish recovered from invasion and organised retaliatory raids. With assistance from France a possibility, England's security itself might be compromised by war in Scotland. His mobile forces of light cavalry, operating from secure fortifications, would make it impossible for a Scottish army to restore control of the Pale, or threaten northern England, without leaving its own lines of communication open to attack. The mounted troops were therefore crucial to the success of the entire operation. This too was an unprecedented feature of Somerset's strategy, and is a reminder of how important the mounted arm had become in early modern English armies.

Somerset's strategy was therefore a daring and sophisticated one, relying on

---

[4] Marcus Merriman, 'The Struggle for the Marriage of Mary Queen of Scots: English and French Intervention in Scotland, 1543–1550' (University of London Ph.D., 1974), pp. 206–208.
[5] *Calendar of State Papers Relating to Scotland, Vol. 1, 1547–63* (Edinburgh, 1898), 31.
[6] *Cal. State Papers Scot.*, vol. 1, 31, Raphaell Holinshed, *The Historie of Scotland* (London, 1805), pp. 552, 559.

modern fortifications, the fighting potential of light cavalry, and an optimistic assessment of the level of support for the cause of union in Scotland. The implementation of this strategy began even before the invasion proper was under way. In late August Somerset was joined in Newcastle by Archibald Armstrong, the young Laird of Mangerton in Liddesdale, and 'forty Scottish gentlemen of the East Borders'. Armstrong was a welcome ally, having already proved himself whilst fighting for Thomas Wharton in Annandale in April of 1547.[7] On 1 September Somerset led a small band of horsemen six miles north of Berwick, into Scotland. He had selected Eyemouth as a suitable site for his first garrison.

Here there was no existing fortification to occupy or adapt. The fort that was constructed on the site reflected the lessons the English had learned at Boulogne. A single full bastion, well furnished with gun ports and casements, was built across the neck of a peninsula that commanded the town's harbour. Curtain walls, 50 feet thick and faced with masonry, projected from the bastion to the cliff edges on either side. These were protected in turn by a 20 foot ditch and counterscarp. Twelve cannon, ranging in size from demi-culverins to twin-barrelled fowlers, completed its defences. Eventually this small fort was to be the base for thirty-four arquebusiers and ten light horse under the command of Thomas Gower, Marshal of Berwick.[8] With the site of his first garrison established, the English commander now made the final preparations for invasion.

Arran's response: the problems of defence

Arran could not have failed to notice these preparations. Throughout August he had been preparing his own defences, this time with more determination than in 1544 or 1545. The castles of Home, Edinburgh, Stirling and Dunbar were supplied with men, munitions, cannon and victuals. The system of beacons and lookout posts which would give warning of invasion was put in readiness. On 17 August, by which time invasion was a certainty, Arran sent out letters ordering contingents from every corner of the land to muster at Fala by 31 August. The message was reinforced by the sight of riders bearing the fiery cross.

Yet Arran faced major problems in mobilising his army. The campaign to drive the English from Langholm in July had involved twenty thousand men. They had served for two weeks, and were now only obliged to serve for another twenty-six days in that year. Furthermore, many in the West March were reluctant to leave their homes at all, fearing – correctly as it turned out – that there might be two invasions. Archibald Campbell, Earl of Argyll, had raised a considerable body of Highland troops in July, but their indiscipline was causing

[7]   *Calendar of State Papers, Domestic, Elizabeth 1601–1603, with Addenda* [*Addenda*], *1547–1565* (London, 1870), p. 323, William Patten, 'The Expedition into Scotland, 1547', in A.F.Pollard (ed.), *Tudor Tracts 1532–1588* (Westminster, 1903), p. 80.
[8]   Marcus Merriman, 'The Fortresses in Scotland', in H.M.Colvin (ed.), *The History of the King's Works*, vol. 4, part 2 (London, 1982), pp. 703–704.

much friction with Lowlanders, 'thir Irismen . . . waist and distoyis all menis gudis quharever thay cum'.[9] Yet, with commendable effort, threats and promises, Arran finally managed to raise an impressive force. His army comprised about twenty-six thousand foot, predominantly armed with pike, four thousand Highland bowmen and fifteen hundred light cavalry.[10]

Despite the losses of Solway Moss, he was also able to field a useful artillery train, perhaps thirty cannon and a number of smaller pieces mounted on waggons. Arran was joined too by many kirkmen, and some of his soldiers fought under a banner bearing the legend AFFICTAE SPONSAE NE OBLIVISCARIS (Forget not your afflicted wife), a reference to the threat now posed to Catholicism in Scotland.[11] These priests were concentrated mostly with Arran's main battle. They would have been less welcome elsewhere in the army, a reflection of the divisions within Scottish society.[12] The vanguard was to be led by the Earl of Angus, England's erstwhile ally. Most of his men were from the south-west, an area with marked Protestant and pro-English sentiments. Indeed many of the Lowland levies might have noted the absence from the army of their lords, the Earls of Cassillis and Glencairn, both in English pay.[13] Mutual distrust and suspicion lay festering at the core of the Scottish army.

Yet political expediency demanded that, for the time being at least, these men serve Arran. In the face of foreign invasion a man had to be seen to take up arms in the defence of his country. And whatever double-dealing game Angus was involved with, in the field he was a proven commander, having been largely responsible for the victory at Ancrum Moor. The same was true of the commander appointed to command the Scottish rearward. George Gordon, Earl of Huntly, had proved his own ability in a hundred Border skirmishes, most notably at Hadden Rigg. Like Angus, Huntly was known to have some sympathy for the idea of union with England, but his appointment to the rank of Chancellor by Arran in 1546 had gone some way to reconciling the two men and made it difficult for him to avoid taking a position of responsibility in the army. Both in terms of the quality of his officers and the sheer size of his army, Arran had reason to be confident.

Time, however, was not on his side. The mustering was painfully slow. The contingents from the north were delayed by a shortage of ferries. Additionally, he faced the possibility that his soldiers would simply begin to drift away before too long, a problem which plagued all Scottish commanders of the sixteenth century. Thus it was important to predict Somerset's plans, and bring him to battle quickly. Two visits by the Italian engineer Sir Giovanni de Rossetti to the

---

9   *Cal. State Papers Scot.*, vol. 1, 23.

10 Patten, 'Expedition into Scotland, 1547', p. 108, Robert Lindesay of Pitscottie, *The Historie and Cronicles of Scotland*, vol. 2 (Edinburgh, 1899), p. 96.

11 Patten, 'Expedition into Scotland, 1547', p. 132.

12 David Caldwell, 'The Battle of Pinkie', in Norman MacDougall (ed.), *Scotland and War, AD 79–1918* (Edinburgh, 1991), p. 74.

13 James Fergusson, '1547, The Rough Wooing', *Blackwoods Magazine*, vol. 262 (1947), p. 187.

Castilians in June 1547 had been a strong hint about Somerset's long term strategy. De Rossetti was known to be in English pay, and the Scottish Lord Advocate, Adam Otterburn, had guessed correctly that he was searching for possible sites to fortify. A full three months before Somerset crossed the Border, Otterburn was warning that he meant to establish forts in Fife and Lothian.[14]

Arran therefore had a broad knowledge of Somerset's intentions. It remained difficult to plan how best to meet the threat since one vital piece of intelligence remained unclear. He did not know Somerset's intended route. Arran guessed that the invasion route would be inland, through the Middle March. An army mustered at Fala would protect Edinburgh from a thrust from that direction. In the event it soon became apparent that Arran had seriously miscalculated.[15]

The double invasion

The English hoped to wrong-foot the Scottish defence by launching two simultaneous invasions. The main thrust would be Somerset's army, nineteen thousand strong, mustered at Berwick-upon-Tweed.[16] This army would proceed along the coast of the Merse, well to the east of the route predicted by Arran. Moving along the coast allowed Somerset to count on the close support of a powerful English fleet. This armada comprised eighty 'shippes, shalupes and boates of warre', ranging in size from the mighty *Harry Grace à Dieu*, displacing 1000 tons, down to the little *Fawcon of Plymouth*, one of the 'Western men with oores' displacing just 20 tons. Altogether the warships were crewed by 9222 men.[17] The main invasion was to be a combined land–sea operation, the logical extension of the successful technique used in the 1544 expedition.

The secondary invasion was to foray into Annandale in the south-west of Scotland, under the command of the Warden of the West March, Lord Wharton. In effect, Wharton's invasion was to be little more than a diversion. He would lead two thousand foot, five hundred horse, and gunners with six small cannon in a campaign which would draw Scottish manpower away from the main invasion. Since Wharton was accompanied by the Earl of Lennox, and two hundred of his reivers were Scottish, it was hoped that others, in a region with strong pro-English sentiments, would join them.[18]

Wharton's force crossed the Border into Annandale on 9 September. They were accompanied by some artillery but little baggage, each man carrying twenty days' victuals with him. They pushed swiftly north, reaching Castle Milk, sixteen miles on, the following day. Here their campaign had an auspi-

---

14 Annie I. Cameron (ed.), *The Scottish Correspondence of Mary of Lorraine* [*Scottish Correspondence*] (Edinburgh, 1927), cxxxvi.
15 Caldwell, 'The Battle of Pinkie', pp. 70–71.
16 Patten, 'The Expedition into Scotland, 1547', pp. 77–78.
17 *Cal. State Papers Scot.*, vol. 1, 29.
18 *Cal. State Papers Scot.*, vol. 1, 42.

cious start. The captain of the castle, James Stewart, was summoned to surrender, and did so without resistance once he saw that the English were accompanied by Lennox. The castle was immediately handed over to a garrison of twenty men, twelve of them 'hagbutters', under the command of one Fergus Graham. To ensure their continuing loyalty Wharton paid the men one month's wages in advance (an unusual experience for sixteenth-century soldiers) and left them with ample provisions. Castle Milk soon became an active part of Somerset's chain of garrisons. Fifty light horse were based there and held Annandale for the King. The castle itself was in a state of some decay, yet the English appreciated its strategic location and it appears centrally on a contemporary 'platte' of the region, a 'platte' that illustrates clearly that the military map was not a seventeenth-century phenomenon.[19]

Arran, preparing to meet Somerset personally in the east, had planned that resistance to Wharton in the west should centre on Annan. He had sent one James Lyone with seven gunners and over fifty men to the town, whose folk he had charged to aid in the defence. Lyone had fortified Annan church. There, on 11 September, he was confronted by the invaders. He was to make a far greater show of resistance than Stewart had managed at Castle Milk, defiantly rejecting the first summons to surrender. The English were left to puzzle overnight how to take the thick-walled church, their six cannon being too light to accomplish the task unaided.

Eventually Wharton and Lennox reached the conclusion that the walls of the church would have to be mined. Their attack began at eight the next morning. The artillery commenced its bombardment, supported by a steady fire from archers and arquebusiers. Under cover of this fire a large timber pavise was manoeuvred against the steeple wall, beneath which six pioneers hacked and dug at the stone. This first attempt to undermine the steeple met with disaster. Those inside 'maid sharpe warre'. Heavy rocks dropped from the parapet smashed the pavise, killing four of the sappers. A second effort was made against the east end of the church. This time a charge was successfully laid and exploded. A section of wall and the roof of the church collapsed, falling timber and masonry killing seven of the defenders, the others fleeing into the steeple. The English cannon now played on the breach and on the steeple door, pinning down those inside whilst the pioneers laid further charges. Lyone realised that further resistance was hopeless and surrendered without conditions at four in the afternoon, delivering the keys of the steeple and the fifty-seven surviving defenders into Wharton's hands.

The English detonated their remaining mines, destroying what was left of both church and steeple, before burning Annan to the ground. Wharton's policy was to spare those who made no resistance, punish those who did. For five days he harried and burned the recalcitrants before returning to Carlisle on 12 September with eighty prisoners and twelve 'principal hostages'. He confidently

[19] Marcus Merriman, 'The Platte of Castlemilk, 1547', *Transactions of the Dumfriesshire and Galloway Natural History Society*, vol. 44, part 3 (1967), pp. 175–181.

asserted that the whole of Annandale would soon serve the King and praised the efforts of the gentlemen of the West March. Although 'want of victual and ordnance' had meant an early return, he hoped that the task of further promoting the cause of union could now be entrusted largely to the assured Scots. However much he boasted of his success though, news had already reached him of the astonishing outcome of Somerset's campaign, news which entirely overshadowed his own little foray.[20]

The invading army in the East March had pushed into hostile territory on 4 September, following the lead of the fleet, which had put to sea two days earlier. On the march the army was divided into the traditional three battles. John Dudley, the Earl of Warwick, Lord Lieutenant of the Army, led the vanguard of three thousand footmen. Dudley was well qualified for this office. An experienced commander, he had captained the English garrison at Boulogne, repelling the *camisado* of October 1544. The main battle, four thousand strong, was commanded by the General of the Army, Somerset himself. A soldier by inclination and aptitude, Somerset may have struggled as the head of government but was in his element at the head of an army. The rearward of three thousand men was led by the current head of a famous Border clan, Thomas, Lord Dacre. A veteran of Solway Moss and the cut and thrust of Border warfare, Dacre was perhaps more of a reiver than a soldier, but that pedigree was not to be despised. It had served England well enough at Flodden.

The core of the English army, the three infantry battles, thus marched under proven commanders. The majority of their troops were still of the traditional bow and bill type, although an increasingly large number of native pike and shot were available. Somerset benefited also from recent developments of the system by which the shire levy was mustered. In particular, the office of Lord Lieutenant was evolving from the exigency creation of the crisis of 1539 into a more permanent feature of English military organisation. Although appointments to Lord Lieutenant were still temporary in 1547, the office carried considerable authority. With the power to assemble and organise the levy now vested in one individual, the process of mustering was considerably streamlined.[21]

Although still serving alongside the companies raised by nobles, the levy provided the backbone of Somerset's force. Many of these men would have been from the north country and thus would have been serving under arms on a semi-permanent basis since 1542. Those who had accompanied Somerset's expeditions in 1544 and 1545 must have been not only experienced but brimming with self-confidence, remembering their succession of easy victories. They were reliable too, for the Lord Protector stamped his authority on the mass of troops he commanded early on in the campaign. In late August a new gallows

---

20 *Cal. State Papers Scot.*, vol. 1, 42, 44, Holinshed, *Historie of Scotland*, pp. 552–553.

21 B.Coward, 'The Lieutenancy of Lancashire and Cheshire in the Sixteenth and Early Seventeenth Centuries', *Transactions of the Historical Society of Lancashire and Cheshire*, vol. 119 (1967), pp. 39–64, Hermann H. Hattaway, 'Some Aspects of Tudor Military History', *The Army Quarterly*, vol. 98 (1969), pp. 53–63.

was erected in Berwick market place, 'for example's sake', and a quarrelsome soldier was hanged for brawling soon after.[22] If the bulk of Somerset's infantry were not yet professionals in the strictest sense of the term, they were without doubt competent and well disciplined.

Besides the ten thousand foot there was a powerful cavalry arm under the overall command of William, Lord Grey of Wilton, High Marshal of the Army. Another veteran of the French wars, Grey had been wounded at Montreuil. Later, like both Dudley and Somerset, he had a spell in command of the garrison of Boulogne.[23] He was ably supported by two lieutenants. Sir Francis Bryan had charge of two thousand light horse, mostly Borderers but also including some Yorkshire men. Sir Ralph Vane had overall command of four thousand heavy cavalry who had mustered in Newcastle in late August, receiving their conduct money and a uniform of red surcoats.[24] These included fully armoured men-at-arms, including Spanish and Burgundian mercenaries and the lighter, but business-like, demi-lancers.

To emphasise the importance attached to this campaign, two units of England's few genuinely professional soldiers formed the central core of the heavy cavalry, Edward Shelley's Bulleners of the Boulogne garrison and Sir Thomas Darcy's Gentlemen Pensioners. Somerset had brought some specialists too. Sir Peter Mewtys, who had served him so well in 1544, was present with six hundred Spanish and Italian arquebusiers. Amongst these mercenaries were some individual military professionals of considerable repute. The Spaniard Julian Romero, later one of Alba's leading lieutenants in the Netherlands, served under Mewtys.[25] In the company of the Earl of Warwick was John Berteville, a French Protestant and soldier of fortune. The presence of such men gave Somerset's army a core of genuine military professionals with expertise in the most modern techniques of war.

The most important mercenary captain of all was Pedro de Gamboa. He had been hired to lead two hundred Italian 'hackbutters on horseback', mounted firearm troops of the most modern kind. These troopers were the final element of Somerset's mounted arm, confirming the extent to which this English army conformed to practices advocated by the most advanced military theorists on the continent. In Du Bellay's *Discourse Militaire* of 1548, the French veteran identifies four essential categories of mounted men: men-at-arms, the lighter chevauxlegers, stradiots and harquebusiers.[26] These categories are exactly equivalent to Somerset's Pensioners, demi-lancers, Border horse and hack-

---

[22] Patten, 'The Expedition into Scotland, 1547', p. 80.

[23] Sir Philip de Malpas Grey Egerton (ed.), *A Commentary on the Services and Charges of Lord Grey of Wilton 1508–1562 by his Son Arthur, Lord Grey of Wilton* (Tonbridge, 1991), vii–viii.

[24] *Calendar of State Papers, Domestic, Edward VI, 1547–1553* (London, 1992), 45.

[25] The career of Julian Romero is recounted by Martin Hume, 'Julian Romero – Swashbuckler', in M.Hume, *The Year after the Armada and other Historical Stories* (London, 1896), pp. 75–121.

[26] Hans Delbrück, *The Dawn of Modern Warfare* (London, 1990), p. 118.

butters on horseback. The strength of this modern cavalry arm was to be a major factor in the outcome of the campaign.

Fifteen pieces of 'great ordnance' also accompanied the army, with munitions and victuals carried in nine hundred carts and 'many waggons'. At the head of this formidable fighting force, Somerset had not forgotten his overall purpose. He had brought fourteen hundred pioneers, under captain John Brende, to build his forts. These were to be devised by Richard Lee, the experienced military engineer who had served him before in Scotland and Boulogne.[27]

This daunting army marched with the same discipline and order that had characterised Somerset's campaigns in 1544 and 1545, reaching Reston, six miles into Scotland, by nightfall on 5 September. Four hundred of Bryan's light cavalry preceded the advance, probing cautiously along the route north a mile or two ahead of Warwick's vanguard. This, in turn, was followed by the main battle and the rearward. The three English battles were each flanked on the inland side by heavy cavalry and accompanied by their own artillery and pioneers, ready for any eventuality.

As they advanced rumour reached them that the Scots were fortifying the Pease, that deep ravine traversed only by difficult and steep paths, in the path of the English advance. There was no way to outflank this obstacle, for it lay across a narrow strip of land between the Lammermuir Hills and the sea, and into which the invading army had been funnelled. This was the inherent disadvantage of taking the eastern route into Scotland, and possibly explains why Arran had assumed that the invasion would arrive from further west. Somerset may have gambled on Arran's miscalculating, for he certainly knew about the defensive potential of the Pease, having crossed it in 1544. He had approached the position with much caution then, although in the event the English had forced a passage without difficulty. With a more resolute defence it would be a hard fight for this defile.

Once again a cautious approach was made, but this time, to their surprise, the English found the Pease completely unoccupied. Shallow trenches had been scratched in the earth, hindering the passage of the English baggage, but their architects had gone. Their brief efforts had been made after last minute orders from Arran. On 1 September he had realised that his musters in Fala were in the wrong place. He had left Edinburgh intending to move his army with all haste to the Pease. Yet the delayed arrival of many of his troops had frustrated this last minute change of plan. The projected defence of the Pease was abandoned, to the great good fortune of the English.[28] Their pioneers levelled the half-dug ditches, the carts and ordnance passed and the English made camp at sunset. Somerset, impatient to be making progress, had gone on ahead one mile with a sizable escort to demand the surrender of the small castle at Dunglass.

The garrison of just twenty-one soldiers was led by Matthew Home who, realising the futility of his position, quickly surrendered. He and his bedraggled

---

27 Patten, 'The Expedition into Scotland, 1547', pp. 77–78.
28 Caldwell, 'The Battle of Pinkie', p. 73.

band of soldiers were sent on their way, having sworn not to bear arms again against the invaders. John Brende's pioneers then set about dismantling the castle, carting much of the stonework to Eyemouth as building material for the English fort. Keen still to emphasise his good intentions towards Scotland, Somerset spared the town of Dunglass from the torch. Just a mile and a half beyond Dunglass were two other small strongholds, little more than fortified houses, Thornton and Innerwick. Both contained small garrisons, which Somerset resolved to deal with the following day.

On the morning of 6 September, Somerset sent his herald alone to Thornton to give its captain, Tom Trotter, the chance to surrender. Trotter mischievously replied that he would come and talk to the English commander in person. Instead he locked sixteen poor soldiers into the house and ordered them to defend themselves for as long as possible. With that, and, taking the keys with him, he rode away, promising to return with reinforcements the next day. His soldiers appeared to believe this unlikely tale, for when summoned to surrender they unwisely refused.

The assault on Thornton was entrusted to Sir Peter Mewtys and his arquebusiers, supported by four cannon. The garrison attempted to hold the English at bay with two bases (small cannon) of their own and by dropping rocks from the higher storeys when the attackers approached the walls. Yet the sustained and accurate fire of the Spanish and Italian veterans drove them away from their windows and loopholes. Under cover of this fire, some of the arquebusiers broke into the lower storey of the house, which was abandoned by the defenders, who had retreated upstairs. With their situation obviously hopeless they now attempted to surrender.

Their assailants, though, were conducting this strange little skirmish as if it were a major siege. The garrison had refused to surrender when summoned so, by the generally accepted customs of war, their lives were forfeit if the house was taken by assault. With their request to surrender denied, the garrison asked that they might be taken and hanged, so that they might 'reconcile themselves to God and not die in malice, with so great danger of their souls'. Their petition was taken to Somerset, who chose instead to spare them.[29]

The garrison at Innerwick was less fortunate. This house, too, was similarly assailed by arquebusiers, but it was not felt necessary to support them with artillery, for the house was only held by nine men. Pinning this insignificant garrison down with accurate fire, the arquebusiers worked their way to the walls and forced an entry into the house. Finding the lower floor deserted and the stairway

---

[29] The captives were committed to the care of the Provost Marshall and, in all probability, released on taking assurance with the English Crown. Keeping poor men as prisoners of war was more trouble and expense than it was worth. In 1588 three Dutch sailors who 'had beene in the Spanish fleete againste her majestie', were captured in Cheshire. On 7 November they were placed in Chester gaol. Just one week later the Mayor was demanding that the Earl of Derby remove them, so that they should no longer be a charge to the city. Chester City Records Office, Mayors' Military Papers, MMP/5/16.

blocked, they simply piled up combustible material and set the house on fire. Again the defenders realised the hopelessness of their situation and offered to surrender. Once more, Somerset chose to spare them, but before he had time to order their withdrawal the war-hardened mercenary arquebusiers had killed the entire garrison.

The defenders of these sorry 'piles' had little chance, but Dunbar Castle, defended by modern artillery fortifications, successfully defied Somerset. The English were forced to bypass the stronghold, coming under cannon fire as they did so, and had to fight off a sortie by light cavalry from the town.

Nine miles further along the coast from Dunbar was Tantallon Castle, stronghold of the Douglas family. Tantallon had also been modernised in recent years and was well provided with defensive ordnance. Like Dunbar, it would have made an excellent base for a garrison, but no move was made against it. On the evening of 6 September the English camped nearby, but recommenced their march north the following morning. The reduction of Dunbar and Tantallon was almost certainly within the capability of the English siege train, yet their fortifications would have made this a lengthy task. It being late in the campaign season, Somerset seems to have made the decision that the destruction of Scottish forces in the field would be the immediate priority. Having calculated on a campaign of only thirty days duration, the English army pressed on to seek a decision with Governor Arran's forces.

The Scottish Border horse now shadowed the advancing army. They hoped, perhaps, to emulate the success of Musgrave's English Borderers at Solway Moss; Somerset's army had good reason to eye the large bands of Scottish troopers with some apprehension. On 7 September the English made a difficult river crossing across Linton Bridge, near Hailes Castle. This was precisely the kind of difficult operation that threatened the order of the English army and, consequently, presented the Scottish cavalry with an opportunity. The waters of the River Tyne were shallow enough for the horse and waggons to ford, but all the foot had to pass over the single bridge.

Hailes Castle lay about a mile to the west, but south of the river. About three hundred Scottish Border horse gathered on a ridge by the castle. The English vanguard was now opposite them, on the far bank. There was some ineffectual fire from Hailes and some of the Scottish horse threatened to cross the river under cover of the castle's cannon. This was no more than a diversion, for a larger band of cavalry was making its way towards Linton, where the English rearward was struggling across the narrow bridge. Recognising the danger, Warwick left the vanguard to help Dacre get his men across the river before the Scottish horse could fall on the tail end of the army.

The English horse were already over the river and this emboldened the lighter Scottish cavalry. One called out that he wished to treat with a nobleman, and unsuspecting English soldiers actually directed him towards Warwick. Taking advantage of a thick fog, about two hundred Scottish riders splashed across the river where Warwick was chivvying his soldiers along. He, and a small band of mounted officers, suddenly saw twelve Scottish horse emerge from the mist.

Lowering their own lances they charged, little suspecting that a much larger number of Scots were lurking in the fog. In the murk, Warwick picked out a Scottish Borderer named Dandy Kerr, and charged at him with levelled lance. Kerr took off into the gloom, and Warwick thundered after him, riding straight into the ambush party. Henry Vane, who rode at Warwick's side, was confronted by five Scottish horse and badly injured. The Earl himself would have been taken, had not John Berteville galloped to his aid with a small band of mounted arquebusiers. There was a brief scuffle, in which Berteville was slightly wounded and one of his men killed, before volleys from the arquebusiers drove the raiders off. This would not be the last time that the Frenchman's quick thinking was to avert disaster for the English, and his courage was recorded by the young English King in his personal chronicle.[30]

The incident demonstrated quite clearly the danger posed by the marauding Scottish horse. Somerset remained determined that his own cavalry should resist the temptation to break ranks and pursue their tormentors. Yet it was impossible for the English to relax. The Scots laid their ambushes, goaded the marching soldiers to break formation and employed cunning *ruse de guerre* to disrupt the advance. At one point they tried to tempt an English galley ashore, to what would have been an inhospitable welcome, by waving the cross of St George on the shore line. Their success now, however, was limited. The English arquebusiers, foot and mounted, kept the Scottish horse at arms length, although they continued to hover disconcertingly close by. When their proximity appeared particularly menacing, Somerset had two field guns turned upon them, but otherwise he would not be distracted and restrained his own impatient cavalry.

On 8 September he met with Lord Clinton. The Admiral had anchored his fleet off Leith, perhaps hoping to capture shipping or even to seize the port itself. Most of the Scottish merchant ships, however, had abandoned Leith for Blackness further up the Firth. Two merchantmen had been taken at sea, although the English themselves had lost a ship in the process. With his original designs frustrated, Clinton had bombarded both Leith and Blackness whilst he waited for the army to arrive. From the sea, he watched as Arran's army encamped at Musselburgh, apparently intending to halt the English on the Esk, blocking their advance on Edinburgh. This indeed was Arran's initial plan, to 'lie still and defend his ground' should Somerset choose to give battle.[31] Having conveyed this intelligence to Somerset, Clinton's first priority was a redeployment of the fleet. The smaller ships, and those carrying victuals, were brought closer to the army. The great ships sailed along the coast from Leith until they lay off Musselburgh, announcing their arrival by firing several salvoes into the tents and pavilions of the Scottish camp.

The English finally drew close to the main body of the Scottish army on 9 September and made their camp at Prestonpans. Here they were resupplied from

---

[30] W.K.Jordan (ed.), *The Chronicle and Political Papers of King Edward VI* (London, 1966), p. 7, Patten, 'The Expedition into Scotland, 1547', p. 93.
[31] Holinshed, *Historie of Scotland*, p. 550.

the sea; a difficult operation with no proper harbour facilities yet in English hands. Indeed, having captured no port and having failed to secure Dunbar and Tantallon, Somerset could not hope to sustain his campaign for much longer. He now needed to seek a decision quickly in the field, but his reconnaissance revealed that this would be no easy task.

Arran had selected a strong position following the line of the River Esk, along Edmonston Edge between Musselburgh and Inveresk, blocking the road to Edinburgh. To their left lay the Firth of Forth, and to their right an area of extensive marsh, the Shire Moss. Before them the ground sloped down to the Esk itself, flowing along the base of the ridge, which presented a further obstacle to assault. The natural strength of the position had been enhanced with field fortifications, trenches and earthworks furnished with cannon and *arquebusiers à croc*. With no open flank to turn, the English faced the prospect of assailing the position head on, fording the Esk under fire, and advancing up the exposed slope of Edmonston Edge.

The skirmish on Fawside Brae

Compounding Somerset's problems, the Scottish horse had gathered on the western end of Fawside Brae, a hill overlooking the English army. Here they watched as the English prepared their camp. Having taunted the English cavalry for several days without provoking any response, the Scottish troopers had now grown very bold indeed. Lord Grey's son Arthur recalled them 'pricking . . . and shootyng within theyr speare lengthes of owre horsmen'.[32] His father had been chafing before the 'bragges and realinges' of the Scots and, over supper on the evening of 8 September, had begged Somerset to allow him to tackle the enemy cavalry. Now he received the support of the Earl of Warwick, and Somerset, although still reluctant, eventually agreed that the English horse should accept the next offer of skirmish.[33]

As the English foot made camp, a body of light horse, backed up by heavier demi-lancers and possibly Gamboa's mounted arquebusiers, was despatched to clear the Scots from the Brae. Between fifteen hundred and two thousand English horse advanced cautiously under Grey's strict control. The leaders of the cavalry troops were ordered to restrain their men as the Scots approached, allowing them to perform 'theyr accustomed dallying and bragging'. Only when the Scottish ranks wheeled or turned were the English to deliver their charge.[34] Ahead of the English advance on Fawside Brae were fifteen hundred Scottish horse supported by five hundred concealed infantry.[35] It would appear that an

---

32 Malpas (ed.), *Lord Grey of Wilton*, p. 10.
33 Holinshed, *Historie of Scotland*, pp. 548–549.
34 Malpas (ed.), *Lord Grey of Wilton*, p. 12.
35 Patten, 'The Expedition into Scotland, 1547', p. 101.

ambush had been laid, the outnumbered Scots planning to draw their English pursuers on to the pikes of their hidden infantry, as they had at Ancrum Moor.

Unfortunately for the Scots, the ploy didn't come off this time. Instead Grey's plan worked to perfection. The Scots were caught entirely by surprise by a sudden charge as they wheeled in front of the English, whom they had baited without response for the past few days. The retreating Scots were overtaken, and for three miles, fought a running battle with sword and lance in which weight and numbers were clearly on the English side. The Scottish cavalry was badly cut up. Their commander, Lord Home, was thrown from his horse and carried injured to Edinburgh Castle, whilst his son was captured. In all, Scottish losses numbered around eight hundred – severe enough to prevent their cavalry from playing any significant part in the next day's battle. Although undoubtably the victors of this encounter, the English did not emerge from the skirmish completely unscathed either, losing around a hundred men, including many captured. These had made the perennial mistake of cavalry in a successful charge, pursuing a fleeing foe deep into his own territory, exhausting their horses in the process and suddenly finding themselves the victims of a dramatic reversal of fortune.[36]

Having cleared the enemy from the Brae, Somerset, Warwick and a small escort ascended the hill, since it afforded them the best view of the surrounding ground. Half a mile to the south-east of them they could see the Scottish camp, the tents and pavilions arranged in long rows east to west like 'four great ridges of barley'.[37] As if that was not a daunting enough sight, the strength of Arran's position, flanked by the Firth to the north, a marsh to the south and fronted by the steep-banked Esk, was obvious. From the hill Somerset could see their ordnance too. Some was positioned behind a low turf wall on the right flank. The rest covered the approaches to the only bridge over the Esk. Besides ignominious retreat, a frontal assault on this position was Somerset's only alternative.

Yet there was still a chance for victory. Experience in the Italian wars had taught Europe's soldiers that even an enemy in a strong defensive position could be beaten by intensive artillery fire. In particular, French gunners who had succeeded in enfilading the Spanish camp at Ravenna in 1512 had played a major part in Gaston de Foix's victory over the Imperialists.[38] Somerset had the necessary ordnance to emulate this success. From the summit of Fawside Brae two invaluable artillery positions were clearly visible. Cannon on Carberry Hill, south of the Shire Moss, would be in range of the Scottish right flank. To the north of Carberry was the low hill of Pinkie Cleugh, on which stood St Michael's church of Inveresk. This was on the east bank of the Esk, in front of the Scottish lines but jutting towards them, and slightly higher than the positions on Edmonston Edge. Cannon here could pound the centre of the Scottish position.

---

[36] Patten, pp. 99–101, Holinshed, *English Chronicles* (London, 1808), vol. 3, pp. 872–873.
[37] Patten, p. 101.
[38] F.L.Taylor, *The Art of War in Italy* (London, 1993), p. 203.

Additionally, the English navy carried a substantial weight of ordnance with which, from the position they had taken up in the Firth of Forth, they could assail the Scottish left flank. The muzzles of a handful of Scottish cannon pointed vainly out to sea to meet this threat, but the floating gun platforms in the Firth rendered the position of the Scottish rearward, their left flank, untenable.

Somerset resolved, therefore, to advance his three battles and their artillery towards St Michael's church. At the same time the English baggage and a detachment of gunners and cannon would haul their waggons and guns up Fawside Brae. The baggage was to be sheltered by Fawside Castle, the guns were to advance to a position from where they could bombard the Scottish line.

Black Saturday

Although shots had already been fired by both sides, there was a final attempt to prevent a major effusion of blood. Huntly challenged Somerset to single combat, but Somerset curtly dismissed the suggestion on the grounds that, as he had charge of the King's person and was Protector of all his realms, his life was not his own to venture.[39] A more constructive suggestion appears to have been made to Arran. Somerset, who long protested his peaceful intent, offered to withdraw his army, even to pay compensation for the damage it had caused, if only the Scots would agree to the marriage of Edward and Mary. The strength of Arran's army and the position it occupied may well have put Somerset into a more conciliatory frame of mind, even to the extent of accepting that Mary should remain in Scotland until of age. The terms were not ungenerous, but Arran was firmly under the sway of the kirkmen. They were not prepared to deal with Protestant England, and news of Somerset's offer was suppressed for, without doubt, there were many in the Scottish ranks who would have accepted it.[40] Those men were now consigned to battle, and many of them condemned to death.

At eight o'clock on the morning of Saturday 10 September the English broke camp and the three battles set out for Inveresk church. They had not marched far when they saw, to their amazement, that the Scots had abandoned their natural fortress and were streaming across the Esk towards them. The order to advance had been given by Arran, but the movement was led by Angus's vanguard. Angus had obeyed reluctantly, refusing the first order to advance point blank. A second order had come, charging Angus to advance 'under pain of treason', and this he had obeyed.[41]

Whatever Angus's misgivings, Arran's reasoning may have been sound. Having surmised Somerset's intentions, Arran faced the prospect of being bombarded out of his position by the combined might of the English navy and the

---

[39] Patten, 'The Expedition into Scotland, 1547', pp. 102–103.
[40] Holinshed, *Historie of Scotland*, pp. 549–550. Pitscottie, *The Historie and Cronicles of Scotland*, vol. 2, pp. 93–95.
[41] Pitscottie, pp. 96–97.

army's substantial artillery train. Few courses of action remained open to him. Retreat was not one of them. With his battered cavalry force unable to screen a withdrawal, the English troopers would have ridden his slow-moving infantry down. Arran thus had only one real option, to use his pike columns as a shock weapon, as modern tactics dictated. Moving fast, the columns need not endure long under English bombardment, nor suffer the inevitable arrow storm. With sufficient momentum, a blow delivered at the right moment could avenge Flodden and send the invaders reeling homeward.

The English army marched towards Inveresk with the intention of making camp once it had seized the position; they had not been expecting to fight that day. Those plans were now thrown into utter disarray.[42] Arran had seized the chance to fling his pike columns at a disorganised enemy on the move. William Patten, who witnessed the Scottish advance, suggested that Arran may even have been hoping to catch the English still in their camp. If they could cover the ground quickly enough, the English would not have time to form up properly, for their three battles were advancing in column, one behind the other, not in line, and could be destroyed piecemeal. Nor, if the attack were delivered with sufficient speed, would the English gunners be able to get their cannon into position. A spectacular victory seemed to lie within Arran's grasp.

The unexpected assault did indeed take the English by surprise, 'disappointing their purpose' of seizing Inveresk Hill, which was hastily occupied by some of Arran's men and planted with artillery. The rapidity of the advance caused the English considerable alarm; Patten commented that the Scots moved at the pace of cavalry rather than infantry.[43] English infantry stumbled their way into a semblance of order, pioneers and gunners struggled to get the cannon forward. It was a race against time, and one which the English might so easily have lost but for two factors, the fleet in the Firth of Forth and the large mounted arm, which could move swiftly against the advancing columns.

Huntly's rearward was in range of the ships' guns, and they opened fire with deadly effect. The first shot killed the Master of Graham and twenty-five of his men.[44] Argyll's lightly armoured Highland archers on the extreme Scottish left hesitated under the fire and could not be persuaded to advance further. More cannon balls crashed into the tightly packed ranks of Huntly's pikemen, killing swathes of them at a time. Huntly, of necessity, checked his advance and moved his column inland. The three battles of the Scottish army now all veered southwards, heading for the high ground of Fawside Brae.

Somerset held a hurried council with his chief lieutenants. They reasoned that possession of Fawside Brae would give the Scots the advantage of ground. Any English advance on Edinburgh would then run the gauntlet of the guns by Inveresk church and risk a flank attack from the main army on the high ground. Whilst the English army buzzed with rumour, the hastily convened council

[42] Patten, 'The Expedition into Scotland, 1547', p. 107.
[43] Patten, pp. 109–110.
[44] Patten, p. 108.

determined their next course of action. The Scots were outpacing the English and Angus's 8000-strong vanguard looked like seizing the high ground first. To give his infantry and artillery time to get into a defensive position, Somerset had only one chance. To halt the pike columns, he would have to advance his cavalry up Fawside Brae ahead of his infantry, from where they could charge into the Scottish pike columns.

A solid phalanx of resolute pike was formidable opposition for charging lancers. Only heavily armoured men-at-arms were suitable for the task, which would fall therefore to the Gentlemen Pensioners and the Bulleners. Yet formed pike were rarely beaten by cavalry, even heavily armoured men-at-arms. The danger was enhanced by their lack of preparedness. Not expecting battle that day, the Pensioners and Bulleners had left their horse bard with the baggage. They would now have to charge the outstretched pike points on unarmoured horses.[45] This would be a dangerous undertaking and Arthur, son of Lord Grey of Wilton, credits his father with both the plan and some heroic words addressed to Somerset: 'Your Grace shall not thynk that I wyll bee a devysor of that which I dare not allso bee an enterpryzor of.'[46] Yet even if there was little hope of breaking the pike columns, Grey at least could halt them long enough for the English vanguard to scale the Brae ahead of Angus, and for the main battle and the rearward to move along the base of the hill to engage the Scottish battles 'to front'. Once halted, the Scottish battles would present a large and vulnerable target, which the combined fire of cannon, arquebus and bow could destroy.

Somerset himself set off up Fawside Brae once again, this time accompanied by his Master of Ordnance and three cannon. Halfway up the hill, Somerset's attention was directed to the Scottish pike columns, who, for some unaccountable reason, had drawn to a temporary halt. For a moment he doubted that they intended to fight.[47] It is probable though, that the Scottish were in some disarray, caused by the speed of their advance and Huntly's sharp manoeuvre away from the gunfire of the English fleet. Arran was probably taking the opportunity to recover a semblance of order. The three Scottish battles were now fairly ragged formations. At best they were too close together, at worst they were coalescing into one disorganised mass. Their survival in the face of Grey's cavalry depended on meeting it in impenetrable ranks of solid, close order pike.

Both sides were bringing more and more guns into action now and a pall of dark smoke hung over the battlefield. The gunners manhandling the Scottish pieces forward laboured to the point of exhaustion, loading, firing, pushing onwards again. 'Herewith waxed it very hot, with pitiful cries, horrible roar, and terrible thundering of guns besides', wrote Patten, adding that 'each man [was] stricken with a dreadful fear . . . death to fly and danger to fight'.[48] Into this maelstrom charged the English heavy cavalry down the slope of Fawside Brae.

45 Patten, p. 116.
46 Malpas (ed.), *Lord Grey of Wilton*, p. 14.
47 Holinshed, *English Chronicles*, vol. 3, p. 876.
48 Patten, 'The Expedition into Scotland, 1547', pp. 112–113.

A wide ditch crossed the path of their advance. This was taken at a leap by many, led by Edward Shelley and Grey himself. Others, however, stumbled and tripped, blocking the path of those behind. Another obstacle lay beyond the ditch. The field in which the pikemen of Angus's vanguard halted to receive the charge was traversed by deep furrows and the English cavalry struggled to gather momentum as they closed with the Scottish infantry.

The front ranks of the pike columns yelled their defiance, daring the English to come on, shaking their pike points and crying 'Come here, lounds!', 'Come here tykes!', 'Come here heretics!' Whatever the impediments to their charge, the English advance was sufficiently forceful to send a shock wave rippling through the Scottish battle. They were 'compelled to sway a good way back and give ground largely' but the pikemen did not break.[49] The leading ranks of the English cavalry were caught helpless before them, unable to advance further yet unable to retreat through the ranks behind them. Angus's pikemen lunged forward, killing many in the leading ranks of the English horse, including the gallant Shelley who had led the charge.

Seeing no way forward, others began to retire back up Fawside Brae, their leaders hoping to reform for another charge, yet for some the 'sober, advised retire' turned into 'a hasty temerious flight', a 'few lewd soldiers' panicked and fled the field.[50] More determined men-at-arms were trying to hack their way into the solid blocks of Scottish infantry, smashing down the pike points thrusting at them with sword and mace, but with little success. Dashing from the Scottish ranks, men with swords and axe ran forward to finish off dismounted knights and hamstring the unbarded horses. Gradually the last of the English men-at-arms were driven off.

Lord Grey himself emerged from the mêlée bleeding badly, having received a pike thrust through the throat and into his mouth. Sir Thomas Darcy, captain of the Pensioners, was shot. His sword hilt was shattered, his right forefinger 'beaten flat' and his body badly bruised by the bullet, which nevertheless failed to penetrate his armour. Sir Andrew Flammack, bearer of the King's Standard, was surrounded by Scots. A fight for possession of the banner ensued. Flammack, clinging defiantly to the staff, was saved by the timely intervention of Sir Ralph Coppinger, a Gentleman Pensioner who came to his rescue, and the two fought their way to safety. Flammack somehow retained possession of the standard itself, but the Scots were left in triumphant possession of its staff, which had snapped off in the struggle.[51]

Bloodily repulsed, the English horse withdrew up Fawside Brae, some of them so speedily that they disordered the oncoming English vanguard, much to the encouragement of the Scots. For a moment they stood victorious on a battlefield strewn with English dead. Yet their victory was short lived, and their fate already sealed. The cannon dragged up Fawside Brae were now in position on

---

[49] Patten, p. 116.
[50] Patten, p. 117.
[51] Malpas (ed.), *Lord Grey of Wilton*, pp. 14–15.

the crest of the hill. The English vanguard, flanked on its right by a wing of archers, moved along the slope of the Brae. Warwick's men had been somewhat unsettled by the speedy withdrawal of the English horse, especially those who had galloped through their own ranks. The Earl had managed to steady them and now they followed the lead of their foremost ranks, three hundred well harnessed men under the command of an experienced captain, John Luttrell. Their advance was constrained to some extent by a low wall, but they looked poised to take Angus in the flank.

The vanguard was followed by the main battle. The lead elements of this had also climbed onto the slopes of the Brae and were in turn supported by Dacre's rearward. The English line thus extended far enough to threaten to envelop the compressed mass of the three Scottish battles. Soon they were coming under fire from both the ordnance on the hill and that accompanying the main battle and rearward. Little reply was made to this fire. Besides the few cannon manhandled forward by exhausted gunners, the Scottish missile strength had melted away. Having refused to advance under the shore bombardment of the English fleet, the Highland bowmen now withdrew from the field entirely.[52]

Nor did the remaining Scottish horse come to the aid of the halted infantry battles. They hung on the edge of Fawside Brae, eyeing the English artillery and baggage train whose carters stood ready with bows and bills, but unwilling to commit itself once more to the fight. A half-hearted advance picked its way gingerly towards the Lord Protector but was driven off by cannon fire. The Scottish horse then disappeared from the field, riding hard for Dalkeith. The pike columns, now robbed of their battle-winning momentum and close order, were alone.

At the ditch which had held up the English cavalry charge, Peter Mewtys had positioned a detachment of arquebusiers who opened fire on the stationary pikemen. Pedro de Gamboa's mounted arquebusiers galloped past the Scots, discharging their weapons into their ranks, but out of reach of their pikes. Their tactics were a sharp contrast to the brutal mêlée fought by the lance-armed heavy cavalry. The archers, forming a wing to the vanguard, with their rapid rate of fire unleashed the arrow storm once more. Worst of all was the continued bombardment from the English cannon, firing hail shot at a devastatingly short range.

Unable to resume their advance up Fawside Brae in the face of this fire, the Scots had to manoeuvre to meet the on-coming English battles. Angus's column was still remarkably steady and he was able to wheel to the left to meet Warwick's vanguard head on. Panic, however, was beginning to grip Arran's battle, although it had been less heavily engaged than the Scottish vanguard. Since Angus's soldiers were moving away from their original line of advance, they appeared to those behind them to be retreating. Those at the rear of the Scottish formations were already slipping away. Groups of one or two at first, then whole

---

[52] Pitscottie, *The Historie and Cronicles of Scotland*, vol. 2, p. 99.

sections, would break until there was a constant flow of men streaming backwards. Arran himself entirely misinterpreted Angus's intentions. His lingering suspicions about Angus's loyalties suddenly appeared to be confirmed, and he cried 'Treason!' to the astonishment of those around him. Arran 'took swiftly to horse'; his soldiers could only follow on foot.[53] The speed with which the men of Arran's battle took to their heels reveals the extent to which mutual fear and distrust sapped the will of the Scottish army. Under pressure it simply fell apart.

Whilst the main battle disintegrated, Huntly had managed to hold his rearward together for the time being. Yet his position was entirely uncertain. There was a surging mass of men ahead of him whilst a legion of fleeing soldiers passed quickly by, heading for the Esk. A pall of thick black smoke hung over the whole battlefield, obscuring vision, confusing the senses. A driving rain was blown into the faces of Huntly's men as they peered forward and tried to make sense of the fighting ahead of them. Suddenly a body of troops emerged from the chaos ahead, well ordered with pikes shouldered. Angus really was retreating now, hoping to rally alongside Huntly's men. This time, however, it was not his intentions that were mistaken, but his nationality. Convinced that the approaching troops were English, the Scottish rearward joined the panicky retreat.[54]

Casting down pikes, swords, jacks and any other encumbrances in their haste, the Scottish infantry may have made good their escape if pursued only by English foot. Remarkably, however, the English horse had rallied. As they had straggled back up Fawside Brae after their abortive charge, Henry Vane had rounded them up and 'with great dexterity' had ordered them in sound array.[55] Now they embarked on a vengeful pursuit of their erstwhile vanquishers. Even the injured Lord Grey took part in the chase, riding as far as the Scottish camp. It was during this pursuit that the overwhelming majority of Scottish casualties were incurred. The circumstances cannot have been more unfortunate; a routed, disorganised infantry fleeing across relatively open ground, pursued by several thousand vengeful cavalry. The result was an appalling shambles. Finally Somerset, shocked by the bloodletting according to Patten, reigned his enraged troopers in.

Angus, like Arran, made good his escape, playing dead whilst the English pursuit hurried by until his own horse was brought to him. Huntly was less fortunate. About a hundred of his men rallied to hold the crossing of the Esk and cover the retreat of their comrades. Eventually they were overrun by English Border horse and the Earl surrendered at lance point, one of fifteen hundred Scots made prisoner that day.

Amongst them was a grey haired old veteran called John MacKenzie of Killin. Thirty-four years before, almost to the day, he had escaped with his life

---

53 Pitscottie, *The Historie and Cronicles of Scotland*, vol. 2, p. 99.
54 Pittscottie, p. 100.
55 Patten, 'The Expedition into Scotland, 1547', p. 122.

from the disaster at Flodden.[56] Although a captive, he had been fortunate again. Between six and ten thousand of his compatriots were slain or drowned crossing the Esk as they fled towards Edinburgh or across the marshy ground before Dalkeith. Amongst them were many prominent nobles, Lord Cathcart, Lord Elphinstone and Lord Fleming and the Masters of some prominent families, Buchan, Livingstone, Methven, Ogilvy, Erskine, Graham and Ross. On the English side, Patten mourns the death of Edward Shelley, and notes injuries to Lord Grey, Sir Thomas Darcy and Pedro de Gamboa, but records no other casualties amongst the officers. Their total casualties probably numbered in the hundreds rather than the thousands, with most inflicted when the cavalry was repulsed. Officially the English claimed only two hundred dead. The true figure was probably closer to eight hundred.[57]

Operational effectiveness of the rival armies at Pinkie

The disparity in casualties has perhaps exaggerated the ease with which the English had won the field. Most of the Scottish losses had occurred after their battles had broken and the fleeing infantry was ridden down. At the crucial moment when Arran's battle had disintegrated, casualties on both sides had probably been very similar. Up to that point the Scottish army had fought remarkably well. Arran's rapid advance across the Esk had taken Somerset completely by surprise; his army was disordered and unprepared for battle. Somerset's previous successes as a field commander had perhaps made him more than a little complacent. Having lost the initiative, the English had been compelled to resort to an act of desperation, a charge by lance-armed cavalry against a body of formed pike.

Once this crisis had been weathered, however, victory came inexorably to the English. The final stages of the battle highlighted the contrast between the military capacities of the two nations. Their cavalry too light to contend in battle with English men-at-arms, the Scottish remained almost wholly dependent on their infantry. Individual courage and prowess was undermined by divided loyalties, fear and suspicion. At the very root of Scotland's defeat was the flight of Arran's battle, before the fight had even come to handstrokes. Those who had stood their ground had, at least, demonstrated a growing skill with the weaponry of modern war. The initial success of the Scottish pike at Pinkie contrasts with the failure of the columns that had been armed with the weapon at Flodden. Similarly, the Scottish gunners had demonstrated competence and mobility. They exacted a steady toll from the English and some of the lighter pieces had advanced in pace with their infantry. Again the contrast with Flodden, where James IV's cannon had been unable to fire downhill and were quickly left behind on Branxton Edge, is striking.

---

56 Fergusson, '1547, The Rough Wooing', p. 189.
57 Caldwell, 'The Battle of Pinkie', pp. 86–87.

Yet these advances pale into insignificance when compared to the strides made by the English. Their victory at Pinkie was a triumph of co-operation between the arms of cavalry, infantry and artillery. Even the fleet had contributed, its shore bombardment marking a crucial intervention in the battle. Such skill was hardly surprising, given the wealth of expertise and experience born of continental warfare to be found in the English ranks. Furthermore, the English benefited from the expensive hired specialists in their employ. Somerset's mercenaries had proved indispensable and they were prominent amongst those awarded for their services after the battle. The Spaniards Pedro de Gamboa, Pedro Negro, Alonso de Villa Sirga and Cristobal Diaz were all knighted. So was the Frenchman John Berteville, who received the honour from the Earl of Warwick, whose life he had saved at Linton Bridge.[58]

Notwithstanding the magnitude of the defeat on Black Saturday, the Scots had avoided complete annihilation. The proximity of Edinburgh and its virtually impregnable castle offered shelter to many of the survivors. These survivors could form the basis of a new Scottish army, and thus Arran could continue to offer resistance. Once again, a staggering victory had not been enough to render Scotland defenceless. As Somerset was well aware, all that he had won as yet was the chance to build his garrisons. The war had only just begun.

---

[58] Hume, *The Year after the Armada and other Historical Stories*, p. 90. Patten gives a full list of those made bannerets and knights by Somerset on 28 September and Warwick on the 29th. See 'The Expedition into Scotland, 1547', pp. 149–151.

CHAPTER SIX

THE WAR FOR SCOTLAND, 1547–1550

The first phase: establishing the garrisons

THE SCATTERING OF Arran's army on Black Saturday left Somerset free to pursue his primary objective, the establishment of an English Pale. Work was already under way at Eyemouth, where masonry from demolished Scottish towers was being used in the construction of a modern artillery fort.[1] Progress was even more rapid in the south-west. In the aftermath of his successful campaign in Annandale, Thomas Wharton had made great strides towards establishing English dominance. Castle Milk was now garrisoned and provided a base for further marauding. Langholm seems to have been recaptured quickly and its captain, Thomas Carleton, was responsible for placing English troops further north at Moffat on the River Annan.[2] Lamington and Dumfries were attacked, the latter surrendering on 20 October. Its citizens took assurance with the English and then took part in an unsuccessful assault on Kirkcudbright. This was, however, a purely temporary setback. Before the end of October the Johnstones' tower of Lochwood was in English hands. By mid-November, Wharton had the tower of Cockpool as well.

With this network of English garrisons in place, the number of Scots who assured rose rapidly. In September 1547 nineteen hundred Scots had pledged to serve Wharton. It was his boast that his garrisons brought order and obedience. The life and property of assured Scots was secured, and they travelled the roads in safety whilst thieves and 'broken men' languished in Carlisle dungeon. By the end of October five thousand Scots had assured. On 12 November the locally powerful John Maxwell, the Master of Maxwell, arrived in Carlisle to swear his loyalty to the English Crown. By then Wharton had 7008 assured Scots in his service. Their oaths, it seems, were not the sole guarantees of their loyalty, for Wharton insisted that hostages be held in Carlisle. If an assured Scot broke his word, his relatives would pay with their lives.[3]

Once assured, these Scots not only fought for England but supplied the

---

[1] Marcus Merriman, 'The Forts of Eyemouth: Anvils of British Union?', *The Scottish Historical Review*, vol. 67 (1988), pp. 142–155.
[2] *Calendar of State Papers, Domestic, Elizabeth 1601–1603, with Addenda [Addenda], 1547–1565* (London, 1870), pp. 331–332.
[3] *Addenda*, p. 329.

English garrisons with victuals 'at a reasonable price'. Sympathetic Scots also formed the basis of a comprehensive intelligence operation that kept the English well informed of troop movements and events at the Scottish court.[4] By the end of the year the establishment of an English Pale in south-west Scotland seemed an accomplished fact, and Wharton's position unassailable.[5] In contrast, the position of the remaining Scottish garrisons in the area seemed altogether less secure. Caerlaverock and Lochmaben would find that they had 'sharp neighbours' that winter, or so Wharton predicted with understandable confidence.[6]

In the month following his victory at Pinkie, Somerset too made rapid progress in establishing more garrisons in the Eastern and Middle Marches. Many of the lairds of East Lothian had marked Protestant sympathies and were now quick to pledge their allegiance, and surrender their homes, to England. Amongst the most important of these was John Cockburn, Laird of Ormiston, whose fortified home at Saltoun was garrisoned on behalf of the English King.

It is clear that Somerset had already decided on the sites for his own new garrisons. He considered both strategic location and the existence of older fortifications which could be incorporated into newer works, to keep costs down. On 13 September Somerset inspected the island of Inchcolm in the Firth of Forth, which commanded the approaches to Leith, just four miles distant. Here the buildings of an Augustine abbey offered an immediate shelter to a small force whilst more elaborate works were built. The island, too, was well supplied with fresh water, and rabbits for food. On 17 September the island was seized and garrisoned. Sir John Luttrell was rewarded for his good service at Pinkie with the captaincy of Inchcolm. His command numbered one hundred arquebusiers, fifty pioneers and seventy mariners. These mariners would crew two small 'row barks' which would patrol the Firth. Once the site was properly fortified in such a useful location and with his small but potent command, it was predicted that Luttrell would soon become 'a Prelate of much power'.[7]

No serious consideration seems to have been given to attempting to take nearby Edinburgh Castle, although it would have been of enormous benefit for Somerset to have done so. Patten claimed 'My Lord's Grace, for considerations moving him to pity . . . spared Edinburgh.'[8] More likely, it was memories of the castle's defiance in 1544 that stayed his hand. Only treachery could deliver such an immensely powerful fort to its enemies.[9] For the time being, Arran was safe

---

4   One of the most useful spies signed his letters to Wharton and John Luttrell as 'Ye Wait Quha'. The only clue to his identity is Wharton's reference to 'my spy Maitland'. See *Addenda*, p. 321.

5   Marcus Merriman, 'The Platte of Castlemilk', *Transactions of the Dumfriesshire and Galloway Natural History Society*, vol. 44, part 3 (1967), p. 176; *Addenda*, pp. 330–354.

6   *Addenda*, p. 330.

7   William Patten, 'The Expedition into Scotland, 1547', in A.F.Pollard (ed.), *Tudor Tracts 1532–1588* (Westminster, 1903), pp. 137–139.

8   Patten, p. 140.

9   In late November 1547 Grey of Wilton was approached by a malcontent called Patrick Kynkayde, whose 'fellow' was the porter of Edinburgh Castle. He offered to arrange to have

within its walls. From the battlements, he could see flames consuming Leith once more as the English army turned southwards on 17 September. Patten rue-fully records that their departure was saluted by twenty-four of Arran's cannon.[10]

Although now heading towards the Border, the English were far from quitting Scotland. Garrisons would be needed further south to subdue the Scottish Low-lands and extend English control beyond the Tweed. Their march took them across the scene of their victory eight days before. Many of the dead still lay unburied where they had fallen. Others had been interred in hastily dug graves in Inveresk churchyard, marked with the odd pitiful rag or piece of clothing to aid future identification.[11] It must have been an eerie experience, and the English hurried on, covering seven miles that day before camping at Cranstoun. Here a small division of forces took place. Sir Andrew Dudley, Warwick's younger brother, was knighted by the Lord Protector. He was to be entrusted with an important command, establishing a base far to the north, on the River Tay. A garrison there would carry the war into an area of Scotland so far virtu-ally untroubled by the presence of the English.

It was also possible that Dudley would find many allies, for the region was thought to be largely Protestant in sympathies. In 1543 mobs had attacked the local convents of grey and black friars. More recently the population of Dundee had supplied food and munitions to the Protestant garrison of St Andrews. When Leo Strozzi took the castle, the people of Dundee had rioted and killed seven of his men.[12] Dudley could thus expect some support, and not just from the local population at large. Indeed it was the active co-operation of a Scottish noble taken prisoner at Solway Moss, Patrick, Lord Gray, that made it possible for the English to establish themselves in Fife. Forewarned of the danger by Adam Otterburn in June, the Dowager Queen had taken some steps to ensure that the coastline of the county be defended. Yet she could do nothing to prevent Gray's castle at Broughty Craig, just outside Dundee, from being delivered into English hands. Dudley and Clinton's flotilla arrived off Broughty on 20 Septem-ber, and the castle's Captain, Henry Durham, duly surrendered to them.[13]

The capture of Broughty was something of a coup. It posed a danger signifi-cant enough that not just the local levies but Governor Arran himself and French auxiliaries would be drawn north in an attempt to expel Dudley. Broughty would become the second largest of the English garrisons and the base for a fleet

the gates opened for a mere 1000 crowns. Grey was clearly tempted but the plan was never executed. Kynkayde disappeared into historical oblivion, possibly with his pockets bulging with English gold. *Calendar of State Papers Relating to Scotland, Vol. 1, 1547–63* (Edin-burgh, 1898), 95.

10 Patten, 'The Expedition into Scotland, 1547', p. 141.

11 Patten, p. 141.

12 F.Mudie, D.Walker and I.MacIvor, *Broughty Castle and the Defence of the Tay* (Dundee, 1970), pp. 16–19.

13 Annie Cameron (ed.), *The Scottish Correspondence of Mary of Lorraine* [*Scottish Corre-spondence*] (Edinburgh, 1927), cxliii, cxxxvi, cxliii.

which would harry and burn the length of the Tay estuary. Dudley, however, had his work cut out for him. He found his new post in a dilapidated state: 'the House was more lyke a kyepar lodge when I came to hit then lyke a fforte'.[14] The walls, at a mere four feet thick, would be easily breached. Dudley immediately set the Italian engineer Giovanni de Rossetti to work, organising defensive trenches and throwing up gun emplacements and rampires for the thin walls. Yet the difficulties that were to beset the Broughty garrison throughout its existence soon became apparent. The distance from the main English supply centres at Berwick and Newcastle, and the dependence on ships that were at the mercy of the weather were to leave Dudley plagued by material shortages. Just three weeks after his arrival he wrote that there was:

> no wudd, cole nor candell nor glasse for any wyndowe, nor scant wyndowe to shut, nor doore, locke, nor bolt, latch nor naile, beynge cleane destitute of all manner of thinges that men should woorke withall, the which I have nead of, as carpenters, masons and bricklayers, Smythes or anye other craftesmen or artificers.[15]

The extensive work required at Broughty would lead to mounting expense. Refortification itself cost £2245, whilst by May 1548 paying and supplying the garrison had added another £16,708 to the bill.[16]

Oblivious to Dudley's problems, Somerset was tightening his grip on the Lowlands. On 19 September his army reached Lauder. Finding the town empty, the English set to pitching their tents. Suddenly twenty Scottish horsemen broke cover and charged through the camp, wounding one who was too slow in his leap for cover. It was a small incident, but the English seem to have been caught by surprise by these 'hedge creepers'.[17] They steadied their nerves by burning a couple of nearby houses in retaliation, but may have wondered if this audacity heralded a more potent Scottish recovery.

For the time being Somerset's good fortune held. His next target was Home Castle, north of Kelso. Thick walled, built on rocky ground and surrounded by marsh, Home Castle had been up-graded recently by French military engineers. It was, therefore, a tempting prize and, for all its strength, a vulnerable one. Its Lord lay wounded in Edinburgh, after his fall from his horse on Fawside Brae, and his son was Somerset's captive. A brief display of firepower was enough to convince Lady Home that resistance was futile. One French account also suggests that, alongside this show of strength, the English constructed a gallows and threatened to hang her son if she did not surrender.[18] The defenders were

---

[14] Marcus Merriman, 'The Fortresses in Scotland', in H.M.Colvin (ed.), *The History of the King's Works*, vol. 4, part 2 (London, 1982), p. 709.

[15] Merriman, 'The Fortresses in Scotland', p. 709.

[16] M.L.Bush, *The Government Policy of Protector Somerset* (London, 1975), p. 28.

[17] Patten, 'The Expedition into Scotland, 1547', p. 142.

[18] J.B.Brown (ed.), 'The French Troops in the Borders in 1548', *Transactions of Hawick Archaeological Society* (1905), p. 39. The evicted Lady Home was accused of taking English money in return for the castle by some of her countrymen. Yet there can be little doubt of her

allowed to leave with their baggage, but their cannon were left to the English. Sixty arquebusiers, forty light horse and one hundred pioneers were placed in the castle.[19]

From Home the English moved on to Roxburgh. Eighty-seven years before an English garrison had been expelled from the castle here. Now their descendants would reoccupy and refortify the ruins left after that earlier siege. Occupying a hill-top site, Roxburgh Castle was positioned between the Tweed and the Teviot, on the narrow neck of land close to the rivers' confluence. This made any approach by hostile forces difficult whilst making supply from the rivers simple.[20] Somerset had long appreciated its potential strength, commenting in 1545 that it was 'one of the strongest seates of a fortress that I have seen'.[21] Under the guidance of Sir Richard Lee, the earlier walls were incorporated into a newer defensive system. Although the new fort was to be relatively small, never housing a garrison of more than five hundred men, it was clearly held to be very important. Somerset himself worked for two hours each day, with a shovel in his hand, as an example to the other lords and knights, who then 'did their parts therin right willingly and uncompelled'. Most of the labour, however, was provided by the common soldiery, each captain sending up the one hundred men of his company to work in one hour shifts.[22] Roxburgh's main function was to be as a supply depot. Plans were put in hand for the construction of a brewery, bakery, kitchens, grain mills, smithy, stabling and storehouses. Its initial garrison, commanded by Sir Ralph Bulmer, comprised three hundred arquebusiers and two hundred pioneers.[23] Once he was certain that Roxburgh was secure, Somerset appointed William, Lord Grey of Wilton, as his chief lieutenant and returned to London and the business of government. Grey, based initially in Norham Castle and later in Berwick, would largely command operations in the east, whilst Wharton in Carlisle would control operations in the west.

These initial successes in the immediate aftermath of Pinkie might have given the English cause for considerable optimism. Their sphere of influence continued to expand. Aytoun Tower, near to the new works at Eyemouth, was captured in early October and soon received its complement of light horse. Yet it quickly became apparent that Grey now faced a number of pressing problems. The most serious of these was the weather. Winter arrived early in 1547. Storms struck hard in October, with incessant hail and rain. This affected all the garrisons, though Broughty Craig, cut off by rough seas, felt the isolation most. The first phase of building work tended to concentrate on ramparts and gun

courage or her wit. Turning on her accusers, most of whom had fled from Pinkie, she 'marvelled they thought we could keep the sobour barmkin of Home against [the English] army, when all the nobles of Scotland could not keep the field!' See *Cal. State Papers Scot.*, vol. 1, 74.

19 Holinshed, *English Chronicles*, vol. 3 (London, 1808), p. 888.
20 *Cal. State Papers Scot.*, vol. 1, 73.
21 Merriman, 'The Fortresses in Scotland', pp. 706–707.
22 Patten, 'The Expedition into Scotland, 1547', p. 147.
23 Holinshed, *English Chronicles*, vol. 3, p. 888.

emplacements rather than barracks and stable blocks. Exposed to the elements and difficult to resupply, the garrisons, and crucially, their mounts, were soon suffering terribly. As early as 18 October 1547 Lord Grey wrote to Somerset warning of the 'scarcity of horsemeat and victuals'. He was already loathe to risk his light cavalry outside the garrisons as they were so poorly mounted, and he urged Somerset to raise fresh horse in Yorkshire. Ominously he also predicted that the heavy cavalry stationed in the garrisons would be unfit for service by the following spring.[24]

The importance attached to the well-being of the horses indicates how vital it was considered to maintain viable forces of English light cavalry in Scotland. Without them it would be impossible to police the Pale. Yet illness, exposure and paucity of supplies continued to take their toll. Soon 588 horses were unfit for duty. Grey informed Somerset that their owners, yeoman farmers from Yorkshire, were too poor to afford remounts. To make matters worse, the heavy rain was seriously hampering English logistics. The mud which caked the roads was soon so thick that Grey told Somerset 'neither horseman nor carriage can pass'.[25] Without adequate victuals and without pay, many of the labourers and some of the soldiers at Eyemouth, Roxburgh, Ayton and Home began to desert.[26]

Grey lamented that the garrisons could not even live off the land. Although corn still lay in great quantities in the fields, the English had no means of transporting it, their old country carts being 'so utterly decayed and tyred'.[27] Carts and draught animals were not the only things Grey needed. At the end of October he was still waiting for two boats to be based at Roxburgh to help ease his transport problems. The spread of disease and the possibility of casualties led him to request that Somerset send him a good physician and a surgeon, for Berwick had but one, and he was 'base and symple'. The possibility of casualties indicates that Grey feared that the fighting might soon escalate. He was determined that the English maintain their superiority in the mounted arm, asking Somerset to send him harness for one hundred demi-lancers.[28]

Grey's fears were well founded. Besides the weather, the garrisons would soon be battling against a reinvigorated Scottish foe, stiffened by French auxiliaries. Rather than union with England, Pinkie had forced Scotland into accepting the subordinate role in an unequal partnership with France. For Scotland's distress was France's opportunity. Arran would pay for French support with an almost total capitulation to French influence. One benefit, however, was the arrival of French troops to help in the expulsion of the English garrisons. The advance guard of fifty captains, 'bringing money to wage ten thousand Scots for

[24] *Cal. State Papers Scot.*, vol. 1, 57, 61.
[25] *Cal. State Papers Scot.*, vol. 1, 61, 63, 70.
[26] *Cal. State Papers Scot.*, vol. 1, 63.
[27] *Cal. State Papers Scot.*, vol. 1, 70.
[28] *Cal. State Papers Scot.*, vol. 1, 73.

a year', landed on Christmas Day 1547.[29] Grey's immediate fears were for his more isolated posts, at Inchcolm and Broughty Craig.

On Inchcolm, Luttrell was frustrated by a lack of suitable ships with which to establish control of the Firth of Forth. With famine and pestilence ravaging the nearby towns, he was convinced that English control of the estuary would be the final straw, forcing his 'stubborn neighbours' to assure. Currently his own small boats were no match for the larger French and Scottish vessels that confined him to the island. Galled that valuable prizes were sailing peacefully by beyond his reach, Luttrell was also aware that an opportunity to offset the financial cost of the garrison was being lost. He was at least confident that he could defend the island as soon as his gun emplacements were finished. However, he clearly had not been able to bend the local Scots to his will and they continued to defy him. In early November a French merchantman ran aground outside Leith and the English took to their boats to snatch the prize. Hard as they rowed, they were beaten to the wreck by Scottish salvagers. The boats of Leith, crammed with men, shielded the stranded French ship and drove Luttrell back to his bleak little island.[30] The uneasy stand-off in the Firth persisted, but the imminent arrival of French troops threatened to make Luttrell's hold on Inchcolm even more tenuous.

In fact Arran had already made the decision that he would strike first at Broughty Craig. In November 1547 the Scottish bishops had donated £5000 towards the cost of the siege, although the Council in Edinburgh had already helped itself to the 'juelles' and 'challasses' of the Church to help fund the war effort. Arran therefore felt he had the resources to remove the English from their most northerly base.[31] Dudley's garrison was proving a useful winter base for elements of the English fleet. Things were not going quite so well in the construction of the new fortifications. Desperately short of raw materials already, the difficulties of resupply were now exacerbated by the atrocious weather. Four ships carrying supplies from Holy Island were caught in a particularly violent storm and blown way off course. Dudley had no idea where his precious stores had gone but guessed forlornly at Shetland or Denmark.[32]

The most pressing need was for timber to reinforce the new earthworks and gun emplacements. But Dudley was short of key personnel as well. He had no pioneers, his only source of manual labour being his soldiers and mariners. They were proving poor workers, 'gevyn all to eatinge and drynkyng and slowfullness'. Dudley was not even very confident of their abilities in a fight, fearing that only three of his gunners knew how to load and discharge their weapons.[33] Without masons or craftsmen, the task of supervising the building work rested solely on the shoulders of the Italian, de Rossetti, who had worked so hard that

---

29 Brown (ed.), 'The French Troops in the Borders in 1548', p. 36.
30 *Cal. State Papers Scot.*, vol. 1, 76, 77.
31 *Cal. State Papers Scot.*, vol. 1, 88.
32 *Cal. State Papers Scot.*, vol. 1, 84.
33 *Cal. State Papers Scot.*, vol. 1, 56.

he himself was now on the sick list. The slow progress and inadequacy of the fortifications raised real dangers. Dudley, like Luttrell, was not able to establish naval superiority, and looked nightly for the arrival of the Earl of Angus, whom he believed would lead the assault on his fort. Political considerations also stayed his hand. He had been urged by Somerset to 'use the country gently', whilst he negotiated with Dundee and sought assurance. Similarly, negotiations were in progress with the Master of Ruthven, who promised (but in the end never delivered) the surrender of Perth.[34]

Dudley would need all his skills as a soldier and a diplomat. Whilst he (gently) threatened Dundee, he worked uneasily with Patrick, Lord Gray, the former master of Broughty. Gray was travelling a crooked path, characteristic of that taken by many members of the Scottish nobility. He extracted hefty sums of money from the English, with frequent obsequious protestations of his faith and loyalty whilst remaining also in the pay of the Scottish Crown. Frustrated by his slow progress, both in fortifying Broughty and winning the assurance of the local Scots, Dudley resolved to take Dundee by force. On 27 October the barque *Ager* and the *Mary Hambrough* bombarded the city from the sea. In the belief that more English ships were on the way and that their town would be razed, the inhabitants took assurance.

This was good news for Dudley. He found much to encourage him when he spoke to Dundee's leading citizens, finding them to favour 'the Word of God', and to be desirous of a good preacher, Bibles and Testaments in English. He saw a chance for profit too. The Tay was crammed with ships of diverse nations, and Dudley thought he could collect the customs duties of Dundee on behalf of the English Crown, to help offset the cost of the war. Yet bright as this outlook was, this turn of events offered little prospect of a solution to the Broughty garrison's mounting supply problems. Living off rotten biscuits and sour beer, which still had to be stored on ships, Dudley's soldiers grumbled loudly. At night they lay 'together like swine as wet as in the field'. Their clothes were in tatters and the cold, sodden and exhausted men grew sick and weak. Their mood was so black that their captain feared them more than he did the Scots. Food, shelter and clothes were not the only problem. The English had spent almost all of their powder and shot bombarding Dundee and in firing at the Scottish light horse that was 'pricking' along the nearby hills. In desperation, Dudley paid the people of Dundee to return as much of the shot that had been fired at them as they could find. Such extemporised solutions could only ease his difficulties temporarily.[35]

Dudley now hoped to fortify Dundee itself, as an alternative to Broughty, and the ailing de Rossetti set to work producing a plat. These plans, however, were quickly abandoned when the long awaited attack on Broughty was finally delivered. On 22 November three thousand Scottish horse and foot, supported by a small artillery train, arrived in the vicinity of Dundee under the command of

---

[34] Gordon Donaldson, *Scotland, James V – James VII* (Edinburgh, 1965), p. 78.
[35] *Cal. State Papers Scot.*, vol. 1, 74.

Arran himself. The English withdrew into Broughty Craig but parties of soldiers and mariners sallied out to skirmish by day and night. Despite their captain's earlier misgivings, the garrison rallied once under siege and staged a determined defence.

The fighting was fierce and Dudley could ill afford his losses. Captain Drewry of the *Phenix* was shot through the leg by an arquebusier, and his master gunner slain by cannon fire. With several of his own pieces destroyed, Dudley was unable to prevent the Scottish sappers from pushing their trenches hard up against the castle walls, nor could he prevent their gunners from blasting a breach into the wall of the tower. A desperate sortie drove the Scots from their trenches and overran their gun line, but Dudley could not take possession of the cannon themselves and was soon driven back inside the castle. Batteries placed on the far side of the Tay made relief from the sea difficult, and the garrison crammed into the small castle were soon running short of food, water and munitions. Dudley was now in dire straits but, although thrice summoned to surrender, he grimly defied his assailants.[36]

Remarkably, his obstinacy was rewarded. Arran had confidently expected an easy conquest but Dudley's sustained resistance caused him to quickly lose heart. He called on the local nobility to come to his assistance 'on pain of death'. Angus, however, who was once again in secret communication with England, withheld his support. Arran's casualties mounted. Frustrated, and perhaps not realising how close he was to victory, he abandoned the siege and withdrew to Stirling on 9 December.[37]

His decision to abandon the siege may well have been influenced by the arrival of English naval forces, under Thomas Wyndham, in the Firth of Tay. Wyndham brought two men-of-war, the *Lion* and the *Tiger*, and several smaller ships.[38] He also brought reinforcements, taken from the garrison of Wark. Numerically, these were a welcome addition to his forces, 170 soldiers in all, including seventy arquebusiers and three experienced captains, the Italians Tiberio and Cattlyne, and the Spaniard Pompey. Their first task was to recover Dundee, which Arran had garrisoned with a troop of light horse and a foot band under one Captain Learmouth. As Wyndham bombarded the town it was simultaneously assaulted by two hundred arquebusiers from the eastern side who forced Learmouth to abandon his position. On 15 December Dundee assured once again.

Wyndham spent the remainder of 1547 raiding up and down the coast of the Firth of Tay. On Christmas Day he stormed the abbey at Balmerino, with the assistance of the people of Dundee. Four days later he sacked the nunnery of Elcho and abducted 'all the nuns and many gentlemen's daughters with them'.[39] Dudley, however, was still unhappy with his situation. In particular, he was

---

36 *Cal. State Papers Scot.*, vol. 1, 96.
37 *Scottish Correspondence*, cxlix, *Cal. State Papers Scot.*, vol. 1, 98.
38 David Loades, *The Tudor Navy* (Aldershot, 1992), p. 143.
39 Mudie *et al.*, *Broughty Castle*, p. 22.

unimpressed by the troops Wyndham had brought, describing them as a vicious and idle company, and was convinced that they were the refuse of the army. Many of them were Scots and had been accompanied by their womenfolk. Since Dudley would not 'suffer ther harlottes here', he had soon incurred their displeasure.[40] Nor were relations between the two officers, Dudley and Wyndham, very positive. It was not clear who was senior, and Dudley was soon complaining to Grey of Wyndham's pretensions.[41]

The supply problems, too, remained critical, although Dudley had taken several casks of wine off captured shipping.[42] With an increased garrison, the pressure on the limited resources was even greater, although many of the sick and injured were shipped back to England. In addition, the English now had an obligation to the citizens of Dundee who, having assured, could no longer trade with their own countrymen. Dudley requested coal, wine and timber for them, as well as repeating his pleas for a good preacher and copies of the Bible, which, he argued, would secure their loyalty more surely than fire and sword.

The logistical problems had been exacerbated by a lack of barrels and casks in which to carry victuals to Broughty from Newcastle. Lord Grey of Wilton had requested that Dudley return empty casks from previous shipments, but Dudley could not oblige. The sandy soil around Broughty had proved unsuitable as a building material. Without timber supports the new earthen ramparts had quickly collapsed. So Dudley had filled the empty wooden casks with earth and built them into his new ramparts. This had been an ingenious extemporisation, but now it had back-fired. Stores rotted in Newcastle for want of casks in which to transport them. To recover them Dudley would have had to dismantle his own defences. To add to his woes, Dudley was also running out of money and his Spanish and Italian soldiers were growing restless over their pay arrears. In January 1548 he began hinting strongly that he wished to be relieved of his command.[43]

His most immediate problem was his limited ability to defend himself in the event of renewed fighting. Broughty Castle itself had withstood one brief siege but, in the face of the experienced French gunners who might accompany the next assault, there were real fears about its defensive capacity. Dudley's first instinct was to fortify Dundee itself. He set his men to work as soon as Learmouth's garrison was expelled, and by 2 January 1548 reported that the town was being fortified as quickly as possible. By 12 January the English had placed cannon in the church steeple. Yet work did not progress quickly enough. A mixed Franco-Scottish force under Argyll approached the town and, to Dudley's fury, the men of Dundee forgot their assurance and fled at his approach.

With barely 150 men to spare from Broughty's garrison, the English could not hope to defend the city, although Dudley swore that with five hundred men

---

40 *Cal. State Papers Scot.*, vol. 1, 129.
41 *Cal. State Papers Scot.*, vol. 1, 144.
42 *Cal. State Papers Scot.*, vol. 1, 127.
43 *Cal. State Papers Scot.*, vol. 1, 107, 129.

he would have held it against all Scotland or died in the attempt. For two or three days Dundee remained a kind of no man's land. A strong probe by two thousand of Argyll's men towards the town was met by heavy arquebus fire, and a high ranking French officer, Captain Villayne, was killed. Argyll then held his forces back, waiting for his artillery.[44] Before moving against Broughty he requested a parley with the English and met briefly with Thomas Wyndham at St Johnston (Perth). Argyll was accompanied by a small bodyguard, including one hundred Scots, whom Wyndham dismissed as 'the simplest men I ever saw' but who all carried arquebuses, presumably supplied by the French. Even more ominous for the English was the presence of fifty French mounted arquebusiers, fully harnessed and 'bragyng to and fro as they had been conquerors of the world!'[45] Dudley and Wyndham were now about to contest their ability to operate freely inland from Broughty with Argyll's forces.

Whilst refusing a request that Dundee remain neutral ground, the English commanders recognised the futility of attempting to maintain any men in the town. Withdrawing his cannon from the steeple, Dudley burned the 'ydolls' in the church, but spared the rest of the town, on Patrick Gray's request. To keep the Franco-Scottish forces off balance, Wyndham undertook to gain the tactical initiative, rather than allow himself to be bottled up in the crumbling little castle. Taking advantage of the mobility afforded by his ships, he struck at the Fife coastline with two hundred men, on the far side of the estuary. Scotscraig was torched and the raiders moved swiftly inland. About five hundred local light horse gathered to try and cut the raiders off, but Wyndham forced a passage back to his ships.

Stung into action, Argyll moved against Broughty. He now had about six thousand men under his command, predominantly Scottish but with a leavening of French auxiliaries and supported by at least twelve cannon. The French led the first assault on Broughty but were met by a sally of soldiers and mariners from the garrison. Wyndham noted that the French came on bravely, and a fierce skirmish ensued until, with their chief captain slain and another shot through the arm, the attackers reluctantly withdrew.

The undaunted Wyndham took to his boats again, landing 130 men on the south coast to burn a mill, houses and wheat. Only thirty moved inland this time, with the other hundred formed up just a quarter of a mile from the boats to protect the line of retreat. This was a more cautious raid, reflecting the growing power of the Franco-Scottish forces in the area. Even so, it was almost too risky a venture. The raiders were pursued back to their boats by a thousand Scottish light horse armed with arquebuses. There was a nasty skirmish at the boats, with both sides taking casualties, before Wyndham managed to get out to sea.[46] The siege itself was drawing towards its inconclusive end. Having no more luck against Broughty's doughty garrison than Arran, Argyll lifted the siege after

[44] *Cal. State Papers Scot.*, vol. 1, 141.
[45] *Cal. State Papers Scot.*, vol. 1, 142.
[46] *Cal. State Papers Scot.*, vol. 1, 142.

just ten days, resolving publicly to move instead, with more power, against the English garrison that had been established away to the south in Dumfries. In fact he had now entered secret negotiations with the English and was to successfully extract some large bribes, via Patrick Gray.[47]

Cold, hungry, lacking munitions for the soldiers and salves for the injured, the garrison of the dilapidated Broughty Craig had now withstood two sharp sieges against heavy odds. Yet Dudley must have been aware that this was not enough. His good fortune could not last forever, and his inability to hold Dundee or win assurance from the local population at large was underlining the essential futility of his endeavours. The high hopes of strong local support were proving illusory. Whatever heroics his men were inspired to, they counted for nothing if they did not advance Somerset's cause. Mere survival was not enough. The garrison of Broughty had to be able to flex its military muscle; otherwise it was little more than an expensive liability.

This truth had already become apparent at Inchcolm. Luttrell had raided from his island base throughout the winter, but to little effect. The feared French assault had never materialised; the first Frenchmen to arrive had been busy at Broughty. Yet Luttrell had not been able to dominate the Forth or influence the surrounding countryside. Inchcolm had been little more than a nuisance, and eventually Somerset had ordered it to be abandoned. Luttrell himself was sent north to take command of Dundee after the second siege of Broughty had been lifted, arriving on 1 March 1548.[48]

There he joined Sir Thomas Palmer, the military engineer, who was surveying the area in order to strengthen the precarious English grip on Tayside. To Luttrell's dismay, Palmer rejected the idea of fortifying Dundee. He had found that the English had a willing workforce, with many of the locals prepared to work for 5 pence a day, providing their own victuals. Yet there was still a critical shortage of building materials. Dudley had made repeated requests to Lord Grey of Wilton for timber, but little had been forthcoming and the garrison at Broughty now feared that they were 'out of syght out of mynd'.[49]

A letter had been despatched to Somerset, pleading that he intervene, at the same time explaining that fortifying Dundee was too great an undertaking to be practical. The town was overlooked by three large hills, which would have to be incorporated as 'bulwarks' within the defensive perimeter if the town was to be held against siege. To do this, Palmer had declared, would be too costly and too time consuming.[50] The disappointed Luttrell would not get the captaincy of Dundee. Instead he was to be charged with the command of an entirely new structure, an earthwork artillery fort constructed on Balgillo Hill, 2000 feet

[47] *Addenda*, p. 360.
[48] *Cal. State Papers Scot.*, vol. 1, 184.
[49] *Cal. State Papers Scot.*, vol. 1, 160.
[50] *Cal. State Papers Scot.*, vol. 1, 160.

north-west of the old castle and a useful vantage point which 'lookedth some-what partly ovre them [the Scots]'.[51]

The plan won Grey's instant approval, so much so that he was finally stirred to action on the Broughty garrison's behalf. Without waiting for authorisation from Somerset, he despatched reinforcements and building materials north. The Master Surveyor of Berwick, William Ridgeway, was also ordered to send one hundred of his pioneers to Broughty, together with two or three 'frames for houses', prefabrication which would allow work to proceed quickly.[52] The fort owed much in its design to Palmer's experience in Boulogne. It boasted a thick rampart, scaled by ladders and protected by a parapet which included four rather irregularly shaped bastions. Around its perimeter ran a protective ditch, 20 feet wide around the bastions and 54 feet around the scarp of the curtain walls. 'Ted-ious' rock limited the depth of the ditch to just 8 feet, but did provide plentiful material for masonry.

The new fort did much to secure the position of the Broughty garrison. The local Scottish forces, deployed to keep an eye on the English, took a keen inter-est in the construction, but attempts by their light horse to get a closer look were driven off by gunfire. With rueful good humour, the disappointed Scots chris-tened the new fort 'Bragyng Trowble'.[53] With Palmer's expertise required else-where, he left the new fort under the command of Luttrell and the hard working de Rossetti. For his unstinting labour the Italian was rewarded with a promotion to the rank of Master of Ordnance, 'the which he rejoyceth not little in'.[54] With precedence given to work on the ramparts themselves, 'stowage houses' were not immediately constructed and storage thus remained a problem. Food and munitions had to remain on board the victuallers' ships, which languished at considerable cost (and risk if French galleys put in an appearance) on the Tay.[55] The fundamental problem of keeping Broughty resupplied had not really been eased, but the site was now much more defensible. In April Grey allowed an establishment of three hundred men for the Broughty garrison. The 'surplus' was withdrawn, along with the unhappy Andrew Dudley. Wyndham, too, left at this time to serve on land in Lothian, leaving Luttrell in undisputed command.[56]

At first things went well. A third attempt to seize Broughty, led by Bishop James Hamilton of Dunkeld, was beaten off without difficulty. Yet before long Luttrell's communications with Grey and Somerset echoed Dudley's earlier complaints. Sickness reduced his garrison by a hundred men, a situation which cannot have been helped by a diet restricted to salted meat. Unstable earthwork

---

51 Mudie *et al.*, *Broughty Castle*, pp. 25–27.
52 *Cal. State Papers Scot.*, vol. 1, 145.
53 Marcus Merriman and John Summerson, 'The Scottish Border', in H.M.Colvin (ed.), *The History of the King's Works, Vol. 4, 1485–1660*, Part 2 (London, 1982), pp. 710–712, *Cal. State Papers Scot.*, vol. 1, 160, 176, 183.
54 *Cal. State Papers Scot.*, vol. 1, 196, 200.
55 *Cal. State Papers Scot.*, vol. 1, 220.
56 *Cal. State Papers Scot.*, vol. 1, 218.

ramparts slid into the defensive ditches. Scottish light horse, supported again by French auxiliaries, tried to sever communications between Broughty Castle and Balgillo Fort and had to be driven off with gunfire, although the English had precious little powder to spare. Some soldiers of the garrison were now owed eighteen months' pay arrears, and only Luttrell's willingness to share their duties and travails kept their grumbling to a minimum. He himself had plenty of grounds for complaint. His repeated requests for money and supplies were ignored. Exasperated, he wrote directly to Somerset commenting that he would rather 'trayle the pyke' again as a simple soldier than command this burdensome post.[57]

The battle for the south-west: ambush at Drumlanrig

Further south, Somerset was keen to capture and establish new garrisons before French forces arrived in strength. He ordered two fresh invasions for February 1548. Grey was to advance from Berwick in the east, and Wharton was to penetrate once more into the west, where he had already made considerable progress. In Lothian all went smoothly for Grey initially. Acting on their own initiative, English officers had successfully stationed light horse and foot at several important locations in the Merse and Teviotdale. Jedburgh, Kelso, Billie Tower and Ayton Castle were all garrisoned. Grey himself had quickly gained possession of Hailes, Yester and several smaller strong points, but then came startling news from the west. Wharton had suffered a severe set back in a battle at Drumlanrig and, at a stroke, England's hold on the south-west had collapsed.

However strong Wharton's position had seemed, his defeat signalled how uncertain the loyalty of the assured Scots really was. The defection of one prominent family, the Maxwells, had been the root cause of Wharton's ill fortune. The Maxwells, like so many of the Scottish nobility, were carefully hedging their bets. With Robert Maxwell a prisoner in England, his younger brother John had taken assurance at Carlisle and surrendered many kinsmen as hostages. Wharton had kept up the pressure on Maxwell, needing his assistance if he was to expel the Scottish garrisons from Lochmaben and Caerlaverock. Maxwell, the Warden of the Scottish West March, continued to profess his desire to advance the cause of the royal marriage, but objected strongly to the despoiling of his own lands by English raiders and other assured Scots. Whilst Wharton grew impatient and suspicious of Maxwell, his main concern remained the Earl of Angus and his brother George Douglas. Wharton hoped to put an end to the double dealing of the Douglases with a strong foray against their lands in the south-west, aided by his Scottish allies Lennox and the vacillating John Maxwell.

Wharton's foray began on 20 February 1548, when three thousand Cumbrians

---

[57] *Cal. State Papers Scot.*, vol. 1, 224, 231.

and assured Scots crossed the Border into Nithsdale and advanced through Dumfries, where they established a baggage park for their waggons and victuals. In typical Border fashion, a raiding party of horsemen was despatched ahead of the main force to burn Durisdeer, under the command of Wharton's son Henry. This tactic allowed raiding parties to maximise the devastation they caused. Yet any division of forces was dangerous in the face of a determined and mobile enemy, as the English had learned at Haddon Rigg. Wharton had his suspicions about the loyalty of some of his assured Scots, and had confided so to some of the gentlemen who accompanied him on the expedition. Yet he thought his force large enough to deal with any trouble, even if some of those in his own ranks were suspect.[58]

In this he had underestimated the number of assured Scots whose loyalty to England was wavering. The division of his own forces was consequently a fatal error. The Scottish commander on this occasion was Angus himself, the victor of Ancrum Moor and a master of the fast-moving Border skirmish. He struck first at the mounted foray heading for Durisdeer. Angus advanced on horseback with 'a chosen power of men' whilst 'also upon everie hill about, great numbers of Scotish footmen' appeared around the English. Apparently acting to a pre-arranged plan, Maxwell's four hundred riders accompanying Henry Wharton suddenly hoisted a black flag onto a lance point and turned on their erstwhile allies, whilst Angus's forces closed in from all sides.[59]

Surprise had not been complete, for Wharton had forewarned his captains of potential treachery and, although scattered, much of the Cumbrian cavalry managed to fight its way to safety. One of the first of them to get away rode hard for Wharton's main battle, which was now approaching Drumlanrig. Reaching Wharton, the survivor recounted a panicky tale of the total defeat of the advanced foray. Angus was now moving against the main battle and, as soon as he appeared, many of the assured Scots in Wharton's band 'took or laid hands upon any Englishman' close by.[60] However, the Scottish Armstrongs of Liddesdale stayed loyal to Wharton and their good service averted a complete disaster.

Ably assisted by the veteran Jack Musgrave, Wharton managed to array his foot into order of battle, causing Angus to hesitate. There followed an uneasy two-hour stand off, with Wharton reluctant to abandon his son but unsure whether he still lived. Finally, with the weather worsening, Wharton began to withdraw hesitantly towards Dumfries. The Scots followed at a distance of only 1000 yards, content at that moment just to keep contact with their quarry, for they knew reinforcements were on their way. The English baggage train at Dumfries had already been overrun (costing Wharton precious victuals, carts, carters and draught animals). Now a large body of Scottish foot was advancing from the south.

It was Angus's misfortune that these reinforcements were beaten to the scene

58 *Addenda*, p. 381.
59 Holinshed, *Historie of Scotland* (London, 1805), p. 556.
60 *Addenda*, p. 362.

by Henry Wharton, who had survived Maxwell's ambush, gathered his scattered horse and now rode to his father's rescue. Relieved to find the English foot well ordered, Henry Wharton charged the Scottish foot, who broke and fled. Wharton reported that about five hundred of them were slain, with many drowned as they tried to escape across the Nith.[61]

The timely reappearance of his son had saved Wharton from complete disaster, but the failure of the foray and Maxwell's defection were of immense significance. English power in the region was broken. Indeed there were fears that Angus would himself seize the initiative and move into the English West March. When the first rumours of the battle reached Carlisle, it was believed that the whole English force was lost. Wharton's youngest son, also called Thomas, wrote to Somerset of 'this poor country now destitute, not only of all the gentlemen, but most of the true men within the wardenry, and also of good horses'.[62] This grim picture was an exaggeration. The elder Wharton returned to Carlisle braying with rage at Maxwell's perfidy, but England still held Castlemilk, Cockpool and Lochwood. The expulsion of these garrisons, not invasion, would remain the Scottish priority. Yet the system of assurance had broken down completely in the west. Those still loyal to England were now hounded by Angus's forces and the isolated garrisons were no longer able to fulfil their obligation to defend them. Wharton vented his fury on the Maxwell hostages held in Carlisle, fourteen of whom he hanged. Both the Maxwells and the Douglases would continue to make overtures to England, but the war with Wharton and his equally bellicose sons was now a bloody personal feud. Angus observed that he and his brother

> always pleased the last King of England, the King that now is, my Lord Protector, Lords of the Council, and Lord Lieutenant, and all others in authority in England, except Lord Wharton, and he can never be pleased with us; and if he will not be satisfied, we will learn him his A B C again.[63]

Angus's claims to have been a loyal servant of England must have rung a little hollow in London. In Carlisle they drove Wharton to fury, but it was an impotent fury. Further co-ordination between Wharton and Grey was no longer possible. A long-standing antipathy between the two men had been exacerbated by competition for troops, especially valuable arquebusiers, during the winter of 1547–48.[64] This antipathy now matured into mutual loathing, each blaming the other for the recent reverses. All of Wharton's confidence seemed to be drained by the setback at Drumlanrig. His initiative evaporated and he proved incapable of action without prompting from London.

Throughout the spring and summer of 1548 the balance of military power in the west tipped in Scotland's favour. Cumbrian troops were drawn off to fight in

---

[61] *Cal. State Papers Scot.*, vol. 1, 148.
[62] *Addenda*, pp. 361–363, pp. 381–382.
[63] *Addenda*, p. 369.
[64] *Cal. State Papers Scot.*, vol. 1, 94.

the east and assured Scots were harried into forsaking their oaths to England. Wharton could not retain their loyalty, for he could no longer offer them protection. Indeed he was more worried about the security of the English West March, which by August was 'destitute of horsemen'.[65] By then the war had entered its most crucial phase, to the east in Lothian.

England on the defensive: The French intervention

Grey had been shaken by Wharton's defeat at Drumlanrig and had withdrawn back to Berwick. Arran, by the same token, was heartened and moved against some of the smaller English garrisons and their assured allies. The Laird of Ormiston's fortified house at Saltoun was successfully mined by Arran's sappers and forced to capitulate. The Governor had the unfortunate garrison hanged. Similarly, Hailes was recaptured before it was able to serve any practical purpose for the English.[66]

Grey looked elsewhere for replacements. Throughout February and March English surveyors were back at work, assessing possible sites for fortification. A new fort was to be established further inland, guarding the supply route across the Border. Somerset and Grey finally decided to build at Lauder. The fort was to be one of the most sophisticated built by the English during the war. Constructed on the sloping crest of a long hill overlooking Leader Water, Lauder was built on three levels with gun platforms and bastions arranged in tiers. Strong internal defence meant that, even if the outer walls were breached, attackers would be confronted with a small central bastion.

Once again, the use of earth for the main building material allowed the English to construct their fort with surprising rapidity, although a shortage of workmen meant that much of the spade work had to be done by the unfortunate soldiery. This was not done without much grumbling, particularly from amongst the Spanish arquebusiers who, Grey reported to Somerset, 'boast themselves men of war not artificers'.[67] Lauder's natural strength meant it required only a small garrison, which was placed under the command of Sir Hugh Willoughby. The personnel of this garrison gives some indication of the normal composition of the smaller garrisons established by the English: a lieutenant, drummer, ensign bearer, two clerks, a surgeon, a day watch, two porters, six 'gunners of the greate Ordynaunce', ten light horsemen, forty Spanish arquebusiers, thirty English bow and bill, three bakers, two millers and one brewer, cooper, slater and millwright.[68]

Lauder was only of secondary importance to English plans. Spring threatened a major French intervention in the Scottish war. Large numbers of French

[65] *Addenda*, p. 393.
[66] *Scottish Correspondence*, clv.
[67] *Cal. State Papers Scot.*, vol. 1, 220.
[68] Merriman, 'The Fortresses in Scotland', pp. 713–716.

troops might not only contest possession of Scotland, but could threaten England's security as well. Somerset's most pressing need, therefore, was for a major fortification in Lothian, to dominate the Scottish heartland and contain the French counter-attack before it could reach England. Given the pressing supply problems that were bedevilling the English, compounded by muddy roads and a lack of draught animals and suitable carts, a port would have been ideal.

The most obvious site was Dunbar, which Somerset had by-passed on his way to Pinkie, and which remained firmly in Scottish hands. Grey thought that the town itself could be taken and fortified, and from there the castle reduced, if he was provided with enough men.[69] The problem was the blockhouse which protected the castle. Somerset had steered well clear on his way north in September 1547, recognising how much time it would take to win such a fortification. If a substantial French field army were to arrive whilst the English were still in their siege lines, Lothian might be lost altogether and the road to Berwick itself would be open. He decided not to take the risk. Grey had already offered him an alternative site for the new fort, at Haddington.

Just eighteen miles from Edinburgh, a garrison at Haddington would prove a painful thorn in the side of the Franco-Scottish forces. In that sense its location was useful, yet Haddington was five miles inland from the port at Aberlady. Right from the new fort's inception, the problem of resupply loomed ominously. This problem apart, the new fort itself would prove a formidable obstacle. Haddington had a few existing defences which could be incorporated into the new work. A central toll house, which Grey had already briefly occupied, was modified to form a central dongeon, filled with earth and raised to provide a high gun platform.[70] Casements were built between the dongeon wall and its protective ditch. These provided positions for arquebusiers should the outer defences be breached and shielded storehouses and lodgings. Around this inner fort was the main fortification. The English threw up an earth curtain wall, thick enough to absorb shot and defended at each corner by mutually supporting bastions. Each bastion had its complement of artillery and gunners, and was named after its captain, Bowes, Wyndham, Taylor and the Italian Tiberio, recently transferred from Broughty. The curtain wall was protected by a fausse bray and topped by fascines, providing cover for smaller artillery pieces and arquebusiers. To the south-east of the main fort was the lightly fortified base court, a walled enclosure which protected troops posted to guard the bridge over the River Tyne and provided a safe area to graze the garrison's livestock.

The finished fort was both spacious for its 2500-strong garrison (with replacements and reliefs, 4529 were to serve in the garrison over the whole period of its existence) and formidable for any potential assailant. Given that the English were racing against the time when substantial forces would arrive from France, it is unsurprising to find that both labourers and soldiers worked hard to

---

[69] *Cal. State Papers Scot.*, vol. 1, 174, 179.
[70] *Cal. State Papers Scot.*, vol. 1, 135.

erect these fortifications quickly. Here, as elsewhere, many of the local population were also employed. While construction was in progress, defences had consisted of a single trench line, but Arran's troops made little attempt to impede the builders, preferring to wait for their French allies. Aware of how critical the situation was, the soldiery seemed more content in their role of 'artificers' here than at Lauder. Grey picked out the company of the remarkable soldier-scholar John Brende for particular praise.[71] By June work had advanced apace and Haddington fairly bristled with artillery: one demi-cannon, two iron and three brass culverins, one iron and four brass demi-culverins, three iron and two brass sakers, six brass falcons, three double bases and fifteen single bases.[72] While his soldiers laboured, Grey himself was not idle. In May Somerset had instructed him to carry the war once more into the heart of Scotland. By gaining the initiative in this way, Grey was able to secure Haddington from attack whilst work was still in progress. The area around Musselburgh was once again visited by an English army, which burned houses and corn as it passed. The same fate befell the countryside in a wide arc around Edinburgh.

Angus's brother, George Douglas, whose double dealing had worn English patience to the limit, narrowly escaped capture when his home at Dalkeith was captured and his eldest son taken hostage. Grey finished his raid by burning the town of Dunbar, although the castle itself continued to defy the English. Grey boasted that he had achieved 'the utter ruin and destruction of that country', but Somerset was not satisfied. His earlier admonitions to his commanders to treat the Scots gently were now forgotten as he urged vigorous action against those who had taken assurance and subsequently lapsed. As the English found it harder and harder to win allies by offering protection, they turned instead to the threat of reprisal. Increasingly the beleaguered garrisons became instruments of punishment. However much he may have desired Scottish allies, Somerset could never bring himself to abandon the policy of coercion.[73]

The fundamental ambiguity at the heart of his strategy, between coercion and conciliation, exasperated the most stalwart of his allies. The Protestant James Henrisoun found himself, and his appeals to a common British identity, marginalised. He now asked Somerset 'whether it were better to conquer hearts without charges, or burn and build forts at great charges, which will never conquer Scotland?'[74] At the same time the ambiguity complicated the task of English field commanders, who frequently ended up paying compensation for deprivations inflicted on 'loyal' Scots by their troops.[75]

To make matters worse for the English, the French had now arrived in force.

[71] *Cal. State Papers Scot.*, vol. 1, 242.

[72] Merriman, 'The Fortresses in Scotland', p. 721.

[73] Bush, *Government Policy of Protector Somerset*, p. 30.

[74] *Cal. State Papers Scot.*, vol. 1, 357. For the career of Henrisoun, see Marcus Merriman, 'James Henrisoun and "Great Britain": British Union and the Scottish Commonweal', in Roger A. Mason (ed.), *Scotland and England 1286–1815* (Edinburgh, 1987), pp. 85–112.

[75] See, for example, *Rutland Manuscripts* (Historical Manuscript Commission, London, 1905), p. 355.

As he had burned Dunbar in June, Grey had seen their fleet anchored offshore, tarrying for the tide. He had counted 120 sails in all, mostly small vessels, but also sixteen galleys, a brigantine and three 'Great Ships'.[76] They carried the men, munitions and gold that promised to turn Scotland's fortunes. Their undisturbed presence in Scottish waters had revealed a fatal error in English strategy, for the English should have countered this threat at sea. Throughout 1547 an English fleet had blockaded northern waters, but this was withdrawn to Newcastle in March 1548 and discharged, to save money. The implications of this false economy were magnified by the lack of any alternative naval forces to contest the French passage. Other English ships were being used to land raiding parties and to support the garrisons far to the north, notably Dudley's command at Broughty Craig. Grey was able to report that one French landing party of sixty men had been driven back out to sea from North Berwick, but this was a minor success.[77] The French could now land troops and supplies into Scottish-held harbours with little or no molestation. Tough and well equipped, their appearance in force thoroughly unsettled the English garrisons. On 16 June Grey reported to Somerset that the Scottish garrison of Edinburgh had removed to Musselburgh to make way for the French, who finally landed at Leith. He initially estimated their strength at ten thousand troops. As they disembarked, Grey had to revise his estimate upwards to ten thousand French, Italian and *Landsknecht* foot, twelve hundred mounted men-at-arms (which Grey claims were still using horse bard) and eight hundred light horse. Their commanders were men of proven competence, Andre de Montalembert, Sieur D'Ésse, Pedro Strozzi and Philip Francis, 'the Rhinegrave' Count of Salm, one of the most famous of the *Landsknechte*'s captains.[78]

The strength of the mounted arm must have been particularly disconcerting, for England needed to maintain superiority in cavalry forces to police the Pale and guard victuallers on the road. But the garrisons' horses were sick and dying. Their owners had not been paid and could not afford remounts. Nor, according to Grey, had Wharton provided him with the necessary light horse from the West March.[79] Well aware of the necessity of having enough reliable light cavalry to meet the French challenge, Grey turned again to the Spaniard Sir Pedro de Gamboa, who mustered one hundred mounted arquebusiers of the type that had fought so well at Pinkie. The Spanish captain seems to have appreciated the situation too, for he demanded, and received, pay of 8 ducats a month for his men, twice the normal rate. For himself he secured an 'overplus' of twenty-two soldiers. These twenty-two existed only on the muster roles; de Gamboa pock-

---

[76] *Cal. State Papers Scot.*, vol. 1, 242.
[77] *Cal. State Papers Scot.*, vol. 1, 245.
[78] *Cal. State Papers Scot.*, vol. 1, 247, 251. For details of the Rhinegrave and Strozzi's later significance, see respectively, David Potter, *War and Government in the French Provinces* (Cambridge, 1993) and Simon Pepper and Nicholas Adams, *Firearms and Fortifications: Military Architecture and Siege Warfare in Sixteenth Century Siena* (Chicago, 1986).
[79] *Cal. State Papers Scot.*, vol. 1, 258.

eted their pay as a bonus for his services.[80] Grey evidently thought de Gamboa was worth the extra cost. By contrast, in Haddington he was actually trying to stamp out the expensive practice of allowing captains to collect 'deadpay' for none existent soldiers.[81]

The English, however, needed de Gamboa, for he was a 'credyble' man, respected by most of the Spanish, whose discipline was now breaking down. In March 1548 Grey had noted that many of the Spaniards, both officers and men, had deserted. At muster days their comrades filled up the ranks with Englishmen and boys to cover their absence. Material conditions for the garrisons were appalling. The Spanish objected to living in the mean 'cabins' built of branches and turf that satisfied English troops, insisting instead on proper housing or, at least, tents. The most pressing problem, however, was pay. At the very least this was four months in arrears, whilst the Roxburgh garrison were owed seven months' back pay.[82] The most serious incident had occurred at Home Castle in February. Here the Spanish soldiers became so impatient for their back pay that they plotted to murder an English captain of the garrison, William Pelham, and sell the castle back to Scotland. A loose-tongued French soldier had revealed the plot, which had consequently been foiled. The Spanish troops had been rounded up and their lieutenant had been condemned to hang, although he subsequently escaped.[83] Grey hoped that de Gamboa would be able to restore order amongst the Spanish troops. Yet they were not the only ones exhibiting the symptoms of frustration and discontent.

Unpaid English troops were also scrambling over the walls at night and heading for home. Many men had actually deserted during the course of Grey's foray to Dalkeith, absconding with stolen cattle or horses in lieu of their missing wages.[84] Responsibility for the payment of the garrisons' wages rested with the Treasurer, John Uvedale, whom Grey urged to the utmost haste in issuing the money. In fact he ended a letter to Uvedale by scrawling the word 'haste' six times and 'for the life' three times across the bottom of the page. Just in case Uvedale still had not got the message he then added a small drawing of a pair of gallows. It was an ill-judged letter, and Uvedale was furious, particularly about the gallows. He declared that he was not sure what was meant by it 'but surely it is a tokene mete for murdrers, theves and others greate offendours, and not for soo true a man and soo olde a servaunte as I have bene at all tymes yn my liff'. Uvedale was in fact doing all he could to prise money from an increasingly

[80] *Cal. State Papers Scot.*, vol. 1, 258.
[81] *Cal. State Papers Scot.*, vol. 1, 233.
[82] *Cal. State Papers Scot.*, vol. 1, 182, 220.
[83] *Cal. State Papers Scot.*, vol. 1, 152, 155, 157, 204. Captain Pelham may well have been the young Sir William Pelham, later one of Elizabeth's leading soldiers. For his later career, see R.W.Amber, ' "Wise and Experimented": Sir William Pelham, Elizabethan Soldier and Landlord, c.1560–87', in A.Ayton and J.L.Price (eds), *The Medieval Military Revolution* (London, 1995), pp. 163–182.
[84] *Cal. State Papers Scot.*, vol. 1, 240.

tight-fisted government, telling Somerset that 'God knowethe what paynes and penury the pore soldeours doo dayly sustayne for lak of money!'[85]

In fairness to Grey, he had been in continuous service since Pinkie the previous September, and was shouldering a tremendous responsibility. The strain was beginning to show, and the disciplinary problems amongst his ill-paid troops only made it worse. Captain Sir James Wylford reported that many of the light cavalry had deserted from Haddington. By 30 June only 120 of the 400 Border horse Grey had sent to Wylford still served him. The others had fled to Cumberland, where Wharton was trying to round them up, or were living amongst the assured Scots, unable to go back to England 'as they war wilde or outlawes'. Grey intended to make an example of those who were recaptured but in the meantime he implored Somerset to replace them, but not with Borderers who 'only look for pillage'. John Brende, now with Grey in Berwick, echoed these sentiments: 'our light horsemen were never so feble, the nombre of them be of the refuse of men'.[86]

The Borderers were not the only problem. Even some of Grey's officers were becoming undisciplined. Two English gentlemen at Haddington, Lambert, a man-at-arms, and Captain Cholmeley of the light horse, had quarrelled over a game of dice. A duel was arranged, but Cholmeley arranged for two or three of his company to assist him in murdering Lambert. He should have brought more, for in the ensuing scuffle Lambert stabbed him to death. Grey could well have done without such distractions as he prepared to meet the French. Aware of the quality of the troops they would bring, he had instructed John Brende to train up as many arquebusiers as possible.[87] He must have feared, though, that the desertions, grumbling over pay and conditions, and sporadic violence in the camps presaged serious trouble in his own ranks. Now his men faced their most serious trial, as the French began to probe the garrisons for weaknesses. John Brende at least remained optimistic. The French were planning 'to eate us up', he wrote to John Paget at court, but he was sure that his men were not dismayed and waited eagerly for their enemies' arrival.[88]

On 4 June Grey had written to Luttrell, now in overall command at Broughty, warning him that his spies had uncovered a plot to assassinate him. The assassin was to be one of the many trusted Scots who worked with or sold victuals to the English garrison. The potential risk to security posed by such Scots had been recognised by Grey, and he had issued instructions that such men were to be kept out of the forts.[89] The optimistic assumptions of the level of support for union in Scotland had now been revealed starkly as illusion. The whole rationale of Somerset's strategy looked increasingly suspect.

---

[85] G.W.Bernard, *The Power of the Early Tudor Nobility* (Brighton, 1985), p. 116, *The Hamilton Papers, Vol. 2, 1543–1590* (Edinburgh, 1892), 450.
[86] *Cal. State Papers Scot.*, vol. 1, 245, 287, *Hamilton Papers*, vol. 2, 459.
[87] *Cal. State Papers Scot.*, vol. 1, 233.
[88] *Cal. State Papers Scot.*, vol. 1, 229.
[89] *Cal. State Papers Scot.*, vol. 1, 233, *Scottish Correspondence*, clxxiii, clxxiv.

Besides the threat of assassination, Luttrell had much reason for concern. Despite the repulse of three Scottish assaults, he was a long way from achieving any measure of control over the region as a whole. He had requested light horse for his own command, but Somerset refused him, instead ordering him 'in no wise to attempt eny encontre, skirmish, or do eny thyng to thadventure of eny of your fort'. In short, Luttrell was to shut himself up in his fort and bide his time. Somerset was now worried by the mounting cost of the campaign. He even ordered Luttrell to send south some of his best troops, a company of *Landsknechte*, to provide reinforcements for Lothian and cut down on the cost of victualling Broughty.[90]

Luttrell disobeyed the order, wisely as it turned out, for he now became the object of the first major French attack. On 16 June sixteen French galleys and a larger brigantine, guided by a small Scottish barque, anchored as close inland to the Fife coast as they could. From here they attempted to bombard Broughty Castle and Balgillo Fort into submission. Whilst the gunners duelled with the cannon of the fort and the castle, the French mariners battled with a strong current. Having moved as close inshore as they dared, the galleys needed to turn their prows, where their heaviest cannon were positioned, towards the castle.[91] Their choice of target reflects the efficacy of the modern, low lying earthworks being built by the English. Unable to damage the new earthwork fort, they concentrated instead on the high stone walls of Broughty Craig. In doing so they presented their flanks to the heavily armed modern fort and the English gunners took full advantage of this tempting target. The French fleet was soon driven off.[92]

Luttrell suspected that they would attempt to close the river to victuallers but was reasonably confident he had enough supplies for the time being. The Broughty garrison had now survived the fourth serious assault mounted against it, much to the disappointment of the local Scottish troops. Luttrell informed Grey laconically, 'my neighbours and I are fallen out, and no day passes without 5 or 600 horse and the country foot about tend to me'. Revelling in his success, and ignoring Somerset's orders, Luttrell led his English and German soldiers into the field. A series of sharp skirmishes forced the Scots, under the command of Thomas Charteris, back about a mile from the castle. Indeed, Charteris's own base at Powrie Castle was taken and burnt by Luttrell's men. Simultaneously, the English commander was able to strengthen his own earthworks further, using two 'ploughs' of captured oxen and eighteen captured horses to haul turf and timber.[93]

Pleased as Grey was with the news from the Tay, it was clear that the French had not pressed the attack with any vigour. It had been a purely naval assault,

90 *Scottish Correspondence*, clxxv.
91 A galley could not fire a 'broadside'. For the layout of the armament on vessels of this kind, see J.F.Guilmartin, *Gunpowder and Galleys* (Cambridge, 1974), p. 298.
92 *Cal. State Papers Scot.*, vol. 1, 254, 256.
93 *Cal. State Papers Scot.*, vol. 1, 256.

without the commitment of land forces. D'Ésse had held a council of war and
had identified Haddington as their main priority. As soon as the whole force had
disembarked at Leith, they prepared to march on England's main garrison.
D'Ésse was in overall command, with the two infantry battles commanded by
Monsieur D'Andelot and the Rhinegrave, the Count of Salm. The Count D'E-
tauges was to take charge of the cavalry. Arran insisted on accompanying this
force, with his own troops comprising about eight hundred light cavalry.[94]

The French found their allies in some disarray. The Scots had still not fully
recovered from the magnitude of their defeat, nor had they been able to prevent
the hostile light cavalry from roaming at will in Lothian. One French officer,
Jean de Beaugué, discovered that the English:

> held the Scots so tight that they dare not venture anywhere unless in very great
> strength; while the English themselves thought so little of them . . . that about
> five hundred cavalry which they had were daring enough to ride day and night
> right up to the gates of Edinburgh itself, over-running all the countryside and
> holding all the people of the district in a continual state of terror and subjec-
> tion.[95]

De Beaugué was not disheartened by the disarray of his allies. He demonstrated
a sound understanding of the root cause of Scotland's distress:

> it must be understood that the Scots are in no way less warlike, nor in anyway
> inferior to the English; but because of intrigues and divisions, and because one
> party would not trust another, they suffered a thousand kind of petty tyrannies,
> and thus allowed the English to gain ascendancy over them.[96]

God, de Beaugué believed, had grown irritated with the Scots and had inflicted
the English upon them as a punishment. Now they had renewed their faith, God
had forgiven them and the French were to be the instruments of their deliver-
ance.[97]

The siege of Haddington

On 29 June 1548 the French army advanced on Haddington divided into two
battles, the Germans under the Rhinegrave, and the French under D'Andelot.
The English light horse, which had been scouring the area around Edinburgh,
gave ground before them. Advancing through Musselburgh, the French scourers
reported that all the English had retreated into Haddington. Before the Franco-
Scottish army reached the town, though, they were met by fire from a company
of English and Italian soldiers under the command of the redoubtable Captain
Tiberio. After a brief but heavy exchange of fire, Tiberio fell back to Hadding-

[94] Brown (ed.), 'The French Troops in the Borders in 1548', p. 37.
[95] Brown (ed.), p. 37.
[96] Brown (ed.), p. 37.
[97] Brown (ed.), p. 37.

ton, and D'Ésse to Trenent near Musselburgh. D'Ésse recommenced his advance before dawn the next day, his progress preventing the movement into Haddington of a hundred Spanish reinforcements under Sir Pedro Negro.[98]

On 30 June D'Ésse arrived with a small vanguard before the imposing new fortification and was again compelled to fight his way forward, losing one of his officers to an arquebus shot. The French commander first tested the garrison's fire power and determination. Twice in the early hours of the morning he advanced foot and horse close to the English ramparts. On both occasions they were met with a storm of arrows and 'hayle shot' from the watchful bowmen and gunners on the walls.[99] His reconnaissance complete, D'Ésse withdrew to Trenant to mobilise his whole force. The English had done all they could to prepare for his return. Having 'doon wondres in their fortefycations', the men were granted a 'holeday'. They marched, ensigns flying, to the top of a nearby hill and watched the French advance.[100]

The French arrived in force the following day. By two o'clock in the afternoon of 1 July the siege had begun in earnest. An English sortie had met the French vanguard, but the brief skirmish could not halt the investment. The garrison withdrew into Haddington. Heavily outnumbered they could do little but harass the French as they settled down to the sharp work of siege. The Rhinegrave's *Landsknechte* soon established their camp, opposite the base court, on the far side of the bridge. The French and Italian troops made their camp near Clarkington and the Scots were based around Haddington nunnery, about a mile outside the town.[101]

The French artillery was slower to arrive. Three pieces had been placed on craggy ground north of the town and briefly duelled with the guns of Bowes' bulwark on 30 June. The French gunners had the worse of the encounter and were withdrawn later that day. The bulk of the French siege train arrived piecemeal off the ships.[102] However, work did commence on their emplacements. Much of the hard work of digging trenches and artillery positions fell to the nine hundred Scottish pioneers gathered together by Monsieur de la Chapelle. Their first task was to dig a trench and traverse opposite the town's Abbey Gate 'to cover the soldiers that should watch and ward, from danger of the shot out of the towne'.[103] Further Scottish reinforcements arrived soon afterwards, when Argyll brought a large contingent of Highlanders south. The siege now began in earnest. The French

incamped themselves in places of advantage about the towne, cast trenches, planted their ordinance, battered the rampires, and kept them within streictlie

---

98 *Cal. State Papers Scot.*, vol. 1, 267.
99 Holinshed, *English Chronicles*, vol. 3, pp. 889–890, *Cal. State Papers Scot.*, vol. 1, 268, *Hamilton Papers*, vol. 2, 441.
100 *Cal. State Papers Scot.*, vol. 1, 269.
101 *Cal. State Papers Scot.*, vol. 1, 272.
102 *Cal. State Papers Scot.*, vol. 1, 267.
103 Holinshed, *English Chronicles*, vol. 3, p. 392.

besieged on each hand, using all the waies they could devise to constreine the Englishmen to yeild.[104]

Haddington's Captain, Sir James Wylford, was particularly worried about the vulnerability of Taylor's and Wyndham's bulwarks, reporting that 'the flanks of these two bulwarks are so open, they shall be sore beaten'.[105] D'Ésse was determined that the garrison should have no rest. His arquebusiers crouched in the siege trenches, rising to snatch shots at the men on the ramparts, ducking down to reload. Yet as the fighting escalated it became clear that John Brende had trained his arquebusiers well, for they now held their own with the veterans of D'Ésse's army. The rival arquebusiers duelled continually and without respite. Lord Methuen reported to the Queen Dowager that 'daly and nychtlie is at all ouris carmosche of hacbuttis'.[106]

The gunners laboured at their cannon too, battering the ramparts and bombarding the interior of the fort, dismounting an English piece positioned on the toll house. Now the French cannon 'beate at the flankes and into the towne, and with harquebus shot no place is free, which things sore annoye the men'.[107] All the time the besiegers tightened their grip, the Scottish pioneers pushing their assault trench to within 30 feet of the English ramparts. Five hundred oarsmen were taken from the French galleys to speed the work of entrenchment. The English desperately tried to disrupt the progress. One week into the siege, a Scottish boy emerged from the town and reported that the English captain, Sir James Wylford, and his lieutenant were slain. This claim was dismissed, correctly, as a ruse designed to provoke a premature assault.[108]

Against the background of incessant arquebus and cannon fire, French patrols probed and tested the English defences. In retaliation the English would sally out, driving away any of the besiegers who ventured too close to the ramparts. Much of the skirmishing took place around St Mary's church, which lay just outside the walls of the fort. The English should have levelled it completely when they decided not to incorporate it into their defences. Instead they had made a rather half-hearted job of its destruction. Now its battered steeple provided a vantage point for French snipers. Several attempts were made to dislodge them. Pedro Strozzi 'coronell of three ensigns of Italians', was injured in one sortie, but the English were gradually driven back inside the fort. On Thursday 5 July Methuen reported that they had not attempted a sally since the previous Tuesday. Instead they were fighting within their own defences, their

---

[104] Holinshed, *Historie of Scotland*, p. 557.
[105] *Hamilton Papers*, vol. 2, 441.
[106] *Hamilton Papers*, vol. 2, 441.
[107] *Hamiliton Papers*, vol. 2, 441.
[108] *Scottish Correspondence*, clxxvi. This is Methuen's version, in a report to the Queen Dowager. According to Palmer and Holcroft, in a letter to Somerset, the boy had told a more defiant tale: that the English 'had so wroght within, that when the Frencshemen should enttre the bulwark where they myne, they should win nothing'. *The Hamilton Papers*, vol. 2, 445.

sentries using improvised war flails to beat back French troops who tried to scale the ramparts.[109]

The most important battle was that waged by the artillery. As at Broughty, the earthwork fortifications again proved their worth. By day the French guns hammered at the earth walls. By night English soldiers laboured hard with pick and shovel to repair the damage. The long anticipated arrival of the French seemed to infuse the garrison with a new sense of purpose. Flagging spirits revived and put vigour into the tired muscles and weary limbs shovelling earth on the ramparts.

D'Ésse was reluctant to deliver a full-scale assault before the ramparts were adequately breached, fearing that the loss of life would be prohibitive. He pushed his cannon as close as possible to Haddington's ramparts, moving them under cover of darkness and protecting them with fascines. On one day a battery of six guns 'fast at the towne side' discharged 340 shots at the earth walls. The results were disappointing, so the next night D'Ésse had the guns shifted to within 'three score paces' of the defensive ditch circling the walls, and fired another two hundred rounds at the ramparts. Fire at this range had more effect, although it was dangerous for the gunners. St Mary's church was now firmly in French hands. They had hoisted 'cutthrottes' (small cannon) into the steeple and from that vantage point were firing down into the town. D'Ésse had commenced mining operations, too, and his sappers were also making headway, particularly in the direction of Wyndham's bulwark.

Thanks to the efforts of their gunners and sappers, the French began to make real progress: 'they made such breaches in sundrie places for easie entrie into the town' and the English garrison grimly awaited the assault.[110] But it did not come. D'Ésse and his officers marvelled at how quickly the beleaguered garrison repaired the breaches at night and how fiercely any approach to the wall was met with arrow and shot. On the evening of 4 July D'Ésse and Arran had accompanied a party of officers to inspect a breach but were driven off by cannon fire, which killed four or five 'and bare away the leages of a dooson at the lest'. St Mary's, too, had come under heavy fire from English gunners and was abandoned with its steeple on the verge of toppling. Mounting casualties amongst the pioneers made them a reluctant work force and the process of trenching slowed. After so much hard fighting the French paused to survey their position and were baffled and frustrated to find that Haddington's defences seemed stronger now than they had done at the commencement of the siege.[111]

Yet the garrison was in dire straits if only D'Ésse had known it. Haddington had not been well victualled. Like all the English garrisons, it had suffered from a chronic lack of draught animals and suitable carts to convey supplies. Nor was the fort well sited, however formidable its defences were proving. Resupply from the harbour at Aberlady was not possible whilst the French were in the

---

109 Holinshed, *English Chronicles*, vol. 3, p. 892.
110 Holinshed, *English Chronicles*, vol. 3, p. 892, *Cal. State Papers Scot.*, vol. 1, 273.
111 *Cal. State Papers Scot.*, vol. 1, 273, 278, Merriman, 'The Fortresses in Scotland', p. 718.

field, and the garrison now faced serious shortages. The gunners and arquebusiers were forced to rip up their shirts to make matches so they could discharge their weapons.[112] Besides the shortages, casualties had inevitably mounted. Amongst the wounded were several senior officers, including Tiberio.[113] However, Wylford was still able to communicate with his superiors. Messengers who slipped out of Haddington at eight o'clock in the morning could be in Berwick by that evening.[114] Grey was thus well aware of how precarious the garrison's situation now was.

Carelessness, however, was to cost the Franco-Scottish force their opportunity. A daring relief operation by the Berwick garrison demonstrated exactly how useful light cavalry could be during a siege campaign. Sir Thomas Palmer was the mastermind behind the venture. He planned to reinforce the garrison with an extra four hundred arquebusiers. Each would be mounted and was to carry extra powder and matches into the fort, giving the garrison the munitions it needed to resist the expected French assault. To get the arquebusiers to Haddington involved advancing through potentially hostile territory so a hefty escort of two thousand horse, one thousand foot and two cannon was provided.

Setting out on 7 July, the foot, commanded by John Brende, advanced only as far as the Pease. Brende's orders were to hold this strategically important position to make sure that the horse could retreat that way once the arquebusiers were safely in Haddington. For the journey to Haddington the horse swung inland across the moors, hoping to deceive the Scottish eyes that monitored their progress. As they approached Haddington the English put the mounted arquebusiers to the fore, with a picked escort of a hundred Cumbrian reivers under John Kerr and Henry Wharton. Practising the skill and guile learned on countless cattle lifting forays, Wharton led his band along the very edge of the Scottish camp and passed into Haddington through the gate between Wylford's and Bowes' bulwarks.

By the time the alarm was raised in the Scottish camp it was too late. A handful of Scottish light horse arrived in time to meet Wharton and Kerr as they and their Borderers emerged again from the fort but these were quickly 'put to flyght'. Wharton's force then made good its escape, a larger force of Scottish cavalry following only so far before Palmer and the main body of English cavalry appeared and discouraged pursuit. Its mission complete, the English then turned for home, except for Palmer, who tarried a while on high ground overlooking the siege. Heartened by the reinforcements, the garrison put renewed vigour into its fight. As Palmer watched, the cannon fire from both sides escalated.[115]

The beleaguered troops within Haddington's walls had received more than

---

[112] Holinshed, *English Chronicles*, vol. 3, p. 892.
[113] *Cal. State Papers Scot.*, vol. 1, 284.
[114] *Cal. State Papers Scot.*, vol. 1, 278. The fact that the messenger could leave the fort during the hours of daylight suggests that the besiegers must have been held at some distance.
[115] *Hamilton Papers*, vol. 2, 442.

just men and munitions. Palmer had conveyed expert advice to Wylford on the conduct of the siege. A portion of Wyndham's bulwark had finally collapsed, after being undermined. Its cannon had been silenced one by one. Now, under heavy covering fire, the besiegers were using faggots and brushwood to fill in the defensive ditch so an assault could be made on the breach. The English inside waited for the issue 'to be tryed at the pointe of the wepon'. Palmer had another idea. Rather than defending the shattered bulwark he had the garrison construct a retrenchment across its base. Behind this was built a new rampart mounting cannon loaded with hail shot and 'as many hacquebutyers and archers as could stand to shoot'. When the French poured through the breach they would be halted at the retrenchment. Trapped in the narrow confines of the old bulwark they would be an easy target for the gunners and bowmen on the new rampart, 'and then when they hadd tastyd of such an assawlt or twayne, ther were no doubt but they would be found coole enowgh'.[116]

This was the classic means of defending a threatened bulwark and demonstrates the extent to which the English had mastered the practice of modern siege warfare.[117] Palmer had learned the lessons of Boulogne well and he was in no doubt that he was watching the decisive battle of the war. Writing to Somerset of Haddington he warned 'kepe that, and ye shall do what ye wyll in Skotland. Lyese that, and ye put all the rest in hassard thar'.[118] For both sides the price to be paid for Haddington was mounting. Men fell to gunfire or arrow shot, or were slain in the mêlées being fought in the defensive ditches and on the battered ramparts. Grey fretted over the mounting number of English dead, whilst in the French camp a grim hourly ritual developed as the dead and wounded were heaped onto waggons and carted away for burial or surgery.[119]

D'Ésse was now growing impatient, both with his lack of progress and his ally's shortcomings. Wharton's reivers had passed close to the Scottish camp without being detected. Doubtless they were highly skilled in this kind of work, but for a besieging army to allow its enemy to be resupplied so easily was carelessness indeed. Now the Scots would not promise to take part in an assault. Many of their men were drifting away, including Argyll, who did at least promise to return at some point with more Highlanders.

Fortune had favoured the English in some of the recent fighting. Two French artillery pieces raised on a mount to fire into the town had been dismounted. French mining operations had been halted when an English counter-mine had been exploded, collapsing their tunnels. A band of sixty arquebusiers, twenty pike and twenty sword and bucklers had sortied out of Haddington to cut corn for their horses, in the fields to the north of the fort. Under covering fire from

116 *Hamilton Papers*, vol. 2, 442.
117 *Hamilton Papers*, vol. 2, 442.
118 *Cal. State Papers Scot.*, vol. 1, 284, *Hamilton Papers*, vol. 2, 442, Holinshed, *English Chronicles*, vol. 3, p. 892.
119 *Cal. State Papers Scot.*, vol. 1, 277.

gunners on the ramparts they had driven off a hundred Scottish light horse and a company of the Rhinegrave's *Landsknechte*.[120]

D'Ésse could, however, take considerable comfort from one significant coup. If the military situation was not going to plan, he had at least scored a major political victory over Somerset. Indeed this victory was significant enough to render the continued English presence in Scotland increasingly futile. In January 1548 Henry II of France had promised the Governor Arran a handsome French duchy. In return he secured a formal contract that Arran would summon the Scottish Parliament. Parliament would obligingly consent to the marriage of Mary Queen of Scots to the Dauphin, Francis. Ironically, given the war then being fought to expel alien garrisons, Arran also promised to deliver Dunbar and Blackness to French garrisons.

In an audacious act of defiance, the Scottish Parliament met with D'Ésse in the nunnery of Haddington, in sight of the enraged but impotent English garrison, accepting Henry's terms on 7 July 1548. Arran was to emerge from the deal as the wealthy Duke of Chatelherault. Scotland, however, would be little more than a French satellite, held for the French Crown as a useful base from which to torment the English. Mary boarded a French ship in Dumbarton in August, for those Scottish lords who had baulked at the idea of sending their infant Queen to England now happily surrendered her to France. Somerset's hopes for a mutually beneficial union between England and Scotland, ending centuries of doleful conflict, may have been sincere. Yet such a union would doubtless have curtailed the power of the Scottish nobility itself. Fear of this loss of personal influence, combined in many cases with a strong anti-Protestant sentiment, ensured France's diplomatic triumph.[121]

The initial English response was an escalation of the war. With a revival of the treaties of Greenwich and a royal marriage resulting in dynastic union looking increasingly unlikely, Somerset had to re-establish a justification for the English presence in Scotland. Thus the old claim of the English Crown's sovereignty over Scotland was now revived. This reactionary step exposed the bankruptcy of Somerset's strategy. The vision of union receded. The English were now embarked on the same kind of futile campaigning in Scotland that had consistently failed to deliver any decisive results during the preceding two and a half centuries. Somerset was unable to grasp this point. He now despatched Francis Talbot, Earl of Shrewsbury, to the North to gather another 'Army Royal'. This was to be large enough to relieve Haddington completely, establish a new fort on the coast where it could be resupplied, and engage and defeat Scottish forces in the field.

Again the northern levies were mustered, and the commissioners of array picked out the likeliest men and set them on the road to Berwick. As the army grew, Lord Grey resolved once more to ensure Haddington survived long

---

120 *Cal. State Papers Scot.*, vol. 1, 290.
121 W.K.Jordan, *Edward VI: The Young King* (London, 1968), p. 269.

enough to be relieved. Following the success of the first relief operation he planned to repeat the venture, hoping this time to lead in the field himself. Somerset, however, instructed him to wait for Shrewsbury in Berwick.[122] Palmer remained in command in the field with a mobile force of two thousand men. Prospects for the expedition looked good. News had reached the English that D'Ésse and Arran had quarrelled after an abortive assault on Haddington by French troops was driven off.

The French commander blamed Arran for failing to come to his assistance. There was little Arran could do. His troops were tired and dispirited and drifted away from the siege in their hundreds. The French decided to delay their next assault until Argyll returned with his Highlanders. The time seemed opportune to place fresh men and munitions into the fort.[123] A mixed force of foot and horse advanced once more to the Pease. A small number of light horse were sent on ahead, riding easily to Haddington, and returned with the news that the French were on the point of withdrawing from the field. Palmer himself resolved to go to Haddington to assess the situation. Again he easily penetrated the siege lines and was able to talk with Wylford, instructing him to send his own light horse out to support the relief force as it arrived. Yet, contrary to the earlier report from the light horse, Wylford warned Palmer to retire, claiming that the enemy were now too strong to pass.

Palmer was too confident to consider such caution. He would have been well advised to listen. D'Ésse had received intelligence that he was coming, and had no intention of allowing the English to play the same trick twice. Four ensigns of *Landsknechte* kept watch all night in the siege trenches, and a similar number of French infantry guarded their base camp. The remainder of the army was ordered to rest, 'with their armour on their backs'. D'Ésse himself, along with Strozzi, D'Andelot, the Rhinegrave and their captains, had a sleepless night, visiting their watches and meeting with their scouts. News of the English approach was finally brought into camp by Lord Home, now fully recovered from the broken leg received at Fawside Brae, the night before Pinkie. D'Andelot and the Rhinegrave arrayed their foot for battle and the French and Scottish horse were called in from their scouring, and prepared to advance to meet the English.

Palmer had brought a large body of men-at-arms and demi-lancers beside the light horse, de Gamboa and his mounted arquebusiers. It was the Spaniards who made first contact with the enemy just outside Haddington. In the vanguard of the English advance, they were soon skirmishing with 150 French horse which had come out to meet them. De Gamboa was confident he could handle the situation. Fearing that impetuous action by the demi-lancers and men-at-arms would result in dangerous disorder, he sent word back to Palmer to 'cause the

---

[122] Sir Philip de Malpas Grey Egerton (ed.), *A Commentary on the Services and Charges of Lord Grey of Wilton 1508–1562 by his Son Arthur, Lord Grey of Wilton* (Tonbridge, 1991), p. 16.
[123] *Cal. State Papers Scot.*, vol. 1, 292.

squadrantes to remayne firm where they were'. The disciplined fire from the Spanish arquebusiers began to drive the French back just as de Gamboa was joined by four hundred light horse, probably from the garrison at Haddington itself.

Having forced this passage through the siege lines, de Gamboa rode to the ramparts of the fort and conversed coolly with Wylford, whilst French arque-busiers sniped at him from the nearby trenches. Aware that the French camp was now fully alerted and was moving 'to cumpase us', de Gamboa headed back to Palmer to warn him of the attempted envelopment. Again he stressed the need to keep the heavy horse in order, 'who shuld always have contynued at large together, and not breke, to have ben our refuge and savegard'. Yet Palmer's gen-tlemen were growing impatient as the battle developed around them. The light horse were now in the thick of the action again as the French were pressing home their attack. Too close for the Spanish to use their arquebuses, the rival horsemen duelled with swords.

At this moment Palmer and the heavy horse could restrain themselves no more, and the men-at-arms and demi-lancers levelled their lances and charged. They thundered past the startled de Gamboa, who recalled that they 'did so well as ever men at armes dyd' in that they unhorsed many of the French riders and drove the rest back towards their camp. Just as de Gamboa had feared though, it was now impossible to restore order, and the English foot were left unprotected. The light horse followed the men-at-arms until they ran headlong into a formed body of French foot. The fact that the English horse did not now simply overrun this unit suggests that they had plenty of well disciplined pike, probably some of the Rhinegrave's *Landsknechte*. They were not just pike though, as de Gamboa noted, 'and as they had many hackbutters and very good, beganne to play amongst us, wherewith thies northen horsemen began to flee'.[124]

Disordered and under heavy fire, the English foot and horse began to with-draw. Two senior English officers, John Brende and Thomas Holcroft, fled to Haddington itself. The rest of the army was pursued for eight miles. Both Palmer and Sir Robert Bowes were captured. Altogether about seven hundred of the English were taken or slain. Far from aiding Haddington, the expedition had weakened it. Much powder had been expended in supporting Palmer's force, and many of the light horse who had issued out of the fort to join in the battle had failed to return. Skilled and experienced soldier as he was, Palmer had acted most rashly. The defeat was largely of his own making.[125]

---

124 *Hamilton Papers*, vol. 2, 452.
125 *Cal. State Papers Scot.*, vol. 1, 293, *Hamilton Papers*, vol. 2, 452, Holinshed, *Historie of Scotland*, p. 557, Holinshed, *English Chronicles*, vol. 3, p. 893. It is curious to note that the need to keep heavy cavalry under careful control is emphasised strongly by Thomas Audley in his 'Treatise on the Art of War', written for Edward VI at about this time. Indeed so closely do Audley's words echo de Gamboa's advice to Palmer that one suspects that Audley had this disaster in mind when he wrote this section and had, perhaps, discussed the action with the Spanish captain. See Thomas Audley, 'A Treatise On The Art of War', *The Journal of the Society of Army Historical Research*, vol. 6 (1927), p. 70.

The losses were felt particularly keenly by Lord Grey. Although personally safe, his own retinue had been the backbone of Palmer's ill-fated venture. The cost to his own household was enormous: seventy-two 'great horses', one hundred geldings and all the arms and armour carried by their riders. Weary and personally out of pocket, Grey also now faced the prospect of demotion with the imminent arrival of Shrewsbury as Lord Lieutenant of the North. He continued to serve, but his financial worries were playing on his mind and there is evidence of considerable friction between himself and other English officials. In August he would ask, in vain, to be relieved of his command.[126]

The Earl of Shrewsbury and the relief of Haddington

The new Lord Lieutenant of the North, the Earl of Shrewsbury, inherited a shocked and unhappy command. On 19 July Shrewsbury arrived in Berwick, where he was greeted by Grey, who continued to serve as his deputy. Relations between the two men, not unnaturally, were a little strained. Shrewsbury was a painstaking commander and he had been assembling his army with some care. Even Grey had acknowledged this. Commenting on the arrival of a company of two hundred men mustered by the Earl, he had written that Shrewsbury should be greatly thanked 'that so diligently and in so good order he hath sent for suche a bande of tall personages wherein . . . there is not one unable man'.[127]

Now, in the wake of the defeat before Haddington, Shrewsbury pursued a cautious approach, to avoid a repetition of the disaster. Haddington would have to fend for itself whilst forces were accumulated in Berwick. In particular, he waited on the arrival of two thousand *Landsknechte* to stiffen his infantry arm, and on Lord Clinton to restore English naval supremacy. The English now also had a pressing need for reinforcements for their shattered cavalry arm. The bulk of the heavy cavalry had been lost; only six men-at-arms and thirty-six demi-lancers were still available for service in Berwick. The Borderers had simply scattered and headed for home in Northumberland and Cumberland, leaving Shrewsbury with just a hundred light horse. Without an effective mounted arm, the English grip on Scotland and the Marches immediately loosened.

Bemoaning the lack of cavalry, John Brende wrote to Somerset of how the reivers of the Scottish West March had plundered both English and assured Scots, returning to their homes laden with booty.[128] The implications for English strategy were profound. If the English could not protect the assured Scots, they could not hope to maintain their loyalty. Shrewsbury wrote to the Earl of Derby, hoping to rectify the shortfall of cavalry by recruiting in Lancashire.[129] Again, however, this would take time. Thought was given to risking some of the avail-

---

126 *Cal. State Papers Scot.*, vol. 1, 324, *Scottish Correspondence*, cliv.
127 Bernard, *The Power of the Early Tudor Nobility*, p. 124.
128 *Cal. State Papers Scot.*, vol. 1, 297.
129 *Cal. State Papers Scot.*, vol. 1, 298.

able cavalry in another attempt to ride into Haddington, but Wylford cautioned against it, unless undertaken at night avoiding all risk of battle. Nor did he want a large number of horsemen added to his garrison, since forage for their mounts would have to be gathered from outside the fort. This would have to be fought for, entailing the expenditure of more powder.

His soldiers were still labouring on the earthworks, repairing damage and even preparing new defences. Despite the battering the fort had received, Wylford confidently reported that the fort was now five times stronger than it had been when the French arrived. The incessant fighting had left the garrison short of powder, matches, arquebuses and lead, but Wylford bid Grey to delay relief until his forces were stronger. In the meantime, Wylford expressed his willingness 'to defende this towne with the pyke and bill onelie'.[130] There was at least some respite for his hard-pressed command. Some of the French artillery was withdrawn from the siege and the majority of D'Ésse's army moved its camp to the nunnery vacated by the Scots. This gave them a little more freedom to move outside the walls of the fort. They took the opportunity to gather corn and to work on their ramparts. Venturing into some of the abandoned trenches, they found the burned remains of scaling ladders. The English concluded that the French were going to lift the siege.

Guessing that an English army would soon be heading north, D'Ésse would probably choose to withdraw to Aberlady, Dunbar or Leith and begin his own fortifications, which would have explained the withdrawal of cannon from Haddington.[131] Shrewsbury intended to keep the French off balance by threatening Leith and the Firth with Clinton's fleet. The English naval force of thirty-eight ships victualled at Holy Island from 26 to 27 July and embarked a thousand soldiers sent from Berwick. D'Ésse now faced a difficult choice. Most of his warships were galleys. They did not carry a heavy weight of ordnance and needed a large number of soldiers on board if they were to be able to defend themselves. To man his ships he would have to denude his army of manpower, a dangerous course of action if an English army were to head north. Even whilst the English fleet still rested at Holy Island, most of the French ships in the Firth put to sea.

John Brende, whose intelligence services seem to have been remarkably good,[132] speculated that they did not wish to be trapped in the Firth. In any event, he noticed that they did not embark soldiers, and guessed, correctly, that they were heading for the west coast from where they would escort the young Queen Mary to France.[133] In so doing they handed back to the English that freedom of naval action that they themselves had won so easily. It would not be

---

[130] *Cal. State Papers Scot.*, vol. 1, 295, 296, 310.

[131] *Cal. State Papers Scot.*, vol. 1, 299.

[132] There is no real mystery about the source of this intelligence. On the one occasion that Brende could only guess at the size of the French fleet, it was because the French would not let any Scots near their harbour. Doubtless D'Ésse had realised that there were many English sympathisers amongst the ranks of his nominal allies. This probably also explains the ease of communication between Haddington and Berwick. See *Cal. State Papers Scot.*, vol. 1, 301.

[133] *Cal. State Papers Scot.*, vol. 1, 301.

long before Clinton's ships were preying on French victuallers, and D'Ésse's soldiers would begin to feel the pinch of hunger. In the short term Clinton's target was the Forth. Originally it had been intended that he make for the Tay to assist Luttrell at Broughty.[134] Shrewsbury, however, thought that naval support was vital to his own operations. Clinton could close Leith and Aberlady to French ships, intercept their victuallers and trap the French galleys in the estuary. Losing control of the Firth would encourage D'Ésse to retire from Haddington, and Shrewsbury told Clinton in no uncertain terms that the garrison's fate was in his hands.[135]

Six of the few French galleys that had remained attempted to intercept the English fleet off the coast at Tantallon. One was sunk by cannon fire; another hit a rock and also sank. The others were easily driven off, although their shallow draft allowed them to evade the English sailing vessels by hugging the coast-line.[136] At the mouth of the Firth Clinton was halted for several days, battling with an adverse wind. By 9 August he had reached Leith. Forty ships, including the remaining French galleys, fled his approach, Clinton commenting that six of his sailing vessels were too strong for the entire French fleet. He pursued twelve of the fleeing vessels, heavily laden victuallers, to Burnt Island, where they had anchored, supposedly protected by three hundred French soldiers. Clinton put five hundred of his own men into boats and had them rowed ashore. Cowed by the sight of the English warships, the defenders, save for five unfortunate mariners who were captured, withdrew from the ships, which were then burned.

From his prisoners Clinton learned that the French were fortifying Leith, with three hundred Scottish pioneers labouring in the trenches. Their engineers, too, were applying the principles of the *trace italienne*, and Leith would be the first town in the British Isles to be protected by the new system. The commander responsible was Pedro Strozzi, not yet recovered from the wound received at Haddington, and carried about the town in a chair by four of his soldiers. Clinton now planned to give him a restless time, keeping him wakeful at night and occupied during the day. The English ships cruised the Firth, threatening to attack Leith itself, whilst keeping the remnants of the French fleet bottled up on Inchcolm, the abandoned site of John Luttrell's old garrison. To complete the re-establishment of English dominance in the Firth, Clinton attacked the French shipping sheltering at Burnt Island.[137]

On land, Shrewsbury and Grey were still facing difficulties. Somerset was growing impatient waiting for Shrewsbury to act and, since the army appeared to be doing nothing, ordered the Earl to discharge two to three thousand men to save money. Shrewsbury argued for more time. His two thousand *Landsknechte* had arrived but he was still short of horse. Another proposal that a small

---

134 *Calendar of State Papers, Domestic, Edward VI, 1547–1553* (London, 1992), 104.

135 *Cal. State Papers Scot.*, vol. 1, 309.

136 *Cal. State Papers, Edward VI*, 145.

137 Stuart Harris, 'The Fortifications and Siege of Leith: A Further Study of the Map of the Siege in 1560', *Proceedings of the Society of Antiquaries of Scotland*, vol. 121 (1991), p. 360.

mounted force try again to enter Haddington had been abandoned because D'Ésse's forces were now vigilantly covering all approaches. Grey worried that if a convoy were successfully intercepted it might encourage the French to assault the fort whilst the garrison was short of powder, or at least to prolong the siege, at a time when there was some indication that they were now considering withdrawal.

Scottish forces still in the field were reported to be low on supplies. This offered the possibility of a reduction in enemy forces in the near future. There were rumours reaching Berwick that the French were once again planning to attempt to storm Haddington within the next few days, but these were discounted since so many Scots were drifting away from the siege. A sortie by Wylford's men had some success, capturing thirty or forty horses and carts before being driven back into the fort by a tough Scottish captain called Jamie Dog. Haddington therefore still seemed to be holding its own and Shrewsbury would not move until he had sufficient horse. His own supply problems were preying on his mind. He needed to reach Haddington quickly once he was committed to an invasion and for that he needed mounted forces. Wylford was advised to conserve his food and powder and avoid the enemy's offer of skirmish if possible.[138]

Shrewsbury and Grey appear to have been nursing a hope that the French would not stay in the field and that the campaign could be won by 'bruit' (rumour) of strength, rather than by force of arms. In a manner typical of early modern military commanders, Shrewsbury did not wish to hazard his carefully husbanded forces in a pitched battle unless he was absolutely certain he had sufficient numbers to ensure victory. Somerset's growing impatience, however, could not be ignored indefinitely.[139] Still waiting for much of his horse to catch up with him, Shrewsbury's army finally followed the well-worn path across the Border on 18 August, with 11,412 foot and 1800 horse.

The army marched in four battles. The forward was 3050 strong, the main battle 3500, the rearward 2842. A separate battle for the recently arrived *Landsknechte* was 2020 strong. The foot contained, for an English army, a high proportion of arquebusiers, at least 1200. The majority of these were still foreign mercenaries. The *landsknecht* battle in particular bristled with firearms, six hundred of the 'Almains' carrying arquebuses.[140]

This army was not as strong as Somerset's had been in September 1547. Yet D'Ésse's forces had been worn down by the bloody struggle for Haddington and the inevitable miseries of plague, hunger and exposure. There is little precise indication of how strong D'Ésse's forces now were, but they cannot have been much above 5000. There was some prospect of reinforcement. The fiery cross had once again been galloped through the Highlands, and the French commander was expecting the return of Argyll with 15,000 men.[141] In the meantime,

---

138 *Cal. State Papers Scot.*, vol. 1, 312, 314, 316, 317, 318.
139 *Cal. State Papers Scot.*, vol. 1, 312.
140 *Cal. State Papers Scot.*, vol. 1, 161.
141 Brown (ed.), 'The French Troops in the Borders in 1548', p. 38.

he could not risk being caught between the numerically superior English forces advancing from the south and the garrison at Haddington. As Shrewsbury approached, D'Ésse finally lifted the siege and withdrew to Musselburgh. The English advance had been startlingly quick. On 23 August Grey and Shrewsbury wrote to Somerset from Spittal, outside Aberlady, presumably having followed the coast north. They had yet to relieve Wylford's weary garrison, but at Spittal they could communicate easily with Clinton and the fleet, and secure a supply route from the coast to the fort.

When Shrewsbury finally did enter Haddington, which he did by 29 August, he was joyfully received. The relief had been most timely for, as Thomas Churchyard noted, 'the town was so battered and beaten, that men on horsebacke might have ridden over the breach'. Wylford's resolution and skill in defence was clearly evident, for he had 'helde out the force of France and the power of Scotlande . . . and did so noblie every waie, neither scarcitie of victuall, nor want of powder could move his invincible mynde'.[142] The soldiers of the garrison themselves were lauded for their seven weeks of hard fighting in defence of their hastily built, and hastily victualled, earthwork fort. The chronicler Raphael Holinshed enthused over their triumph:

> such was the undaunted valiancie of that noble crew and garrison, that even the verie enimies themselves could not but yeeld high commendations to the captains and soliours for the hardie forwardness and manhood, which at all times they had found and tried in them . . . And verilie their fame deserveth to be had in memorie for ever, not onlie for their woorthie atcived exploits doone by force of hande, to the beating back backe and repelling of the enimies, but also for their patient sustaining of hunger, thirst, continuall watching, nakedness, sickenesse, and all other such calamities and miseries.[143]

Many of this 'noble crew' were too sick or wounded to serve any further and these were evacuated to Berwick. Their place in Haddington was taken by some of the men who had accompanied Grey and Shrewsbury north.

Having reinforced and resupplied Haddington, Shrewsbury had two further objectives. The first was to establish and fortify a new garrison at a more suitable location than Haddington, preferably on the coast. The second was to engage D'Ésse's Frenchmen, now entrenched in Musselburgh, a site the English badly wanted for themselves. Musselburgh was undoubtedly Somerset's first choice for the new fort, but his commanders in the field were altogether more hesitant. Before they could move against D'Ésse, Argyll and his fifteen thousand Highlanders had joined him in his camp.[144] The lightly armed and armoured Highlanders alone were unlikely to have deterred Shrewsbury, even in

---

142 Thomas Churchyard, *A Generall Rehearsall of Warres, Wherein is five hundred severall services of land and sea* (Edward White, London, 1579), p. 63.
143 Holinshed, *English Chronicles*, vol. 3, p. 904.
144 Holinshed, p. 904.

such numbers. Yet in its strong encampment, and with its solid core of French, Italian and German soldiers, D'Ésse's army was a very tough proposition.

There would be no repetition of Pinkie now. The speed at which Shrewsbury had advanced suggests he had brought little or no heavy ordnance with him, whilst D'Ésse surely had his trenches well protected with guns. The English could have got cannon from Haddington, but only at the cost of weakening its defences. The fleet alone would be unable to dislodge the French from their camp, and Clinton was anxious to be sailing north to Broughty, as his orders had originally stated.[145] To win Musselburgh, then, would mean assaulting D'Ésse's fortified encampment, and Shrewsbury baulked at the prospect. The French commander had effectively called his bluff and Shrewsbury withdrew to look elsewhere for a site for the new garrison.

Marching southwards, back towards England, he settled on Dunglas, near the 'pile' Somerset had ruined the previous year. A fortification here would command the Pease, and thus be a useful bulwark against a French counter-invasion of the English East March. As a feeder fort from which to victual Haddington though, it was a poor substitute for Musselburgh or Aberlady.

Somerset was furious. He had wanted D'Ésse's army broken, and in his rage had even complained bitterly to Odet de Selve, the French ambassador, of Grey and Shrewsbury's manifest shortcomings.[146] The Lord Protector had wanted the Pease to be fortified, but he marvelled that Shrewsbury kept the whole army in the field whilst he was doing so. The cost of wages and victuals mounted, and Somerset would rather have spent the money on the fleet, now sailing for Broughty.[147] The King's gold paid instead for a sophisticated little fort. Its elaborate design made it, at £2301, the most expensive of the English forts to construct.[148]

Built on a low hill overlooking the hamlet of Dunglas, the fort was almost star-shaped, its design dominated by four projecting angled bastions. Its architect was Sir Richard Lee, another veteran of Boulogne. His design incorporated those characteristic features of the other English forts, mutually supporting bastions, thick ramparts and gun emplacements well sited to provide flanking fire. Typically, the English pioneers and soldiers worked fast, although the shortage of carts which had hampered logistics throughout the campaign was acutely felt once again. By the middle of October the ramparts were built and turfed and the garrison was in place. Dunglas would eventually be home to 686 light horse and arquebusiers.

Like Haddington, however, the fort was really in the wrong place. It was not convenient for a harbour and was too far from Haddington to provide adequate support in the event of a resumption of the siege. The French dismissed Dunglas

---

[145] *Scottish Correspondence*, clxxx.
[146] Bernard, *The Power of the Early Tudor Nobility*, p. 127.
[147] *Cal. State Papers Scot.*, vol. 1, 325.
[148] Bush, *Government Policy of Protector Somerset*, p. 28.

as of little consequence, and yet it continued to drain the English treasury; the wage bill for its garrison eventually climbed to £5954.[149]

Shrewsbury's tenure of command ended once he crossed the Border back into England and the burden passed back to the weary and, by now, personally impoverished Lord Grey. Summoning up his energy once more, the Warden of the East March led a series of devastating raids into Teviotdale and Liddesdale. His target was those assured Scots whose loyalty to England had lapsed. Following the defeat of the relief column outside Haddington and Shrewsbury's failure to engage the French, a great many more Scots who had taken assurance were now reconsidering their allegiance. North of the Border, support for England was eroding quickly. The political and ideological elements of Somerset's strategy had ceased to be of any real importance. The war was largely a question of military strength.

D'Ésse's counter-attack

Confronted with further English deprivations on the Border and the continued stubborn presence of the English garrisons in Scotland, D'Ésse considered his options. He badly needed a victory, for the discipline of his ragged army was breaking down and his soldiers were becoming deeply unpopular with their Scottish hosts. Bored and frustrated French and German soldiers had rioted in Edinburgh, following an argument over the sale of an arquebus. An Englishman, Thomas Carlisle, taken prisoner at Haddington when Palmer's relief expedition had been routed, was a witness to the violence. He claimed that the soldiers had been completely out of control and that for over an hour 'the French could no soner espie a Scotisheman, woman, or childe, comme out of their dores, or put their heddes out at a wyndoo, but straight way was marked with an harquebut, so as of that nacion they spared none'. Amongst those killed was James Hamilton, the Provost of Edinburgh.[150] In the wake of the riot, the French and *Landsknechte* had been marched to Musselburgh, the gates of Edinburgh slamming firmly behind them as they left. A few Frenchmen were left behind and Carlisle reports that they were hunted down and butchered by the enraged citizenry.[151]

D'Ésse was anxious to get his army back into the field, where a success might repair some of the damage done by this unfortunate incident. With English standards still flying over Haddington, the presence of its garrison so close to Edinburgh continued to taunt the French commander. What siege had failed to take perhaps stealth could now win. In the early hours of the morning of 9 October a substantial force of French and *Landsknecht* troops crept towards

---

[149] Merriman, 'The Fortresses in Scotland', pp. 722–725.
[150] Sir Henry Ellis (ed.), *Original Letters Illustrative of English History*, 3rd series, vol. 3 (London, 1846), p. 292, Holinshed, *Historie of Scotland*, p. 559.
[151] Ellis (ed.), p. 293.

the unsuspecting fort. English pickets on the roads into Haddington were swiftly overrun before they could raise the alarm. Selecting the base court as the easiest point of entry, the *camisado* was delivered whilst the majority of the garrison still slept.

The unfortunate men of the watch were struck down at their posts and the attackers swarmed towards the gate that led into the heart of the fort. Their triumphant yells of victory woke the slumbering garrison, who, half-dressed and half-asleep, were seized by panic and confusion. Only one man kept his head, the French mercenary Jean de Berteville, who had served England so well at Linton Bridge and Pinkie in 1547. The French were packed into the base court on the verge of battering their way through the gate. The vulnerability of this point had, however, been recognised by Haddington's architects. To defend it, a loaded double-barrelled cannon had been positioned at an embrasure on the main wall, trained on the gate. Moments before that gate gave way, de Berteville fired the cannon, at point-blank range, into the close-packed ranks of D'Ésse's men.[152]

The survivors recoiled from the gate, giving the English time to organise a counter-attack. Issuing through a hidden postern gate into the base court, English billmen and halberdiers drove the attackers back over the walls. D'Ésse threw three more desperate assaults at the ramparts but each was beaten off in turn by the now alert garrison. When dawn came the defenders counted three hundred French dead in the base court alone, and watched as D'Ésse retreated, taking a further sixteen waggon loads of wounded and slain with him. In Edinburgh it was reported that as many as five hundred had been killed or injured in total. The townsfolk of Edinburgh had still not forgiven the French for their recent behaviour in the city and Thomas Carlisle noted that they 'reyoiceth as moche of this overthrow as we do'.[153]

Fearful as the cost of this repulse had been, D'Ésse's overall position remained strong. The assurance system had now all but collapsed because the English were pinned down in their fortifications. One English officer, Thomas Fisher, complained bitterly to Somerset that the French in Edinburgh and Leith were being supplied with food by assured Scots 'and yet in theis parties, we cease not to graunt assurances'. He added that the assured Scots of Lothian had failed in their duty to provide intelligence during the attempted *camisado* on Haddington:

> Hoe had it byn possible for such a powere as the Frenche and Almaynes were, not under three thousand . . . to com in the night tyme thorough our assured mens townes . . . and never a one of them shuld heare, either of their comyng or passing, as they say they did not?[154]

Despite English attempts to maintain the system, Scots no longer had any

---

[152] Churchyard, *A Generall Rehearsall of Warres*, pp. 65–66.
[153] Ellis (ed.), pp. 295–296.
[154] Ellis (ed.), p. 208.

reason to take assurance seriously, since the garrisons were incapable of exerting authority beyond their own battered walls. Crucially, they lacked sufficient mounts for patrols, and Somerset told Wylford that he must not hazard sending unsupported infantry into the field lest it should encounter a larger body of enemy cavalry. Instead Wylford was to lie low and 'kepe fast the key in hande', by repairing the damaged ramparts of his fort.[155] Winter was coming in again, cold, wet and muddy. Sleet and driving rain would do much of D'Ésse's work for him.

The garrison at Haddington was hungry and cold. The two ensigns of German *Landsknechte* who had recently arrived were particularly morose. They demanded sheltered billets, although there were precious few intact houses still standing inside the town. Wylford was looking greedily at the rich land around Musselburgh. New plans had been laid to build a garrison at Inveresk church, on the battlefield of Pinkie. These had to be shelved because of the lateness of the season, and Haddington remained dependent on food brought from England. Wylford had acquired a huge quantity of salted fish for the town, and that would have to be the staple diet for the winter.

All other victuals and munitions struggled north in convoys, with the dilapidated carts pushed and pulled through the clinging mud. Their progress was slow and their cost was inordinate, for the Marches remained hostile territory. The convoys needed powerful escorts to reach the isolated garrisons. The French themselves had now established bases for their own operations. French troops occupied Leith, Dunbar, Aberlady and Musselburgh, all sites that the English themselves coveted but now had little hope of capturing. From these bases they harried the English supply lines.

The Dunbar garrison had a notable success in early 1549. They were ideally positioned to ambush English waggons crawling north towards Haddington. The convoy system was poorly organised. There were daily convoys of just two or three carts which needed at least forty light horse to safeguard their passage, and even then the convoys could fall victim to a well laid ambush.[156] On one occasion the garrison's cavalry clashed with a convoy's escort. An English officer's horse was killed beneath him and he was captured. To their delight, the French discovered that their prisoner was none other than Haddington's captain, James Wylford.[157]

Whilst Haddington's continued survival depended on a precarious land lifeline to Berwick, the garrison of Broughty needed shipping. After leaving the Firth of Forth in September, Clinton had taken the English fleet northwards, but he had achieved little. Attempts to land at St Monans had been repulsed by forces under James Stuart, Prior of St Andrews, the illegitimate son of James V. Clinton's losses had been heavy, at least three hundred, whilst the French officer

155 *Cal. State Papers Scot.*, vol. 1, 338.
156 *Cal. State Papers Scot.*, vol. 1, 332.
157 Holinshed, *English Chronicles*, vol. 3, pp. 906–907.

Jean de Beaugué claimed seven hundred.[158] Many of these were taken prisoner, amongst them the historian and poet Thomas Churchyard, then a young soldier. Similarly, an attempt to get ashore at night near Montrose was foiled by John Erskine of Dun and a force of local fencibles.[159]

Operations in the Tay estuary, in conjunction with Luttrell's troops, had also yielded little in the way of success. In the first week of November Clinton had shipped men of the Broughty garrison into Dundee. The townsmen had largely lapsed in their assurance to the English Crown, and Luttrell no longer felt any compunction to treat them gently. Having driven the inhabitants from the town, the English soldiery fell to looting. Their disorder was their undoing, for the redoubtable Jamie Dog, who had fought so well at Haddington, had arrived in the north. Dog led a spirited counter-attack which drove the English back to their ships, leaving thirty slain on the beach, including, according to some accounts, Luttrell's own brother.[160] But Dog's forces were not strong enough for him to hold Dundee, and a more ordered English attack retook the town, but their grip was precarious.

French galleys were attempting to intercept English supply ships as they sailed north and it was only with the help of Clinton's warships that the victuallers could fight their way through.[161] The Broughty garrison could not rely on the continued support of the fleet. With winter imminent, Clinton bid Luttrell farewell and sailed home for England, taking most of his ships with him.[162] After this departure Luttrell struggled both with a lack of supplies and the consequences of the worsening weather. Heavy rain, far more than cannon, revealed the inherent structural weaknesses of earth-built forts. In late November 1548 Luttrell wrote to Somerset complaining that:

> I assuar yowr grace thatt bothe the forte and castell ys presentlye yn grett imperfeccyon, evenn almost sawtable [assaultable] rownde abowt by reasone of the fallinge downe of ther turfe worke wyche, being veray thyccke, hath drawyn downe myche yerthe with the same, so as I cane nott vammuvre the fort, bycaws experyence techythe me suffycyentlye thatt ony new wayght thatt ys forcyd apone the olde worke makythe the fondatyone to fle and bryngythe downe the hole.[163]

Just three or four shiploads of lime might have served to make the walls more stable, but none had been forthcoming and Luttrell concluded unhappily that if

---

[158] Brown (ed.), 'The French Troops in the Borders in 1548', p. 38.

[159] George Buchanan, *The History of Scotland*, vol. 3 (Edinburgh, 1821), p. 62, Churchyard, *A Generall Rehearsall of Warres*, p. 64.

[160] *Cal. State Papers Scot.*, vol. 1, 332.

[161] Churchyard, *A Generall Rehearsall of Warres*, pp. 64–65.

[162] Holinshed, *Historie of Scotland*, p. 538, Brown (ed.), 'The French Troops in the Borders in 1548', p. 38, *Cal. State Papers Scot.*, vol. 1, 332.

[163] *Scottish Correspondence*, cxci.

Broughty were besieged again 'thennymye shall not nede to laye ony batterye unto hytt for theye shall fynde hytt fallen downe redy to ther handys'.[164]

To keep the local Scottish forces at arm's length, Luttrell had established an outlying camp to the east of Balgillo Fort, manned by *Landsknechte*. In the meantime, despite his difficulties, Luttrell was determined still to carry out the original design of exerting pressure on the whole of Fife. Yet the futility of Broughty's existence was becoming more and more apparent. The population of Dundee, whose assurance had been counted such a success, had dwindled to those few 'powre people as servys to bake and brew'. The tentative steps towards a reoccupation of Dundee had been abandoned by the English when the Rhinegrave and his *Landsknechte* had arrived in Fife.

Frustrated by his lack of success at Haddington, D'Ésse had now turned his attention to some of the other English garrisons. He himself was planning to move against English forces in the Borders whilst he entrusted operations around the Tay to the Rhinegrave and the Count D'Etauges. Characteristically, Luttrell was not content to cower behind his imperfect ramparts, waiting timidly for the inevitable assault. Intolerant of any attempt to get close to the walls of either Broughty Castle or Balgillo Fort, the English and the *Landsknechte* of the Broughty garrison sortied out to drive away the intruders.

German crossed pike with German. French and Italian arquebusiers duelled along the banks of the estuary. English bows and bills clashed with Scottish pikes and light horse. As the battle ebbed and flowed, the skill and valour of the Rhinegrave won English admiration, but his forces could never quite reach the decayed walls of the castle or the collapsing earthworks of Balgillo Fort. With the fighting at its height, D'Etauges was killed and the French withdrew. For the fifth time the garrison at Broughty had fended off disaster.[165]

Even with the French gone, Luttrell did not attempt to reoccupy Dundee. A small force of Scottish horse and foot were now in residence. Luttrell wanted more light horse of his own to deal with them. He had mounted ten arquebusiers 'upon meane naggis' to supplement his forces and these had done well, hindering the revictualling of the Scots in Dundee. In a characteristic display of bravado, Luttrell sent the Scottish captain, Jamie Dog, a letter of defiance: 'yf ye knew how lytell I exteme eyther your powre or your warrys, yow wold lesse thretenn me thenn ye do'.[166] Yet his communications with the Lord Protector reveal that behind his bluster he was still concerned 'neyther havinge any cole for fyer nor so myche as maye serve the smythys here, so as I am nott able to kepe the horsys that serve here shod'. Adding to his list of woes his lack of 'monaye, bread and beare', Luttrell pressed Somerset to act soon, that his bedraggled garrison 'be relyved with spede'.[167]

In the event, and despite all his good services, all Luttrell got from Somerset

164 *Scottish Correspondence*, cxci.
165 Holinshed, *English Chronicle*, p. 906.
166 *Scottish Correspondence*, cxc.
167 *Scottish Correspondence*, cxci.

was a sharp rebuke. The Lord Protector demanded that Luttrell release both the few small vessels that he still had and his precious *Landsknechte*, for service in Lothian. If he failed to do so, at once, he would 'answir the kingis majestie upon [his] upmost peril'. Somerset's spite seems to have been fuelled by the failure to occupy Dundee, for he told Luttrell that this lost opportunity was 'partly by your defaulte'. Mounting financial costs and the intractable problem of victualling had led Somerset to put the whole scheme for establishing a Pale into abeyance. His attention was almost wholly occupied by the threats to his hold on power in London. In January 1549 a conspiracy led by his own brother, Thomas Seymour the Lord Admiral, had been uncovered.

Besides distracting the Lord Protector, the escalating political crisis would draw resources away from Scotland. The garrisons were to be held over winter, but no attempt was to made to extend their influence. Luttrell was instructed that:

> you shall for this tyme lie there as you were ded for the while, kepyng only that fort, and not entermedle in eny wis with any skirmish or attempt . . . you must avoid allwais eny such thyng as might be occassioun of scyrmish or hassard of the hole pece.[168]

Whatever dreams Somerset may have harboured about redoubling efforts in the spring of 1549, this order was a tacit admission that his overall strategy had failed. The garrisons had to be active, otherwise they could neither protect nor cajole the local population, a role vital to promote assurance. Without widespread assurance the garrisons were nothing more than isolated outposts in a hostile land, potentially vulnerable to attack or starvation. Luttrell was right. He needed light horse, to ride through the streets of Dundee and St Johnson (Perth), to encourage allies and dishearten enemies. To delay was to invite those enemies to gather their strength and pick off the English garrisons one by one. This opportunity was not lost on D'Ésse, for he now moved against the English bases in the Borders.

Even with the majority of his leading officers returning to France, where a renewal of fighting around Boulogne seemed imminent, D'Ésse resolved to chip away at the English garrisons. His first objective was to counter the continued pressure to assure still being applied to Scottish Borderers. Leading a combined Franco-Scottish force, D'Ésse moved against two Spanish captains, Pedro Negro and Julian Romero, based in Jedburgh. D'Ésse found the Border country devastated by seven years of near continual warfare. The Scottish troops, who brought only what provisions they could carry, were soon out of food, and D'Ésse was forced to halt whilst fresh supplies were fetched from further north. Negro and Romero took advantage of the delay to slip across the Border to England and safety.

Disappointed not to have caught them, the French returned for the moment to Edinburgh. Here they found that the Queen Dowager had been joined by Huntly,

---

[168] *Scottish Correspondence*, cxciv.

captured at Pinkie but now released from his captivity. On 5 December 1548 Huntly had been given licence to return to Scotland for two and a half months to work for England's interest. Yet, once free, the Earl had forsaken his promises to the English government, leaving Somerset to rail against 'the false and subtill departure of the Earle of Hontly who so mych did dissemble with us'.[169] Despite their mutual mistrust, Arran recognised Huntly's importance as an ally and appointed him Chancellor. His return heralded a distinct surge in Scottish fortunes.

Plans were already in hand for a *coup de main* to recover Home Castle, held by the English since September 1547. Lord Home himself, anxious to recover his home, was behind the daring stroke. Eight of his retainers had been working for the English, helping with building work and gathering victuals for the garrison. Maintaining the friendliest of relationships with the soldiers, they were soon thoroughly acquainted with the routine of the watch. The unsuspecting English cheerfully paid them for provisions and encouraged them to fetch more, sure that Home and the French were far away in Edinburgh. Seven of them returned one stormy night in late December, asking for shelter, and their friends in the garrison were happy to oblige.

The eighth led Lord Home and the rest of his troops to the walls of the castle. A sixty-year-old member of the Home clan (possibly Lord Home himself), was credited with scaling the wall and slaying the sentry on the ramparts. Joining the seven men already inside the castle, it was an easy matter for him to open the gates for those outside. The garrison, half-asleep and caught utterly unawares, were quickly put to the sword. Celebrating the victory, Lady Home urged the Queen Dowager to send her more men to help hold the castle and stressed the vulnerability of other English garrisons, notably that at Kelso.[170] The next target, however, was to be Fast Castle.

There the English sentries had lounged nonchalantly as compliant local Scots had unloaded victuals from their carts and carried them into the castle. Suddenly, swords appeared from under cloaks and the carters turned on the lax sentinels. Seizing the gatehouse, the daring band held the garrison at bay whilst the rest of their company, who had been hiding outside, rushed through the open gate. Fast Castle was soon back in Scottish hands.[171]

At this point D'Ésse would have liked to move against Broughty again, but he was urged by the Dowager Queen to return to the Borders. Despite the recent success at Home and Fast Castle, a French officer recalled the Queen's fears that 'all the folk of Tweedale would join the English unless some assistance was sent to them, and would have no faith in our power to help them, having seen that the

---

[169] *Scottish Correspondence*, cxciv.
[170] *Scottish Correspondence*, cxciii.
[171] Brown (ed.), 'The French Troops in the Borders in 1548', p. 40, Holinshed, *The Historie of Scotland*, p. 561, Robert Lindesay of Pitscottie, *The Historie and Cronicles of Scotland*, vol. 2 (Edinburgh, 1899), p. 105, *Scottish Correspondence*, cxciii.

English had once made us retreat'.[172] So, putting his reservations to one side, D'Ésse moved into an area desolated by seven years of war and still strongly occupied by English and pro-English forces. The main objective was to prevent the English from fortifying Jedburgh but, following the successes at Home and Fast Castles, the decision was taken to recover first Ferniehurst.

The sixty-strong garrison there were notorious for their cruelty, their captain having 'omitted no act of the immorality of the most inhuman Moors of Africa'.[173] The plan to storm the castle lacked the subtlety shown at Home and Fast castles. The whole army moved against Ferniehurst, preceded by two hundred arquebusiers to clear the path. The garrison sortied out, as was the English custom, to meet the attackers before they reached the castle walls. The English arquebusiers, about twenty-five in number, selected a narrow defile from which to block the French advance. Yet the French did not slow their pace to exchange fire with an enemy in good cover. Instead they charged the defile, relying on momentum to carry them through rather than firepower. Their rapid onset had the desired effect and the English turned and fled back towards the castle. Only fifteen were quick enough to get safely through the castle gates, which slammed shut in the faces of their pursuers.

The French skirmishers had not carried scaling ladders with them but, flushed with success, resolved to assault the castle anyway. They were joined by Huntly and his company of Scots, who were equally eager to storm the castle immediately. Using tables taken from nearby houses as makeshift pavises, the French and Scots hurled themselves at the low wall surrounding the courtyard. Braving a hail of stones and arrows from the ramparts, the leading ranks tried to scale the wall but were beaten back. The attack was stalled until D'Ésse arrived in person, bringing more arquebusiers and artillery. Their sustained fire drove the defenders from the wall and back into the central dongeon. With the defenders cleared from the ramparts, the Scots were able to hammer down the gate and swarm into the castle.

The garrison were now bottled up inside the dongeon. The windows and doors were covered by the French arquebusiers as others swung picks and axes at the wall of the keep to effect a breach. Their fate sealed, the garrison attempted to surrender to the French, for they feared for their lives at the hands of the vengeful Scots. There was little the French could do to protect them. As he emerged from the dongeon, the Captain was beheaded with a single blow and his body hacked to pieces. If the French were somewhat shocked by their allies' behaviour, they grieved little for men they thought were receiving just payment for past cruelties. Indeed, they freely accepted money for the prisoners they did take, who were sold to the Scots for execution.[174]

The significance of the capture of these three small castles (the garrisons ranged in size from thirteen at Fast, to sixty-seven at Home) was more moral

172 Brown, pp. 40–41.
173 Brown, p. 40.
174 Holinshed, *Historie of Scotland*, pp. 561–562, *Scottish Correspondence*, cxcix.

than strategic. These were old bastions, not earthwork artillery fortifications, and their loss was more of an irritant than a disaster for Somerset. Arran and D'Ésse contemplated an attack on Roxburgh, which would have hurt the English badly, but a reconnaissance in force under Chapelle de Biron revealed that the fort was altogether too strong to risk assault. Nevertheless, the capture of Home in particular was a cause of some jubilation in Scotland, and D'Ésse now felt emboldened enough to take the war south of the Border.

Having established a base in Jedburgh, Franco-Scottish forces executed a series of raids into Northumberland. For the most part these were raids conducted by bands of light cavalry, consisting of fifty Scottish reivers accompanied by five or six French officers. Their targets were villages and farms, which were burned and looted in traditional fashion. Two larger *chevauchées* also took place, one under Chapelle de Biron and another under D'Ésse himself. De Biron struck deep into England with a mixed force of cavalry and infantry, harrying the countryside to the gates of Newcastle. D'Ésse did not advance so far, but struck instead at Ford Castle.

He was delayed by the stubborn resistance of the garrison, led by Thomas Kerr. Outnumbered and outgunned, the English were eventually driven within the walls of one tower, but from there they continued to hurl defiance at D'Ésse. Aware of the growing strength of the English Border horse that gathered to watch his siege, D'Ésse finally admitted defeat. Levelling those parts of the castle he had captured, he withdrew back towards Scotland. His Scottish troopers had not been idle whilst the French were stalled before the walls of Ford and had looted and burned ten villages within a half-mile radius. Altogether they gathered booty to the value of 9000 crowns. Well content with the campaign's outcome, they set off for their homes, leaving the French alone in Jedburgh to face the English force that was gathering to make a reprisal raid.[175]

The desertion of his Scottish allies was not D'Ésse's only problem. Attrition, disease and now hunger were taking a steady toll on his little army. There was little food to be had in the devastated Border country, and his troops had to fend for themselves. The *Landsknechte* proved expert foragers, but the whole army could not live by what could be hunted or fished from the Jed. Very soon the French force was reduced to just two thousand effectives, five hundred horse, the rest infantry. D'Ésse had received reports that the English had mustered eight thousand men at Roxburgh. As soon as it became apparent that they intended to move against Jedburgh, D'Ésse withdrew, first to Melrose and then back to Lothian.

De Beaugué writes in a somewhat celebratory tone about the escape, bearing in mind that the English stranglehold on the Marches had only been loosened, not broken. He was correct, however, to point out that the English pursuit was not delivered with any vigour.[176] A French rearguard was driven from its

---

175 Holinshed, *Historie of Scotland*, p. 562.
176 Brown (ed.), 'The French Troops in the Borders in 1548', pp. 43–45.

position at Ancrum Bridge but thereafter the English, for want of victuals, returned to Wark rather than pursue D'Ésse. Nor did the garrisons at Haddington or Dunglass attempt any interception of the retreating forces. This can only indicate that the English forces, too, were suffering the effects of hunger, disease and the steadily mounting cost of skirmish, ambush and raid. Their small garrison at the abbey at Coldingham was finally ejected, but the other garrisons grimly clung on to their battered positions.[177] As winter gave way to spring, both sides seem to have fought themselves to a standstill.

Only in June of 1549 did the English try to revive their flagging fortunes. Faced with serious peasant insurrection in England itself, Somerset seems to have grasped once again the notion of cost-effective island bases in the Firth of Forth, to cut off trade, seize prizes and harry the coast around Edinburgh. To this end, a large English fleet of twenty-five men-of-war attempted to bombard the castle on Bass Rock into submission. The island of Bass Rock lay at the mouth of the Forth, opposite the stronghold of Tantallon. It had not previously figured in English plans but could have made a useful operational base for marauding men-of-war. Its captain, however, could not be persuaded to yield the castle. Built on a high outcrop of rock, this stronghold had little to fear from a naval bombardment, and the English lacked the troops to attempt a formal assault. Consequently their desultory attack was fended off without difficulty.

The English fleet sailed on into the familiar waters of the Forth. Leith was again bombarded, and Scottish and French vessels pursued and captured. Four ensigns of English soldiers and one ensign of Italians were landed on Inchkeith to guard the pioneers who were put to work fortifying the island. The English 'Generell' on Inchkeith was John Cotton, 'a capitaine of goode account', assisted by an Italian, Jasper Pizzoni, and George Appleby, an esquire who had led a company of foot from Derbyshire.[178] For twelve days the fleet lay at anchor off Leith, before putting back to sea and leaving the infantry on Inchkeith to fend for themselves. The cost of keeping the fleet in Scottish waters militated against a long stay and, once the fortifications were complete, the new garrison should have been reasonably secure.

The obvious distress of D'Ésse's forces indicated that he would pose little immediate threat. Yet the English had not calculated with the reinforcements that had arrived from France in early June under Paul de la Barthe, Sieur de Thermes, who was destined to replace D'Ésse. Thermes was one of France's most talented soldiers, having made his name as a commander of light cavalry in Piedmont in 1543. At Ceresoles in 1544 he had led a crucial charge at the height of the battle, and had been instrumental in securing the final victory. His despatch to Scotland emphasises the importance of the campaign to France. He brought with him fresh troops, one hundred men-at-arms, two hundred light horse and a thousand foot. For the time being D'Ésse and his successor worked

---

[177] George Ridpath, *The Border History of England and Scotland* (Berwick, 1848), pp. 390–391.

[178] Churchyard, *A Generall Rehearsall of Warres*, p. 65.

together. They resolved to remove the Inchkeith garrison before it could become properly established. Whilst the Scots gathered together an extemporised fleet of row barks and fishing vessels from all the secret havens of the Forth, Chapelle de Biron undertook a daring reconnaissance. He was accompanied by the captain of the French galleys, Monsieur de Villegaignon. Together they rowed to within arquebus shot of the island and counted the English troops. They returned convinced that the English positions could be taken.

The assault was delivered just sixteen days after the English had first landed. At dawn Thermes' soldiers boarded their boats and pushed out into the Forth. De Villegaignon's galleys skirted the island to draw the fire of the garrison. But the English sentries were watchful and quickly saw that the real threat came from the boats being rowed purposefully towards the shoreline. As these approached the beach they were met with heavy fire from the Italian arquebusiers and a storm of arrows from the Derbyshire bowmen. The French and Scottish soldiers had to fight their way ashore. Bravely pushing forward under a hail of missile fire, they finally came to handstrokes but found the defenders unwilling to concede ground.

De la Chapelle was badly injured, first shot through the hand then knocked to the ground, 'his burguenet [helmet] beaten . . . into his head'.[179] His standard bearer was even less fortunate, slain by a pike wielded by Captain Cotton. Gradually numbers began to tell and the English were forced back off the beach onto the high ground. There they formed up into a 'plump' for their last stand, their numbers quickly whittled away in the mêlée. Cotton, Pizzoni and Appleby fell one after the other, leaving the English without officers and without hope of victory. Finally, after a stout defence, they yielded and the Inchkeith garrison was snuffed out before it was even properly established. D'Ésse, after all the frustrations and setbacks of his months in Scotland, at least ended his period in command with a hard-won but satisfying victory.[180]

Thermes now turned his attention to Haddington, the obstinate English garrison in the heart of Lothian. The precarious lifeline to England had been maintained through the spring and early summer of 1549. The garrison often went hungry, barefoot and ragged. Yet they clung stubbornly to their battered and muddy ramparts. Thermes doubted that the fort could be taken by assault, but he resolved to starve the English into submission. In August he seized Aberlady, the haven which the English had been using to land supplies for Haddington from the fleet.

[179] Holinshed, *Historie of Scotland*, pp. 564–565.
[180] British Library MS Cotton Titus B.V. f33.

Peasant revolt and a war on two fronts: England's dilemma

The English had long since planned to fortify Aberlady themselves, but their position had never been quite strong enough. Growing domestic crisis was to further sap English strength. In July the outbreak of peasant revolt in England diverted both troops and resources away from the Scottish war.

The most serious revolts took place in Devon, Cornwall and East Anglia. In the eastern counties agitation was largely the product of the transition from the manorial system of agriculture, with its basis in communal rights and duties, to an economic system in which individual landowners maximised the return on their property. The essence of this transition is encapsulated in the word 'enclosure'. Enclosure saw landholdings amalgamated and worked independently by farmers of means. This trend deprived the rural poor not only of their rights to common land but often they lost even the meagre strips of earth from which they earned their subsistence. Hungry and angry, it was not long before the dispossessed reached for their bows.

Revolt in the western counties had a more marked religious element. Attachment to Catholicism caused a reaction to the religious reforms initiated under the protectorship of Somerset. Rebels demanded a return to the religious practices of the final years of Henry VIII's reign, suppression of the English Bible and even the restoration of some monasteries. Like their discontented eastern countrymen, those in the west finally showed their willingness to resort to arms. Large, but poorly equipped, rebel armies had even attempted formal sieges, at Exeter and Norwich.[181] The weary and impoverished Lord Grey of Wilton, whose wish to be relieved of his onerous command in Scotland had finally been granted in May, was now recalled to fight rebels in the south.

His replacement as Warden of the East and Middle Marches was the young and energetic Henry Manners, Earl of Rutland. Deprived of some of his best troops, as the pick of the mercenaries were sent south, Rutland nevertheless resolved to reverse the recent English setbacks. Ongoing negotiations with the Earl of Bothwell finally saw the Hermitage, the chief strength of Liddesdale, delivered to the English. The grim and forbidding fortress in the midst of the devastated Border country was garrisoned by Italian and Spanish soldiers, who must have heartily wished they were back home in Siena or Codorba.[182]

Rutland had taken the initiative in the east too, pushing forward to Dunglas by 4 July 1549. He remained in that vicinity until the 26th and was able to revictual Haddington. He advanced with such speed that French forces blocking

---

[181] See Julian Cornwall, *Revolt of the Peasantry 1549* (London, 1977) and Stephan Land, *Kett's Rebellion: The Norfolk Rising of 1549* (Ipswich, 1977). Cornwall, in particular, pays careful attention to the military history of these peasant revolts. The social significance of the late medieval peasant wars is discussed in Frantisek Graus, 'From Resistance to Revolt: The Late Medieval Peasant Wars in the Context of Social Crisis', in James Bak (ed.), *The German Peasant War of 1525* (London, 1976), pp. 1–9.

[182] Bush, *Government Policy of Protector Somerset*, p. 17.

the road to the fort were caught completely by surprise. The sight of English horse and a formed battle of *Landsknechte* bearing down on their unprepared camp caused a hasty withdrawal. For the English the only disappointment of the day was the loss of much of their German infantry's baggage. This had been left unguarded when they had moved against the French and had been looted by Scottish Border horse.[183]

Rutland's vigour, however, was not going to be enough to revive England's military fortunes. The revival of the war in France quickly brought disaster. On 8 August Henry II personally led an invasion of the Boulonnais. He had overrun the outlying forts and bottled the garrison up in Boulogne itself, which was then blockaded. The Rhinegrave and his *Landsknechte* had struck with more success than they had ever enjoyed in Scotland, storming two English forts, at Ambleteuse and Blackness. Both had been relatively new structures, constructed in the same fashion as the forts in Scotland. Consequently they had the same defects, with wet weather causing the earth ramparts to collapse.[184]

Now the English were fighting a war on two fronts, as well as persistent domestic insurrection. They had not the men, nor the money, nor indeed the will, to sustain the struggle. In September Rutland made the momentous decision to abandon Haddington. With Aberlady in French hands, the provisioning of Haddington would depend on forcing passage through the dangerous overland route. It would entail the regular commitment of a major expeditionary force, requiring thousands of men and hundreds of carts just to keep the garrison in supply.

Fortifying the town itself had been relatively cheap, costing the treasury just £1423. Maintaining the garrison had been prohibitively expensive. The 4529 soldiers who served in Haddington between September 1548 and November 1549 cost a staggering £31,641 in wages and munitions.[185] England could no longer bear the cost. The next expedition to the battered Lothian town would be the last. Rutland forced the siege lines once more, extracted the garrison and their cannon, levelled the fortifications and withdrew to England 'to the great rejoicing of Louthian, to whom that towne had given occasion of great troubles and calamities'.[186]

If Rutland had been hoping that the abandonment of Haddington would simplify his problems he was mistaken. The condition of the remaining garrisons was pitiful beyond words. The soldiers were cold, hungry, ragged and sick. On 14 October Rutland reported to the council that:

> the men of warre also here must be vittelled, which in this barren countrie without the Kinge's majeste's provisions is not to be gotten. And in dede the Engleshe men here be verey fewe in nombre and daily decrease by sickness and ronning away; albeit the captens for their enterteynement sake can be con-

183 Holinshed, *Scottish Historie*, p. 565. *Rutland Manuscripts*, pp. 364–366.
184 H.M.Colvin, 'The King's Works in France', in H.M.Colvin (ed.), *The History of the King's Works, Vol. 3, 1485–1660*, Part 1, pp. 337–395.
185 Bush, *Government Policy of Protector Somerset*, p. 28.
186 Holinshed, *Historie of Scotland*, p. 565.

tented to abyde, generally all men eschue fortes for the misery and sicknes in them . . . To put strangers [mercenaries] into them, besides that it is dangerous, they cannot [be] persuaded ther unto.[187]

Rutland called for at least a thousand fresh men from England, and, to emphasise the dire necessity he was in, he raised the prospect of an imminent Scottish invasion of Northumberland.

Scottish confidence had certainly risen in the wake of the withdrawal from Haddington, but Thermes' first military priority remained the reduction of the surviving English garrisons. The prospects for the outright expulsion of the English now looked very good. Not only were the starving garrisons in little position to offer the kind of resolute resistance they had in the previous year, but Somerset himself now looked as if he were to be a casualty of the crisis consuming England. He faced not just revolt, but financial disaster. Almost £15,000 had been spent on building the new fortifications, but this figure was dwarfed by the cost of their upkeep and paying their garrisons, now spiralling towards £60,000. In total Somerset's Scottish policy had cost the English exchequer a punitive £580,000.[188]

The financial burden of the war was falling heavily on the people of England themselves. A 400-strong band of Irish kern, passing through Chester in the final stages of the war, were paid and victualled at the expense of prominent locals, headed by the Lord Mayor himself.[189] The government no longer had the money to pay for transporting soldiers, and men were left stranded not just in Chester but thousands more in Calais and the North. The cost of sending these troops home would eventually be met by expending 100,000 crowns from the first French payment for the return of Boulogne.[190]

Unable to restore order in the rebellious counties, and unwilling to withdraw from the cripplingly expensive war in Scotland, the Lord Protector lost control of the Privy Council to his rival, the Earl of Warwick. Somerset was soon in the Tower, and he stayed there until February 1550. On his release he would briefly regain a degree of authority in an uneasy alliance with Warwick, who had adopted the title Lord President. Warwick had, however, achieved such a degree of ascendancy over the Council, and the mind of the young King, that Somerset's eventual fate was sealed. He finally went to the block in January 1552. In the meantime, Warwick determined to restore domestic stability with the aid of reliable mercenary forces (Julian Romero and Pedro de Gamboa amongst them) and to end the economic crisis via political reform and financial retrenchment.

The agony of the garrisons was prolonged for a little longer. It must now have been readily apparent that there was no hope of establishing an English Pale, and the only point in holding out was to try and wrest some concessions from the Scottish government. Rutland was negotiating for the release of English

---

[187] *Rutland Manuscripts*, pp. 192–193.
[188] David Loades, *Essays in the Reign of Edward VI* (Bangor, 1994), p. 36.
[189] Chester City Records Office, Mayors' Military Papers, MMP/1/4, MMP/1/5, MMP/1/6.
[190] *Acts of the Privy Council of England, Vol. 2, 1547–1550* (London, 1890), p. 93.

prisoners, in particular for James Wylford, who had captained Haddington so valiantly and now lay sick and close to death in a Scottish dungeon.[191] The Scots were amenable to his approaches, and indeed they could afford to be. They were now negotiating from a position of some strength.

Warwick was keen to end the war with France quickly, and accepted humiliating terms which saw Boulogne handed back to France immediately, rather than in 1554, as had been agreed in 1546. Further, the English received a payment of just 400,000 crowns instead of the originally promised 800,000. Yet Warwick still seemed to want to maintain some garrisons in Scotland. He established two commissions to organise their refortification and revictualling. The hope remained that Scotland might still agree to the marriage of Mary to Edward in return for the ceding of the remaining garrisons.[192] Military reality, however, meant that Scotland did not have to consider such deals. The failure of the garrisons was now made absolutely manifest by events at Broughty Craig.

The collapse of English power in Scotland

Sir John Luttrell's command had been clinging to its precarious existence throughout 1549. Ordered by Somerset to lie quiet, Luttrell had been able to do little else. The isolated position of his garrison had meant that it suffered the effects of plague, exposure and long periods without pay more than most. Luttrell himself was ill and, like Grey of Wilton, had been forced to dig deep into his own pocket to meet the continued expenses of the garrison. In July 1549, finding himself heavily in debt and suspecting himself 'neyther . . . meat for servys, nor long for the world' he had begged Somerset to relieve him of his command. He urged that the speediest efforts be made to alleviate the suffering of his troops observing that:

> I have nott this v weekis harde owt of Ynglond, nor yett sythe the comynge of Sir Petro Negro and his bande [in March, 1549] ther hathe nether benn monaye sent unto him, nor any kinde of thinge to clothe the powre soldyers here who bothe ar nakyd and barefoot, neyther havinge fyar to keape them warme nor wherwithall to dresse ther meate . . . I assuar your grace, neyther I nor anye other yowr grace shall please to apoynt hyther shall be able to kepe thes peces here from thennymyes handis.[193]

With Somerset's harsh and unfair accusation over the loss of Dundee still rankling, Luttrell's patience was finally giving way:

> I havy yn all thingis donn my dutye, I trust lyke a willinge subject, and shall do to the deathe. Butt I am obyd unto and consyderyd as tho yn my paynfull

191 *Rutland Manuscripts*, pp. 194–197.
192 *Rutland Manuscripts*, pp. 192–200.
193 *Scottish Correspondence*, ccxvi.

servys and good wyll I hadd attaynyd only for my rewarde yowr gracys utter yndignatyonne.[194]

Somerset, however, was deaf to Luttrell's pleas. If the weather had been unseasonably cold and wet in July, it paled into insignificance next to the misery of the winter of 1549–50. Although they barely had the strength to man the walls Luttrell and his weary band of Englishmen, *Landsknechte* and Italians soldiered on. Neither the dilapidated castle nor Balgillo Fort, whose muddy ramparts were collapsing under their own weight, were in any condition to withstand a serious assault. In early February 1550, Thermes arrived with a train of siege artillery and pounded the already enfeebled defences. The exhausted garrison no longer had the strength to take the battle to the French gun lines, or shore up their crumbling walls. The end came at midnight on 12 February. A Franco-Scottish *camisado* stormed the low ramparts of Balgillo Fort and those who were not killed quickly surrendered. The old castle, its situation hopeless, capitulated soon after.[195]

Scotland's military star was now in the ascendant. Franco-Scottish forces, comprising pike, arquebusiers, mounted arquebusiers, Border horse and artillery, were in a position to reduce the remaining garrisons one by one. Warwick already appears to have admitted defeat; plans had been in hand for the withdrawal of the Lauder garrison from Scotland since 21 February. In late March Franco-Scottish forces arrived in front of Lauder. The garrison here made the customary sortie to meet the attackers in the open field. There was a fierce skirmish before the English were driven back inside their gates, and the two sides settled down to a siege.

Amongst the defenders was Thomas Churchyard who, having escaped from captivity, had joined the garrison at Lauder. He describes a determined resistance. Early on in the siege a sortie of light horse, disguised as Scots, had successfully raided the French camp. The English ordnance, commanded by a Captain Manneryng, initially kept Thermes at arm's length. However, Lauder's garrison was soon under pressure. A French assault penetrated the fort's base court and the losses incurred in driving the attackers back out were heavy. Once again, though, the major problem was logistical. A convoy of supplies had reached the fort on 22 March, shortly before the Scots had arrived. This had been timely, for the garrison had already been short of food to the point where 'the eating of horses did argue'.[196] Once the siege was under way, however, no more supplies had reached the fort. Having rapidly fired off all his munitions, Sir James Willoughby, the English captain, was arranging to have pewter cups

---

[194] *Scottish Correspondence*, ccxvi.

[195] Luttrell was returned to England in exchange for the sons of Sir George Douglas and the Master of Semple, held prisoner south of the Tweed. He was rewarded by Warwick for his long and steadfast service with a generous gift of land in June 1550. However, he never really recovered from the privations and stress he had endured and died in July 1551. See *Scottish Correspondence*, p. 322, n. 4.

[196] Churchyard, *A Generall Rehearsall of Warres*, pp. 66–68.

melted down to cast bullets when news arrived that a peace treaty had been agreed with France.[197] Lauder, Dunglass and all the other surviving English garrisons were to be evacuated. The war was over.

William Patten records that early in the 1547 campaign, as his army first advanced into Scotland, Somerset had had a strange dream. In it he received a hearty welcome from the King on his return to Court, yet he could remember having achieved nothing at all. Indeed when he 'considered the King's . . . great costs, and the great travail of the great men and soldiers [all] to have been done in vain', he had been roused from his uncomfortable sleep. Writing in early 1548, Patten thought it worthy of note that precisely the opposite of Somerset's fears seemed to have come to pass.[198] Two years later he may have recognised the dream for the unerring prophecy that it was.

[197] See D.L.Porter (ed.), 'Documents Concerning the Negotiation of the Anglo-French Treaty of March 1550', *Camden Miscellany*, 4th ser., vol. 29 (1984).
[198] Patten, 'The Expedition into Scotland, 1547', pp. 83–84.

CONCLUSION

As the last battered remnants of the English army abandoned their castles and earthworks and slunk homewards in 1550, Scottish pioneers with picks and axes took their places. Determined that, were the English to return, they would find no bases, the decision was taken to level the forts. Today only the barest traces remain at Lauder, Eyemouth and Dunglas. Of Haddington and Balgillo Fort nothing remains. This physical removal has perhaps played its part in the scant historical treatment afforded to those three crucial years in British military history, 1547 to 1550.

Those years saw the *trace italienne* arrive in the British Isles, with the construction of modern earthwork artillery fortifications an integral part of Somerset's strategic design. The forts were built by a tactically efficient army, composed of a well balanced synthesis of light and heavy cavalry, artillery and infantry. This army was supported by naval forces, who not only assisted in troop movement and supply, but proved capable of amphibious operations and shore bombardment. The ordinary soldiers were raised by a reliance on the neo-feudal obligations of nobles and their retinues, and on the levy provided by a venerable national militia. Much doubt has been expressed about the efficiency of such an archaic system. Yet on every occasion that the levy was called upon to actually defend its country it had been entirely successful, at Flodden in 1513, Solway Moss in 1542 and on the Isle of Wight in 1545. Elizabethan soldiers actively debated the militia's best response to invasion, 'to give . . . present battaile, or to temporize and defer the same'.[1] In 1542 Thomas Wharton had demonstrated that, properly handled, even a severely outnumbered levy force could move swiftly and decisively against an invader.

Nor should the continued existence of the levy disguise the presence of genuine professionals within the English army's ranks. These individuals served for pay and were available for service for long periods, making possible a sustained three year campaign to occupy and hold territory. Amongst them were some highly skilled individual specialists, military engineers, surveyors, light cavalry commanders and gunners. Where native troops could not provide particular specialisms, foreign soldiers were employed in the same manner that the major continental powers employed mercenaries. Over the course of Henry VIII's reign an increasing number of English troops made the transition from bow and bill to pike and shot. As this gradual shift took place their numbers were supplemented by the *Landsknechte* and by Spanish and Italian arquebusiers. Similarly, whilst Henry slowly built up a native heavy cavalry arm, he was quite prepared to employ Burgundian men-at-arms and German *Reiter* to

[1] British Library, MS Harleian Collection, 4685.

ensure that English armies in the field remained comparable to their continental counterparts.

The influence of these professional soldiers, native or foreign, gave the army a tactical sophistication that has, so far, been largely unrecognised. English infantry units, combinations of bow, bill, pike and arquebusier, proved capable of operating in small, flexible units of a few hundred men. The earthwork forts from which they operated were extremely resilient, and the garrisons of Haddington and Broughty in particular successfully defied the tough and experienced French veterans who were hurled at them time and again. English field artillery was mobile enough to accompany fast moving cavalry on Border *chevauchées*. The English also proved adept at amphibious operations and shore bombardment. In short, in terms of military practice, there is little reason for seeing the English armies of the mid-sixteenth century as intrinsically backward or less tactically capable than their continental counterparts. There was no revolution in their military practice. In particular the gun was slow to establish itself, for the English already possessed a fine missile arm in the longbow. Instead, English armies of the sixteenth century continued to adapt existing practice and to develop or adopt new practices when necessary. There was a strong continuity between early sixteenth- and fifteenth-century armies, but this should not be taken as evidence of a moribund military establishment. The successful combined arms force that Somerset took to Scotland in 1547 was not the product of a military revolution. Rather there had been a steady accreditation of novel military techniques, combined with the gradual adaptation of existing practices. English armies were heavily influenced by experience of warfare on the continent, but their nature was always governed by the constraints imposed by insular warfare.

A similar point can be made in regard to Scottish military effectiveness over the course of the first half of the sixteenth century. Scotland, like England, relied primarily on a long-standing levy system to raise large bodies of troops. This system remained essentially the same as had operated in the fifteenth century. Yet this organisational continuity did not entirely preclude military innovation. Scotland demonstrated an early commitment to the battlefield combination of pike and shot, which offered some prospect of success against the combined arms forces fielded by England. The early emphasis on shock action, demonstrated by the imitation of 'the Almain's manner' at Flodden and the high pay afforded to pikemen, was tempered over time by an increased emphasis on firepower. By mid-century Scottish commanders were, in principle at least, aiming for an equal division of their infantry between pike and shot, a proportional distribution well in line with continental practice. Thus, within the limitations imposed by the organisational framework of Scottish armies, there was a clear indication of tactical and technological development. The presence of French troops, particularly during the campaign to expel Somerset's garrisons during 1547–1550, was of the greatest significance to this process. Once again, continental influence combined with the particular circumstances of warfare in Scotland to dictate the nature of military practice.

Tactical ability was, therefore, in evidence in both English and Scottish armies of the first half of the sixteenth century. Although the military history of the period seems dominated by the pitched battles at Flodden in 1513 and Pinkie in 1547, for the most part soldiers were employed in relatively small-scale operations that demanded a high level of weapon skill and unit cohesion. The notion of early sixteenth-century warfare as a question of unwieldy mass against unwieldy mass rests uneasily with a reality in which most soldiers were employed in operations likely to give rise to forms of combat requiring initiative and tactical ability. Convoy escort, the *camisado* surprise attack, *chevauchée* and ambush, amphibious operations; soldiers would find themselves fighting in these circumstances far more often than in the mass formations of major battles. The destruction of the 'Ill Raid' at Millfield in 1513, Wharton's defence of the English West March at Solway Moss, Scottish success at Haddon Rigg in 1542 or Ancrum Moor in 1545, Palmer's successful dash into Haddington in 1548, and D'Essé's successful ambush of a relief force soon after, all suggest a high degree of proficiency in low-level tactics.

Yet the prominence of such actions in the Anglo-Scots wars, whilst indicative of tactical ability, also demonstrates the strategic limitations under which both nations operated. The major battles decided very little, warfare became a protracted affair of destructive raid and counter-raid, pursued with varying degrees of intensity according to the political climate. Both Scotland and England utilised war in pursuit of political objectives. From James IV announcing his personal rule and forcing Henry VII to the negotiating table to Protector Somerset seeking to secure his King's royal bride and dynastic union, war seemed a natural corollary to open diplomacy and political intrigue. Yet neither nation could formulate, or implement, military strategies that would actually deliver decisive results. For Scotland the question of strategic objectives was complicated by the alliance with France. French pressure on Scotland to maintain an offensive strategy towards England was naturally self-interested. Politically the French alliance was important to Scotland, but there were increasing doubts about the wisdom of taking military action against England.

After the disaster at Flodden in 1513, Scotland's levy-based army lost all credibility as an offensive force. It became in effect an organisation of fencibles, which could mobilise for home defence but which could not be used outside Scotland itself. Cross-border operations could only be conducted by French auxiliaries, who were usually deeply unpopular with their Scottish allies, or by Borderers, whose primary concern was amassing plunder, or by forces composed solely of noble retinues, whose self-serving lords were usually too busy squabbling amongst themselves to provide effective field command. Scottish attempts to reinitiate an offensive strategy against England in 1521, 1523, 1542 and 1545 were all failures. Although Scottish (and French auxiliary), forces could foray into England, the level of destruction they could achieve did not justify the continued English belief that a serious menace to national security still existed in the North.

The perceived need to counter that menace played a significant part in

English strategic calculations. Yet, primarily, the Crown's focus remained fixed on continental Europe until 1547. Henry VIII's fundamental desire was to reopen the Hundred Years War. The threat of Scottish intervention in the Marches was a serious distraction from that policy, but not one to which Henry would give his full attention. England was never able to develop the logistical apparatus necessary to sustain a military campaign in Scotland. Henrician strategy towards Scotland was crude and unrealistic. His armies could inflict massive material damage but their presence was always fleeting and usually confined to a specific area, the Marches. Thus, in 1544 and 1545 highly destructive English forays operated with virtual impunity in the field, but failed to further the cause of dynastic union or substantially weaken Arran's grip on power. Protector Somerset's attempt to sustain military pressure in Scotland by seizing and holding key garrisons and by harnessing the support of pro-union Scots was a recognition of the inadequacy of the Henrician approach. Yet ultimately Somerset's strategy offered no greater prospects for achieving his political goals. His initial desire to wage an ideological war for a 'Greater Britain', rather than an aggressive war against an independent Scotland, was undermined by the iron-fisted manner in which his strategy was implemented. The underlying similarities to previous English endeavours soon became apparent, most notably in the eventual revival of the English Crown's claim to suzerainty. Forced to rely on his garrisons as instruments of military coercion, Somerset became embroiled in a protracted war of occupation without the requisite logistical structure to supply his forces in the field or, ultimately, the resources to finance such a conflict. In the face of French intervention on an unprecedented scale and internal peasant insurrection, the English war effort simply collapsed.

Somerset's strategy did not just fail. Its consequences were exactly the opposite of what the Protector had set out to achieve. Scotland was reduced to a mere satellite of France. Edward VI's prospective bride was engaged to the Dauphin, wrecking the prospect of dynastic union between England and Scotland. Boulogne was surrendered with humiliating haste and Somerset lost his own hold on power. This was only the most striking example of how the recourse to war in furtherance of political aims proved consistently counter-productive and self-defeating for both Scotland and England. James IV's early military success clouded his judgement in 1513, with fatal consequences. Albany's desire to use Scottish troops to fight French battles in 1523 undermined his own position as regent and caused French influence in Scotland to wane for several years. James V's plans to apply military pressure to the North of England led to the rout at Solway Moss. The defeat gave Henry VIII a potent political opportunity to further his own ambitions in Scotland via the good agency of the prisoners taken on the field. His diplomatic blundering and rapid resort to the sword only drove Scotland more firmly into the orbit of France, a process accelerated by the escalation of warfare under Somerset. In a great many respects the course of Anglo-Scottish relations during the early sixteenth century was governed by the consequences of strategic failure.

For the most part conflict simply fostered further conflict, neither achieving decisive results nor allowing for the possibility of a constructive peace. The English military collapse in 1550 did at last draw this depressing and frustrating state of affairs to a close. The resumption of conflict on the Border in 1557–59 was essentially an extension of the Valois-Hapsburg conflict rather than a renewal of the ancient Anglo-Scots wars. With Mary Tudor of England married to Philip of Spain, and Mary Queen of Scots married to the French Dauphin, Francis, it was almost inevitable that Europe's wider conflict would draw in the island nations. Yet the fighting in the Marches was desultory. The largest Scottish army levied for an invasion of England refused to cross the Border, leaving a depleted force of French auxiliaries to vainly assault Wark in a repetition of the events of 1523. Although it may not have been immediately apparent to contemporaries, the tenor of Anglo-Scottish relations had changed. The Border would see another half century of foray, 'hot trod' pursuit, blood-feud and blackmail, but the national armies of Scotland and England would never face each other in the field again.

Indeed, in 1560 England's new Queen, Elizabeth I, would send auxiliaries to fight shoulder to shoulder with the Scottish army of the Protestant Lords of the Congregation in their struggle to expel French troops from Scotland. The gathering pace of the Scottish Reformation had inevitably led to a challenge to French influence. Elizabeth's distaste for rebellion against a lawful sovereign proved less strong than her fear of Francis and Mary's pretence to the English throne. England and Scotland now shared a viable strategic objective: to drive the French from the British Isles. The major French garrison at Leith was invested. Its defenders fought with their customary skill and courage. They fended off several assaults before finally being starved into submission. The English auxiliaries retired quietly back across the Border, their task completed. The success of this Anglo-Scottish military venture stands in marked contrast to the futility of the preceding fifty years of conflict.

GLOSSARY

Almain A German soldier, a *Landsknecht*.

Almain Rivet Mass produced armour of variable quality produced in Germany and the Low Countries.

Arbalest A crossbow.

Archer (i) A man armed with a bow. (ii) French mounted soldier, originally armed with longbow or crossbow but, by the early sixteenth century, evolved into a true cavalryman armed with a lance.

Arquebus A trigger operated firearm, weighing about 10 pounds and firing a half ounce lead ball. Fitted with a matchlock firing mechanism and braced against the shoulder, the arquebus was developed from the earlier *handgun* in the late fifteenth century. The matchlock was a rotating arm attached to the trigger which held the lighted match in place. This allowed the gun to be steadied with both hands, thus allowing for more accurate firing. Used throughout the sixteenth century but generally supplemented by the heavier *musket* from the 1530s onwards. Its (relatively) light weight and (again relatively) high rate of fire meant that most armies retained *arquebusiers* or men armed with the slightly heavier 'caliver'.

Arquebus à Croc A heavy, large calibre firearm mounted on a waggon. Effectively this was a small piece of field artillery.

Arquebusier A soldier armed with an *arquebus*.

Auxiliaries Troops lent to an army by a friendly power.

Bard Armour for horses, rarely used after c.1550.

Base A small artillery piece, weighing about 200 pounds, with a calibre of about 1.25 inches and firing a projectile weighing about 0.5 pounds.

Bastion An emplacement for artillery projecting from the walls of a fortification.

Bastle House Fortified dwelling of the Anglo-Scottish Marches.

Battle A military formation. Traditionally fifteenth- and sixteenth-century armies were divided into three battles, the vanguard, the main battle and the rearward. Although usually associated with units several thousand strong, by the late 1540s the term battle was also being applied to much smaller units, perhaps numbering only two or three hundred.

Bill A staff weapon combining an axe blade and spear point. Developed from the peasant's hedging bill, this was the standard mêlée weapon of English infantry throughout the first half of the sixteenth century.

Blockhouse A detached, heavily fortified gun emplacement, often built to strengthen existing, but old fashioned, castles or in defence of harbours.

Border Horse Light cavalry raised in the Anglo-Scottish Marches. Sometimes referred to as *Northern horse*.

Brigandine Lightweight, padded body armour, consisting of overlapping metal plates sewn within a leather or canvas jacket.

Buckler A small shield, usually used in conjunction with a sword.

Bullener English heavy cavalryman of the Boulogne garrison.

Bulwark See *Bastion*.

Burgonet A peaked military helmet.

Camisado A surprise attack, particularly one that aims to break into an enemy fortification by stealth.

Cannon In this period this word usually referred to a large artillery piece, weighing in excess of 8000 pounds and firing a ball of over 20 pounds in weight. Smaller versions were referred to as 'demi-cannon'.

Caracole A tactic used by pistol-armed cavalry in which successive ranks of a column rode up to their target, discharging their weapons rank by rank.

Casement A vaulted chamber in the wall of a fortress, built to house artillery.

Chevauchée A large-scale destructive raid designed to destroy resources and terrorise an enemy population in order to discredit its government or force it to negotiate.

Cheveauléger French cavalryman of the mid-sixteenth century armed with lance and pistol.

Claymore In the sixteenth century a two-handed sword associated with Highlanders. In the seventeenth and eighteenth centuries the word was used to describe the basket-hilted, single-handed sword used by Scottish troops.

Condottiere Italian mercenary captain. In the fifteenth century a heavily armoured man-at-arms, later applied more generally to any professional soldier who raised and led mercenary units.

Corselet (i) Plate armour protecting the body but not the arms and legs. (ii) A soldier wearing the same.

Counter-march The technique whereby successive ranks of *shot* advanced, fired and then retired to reload in sequence, allowing units to maintain a high rate of fire.

Counterscarp The outer wall built along the edge of a defensive ditch. This was a useful position for a besieger's artillery, so often the first objective of an attack during a siege.

Coustillier A late fifteenth-century French or Burgundian light cavalry man.

Cracker English irregular soldier, particularly associated with the 1522–23 campaign in France.

Cuirass Back and breastplate.

Cuirassier An armoured cavalryman.

Culverin A cannon weighing between 4500 and 6500 pounds, with a calibre of about 5 inches, firing a 15–20 pound projectile. Smaller culverins, those weighing less than 5000 pounds, might be referred to as 'bastard culverins' or 'demi- culverins'.

Culverineer A hand gunner.

Curtain The wall of a fortification running between the *bastions* and gatehouses.

Curtow A large cannon used in siege operations, firing a projectile of around 60 pounds.

Dag English name for *pistol*.

Demi-lancer A lance-armed cavalryman wearing half or three quarter armour.

Doppelsoldner A veteran *Landsknecht* in receipt of double pay, who would fight in the front rank of a pike column.

Embrasure Splayed aperture in a wall, through which cannon could be fired.

Ensign (i) A unit of men, usually around 350 strong. (ii) A unit standard. (iii) The officer who bore this standard.

Falcon A field artillery piece weighing about 700 pounds with a 2.5 inch calibre and firing a 2 pound ball. A slightly smaller version might be referred to as a 'falconet', a 'cut-throat' or a 'murderer'.

Fascine A bundle of brushwood used to plug a gap in a defensive wall, or by attackers to fill in a defensive ditch.

Fausse-Bray Mound on which to place artillery, built either to defend a fortification or, by a besieger, to overlook a defensive rampart.

Fiery Cross A burning cross carried by a horseman from village to village. This was the dramatic expedient by which Scotland raised troops during an emergency. A similar device was used on both sides of the Border to summon men to the 'hot trod' pursuit.

Foot Any infantry force.

Foot Band A tactical unit of English infantry, 100 to 350 strong, and associated with a particular noble or captain.

Foray A military or quasi-military expedition usually carried out by light cavalry to lift cattle, raid settlements and generally cause havoc to one's enemies in the pursuit of national or personal quarrels.

Forlorn Hope A detached body of troops undertaking a particularly dangerous task, possibly a skirmish line in battle, or the first men into a breach during a siege.

Galloglass Irish mercenaries of Scottish descent. Famously hardy and well-disciplined, usually armed with two-handed sword or battle axe.

Gendarme A man-at-arms in full plate armour and armed with a lance.

Gentlemen Pensioners A semi-permanent body of heavy cavalry raised by Henry VIII.

Glacis The exposed sloping ground over which attacking troops had to advance to reach defensive walls. It sometimes concealed a covered passage, through which the defenders could move troops.

Gun Loop Aperture through which hand-held firearms could be fired.

Hackbutt The English word for *arquebus*.

Halberd A staff weapon, usually around two metres in length combining an axe head and spear point. Often associated with Swiss infantry, but used, in decreasing numbers, by most European armies throughout the sixteenth century.

Handgun Any hand-held firearm, in use from the early fourteenth century onwards. Usually fired whilst braced against the breastbone, with one hand holding a lighted match to the touch-hole, the other supporting the weapon. Supplanted by the *arquebus* in the late fifteenth century.

Harness Personal military equipment, helmet, body armour and weapon.

Harquebusier See *Arquebusier*.

Herce A formation of archers, usually protected by a stockade of wooden stakes, positioned to support dismounted men-at-arms. Associated particularly with the Hundred Years War, but English soldiers still used the expression in the latter half of the sixteenth century when describing units of men armed with the longbow.

Horse Any mounted force.

Jack Lightweight body armour, similar to the *brigandine*. Constructed of overlapping plates of metal sewn into a leather or canvas garment.

Jedburgh Axe A staff weapon with a long, thin blade which could be used as a lance when mounted and as an axe when dismounted.

Kern Irish light infantry armed with javelins, bows and swords. Widely employed by the English both in France and Scotland.

Lance (i) The staff weapon carried by cavalry. (ii) A military unit comprising a man-at-arms, his squire and a varying number of other soldiers. French and Burgundian lances generally consisted of six men. English lances may have had as many as nine.

Landsknecht German mercenary, usually armed with pike or *arquebus*.

Leith Axe A staff weapon similar to the *halberd* or *bill* and carried by Scottish troops.

Lochaber Axe (i) A heavy single-bladed, possibly one-handed, axe particularly associated with Highland troops. (ii) A generic term for any staff weapon carried by Scottish soldiers.

Longbow Missile weapon used by both English and Scottish forces. Most bows used in battle probably had draw weights of around 100 pounds and could penetrate 1 to 2 millimetres of plate armour at 10 metres.

Mace A heavy metal club, usually used by cavalry. Generally replaced by the *pistol* but retained by commanders as a symbol of rank.

Morion A high-crested military helmet.

Mount Artificial hill on which a besieger would place artillery.

Munition Armour Mass produced armour for the common soldiery.

Musket A heavy, large calibre firearm, weighing up to 18 pounds and firing a two ounce lead ball. Fired from a rest, it out performed the *arquebus* in all respects except rate of fire. A late sixteenth-century musket could penetrate between 2 and 4 millimetres of plate armour at 100 metres, but its limited mobility was a liability in combat.

Northern Horse Light cavalry raised in the north of England, including Cheshire, Lancashire and Yorkshire, but especially from the Border counties.

Ordnance Military equipment generally, but most usually artillery.

Pavise A large shield, usually used to protect crossbowmen or handgunners during sieges. Supposedly used by some Scottish troops at Flodden, but largely rendered obsolete by gunpowder weapons.

Pele A type of small, square defensive tower common to the Anglo-Scottish Marches. Sometimes referred to as a 'pile'.

Petard Explosive charge laid against weak points of fortifications.

Pike The standard infantry mêlée weapon of sixteenth-century European infantry. Between 12 and 20 feet in length, its use required a high degree of co-ordination for effective use. It was most effective in the hands of Swiss, *landsknecht* and Spanish infantry.

Pioneers Military labourers used in building fortifications or field emplacements.

Pistol Hand-held firearm fitted with a wheel-lock mechanism, making it an easy weapon to use from horseback. It originated in either Italy or Germany in the 1520s and was in wide use by most West European cavalry by the 1540s.

Plat-Maker Military surveyor and architect.

Point-blank The range at which the trajectory of a missile, arrow, quarrel or ball, is straight rather than curved.

Pole Axe Two-handed battle axe usually carried by dismounted men-at-arms. Seldom seen after the early decades of the sixteenth century.

Pricker English word for light cavalryman.

Proof Armour tested against bow or gun at point-blank range.

Rampire Earthwork built up against the walls of an existing stone fortification to strengthen it against artillery.

Ravelin Detached *bastion*.

Reiter German heavy cavalryman, usually armed with *pistols* from the 1540s onwards.

Reiver A light horseman from the Anglo-Scots Border, widely employed by both English and Scottish armies.

Saker A medium artillery piece weighing about 1500 pounds, with a 3.5 to 4 inch calibre, firing a 5 to 7 pound projectile.

Sallett A style of helmet, usually with visor, providing good protection for head and neck. Common in all European armies in the late fifteenth and early sixteenth centuries.

Sapper Soldier employed in military engineering, usually tunnelling and placing explosive charges under fortifications.

Serpentine An artillery piece weighing about 3000 pounds, of 4 inch calibre, and firing a projectile weighing around 7 pounds.

Scarp Sloping lower section of a fortification's walls.

Shot A common expression for infantry armed with missile weapons, including, in English armies, archers.

Slaghe Sword Two-handed sword used by *whifflers*.

Sleeve A linear formation of infantry, one or two ranks deep, armed with missile weapons and positioned around a unit of pike and halberdiers.

Spears Lance-armed cavalry.

Staff Light lance or spear carried by *northern horse* or *demi-lancers*.

Stradiot Albanian mercenary light cavalry. Employed by the English for use in Scotland.

Targe A small shield, usually used in conjunction with a sword or, by Highland troops, with a *Lochaber axe*.

Trace Italienne A style of military architecture developed in late fifteenth-century Italy, designed both to maximise the potential of the defender's artillery and to provide the best possible defence against the attacker's.

Trench Master Officer in charge of trenching during siege operations.

Victualler (i) An individual responsible for providing supplies to an army in the field. (ii) A ship carrying supplies for an army.

Vintner English soldier responsible for a group of twenty men.

Wappinshaw A Scottish troop muster, with strict regulations governing the appropriate arms and armour to be brought by each man.

Whiffler English soldier responsible for maintaining order on the march and, by the 1540s, in battle.

Wing A small detached unit of infantry normally armed with missile weapons, positioned on the flank of a larger unit.

BIBLIOGRAPHY

Primary Sources

Manuscripts

British Library
  Additional Manuscript 32648
  Cotton Caligula BVII
  Cotton Titus BV
  Harleian Collection 4685
Chester City Record Office
  Mayors' Military Papers [MMP]/1/1–6
    MMP/5/16
    MMP/7/9,10,32
Manchester Central Reference Library
  L1/40/01/1–2
  M35/7/4

Printed source collections

Acts of the Privy Council of England, vols 2 and 3, *1547–1550* and *1550–1552*, ed. John Roche Dasent (HMSO, London, 1890 and 1891).

Calendar of Letters, Despatches And State Papers Relating To The Negotiations Between England And Spain, Vol. 13, July 1554 – November 1558, ed. Royall Tyler (HMSO, London, 1954).

Calendar of State Papers, Domestic, Edward VI, 1547–1553, ed. C.S.Knighton (HMSO, London, 1992).

Calendar of State Papers, Domestic, Elizabeth I, 1601–1603, with Addenda 1547–1565, ed. Mary Anne Everett Green (Longman, London, 1870).

Calendar of State Papers Relating to Scotland, Vol. 1, 1547–63, ed. Joseph Bain (HM Register General House, Edinburgh, 1898).

Calendar of State Papers, Venice, Vol. 2, 1509–1519, ed. Rawdon Brown (Longman, London, 1867).

The Hamilton Papers, 2 vols, *1532–1543* and *1543–1590*, ed. Joseph Bain (HM Register General House, Edinburgh, 1890 and 1892).

Letters and Papers, Foreign and Domestic of the Reign of Henry VIII, 1509–1547, 21 vols in 33 parts, ed. J.S.Brewer (vols 1–4), ed. J.Gairdner (vols 5–13), ed. J.Gairdner and R.H.Brodie (vols 14–21) (London, 1862–1910).

The Manuscripts of His Grace The Duke of Rutland, vol. 4 (Historical Manuscripts Commission, London, 1905).

The Register of the Privy Council of Scotland, Vol. 1, 1545–1569, ed. John Hill Burton (HM General Register House, Edinburgh, 1877).

State Papers, Henry VIII, 11 vols (His Majesty's Commission, London, 1831–1852).

Annie I. Cameron (ed.), *The Scottish Correspondence of Mary of Lorraine*, Scottish History Society, 3rd ser., vol. 10 (Edinburgh, 1927).

Henry Ellis (ed.), *Original Letters Illustrative of English History*, 1st ser., vol. 1 (Harding, Triphook and Lepard, London, 1824).

Henry Ellis (ed.), *Original Letters Illustrative of English History*, 3rd ser., vol. 1 (Richard Bentley, London, 1846).

Henry Ellis (ed.), *Original Letters Illustrative of English History*, 3rd ser., vol. 3 (Richard Bentley, London, 1846).

James Ferguson (ed.), *Papers Illustrating the History of the Scots Brigade in the service of the United Netherlands*, vol. 1 (Scottish History Society, Edinburgh, 1899).

Henry James (ed.), *Facsimiles of National Manuscripts from William the Conqueror to Queen Anne*, Part 2 (Southampton, 1865).

John Glas Sandeman (ed.), *Facsimiles of the Ordinances and Statutes of the Spears of Honour, 1509, and the Oath and Articles of the Gentlemen Pensioners, 1600* (Hayling Island, 1912).

Alfred Spont (ed.), *Letters and Papers Relating to the War with France 1512–1513*, Navy Records Society, vol. 10 (1897–98).

Patrick Fraser Tytler (ed.), *England Under the Rule of Edward VI and Mary Illustrated in a Series of Original Letters*, vols 1 and 2 (Richard Bentley, London, 1839).

Marguerite Wood (ed.), *Flodden Papers: Diplomatic Correspondence Between The Courts of France and Scotland 1507–1517*, Scottish History Society, 3rd ser., vol. 20 (Edinburgh, 1933).

Chronicles and contemporary commentaries

W.A.J.Archbold (ed.), 'A Diary of the Expedition of 1544', *English Historical Review*, vol. 16 (1901), pp. 503–507.

Z.M.Arend and R.Dyboski (eds), *Knyghthode and Bataile* (Early English Text Society, London, 1935).

Roger Ascham, *Toxophilus* (Constable, Westminster, 1902).

Thomas Audley, 'A Treatise On The Art of War', *The Journal of the Society of Army Historical Research*, vol. 6 (1927), pp. 65–78, 129–133.

Ian F. Baird (ed.), *Scotish Feilde and Flodden Feilde, Two Flodden Poems* (Garland, London, 1982).

Humfrey Barwick, 'A breefe Discourse, Concerning the force and effect of all manuall weapons of fire', in E.G.Heath (ed.), *Bow versus Gun*.

J.B.Brown (ed.), 'The French Troops in the Borders in 1548', *Transactions of Hawick Archaeological Society* (1905), pp. 35–45.

J.Bruce (ed.), *Historie of the Arrivall of King Edward IV, AD 1471* (Camden Soc., London, 1838).

George Buchanan, *The History of Scotland*, 3 vols (James Kay, Edinburgh, 1821).

A.T.P.Byles (ed.), *The Book of Fayttes of Armes and Chyvalrye* (Early English Text Society, London, 1932).

Thomas Churchyard, *A Generall Rehearsall of Warres, Wherein is five hundred severall services of land and sea* (Edward White, London, 1579).

Thomas Coningsby, *Journal of the Siege of Rouen, 1591* (Pallas Armata Reprints, Tonbridge, 1992).

Archibald Constable (ed.), *John Major's History of Greater Britain* (Scottish History Society, Edinburgh, 1892).

M.B.Davies (ed.), 'Suffolk's Expedition to Montdidier 1523', *Fouad I University, Bulletin of the Faculty of Arts*, vol. 7 (1944), pp. 33–43.

M.B.Davies (ed.), 'The "Enterprise" of Paris and Boulogne', *Fouad I University, Bulletin of the Faculty of Arts*, vol. 11 (1949), pp. 37–95.

M.B.Davies (ed.), 'Boulogne and Calais from 1545 to 1550', *Fouad I University, Bulletin of the Faculty of Arts*, vol. 12 (1950), pp. 1–90.

Gladys Dickinson (ed.), *Two Missions of Jacques De La Brose* (Scottish History Society, Edinburgh, 1942).

Sir Philip de Malpas Grey Egerton (ed.), *A Commentary on the Services and Charges of Lord Grey of Wilton 1508–1562 by his Son Arthur, Lord Grey of Wilton* (Pallas Armata Reprints, Tonbridge, 1991).

John X. Evans (ed.), *The Works of Sir Roger Williams* (Oxford, Clarendon Press, 1972).

George Ferrers *et al.*, *The Winning of Calais by the French, January 1558 AD* (Pallas Armata Reprints, Tonbridge, 1991).

Thomas Gale, *Certaine Workes of Chirurgerie Newly Compiled and Published by Thomas Gales Maister of Chirurgerie* (Rouland Hall, London, 1563)

Thomas Gale, *Certaine Workes of Galens, Called Methodus Medendi, with a briefe Declaration of the Worthie Art of Medicine, the Office of a Chirurgion, and an Epitome of the third booke of Galen, of Natural Faculties* (Thomas East, London, 1586).

J.R.Hale (ed.), *Certain Discourses Military by Sir John Smyth* (Cornell University Press, Ithaca, 1964).

J.R.Hale (ed.), 'On a Tudor Parade Ground: The Captain's Handbook of Henry Barrett, 1562', in Hale, *Renaissance War Studies*, pp. 271–284.

Edward Hall, *The Triumphant Reigne of Kyng Henry the VIII*, 2 vols (T.C. and E.C.Jack, London, 1904).

Denys Hay (ed.), *The Anglia Historia of Polydore Vergil* (Camden Soc., London, 1950).

Sidney Heritage (ed.), *England in the Reign of King Henry VIII, Part 1, Starley's Life and Letters* (Early English Text Society, London, 1878).

Raphaell Holinshed, *English Chronicles*, vol. 3 (London, 1808).

Raphaell Holinshed, *The Historie of Scotland* (London, 1805).

Paul L. Hughes and James F. Larkin (eds), *Tudor Royal Proclamations*, vol. 1 (Yale University Press, London, 1964).

W.K.Jordan (ed.), *The Chronicle and Political Papers of King Edward VI* (George Allen and Unwin, London, 1966).

John R. Kenyon (ed.), 'Ordnance and the King's Fortifications in 1547–48: Society of Antiquaries MS 129. Folios 250–374', *Archaeologia*, vol. 107 (1982), pp. 165–213.

David Laing (ed.), 'A Contempoary Account of the Battle of Flodden, 9th September 1513', *Proceedings of the Society of Antiquaries of Scotland*, vol. 7 (1866–68), pp. 141–152.

Elizabeth Lamond (ed.), *A Discourse of the Commonweal of this Realm of England* (Cambridge University Press, Cambridge, 1893).

John H. Leslie (ed.), 'Diary of the Siege and Capture of Boulogne', *Journal of the Society for Army Historical Research*, vol. 1 (1922), pp. 188–99.

John Leslie, *The Historie of Scotland*, trans. James Dalrymple and ed. E.G.Cody and W.Murison (Scottish Text Society, Edinburgh, 1895).

Robert Lindesay of Pitscottie, *The Historie and Cronicles of Scotland*, 2 vols, ed. A.J.G.Mackay (William Blackwood, Edinburgh, 1899).

Niccoló Machiavelli, *The Art of War* (Da Capo, New York, 1965).

William Mackay (ed.), *The Wardlaw Manuscript Entitled 'Polichronicon Seu Policratica Temporum, Or The True Genealogy of the Frasers', 916–1674* (Scottish History Society, Edinburgh, 1905).

John Gough Nichols (ed.), *The Chronicle of Calais in the Reigns of Henry VII and Henry VIII* (Camden Soc. London, 1846).

William Patten, 'The Expedition into Scotland, 1547', in Pollard (ed.), *Tudor Tracts*, pp. 54–158.

A.F.Pollard (ed.), 'The Manner of the Triumph at Calais', in Pollard (ed.), *Tudor Tracts*, pp. 1–8.

A.F.Pollard (ed.), 'The Late Expedition in Scotland', in Pollard (ed.), *Tudor Tracts*, pp. 39–51.

A.F.Pollard (ed.), *Tudor Tracts 1532–1588* (Constable, Westminster, 1903).

John Proctor, *The History of Wyat's Rebellion with the order and manner of resisting the same* (Pallas Armata Reprints Tonbridge, 1991).

Ian Roy (ed.), *Blaise de Monluc: The Valois-Habsburg Wars and the French Wars of Religion* (Longman, London, 1971).

Ian Roy, 'Muster Roll for the Hundred of North Greenhoe (circa 1523)', in *Norfolk Records Society*, vol. 1 (1931), pp. 41–68.

John Skelton, *A Ballade of the Scottysshe Kynge* (Elliot Stock, London, 1882).

G. Gregory Smith (ed.), *Scottish History By Contemporary Writers, no. 1: The Days of James IV, 1288–1513* (David Nutt, London, 1900).

Charlotte Augusta Sneyd (ed.), *A Relation or Rather a True Account of the Island of England* (Camden Soc. London 1847).

Polydore Vergil, ed. Sir Henry Ellis, *Polydore Vergil's English History* (Camden Soc., London, 1844).

John Warkworth, *A Chronicle of the First Thirteen Years of the Reign of King Edward the Fourth*, ed. J.O.Haliwell (Camden Soc., London, 1839).

Secondary Sources

Books and chapters in books

Nicholas Adams and Simon Pepper, *Firearms and Fortifications: Military Architecture and Siege Warfare in Sixteenth-Century Siena* (University of Chigaco Press, Chigaco, 1986).

R.W.Ambler, ' "Wise and Experienced": Sir William Pelham, Elizabethan Soldier and Landlord, c.1560–87', in Ayton and Price (eds), *The Medieval Military Revolution*.

Andrew Ayton and J.L.Price (eds), *The Medieval Military Revolution* (Tauris Academic Studies, London, 1995).

James Bak (ed.), *The German Peasant War of 1525* (Frank Cass, London, 1976).

Sarah Barber and Stephen Ellis (eds), *Conquest and Union: Fashioning a British State, 1485–1725* (Longman, London, 1995).

Barrett Beer, *Northumberland: The Political Career of John Dudley* (Kent State University Press, 1973).

Barrett Beer, *Rebellion and Riot: Popular Disorder in England during the Reign of Edward VI* (Kent State University Press, 1982).

Matthew Bennett, 'The Development of Battle Tactics in the Hundred Years War', in Curry and Hughes (eds), *Arms, Armour and Fortifications in the Hundred Years War*, pp. 1–20.

Matthew Bennett, 'La Règle du Temple as a Military Manual, or How to Deliver a Cavalry Charge', in Harper-Bill *et al.*, *Studies in Medieval History*, pp. 7–20.

G.W.Bernard, *The Power of the Early Tudor Nobility* (The Harvester Press, Brighton, 1985).

Caroline Bingham, *James V, King of Scots 1512–1542* (Collins, London, 1971).

Jeremy Black (ed.), *The Origins of War in Early Modern Europe* (John Donald, Edinburgh, 1987).

Claude Blair, 'The Word *Claymore*', in Caldwell (ed.), *Scottish Weapons and Fortifications*, pp. 378–387.

Robert Borland, *Border Raids and Reivers* (Thomas Fraser, Dalbeattie, 1899).

Lindsay Boynton, *The Elizabethan Militia* (Routledge, London, 1967).

Ernle Bradford, *The Great Siege, Malta 1565* (Penguin, Harmondsworth, 1976).

Ernle Bradford, *The Story of the Mary Rose* (Hamish Hamilton, London, 1982).

Brendan Bradshaw and John Morrill, *The British Problem, c.1534–1707* (Macmillan, Basingstoke, 1996).

Richard Britnell, *The Closing of the Middle Ages? England, 1471–1529* (Blackwell, London, 1997).

Jennifer M. Brown (ed.), *Scottish Society in the Fifteenth Century* (Edward Arnold, London, 1977).

P. Hume Brown, *History of Scotland*, 3 vols (Cambridge University Press, Cambridge, 1909).

Ruth R. Brown and R.D.Smith, *Guns from the Sea: Ships' Armaments in the Age of Discovery* (Royal Armouries, London, 1988).

John Hill Burton, *The History of Scotland*, 8 vols (William BLackwood, Edinburgh, 1873).

M.L.Bush, *The Government Policy of Protector Somerset* (Edward Arnold, London, 1975).

David Caldwell (ed.), *Scottish Weapons and Fortifications 1100–1800* (John Donald, Edinburgh, 1981).

David Caldwell, 'Royal Patronage of Arms and Armour Making in Fifteenth- and Sixteenth-Century Scotland', in Caldwell (ed.), *Scottish Weapons and Fortifications*, pp. 73–93.

David Caldwell, 'Some Notes on Scottish Axes and Long Shafted Weapons', in Caldwell (ed.), *Scottish Weapons and Fortifications*, pp. 253–314.

David Caldwell, 'The Battle of Pinkie', in MacDougall (ed.), *Scotland and War*, pp. 61–94.

Adrian B. Caruana, *Tudor Artillery 1485–1603*, Historical Arms Series no. 30 (Museum Restoration Service, Alexandria Bay, New York, 1992).

Carlo M. Cipolla, *Guns and Sails in the Early Phase of European Expansion 1400–1700* (Collins, London, 1965).

W. Laird Clowes, 'The Navy', in Triall (ed.), *Social England*, vol. 3, pp. 202–228.

H.M.Colvin (ed.), *The History of the King's Works, Vol. 3, 1485–1660*, part 1 (HMSO, London, 1975).

H.M.Colvin (ed.), *The History of the King's Works, Vol. 4, 1485–1660*, part 2 (HMSO, London, 1982).

H.M.Colvin, 'The King's Works in France', in Colvin (ed.), *The King's Works*, vol. 3, part 1, pp. 337–394.

John D. Comrie, *History of Scottish Medicine*, vol. 1 (Ballière, Tindall and Cox, London, 1932).

Philippe Contamine, *War in the Middle Ages* (Blackwell, Oxford, 1986).

Julian S. Corbett, *Drake and the Tudor Navy*, 2 vols (Longman, London, 1898).

Paul Cornish and Angus McBride, *Henry VIII's Army* (Osprey, London, 1987).

Julian Cornwall, *Revolt of the Peasantry* (Routledge and Kegan Paul, London, 1977).

André Corvisier, *Armies and Societies in Europe, 1494–1789* (Indiana University Press, Bloomington, 1979).

Ian Cowan, P.H.R.MacKay, Alan Macquarrie, *The Knights of St John of Jerusalem in Scotland* (Scottish History Society, Edinburgh, 1983).

Charles Cruickshank, *Elizabeth's Army* (Oxford University Press, London, 1946).

Charles Cruickshank, *Henry VIII and the Invasion of France* (Alan Sutton, Stroud, 1990).

Anne Curry, 'The First English Standing Army? – Military Organisation in Lancastrian Normandy, 1420–1450', in Ross (ed.), *Patronage, Pedigree and Power*, pp. 193–214.

Anne Curry, 'English Armies in the Fifteenth Century', in Curry and Hughes (eds), *Arms, Armour and Fortifications*, pp. 39–68.

Anne Curry and Michael Hughes (eds), *Arms, Armies and Fortifications in the Hundred Years War* (The Boydell Press, Woodbridge, 1994).

Gerald De Gaury, *The Grand Captain, Gonzalo de Cordoba* (Longman, London, 1955).

Hans Delbrück, *Medieval Warfare* (Bison Books, London, 1990).

Hans Delbrück, *The Dawn of Modern Warfare* (Bison Books, London, 1990).

Kelly DeVries, *Medieval Military Technology* (Broadview, New York, 1992).

William Croft Dickinson, *Scotland from the Earliest Times to 1603* (Thomas Nelson, Edinburgh, 1961).

Gordon Donaldson, *Scotland, James V – James VII* (Oliver and Boyd, Edinburgh, 1965).

Ian Donnachie and George Hewitt, *A Companion to Scottish History* (Batsford, London, 1989).

Christopher Duffy, *Siege Warfare* (Routledge, London, 1979).

Keith Durham and Angus McBride, *The Border Reivers* (Osprey, London, 1995).

John Dwyer, Roger Mason and Alexander Murdoch (eds), *New Perspectives on the Politics and Culture of Early Modern Scotland* (John Donald, Edinburgh, 1982).

Lord Ellesmere, *The Sieges of Vienna by the Turks* (John Murray, London, 1879).

Fitzwilliam Elliot, *The Battle of Flodden and the Raids of 1513* (Pallas Armata Reprints, Tonbridge, 1991).

J.H.Elliot, *Imperial Spain 1469–1716* (Penguin, London, 1990).

David Eltis, *The Military Revolution in Sixteenth-Century Europe* (Tauris Academic Studies, London, 1995).

G.R.Elton, *The New Cambridge Modern History*, vol. 2 (University of Cambridge Press, Cambridge, 1958).

Peter Englund, *The Battle of Poltova* (Victor Gollancz, London, 1992).

Cyril Falls, *Elizabeth's Irish Wars* (Constable, London, 1996).

Sir James Fergusson, *The White Hind and Other Discoveries* (London, 1963).

Mark Fissel, *War and Government in Britain, 1598–1650* (Manchester University Press, Manchester, 1991).

Anthoney Fletcher, *Tudor Rebellions* (Longman, Harlow, 1986).

J.W.Fortescue, *A History of the British Army*, vol. 1 (Macmillan, London, 1899).

George MacDonald Fraser, *The Steel Bonnets* (Collin Harvels, London, 1989).

Ian Friel, 'Winds of Change? Ships and the Hundred Years War', in Curry and Hughes (eds), *Arms, Armour and Fortifications*, pp. 183–194.

Richard A. Gabriel and Karen S. Metz, *A History of Military Medicine*, vol. 2 (Greenwood, New York, 1992).

Anthony Goodman, *The Wars of the Roses* (Routledge, London, 1991).

Mark Greengrass (ed.), *Conquest and Coalescence: The Shaping of the State in Early Modern Europe* (Edward Arnold, London, 1991).

Donald Gregory, *The History of the Western Highlands* (Thomas Morison, Glasgow, 1881).

John Francis Guilmartin, *Gunpowder and Galleys* (Cambridge University Press, Cambridge, 1974).

John Francis Guilmartin, 'The Military Revolution: Origins and First Tests Abroad', in Rogers (ed.), *The Military Revolution Debate*, pp. 299–336.

Steven Gunn, 'The French Wars of Henry VIII', in Black (ed.), *The Origins of War in Early Modern Europe*, pp. 28–51.

Steven Gunn, *Charles Brandon, Duke of Suffolk 1484–1545* (Blackwell, Oxford, 1988).

George Gush, *Renaissance Armies 1480–1650* (Patrick Stephens, Cambridge, 1975).

John Guy, *Tudor England* (Oxford University Press, Oxford, 1990).

J.R.Hale, *Renaissance War Studies* (The Hambledon Press, London, 1983).

J.R.Hale, *War and Society in Renaissance Europe, 1450–1620* (Fontana, London, 1985).

J.R.Hale, 'The Defence of the Realm, 1485–1558', in Colvin (ed.), *The King's Works*, vol. 4, part 2, pp. 367–401.

J.R.Hale, 'International Relations in the West: Diplomacy and War', in Potter (ed.), *The New Cambridge Modern History*, vol. 1, pp. 259–291.

J.R.Hale, 'Armies, Navies and the Art of War', in Elton (ed.), *The New Cambridge Modern History*, vol. 2, pp. 481–509.

Bert S. Hall, *Weapons and Warfare in Renaissance Warfare* (John Hopkins University Press, Baltimore, 1997).

Robert Hardy, *Longbow* (Patrick Stephens, Sparkford, 1995).

Robert Hardy, 'The Longbow', in Curry and Hughes (eds), *Arms, Armour and Fortifications*, pp. 161–182.

Christopher Harper-Bill, Christopher Holdsworth, Janet Nelson (eds), *Studies in Medieval History presented to R. Allen Brown* (Woodbridge, 1989).

G.A.Hayes-McCoy, *Irish Battles* (Appletree Press, Belfast, 1989).

E.G.Heath (ed.), *Bow versus Gun* (EP Publishing, Wakefield, 1973).

James Michael Hill, *Celtic Warfare 1595–1763* (John Donald, Edinburgh, 1986).

Thomas Hodgkin, *The Wardens of the Northern Marches* (John Murray, London, 1908).

Michael Howard, *War in European History* (Oxford University Press, Oxford, 1976).

Siegfried Hoyer, 'Arms and Military Organisation in the German Peasant War', in Scribner and Benecke (eds), *The German Peasant War of 1525*, pp. 98–108.

Martin A.S. Hume, *The Year after the Armada and other Historical Studies* (Fisher Unwin, London, 1896).

Whitney Jones, *The Mid-Tudor Crisis, 1539–1563* (Macmillan, London, 1973).

W.K.Jordan, *Edward VI: The Threshold of Power* (Allen and Unwin, London, 1970).

W.K.Jordan, *Edward VI: The Young King* (Allen and Unwin, London, 1986).

John Keegan, *The Face of Battle* (Penguin, London, 1991).

John Kenyon, 'Coastal Artillery Fortification in England in the Late Fourteenth and Early Fifteenth Centuries', in Curry and Hughes (eds), *Arms, Armour and Fortifications*, pp. 145–150.

R.A.Konstam, 'Sixteenth-Century Naval Tactics and Gunnery', in Ruth R. Brown and R.D.Smith (eds), *Guns from the Sea: Ships' Armaments in the Age of Discovery*, pp. 17–23.

Steven K. Land, *Kett's Rebellion: The Nolfolk Rising of 1549* (The Boydell Press, Ipswich, 1977).

Gerald F.T. Leather, *New Light on Floddon* (Berwickshire Naturalists' Club, Berwick, 1937).

David Loades, *The Tudor Navy* (Scolar Press, Aldershot, 1992).

David Loades, *Essays in the Reign of Edward VI* (Headstart Lecture Series, Bangor, 1994).

David Loades, *Power in Tudor England* (Macmillan, London, 1997).

John A. Lynn (ed.), *Feeding Mars: Logistics in Western Warfare from the Middle Ages to the Present* (Westview, Oxford, 1993).

Norman MacDougall, *James IV* (John Donald, Edinburgh, 1989).

Norman MacDougall (ed.), *Scotland and War, AD 79–1918* (John Donald, Edinburgh, 1991).

Iain MacIvor, 'Artillery and Major Places of Strength in the Lothians and the East Border, 1513–1542', in Caldwell (ed.), *Scottish Weapons and Fortifications*, pp. 94–152.

William Mackay MacKenzie, *The Secret of Flodden* (Grant and Murray, Edinburgh, 1931).

J.D.Mackie, *The Earlier Tudors, 1485–1558* (Clarendon Press, Oxford, 1952).

R.L.Mackie, *King James IV of Scotland* (Oliver and Boyd, Edinburgh, 1958).

Alan Macquarrie, *Scotland and the Crusades, 1095–1560* (John Donald, Edinburgh, 1997).

William H. McNeil, *The Pursuit of Power* (University of Chicago Press, Chicago, 1982).

Michael Mallett, *Mercenaries and their Masters* (Bodley Head, London, 1974).

Michael Mallet and J.R.Hale, *The Military Organisation of a Renaissance State* (Cambridge University Press, Cambridge, 1984).

Roger A. Mason (ed.), *Scotland and England 1286–1815* (John Donald, Edinburgh, 1987).

Roger A. Mason, 'Scotching the Brute: Politics, History and National Myth in Sixteenth-Century Britain', in Mason (ed.), *Scotland and England*, pp. 60–84.

Marcus Merriman, 'James Henrisoun and "Great Britain": British Union and the Scottish Commonweal', in Mason (ed.), *Scotland and England*, pp. 85–112.

Marcus Merriman and John Summerson, 'The Scottish Border', in Colvin (ed.), *The King's Works*, vol. 4, part 2, pp. 607–728.

Gilbert John Millar, *Tudor Mercenaries and Auxiliaries 1485–1547* (University of Virginia Press, Charlottesville, 1980).

Douglas Miller, *The Landsknechts* (Osprey, London, 1976).

Stephen Morillo (ed.), *The Battle of Hastings* (The Boydell Press, Woodbridge, 1996).

Sir Francis Mudie *et al.*, *Broughty Castle and the Defence of the Tay* (Abertay Historical Society, Dundee, 1970).

Ranald Nicholson, *Scotland: The Later Middle Ages* (Oliver and Boyd, Edinburgh, 1979).

Robert O'Connell, *Of Arms and Men* (Oxford University Press, Oxford, 1989).

Charles Oman, 'The Art of War', in Triall (ed.), *Social England*, vol. 3, pp. 70–202.

Charles Oman, *A History of the Art of War in the Sixteenth Century* (Greenhill, London, 1987).

Charles Oman, *A History of the Art of War in the Middle Ages*, 2 vols (Greenhill, London, 1991).

Geoffrey Parker, *The Military Revolution* (Cambridge University Press, Cambridge, 1992).

Geoffrey Parker, 'In Defence of the Military Revolution', in Rogers (ed.), *The Military Revolution Debate*, pp. 337–366.

V.J.Parry and M.E.Yapp (eds), *War, Technology and Society in the Middle East* (Oxford University Press, London, 1975).

V.J.Parry, 'La manière de combattre', in Parry and Yapp (eds), *War, Technology and Society in the Middle East*, pp. 218–256.

Raymond Campbell Paterson, *My Wound is Deep: A History of the Later Anglo-Scots Wars 1380–1560* (John Donald, Edinburgh, 1997).

Djurdjica Petrovic, 'Fire-arms in the Balkans on the Eve of and after the Ottoman Conquests of the Fourteenth and Fifteenth Centuries', in Parry and Yapp (eds), *War, Technology and Society in the Middle East*, pp. 164–194.

David Potter, *War and Government in the French Provinces, Picardy 1470–1560* (Cambridge University Press, Cambridge, 1993).

G.R.Potter (ed.), *The New Cambridge Modern History*, vol. 1 (Cambridge University Press, Cambridge, 1971).

William H. Prescott, *The Art of War in Spain: The Conquest of Granada 1481–1492*, ed. Albert D. McJoynt (Greenhill, London, 1995).

Michael Prestwich, *Armies and Warfare in the Middle Ages: The English Experience* (Yale University Press, London, 1996).

Jasper Ridley, *Henry VIII* (Constable, London, 1984).

George Ridpath, *The Border History of England and Scotland* (Philip Ridpath, Berwick, 1848).

Michael Roberts, *Essays in Swedish History* (Weidenfeld and Nicolson, London, 1967).

Ralph Robson, *The English Highland Clans: Tudor Responses to a Medieval Problem* (John Donald, Edinburgh, 1989).

Clifford J. Rogers (ed.), *The Military Revolution Debate* (Westview, Boulder, 1995).

Clifford J. Rogers, 'The Military Revolution in History and Historiography', in Rogers (ed.), *The Military Revolution Debate*, pp. 1–12.

Clifford J. Rogers, 'The Military Revolutions of the Hundred Years War', in Rogers (ed.), *The Military Revolution Debate*, pp. 55–94.

Charles Ross (ed.), *Patronage, Pedigree and Power in Later Medieval England* (Alan Sutton, Gloucester, 1979).

Charles Ross, *Richard III* (Methuen, London, 1992).

Andrew Saunders, *Norham Castle* (English Heritage, London, 1998).

J.J.Scarisbrick, *Henry VIII* (Eyre and Spottiswood, London, 1968).

H.R.Schubert, *History of the British Iron and Steel Industry* (Routledge and Kegan Paul, London, 1957).

Bob Scribner and Gerhard Benecke (eds), *The German Peasant War of 1525 – New Viewpoints* (George Allen and Unwin, London, 1979).

L.R.Shelby, *John Rogers: Tudor Military Engineer* (Clarendon Press, Oxford, 1967).

Robert Smith, 'Artillery and the Hundred Years War: Myth and Interpretation', in Curry and Hughes (eds), *Arms, Armour and Fortifications*, pp. 151–160.

David Stewart, *Sketches of the Character, Manners and Present State of the Highlanders of Scotland* (John Donald, Edinburgh, 1977).

Christopher J. Tabraham and George L. Good, 'The Artillery Fortification at Threave Castle, Galloway', in Caldwell (ed.), *Scottish Weapons and Fortifications*, pp. 55–72.

Frank Tallett, *War and Society in Early-Modern Europe, 1495–1715* (Routledge, London, 1992).

F.L.Taylor, *The Art of War in Italy, 1494–1529* (Greenhill, London, 1993).

H.D.Traill (ed.), *Social England: A Record of the Progress of the People*, vol. 3 (London, 1895).

Melvin Tucker, *The Life of Thomas Howard* (Moulton, The Hague, 1964).

M.Vale, *War and Chivalry* (Duckworth, London, 1981).

Martin Van Creveld, *Technology and War* (Free Press, New York, 1989).

Richard Vaughan, *Charles the Bold, the Last Valois Duke of Burgundy* (Longman, London, 1973).

R.B.Wernham, *Before the Armada: The Growth of English Foreign Policy 1485–1588* (Jonathan Cape, London, 1966).

Arthur Williamson, 'Scotland, Antichrist and the Invention of Great Britain', in Dwyer, Mason and Murdoch (eds), *New Perspectives on the Politics and Culture of Early Modern Scotland*.

Jenny Wormald, *Lords and Men in Scotland: Bonds of Manrent 1442–1603* (John Donald, Edinburgh, 1985).

Jenny Wormald, *Mary Queen of Scots: A Study in Failure* (George Philip, London, 1988).

Theses

James S. Cameron, 'Crown Magnate Relations in the Personal Rule of James V, 1528–1542' (St Andrews University Ph.D., 1994).

John Goring, 'The Military Obligations of the English People 1511–1558' (London University Ph.D., 1955).

Thomas Howard, 'The Early Career of the 3rd Duke of Norfolk' (University of West Virginia Ph.D., 1984).

Marcus Merriman, 'The Struggle for the Marriage of Mary Queen of Scots: English and French Intervention in Scotland, 1543–1550' (London University Ph.D., 1974).

Articles

Brian G. Awty, 'The Arcana Family of Cesena as Gunfounders and Military Engineers', *Transactions of the Newcomen Society*, vol. 59 (1987–88), pp. 61–80.

Brian G. Awty, 'Parson Levett and English Cannon Founding', *Sussex Archaeological Collections*, vol. 127 (1989), pp. 133–145.

Cadwallader J. Bates, 'Flodden Field', *Archaeologia Aeliana*, vol. 16 (1892), pp. 351–372.

Diane Bornstein, 'Military Manuals in Fifteenth-Century England', *Medieval Studies*, vol. 37 (1975), pp. 469–477.

M.J.Braddick, 'An English Military Revolution?' *The Historical Journal*, vol. 36 (1993), pp. 965–975.

Gainsford Bruce, 'The English Expedition into Scotland in 1542', *Archaeologia Aeliana*, 3rd series, vol. 3 (1907), pp. 191–212.

John Bury, 'Early Writings on Fortifications and Siegecraft: 1502–1554', *Fort*, vol. 13 (1985), pp. 5–48.

T. Blake Butler, 'King Henry VIII's Irish Army List', *The Irish Genealogist*, vol. 1 (1937), pp. 3–13, 36–38.

François Buttin, 'La lance et l'arrêt de cuirasse', *Archaeologia*, vol. 99 (1965), pp. 77–177.

David Caldwell, 'A Sixteenth-Century Group of Gun Towers in Scotland', *Fort*, vol. 12 (1984), pp. 15–24.

John Whiteclay Chambers, 'The New Military History: Myth and Reality', *The Journal of Military History*, vol. 55 (1991), pp. 395–406.

R. Coltman Clephan, 'An Outline of the History of Gunpowder and that of the Hand-Gun, from the Earliest Epoch of the Earliest Records to the End of the Fifteenth Century', *The Archaeological Journal*, vol. 66 (1909), pp. 145–170.

R. Coltman Clephan, 'The Military Handgun of the Sixteenth Century', *The Archaeological Journal*, vol. 67 (1910), pp. 109–50.

Weston F. Cook, Jr, 'The Cannon Conquest of Nasrid Spain and the End of the Reconquista', *The Journal of Military History*, vol. 57, part 1 (1993), pp. 43–70.

Weston F. Cook, Jr, 'Warfare and Firearms in Fifteenth Century Morocco, 1400–1492', *War and Society*, vol. 11, part 2 (1993), pp. 25–40.

B.Coward, 'The Lieutenancy of Lancashire and Cheshire in the Sixteenth and Early Seventeenth Centuries', *Transactions of the Historical Society of Lancashire and Cheshire*, vol. 119 (1967), pp. 39–64.

C.G.Cruickshank, 'King Henry VIII's Army: Camp', *History Today*, vol. 18 (1968), pp. 852–857.

C.G.Cruickshank, 'King Henry VIII's Army: Munitions', *History Today*, vol. 19 (1969), pp. 40–45.

C.S.L.Davies, 'Provisions for Armies, 1509–50: A Study in the Effectiveness of Early Tudor Government', *The Economic History Reveiw*, 2nd series, vol. 17 (1964–65), pp. 234–248.

Harold Davis, 'John Brende: Soldier and Translator', *The Huntington Library Quarterly*, vol. 1 (1937–38), pp. 421–426.

Kelly DeVries, 'Military Surgical Practice and the Advent of Gunpowder Weaponary', *Canadian Bulletin of Medical History*, vol. 7 (1990), pp. 131–46.

Kelly DeVries, 'Catapults are not Atomic Bombs: Towards a Redefinition of "Effectiveness" in Premodern Military History', *War in History*, vol. 4 (1997), pp. 454–470.

Gladys Dickinson, 'Some Notes on the Scottish Army in the First Half of the Sixteenth Century', *The Scottish Historical Review*, vol. 28 (1949), pp. 133–145.

Viscount C.H.Dillon, 'Irish Troops at Boulogne in 1544', *The Journal for the Society of Army Historical Research*, vol. 1 (1922), pp. 81–84.

Viscount C.H.Dillon, 'The English Soldier of the Sixteenth Century', *The Journal for the Society of Army Historical Research*, vol. 1 (1921–22), pp. 200–204.

Harold A. Dillon, 'Arms and Armour at Westminster, the Tower, and Greenwich, 1547', *Archaeologia*, vol. 51 (1888), pp. 219–280.

R.M.Downes, 'What Medicine Owes to War and War Owes to Medicine', *Journal of the Royal Army Medical Corps*, vol. 67 (1936), pp. 381–394.

Professor Duns, 'Notes on a Helmet found at Ancrum Moor', *Proceedings of the Society of Antiquaries of Scotland*, vol. 6, 3rd ser. (1895–96), pp. 317–322.

Gareth Dupré, 'At Long Last! Research Concludes Longbow Mystery', *Mary Rose Newsbrief*, no. 54 (Autumn 1997), p. 1.

Steven G. Ellis, 'A Border Baron and the Tudor State: The Rise and Fall of Lord Dacre of the North', *The Historical Journal*, vol. 35 (1992), pp. 253–277.

Thomas Epser, 'The Replacement of the Longbow by Firearms in the English Army', *Technology and Culture*, vol. 6 (1965), pp. 382–93.

D.M.R.Esson, 'The Italian Campaigns of Consalvo de Cordoba, Part 1', *The Army Quarterly*, vol. 80 (1958–60), pp. 235–246.

D.M.R.Esson, 'The Italian Campaigns of Consalvo de Cordoba, Part 2', *The Army Quarterly*, vol. 81 (1960–61), pp. 105–120.

James Fergusson, '1547: The Rough Wooing', *Blackwoods Magazine*, vol. 262 (1947), pp. 183–94.

Charles Ffoulkes, 'Some Aspects of the Craft of the Armourer', *Archaeologia*, vol. 79 (1929), pp. 13–28.

M.D.Field, 'Military Professionalism and the Mass Army', *Armed Forces and Society*, vol. 1 (1974–1975), pp. 191–214.

Richard D.Forrest, 'Development of Wound Therapy from the Dark Ages to the Present', *Journal of the Royal Society of Medicine*, vol. 75 (1982), pp. 268–273.

Claude Gaier, 'The Origin of Mons Meg', *Journal of the Arms and Armour Society*, vol. 5 (1967), pp. 425–431.

Hereford B. George, 'The Archers at Crécy', *The English Historical Review*, vol. 10 (1895), pp. 733–738.

Jeremy Goring, 'The Dress of the English Soldier in the Early Tudor Period', *Journal of the Society of Army Historical Research*, vol. 33 (1955), pp. 136–138.

Jeremy Goring, 'The General Proscription of 1522', *The English Historical Review*, vol. 86 (1971), pp. 681–705.

Jeremy Goring, 'Social Change and Military Decline in Mid-Tudor England', *History*, vol. 60 (1975), pp. 185–197.

A.C.F.Green, 'The Loss of Calais', *The Army Quarterly*, vol. 80 (1959–60), pp. 173–178.

S.J.Gunn, 'The Duke of Suffolk's March on Paris in 1523', *The English Historical Review*, vol. 400 (1986), pp. 561–634.

R.K.Hannay, 'Letters of the Papal Legate in Scotland, 1543', *Scottish Historical Review*, vol. 11 (1914), pp. 1–25.

Hermann H. Hattaway, 'Some Aspects of Tudor Military History', *The Army Quartely*, vol. 98 (1969), pp. 53–63.

David Head, 'Henry VIII's Scottish Policy: A Reassessment', *The Scottish Historical Review*, vol. 61 (1982), pp. 1–24.

Charles L. Heizmann, 'Military Sanitation in the Sixteenth, Seventeenth and Eighteenth Centuries', *Annals of Medical History*, vol. 1 (1917–18), pp. 281–300.

James Michael Hill, 'The Distinctiveness of Gaelic Warfare, 1400–1750', *European History Quarterly*, vol. 22 (1992), pp. 323–245.

Thomas Hodgkin, 'The Battle of Flodden', *Archaeologia Aeliana*, vol. 16 (1892), pp. 1–44.

O.F.G.Hogg, 'The "Gunner" and Some other Early Masters of Ordnance', *Journal of the Royal Artillery*, vol. 62 (1935/36), pp. 463–473.

James R. Hooker, 'Notes on the Organisation and Supply of the Tudor Military under Henry VII', *Huntington Library Quarterly*, vol. 23 (1959), pp. 19–31.

Michael Howard *et al.*, 'What is Military History?' *History Today*, vol. 35 (1984), pp. 5–13.

H.A.L.Howell, 'An Historical Retrospect of the Army Surgeon in Britain, Prior to the Sixteenth Century', *Journal of the Royal Army Medical Corps*, vol. 1 (1903), pp. 111–124.

H.A.L.Howell, 'The Army Surgeon and the Care of the Sick and Wounded in British Campaigns during the Tudor and Stuart Periods', *Journal of the Royal Army Medical Corps*, vol. 2 (1904), pp. 606–615, pp. 737–745.

Knud Jespersen, 'Social Change and Military Revolution in Early Modern Europe: Some Danish Evidence', *The Historical Journal*, vol. 26 (1983), pp. 1–13.

Colin Jones, 'New Military History for Old? War and Society in Early Modern Europe', *European Studies Review*, vol. 12 (1982), pp. 97–108.

Peter Jones, 'The Metallography and Relative Effectiveness of Arrowheads and Armor during the Middle Ages', *Materials Characterisation*, vol. 29 (1992), pp. 111–17.

Thomas Jones, 'A Welsh Chronicler in Tudor England', *The Welsh History Review*, vol. 1 (1960–63), pp. 1–17.

Maurice Keen, 'Brotherhood in Arms', *History*, vol. 47 (1962), pp. 1–17.

John R. Kenyon, 'Early Artillery Fortifications in England and Wales', *Fort*, vol. 1 (1976), pp. 33–36.

J.R.Kirkup, 'The History and Evolution of Surgical Instruments', *Annals of the Royal College of Surgeons of England*, vol. 63 (1981), pp. 279–285.

Charles Klinger, Owen H. Wangensteen and Sarah D. Wangensteen, 'Wound Management of Amboise Paré and Dominique Larrey, Great French Military

Surgeons of the 16th and 19th Centuries', *Bulletin of the History of Medicine*, vol. 46 (1972), pp. 207–234.

Peter Krenn, Paul Kalaus and Bert Hall, 'Material Culture and Military History: Test-Firing Early Modern Small Arms', *Material History Review*, vol. 42 (1995), pp. 101–109.

Daniela Lamberini, 'Practice and Theory in Sixteenth-Century Fortifications', *Fort*, vol. 15 (1987), pp. 5–20.

Andrew Lang, 'The Cardinall and the King's Will', *The Scottish Historical Review*, vol. 3 (1906), pp. 410–422.

Gaillard T. Lapsley, 'The Problem of the North', *The American Historical Review*, vol. 5 (1900), pp. 440–466.

L.G. Carr Laughton, 'Early Tudor Ship-Guns', *The Mariner's Mirror*, vol. 46 (1960), pp. 242–85.

Fernando González De León, ' "Doctors of the Military Discipline": Technical Expertise and the Paradigm of the Spanish Soldier in the Early Modern Period', *The Sixteenth-Century Journal*, vol. 27 (1996), pp. 61–85.

N.B.Lewis, 'The Organisation of Indentured Retinues in Fourteenth-Century England', *Transactions of the Royal Historical Society*, 4th ser., vol. 27 (1945), pp. 29–39.

Christopher Lloyd, 'Sussex Guns', *History Today*, vol. 23 (1973), pp. 785–791.

E.M.Lloyd, 'The "Herse" of Archers at Crécy', *The English Historical Review*, vol. 10 (1895), pp. 538–541.

Richard Lomas, 'The Impact of Border Warfare: The Scots and South Tweedside, c.1290–1520', *The Scottish Historical Review*, vol. 75 (1996), pp. 143–167.

Ronald Love, ' "All the King's Horsemen": The Equestrian Army of Henri IV, 1585–1598', *Sixteenth-Century Journal*, vol. 22 (1991), pp. 510–533.

J.D.Mackie, 'The English Army at Flodden', *Miscellany of the Scottish History Society*, vol. 8 (1951), pp. 35–85.

J.G.Mann, 'Notes on the Armour of the Maximilian Period and the Italian Wars', *Archaeologia*, vol. 69 (1929), pp. 217–244.

Sir James Marshall-Cornwall, 'An Expedition to Aquitaine, 1512', *History Today*, vol. 23 (1973), pp. 640–647.

Colin J.M. Martin, 'Ancrum Moor: A Day of Reckoning', *The Scots Magazine*, vol. 83 (1965), pp. 146–52.

Alastair M.T. Maxwell-Irving, 'Early Firearms and their influence on the Military and Domestic Architecture of the Borders', *Proceedings of the Society of Antiquaries of Scotland*, vol. 103 (1970–1), pp. 192–224.

Donald N. McCloskey, 'History, Differential Equations and the Problem of Narration', *History and Theory*, vol. 30 (1991), pp. 21–36.

John McEwen, 'The Battle of Flodden', *History Today*, vol. 8 (1958), pp. 337–345.

Sean McGlynn, 'The Myths of Medieval Warfare', *History Today*, vol. 44 (1994), pp. 28–34.

Alexander McKee, 'Henry VIII as Military Commander', *History Today*, vol. 41 (1991), pp. 22–29.

Andrew McKerral, 'West Highland Mercenaries in Ireland', *The Scottish Historical Review*, vol. 30 (1951), pp. 1–14.

Marcus Merriman, 'The Platte of Castlemilk', *Transactions of the Dumfriesshire and Galloway Natural History Society*, vol. 44, part 3 (1967), pp. 175–181.

Marcus Merriman, 'The Assured Scots', *The Scottish Historical Review*, vol. 47 (1968), pp. 10–34.

Marcus Merriman, 'The Forts of Eyemouth: Anvils of British Union?', *The Scottish Historical Review*, vol. 67 (1988), pp. 142–155.

Gilbert John Millar, 'Henry VIII's Preliminary Letter of Retainer to Colonel Frederick Von Reiffenberg for the Raising of 1500 Men-At-Arms', *The Journal for the Society of Army Historical Research*, vol. 67 (1989), pp. 220–225.

Gilbert John Millar, 'The Albanians: Sixteenth-Century Mercenaries', *History Today*, vol. 26 (1976), pp. 468–472.

Gilbert John Millar, 'Mercenaries under Henry VIII, 1544–46', *History Today*, vol. 27 (1977), pp. 173–182.

Stephen Morillo, 'Guns and Government: A Comparative Study of Europe and Japan', *The Journal of World History*, vol. 6 (1995), pp. 75–106.

J.E.Morris, 'The Archers at Crécy', *The English Historical Review*, vol. 12 (1897), pp. 427–336.

William Murray, 'Flodden: Before and After', *Transactions of the Hawick Archaeological Society* (1913), pp. 38–43.

Cynthia Neville, 'Local Sentiment and the "National" Enemy in Northern England in the Later Middle Ages', *Journal of British Studies*, vol. 35 (1996), pp. 419–437.

Sean O'Domhnaill, 'Warfare in Sixteenth-Century Ireland', *Irish Historical Studies*, vol. 5 (1946–7), pp. 29–54.

B.H. St J. O'Neil, 'Stefan Von Haschenperg: An Engineer to King Henry VIII, and his Work', *Archaeologia*, vol. 91 (1945), pp. 137–55.

Adam Patrick and R.S.Roberts, 'A Consideration of the Nature of the English Sweating Sickness', *Medical History*, vol. 9 (1965), pp. 272–278, pp. 385–389.

J. Balfour Paul, 'Edinburgh in 1544 and Hertford's Invasion', *The Scottish Historical Review*, vol. 8 (1911), pp. 113–131.

Gervase Phillips, 'The Army of Henry VIII: A Reassessment', *The Journal of the Society for Army Historical Research*, vol. 75 (1997), pp. 9–23.

A.F.Pollard, 'The Protector Somerset and Scotland', *The English Historical Review*, vol. 13 (1898), pp. 464–472.

George Raudzens, 'War Winning Weapons: The Measurement of Technological Determinism in Military History', *The Journal of Military History*, vol. 54 (1990), pp. 403–33.

Gareth Rees, 'The Longbow's Deadly Secrets', *New Scientist*, vol. 138 (1993), pp. 24–25.

George Reisch, 'Chaos, History and Narrative', *History and Theory*, vol. 30 (1991), pp. 1–20.

G.V.Scammell, 'War at Sea under the Early Tudors: Some Newcastle upon Tyne Evidence', *Archaeologia Aeliana*, vol. 38–39 (1960–61), pp. 73–205.

H.R.Schubert, 'The First Cast-Iron Cannon Made in England', *The Journal of the Iron and Steel Institute*, vol. 146 (1942), pp. 131–140.

H.R.Schubert, 'The Superiority of English Cast-Iron Cannon at the Close of the Sixteenth Century', *The Journal of the Iron and Steel Institute*, vol. 161 (1949), pp. 85–86.

Sir Bruce Seton, 'The Flodden Campaign – 1513: A Study in Mediaeval Mobilisation in Scotland', *The Journal of the Society for Army Historical Research*, vol. 3 (1924), pp. 175–191.

Dennis Showalter, 'Caste, Skill, and Training: The Evolution of Cohesion in European Armies from the Middle Ages to the Sixteenth Century', *The Journal of Military History*, vol. 57 (1993), pp. 407–30.

G.A.Sinclair, 'The Scots at Solway Moss', *Scottish Historical Review*, vol. 2 (1904), pp. 372–377.

David Stewart, 'The English Army Surgeon in the Sixteenth Century', *Journal of the Royal Army Medical Corps*, vol. 88 (1947), pp. 231–247.

David Stewart, 'Disposal of the Sick and Wounded of the English Army during the Sixteenth Century', *Journal of the Royal Army Medical Corps*, vol. 90 (1948), pp. 30–38.

David Stewart, 'Sickness and Mortality Rates of the English Army in the Sixteenth Century', *Journal of the Royal Army Medical Corps*, vol. 91 (1948), pp. 23–35.

David Stewart, 'The Causes of Disease in the Sixteenth-Century Army', *Journal of the Royal Army Medical Corps*, vol. 92 (1949), pp. 35–41.

David Stewart, 'Military Surgery in the Sixteenth Century', *Journal of the Royal Army Medical Corps*, vol. 92 (1949), pp. 229–237.

Paul Stewart, 'The Santa Hermandad and the First Italian Campaign of Gonzalo of Córdoba, 1495–1498', *Renaissance Quarterly*, vol. 28, part 1 (1975), pp. 29–37.

Charles Chenevix Trench, 'From Arquebus to Rifle: The Pursuit of Perfection', *History Today*, vol. 23 (1973), pp. 407–417.

J.A.Tuck, 'War and Society in the Medieval North', *Journal of Northern History*, vol. 21 (1985), pp. 33–52.

John Vogt, 'Saint Barbara's Legion: Portuguese Artillery in the Struggle for Morocco, 1415–1578', *Military Affairs*, vol. 41 (1977), pp. 176–182.

James Watt, 'Surgeons of the *Mary Rose*: The Practice of Surgery in Tudor England', *Mariner's Mirror*, vol. 69 (1983), pp. 3–17.

Henry J. Webb, 'English Military Surgery during the Age of Elizabeth', *Bulletin of the History of Medicine*, vol. 15 (1944), pp. 261–275.

Dean Guntner White, 'Henry VIII's Irish Kern in France and Scotland, 1544–1545', *Irish Sword*, vol. 3 (1958) pp. 213–25.

A.R.Williams, 'Medieval Metalworking – Armour Plate and the Advance of Metallurgy', *The Chartered Mechanical Engineer* (September 1978), pp. 109–14.

A.R.Williams, 'Metallographic Examination of Sixteenth-Century Armour', *Historical Metallurgy Group Bulletin*, vol. 6 (1972), pp. 15–23.

James Williamson, 'A Tudor Army', *Blackwoods Magazine*, vol. 196 (1914), pp. 195–206, pp. 346–358.

INDEX